PC Hardware
ANNOYANCES™

How to Fix the Most ANNOYING Things
About Your Computer Hardware

Stephen J. Bigelow

O'REILLY®

Beijing · Cambridge · Farnham · Köln · Paris · Sebastopol · Taipei · Tokyo

PC Hardware Annoyances™
How to Fix the Most Annoying Things About Your Computer Hardware

by Stephen J. Bigelow

Copyright © 2005 O'Reilly Media, Inc. All rights reserved.
Printed in the United States of America.

Illustrations © 2004 Hal Mayforth c/o theispot.com

Published by O'Reilly Media, Inc., 1005 Gravenstein Highway North, Sebastopol, CA 95472.

O'Reilly books may be purchased for educational, business, or sales promotional use. Online editions are also available for most titles (*safari.oreilly.com*). For more information, contact our corporate/institutional sales department: 800-998-9938 or *corporate@oreilly.com*.

Print History:	Editor:	Brett Johnson
November 2004: First Edition.	Production Editor:	Genevieve d'Entremont
	Art Director:	Michele Wetherbee
	Cover Design:	Volume Design, Inc.
	Interior Designer:	Patti Capaldi

RepKover™
This book uses RepKover™, a durable and flexible lay-flat binding.

0-596-00715-9
[C]

Contents

Introduction

I started writing about computers and technology back in 1988. No, I wasn't there when the first IBM PC rolled off the assembly line...but pretty close. Since then, I've had the privilege of seeing PC technology evolve from clunky, incompatible contraptions into sleek expressions of processing performance. The best part is that the evolution is continuing even as you read this.

But with all of the advances and standardization that has taken place over the last 15 years or so, it's harder than ever to get your questions answered or problems solved. PCs and their peripherals still offer a real set of challenges for everyday users. Setup, configuration, compatibility, and performance issues weigh on all users at one time or another, and most error messages remain every bit as cryptic as they were back in the days of DOS 2.0. Today, however, most PCs ship with little (if any) printed documentation, and only the very determined—or very bored—can wait hours on hold before finally talking to a human being at technical support. I swear if I hear another Musak version of "Muskrat Love," I might just have a seizure.

IS PC HARDWARE ANNOYANCES RIGHT FOR YOU?

If you haven't looked at the cover yet, this book is about PC hardware annoyances—the issues and problems associated with the drives, monitors, printers, scanners, RAM, chips, boards, and other assorted gadgets tucked inside or attached to your desktop or laptop system.

You don't need to be a computer geek to use this book, but it helps to understand some basics. You'll get the most from this book if you're comfortable using Windows XP, and know which end of a screwdriver to hold when it comes time to open the system. If not, don't worry—I've included step-by-step instructions for important procedures. It doesn't matter whether you've been using PCs for 20 years or still can't find the mouse port on your very first system. The annoyances cut across a wide range of topics and difficulty levels to keep things interesting, while keeping the heavy troubleshooting and geek-speak to a minimum.

HOW TO USE THIS BOOK

The book is organized into big categories—desktops, notebooks, hard drives, printers, networks, and so forth. Within each chapter, the annoyances are grouped by topic. For example, the desktop chapter includes setup, keyboard, mouse, startup, BIOS/CMOS, memory, processor, port, and maintenance annoyances. This makes it easier to browse around and jump to the pages that most interest you—and solve a knotty problem that's been driving you crazy.

CONVENTIONS USED IN THIS BOOK

The following typographic conventions are used in this book:

Italic
> Indicates new terms, URLs, filenames, file extensions, directories, and program names.

`Constant width`
> Used to show the contents of files, commands and options, or the output from commands.

`Constant width bold`
> Indicates commands or other text that should be typed literally by the user.

Menus/Navigation
> This book uses arrow symbols to signify menu instructions. For example, "File → Print" is a more compact way of saying, "Click File on the command bar at the top of the screen and choose Print from the drop-down menu." However, if an instruction directs you to click a tab, check an option, or click a button in a dialog box, we'll tell you.

Pathnames
> Pathnames show the location of a file or application in Windows Explorer. Folders are separated by a backward slash. For example, *C:\Windows\System32*.

ABOUT THE AUTHOR

Stephen J. Bigelow started out in 1987 with a BSEE, and took a manufacturing engineering job where he worked extensively with computer technologies, programming, and interfacing. But after far too many years suffering in the mind-numbing, soul-sucking layoff lottery of corporate hell, he decided to actually do something meaningful with his life.

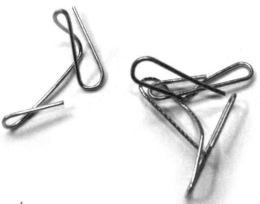

Since then, Bigelow has written numerous popular PC repair books, including *Bigelow's PC Hardware Desk Reference* (McGraw Hill). He has also written numerous technical articles for *Computer Currents*, *Computer User*, and pretty much any other publication that would actually pay him.

Today, Bigelow continues to learn about computers and networks, writing extensively for *Processor Magazine*, *SmartComputing*, and CNET.com. His work has also been seen in *eWeek* and *PC Today*.

ACKNOWLEDGMENTS

One of the great things about this job is that I get to learn new things almost every day. This book would not have been possible without the many varied questions and helpful personal experiences that so many computer users have shared with me over the years. I hope that I've given back even a fraction of what you all have given me.

I'd also like to acknowledge the patient support and encouragement of Robert Luhn, Brett Johnson, Jim Aspinwall, and the entire O'Reilly staff. It's said that you can't make a silk purse from a sow's ear, but you folks make it look easy.

O'REILLY WOULD LIKE TO HEAR FROM YOU

Please address comments and questions concerning this book to the publisher:

O'Reilly Media, Inc.
1005 Gravenstein Highway North
Sebastopol, CA 95472
(800) 998-9938 (in the United States or Canada)
(707) 829-0515 (international or local)
(707) 829-0104 (fax)

We have a web page for this book, where we list errata, examples, and any additional information. You can access this page at:

http://www.oreilly.com/catalog/pchardwareannoy/

To comment or ask technical questions about this book, send email to:

bookquestions@oreilly.com

For more information about our books, conferences, Resource Centers, and the O'Reilly Network, see our web site at:

http://www.oreilly.com

Desktop
ANNOYANCES

I remember my first desktop PC. It was a Packard Bell
8086 with two floppy drives and CGA graphics. The con-
traption terrorized my cats with its constant noise, and
usually threw enough heat to warm my office in our frig-
id New England winters. Of course, a 20MB (yes, megabyte) hard drive and a newfangled VGA graphics adapter
were prized upgrades that worked quite well—once I
managed to get them working in the first place. Times
have changed. Today's 3GHz+ desktop systems offer remarkable compatibility and stability across a myriad of
hardware devices. Still, there are plenty of times when it
seems that your PC genuinely hates you, and not even a
deal with God can get things running the way you want.
This chapter offers practical solutions to keep you from
pulverizing your pesky desktop.

SETUP ANNOYANCES

CABLING AND IMAGE QUALITY

The Annoyance: The image on my LCD monitor looks a little fuzzy no matter what resolution or refresh rate I use. I already downloaded the latest drivers. What else can I do?

The Fix: Electrical noise usually causes an image to seem "fuzzy," but always start with the basics and perform a few quick sanity checks. Make sure you tighten (secure those little thumbscrews) the analog RGB video cable between the monitor and the PC's video adapter. Look for any kinks, nicks, or damage to the video cable. If it looks like the cable just came through an Enron shredder, replace it right away. Reroute the video cable away from any AC power cables or high-energy devices (equipment that can produce substantial electrical interference), such as coffee makers or motorized devices.

If you want to display top-quality images, dump that old RGB cable in favor of a *Digital Visual Interface* (*DVI*) connection (see Figure 1-1). A DVI cable uses digital signals rather than analog levels, so DVI tends to produce a cleaner image. There's just one catch: both the video card and the LCD monitor must have DVI connections handy.

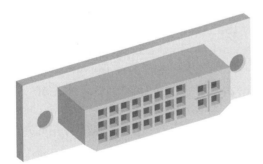

Figure 1-1. A DVI connection will typically produce a slightly better image than an analog RGB video connection.

> Make sure you use the manufacturer's recommended display driver for your particular LCD model. A generic CRT driver may not provide optimal results. Also, try the resolution designed for the LCD. For example, an Acer F51 works best at 1024×768.

COLORS AND CONNECTIONS

The rear of your PC has enough connections to befuddle Dr. Frankenstein. Worst of all, PC makers either fail to mark the connectors or use some kind of modern hieroglyphics that you need a Rosetta Stone to decipher. Fortunately, newer PCs use different colors to identify each connection. The key colors to remember:

- ☒ **Green: PS/2 Mouse**
- ☒ **Violet: PS/2 Keyboard**
- ☒ **Red: 25-pin Parallel Port**
- ☒ **Dark Blue: 15-pin (high-density) Video Port**

And those perplexing little audio jacks:

- ☒ **Lime: Speaker or Headphone Output**
- ☒ **Light Blue: Line (external) Input**
- ☒ **Orange: Microphone Input**

WIRELESS KEYBOARDS NEED ATTENTION

The Annoyance: I installed a new wireless keyboard and mouse combo, but I can't get my system to recognize them.

The Fix: A whole slew of issues can really gum up the works here. Make sure you connected the wireless receiver (usually a small USB device, similar to the wireless mouse's recharging cradle) to a working USB port. Also, the receiver should appear in your Device Manager according to the manufacturer's installation instructions. Sure, you already checked it five times, but do it again, for me.

Now look at the batteries in both the mouse and the keyboard. Check the battery orientation to make sure you installed them correctly. If necessary, replace the batteries with a fresh set. Remember, batteries only last about two months (though the really optimistic manufacturers claim six months). Rechargeable mouse batteries should fully charge before you fire up the system.

Still no response? No worries. Wireless devices support several different channels, so you probably need to synchronize the keyboard and mouse. The steps vary with each manufacturer, but for kits like the Logitech Cordless MX Duo, you simply press the Connect button on the receiver, and then press the corresponding Connect button on the mouse and keyboard. Violà!

OVERCOMING REPETITIVE STRESS PROBLEMS

The Annoyance: Typing drives me crazy. It hurts my hands, wrists, and arms. Got any advice?

The Fix: Ah, you may be an unfortunate victim of repetitive stress injury (your insurance company...um, doctor just calls it RSI). Some research suggests that long periods of repetitive motion (like typing and flicking a mouse back and forth) and improper positioning of your hands and body may systematically injure your nerves, tendons, and muscles. The results can range from pain, numbness, and tingling, to weakness, swelling, burning, cramping, and stiffness. Affected areas can include your hands, arms, shoulder, neck, and back. Bottom line: don't mess around—see your doctor as soon as possible.

Fortunately, you can use some clever tricks to help stave off (and sometimes possibly reverse) RSI. Logitech provides a set of Comfort Guidelines for a preferred workspace setup. Download the multilingual PDF from

http://www.logitech.com/pub/comfort/comfort-us.pdf. Recognized medical resources, such as WebMD (*http://www.webmd.com*), can also provide details and suggestions to help deal with RSI, and Deborah Quilter's RSI help site (*http://www.rsihelp.com*) digs right into the nitty-gritty details. Finally, the following tips might help you:

- Reduce computer use. For example, take a walk or see a movie rather than play a video game.
- Position your workstation properly. Set the monitor directly in front of you, with the screen at eye level. The keyboard and mouse should be low enough to position your elbows at 90 degrees.
- Sit up straight. Your spine should be upright.
- Technique is vital. Never rest your wrists on a desk, wrist pad, or armrests while you type or use the mouse.
- Take a short break every 20–30 minutes. Stretch frequently while at the computer.
- Regular cardiovascular exercise (like walking) helps with circulation, and upper body strengthening and stretching exercises can help your arms and wrists.
- Do not continue working with the computer if you experience pain or fatigue—see your doctor immediately.

---

t i p

Check out the Occupational Safety and Health Administration (OSHA) web site (*http://www.osha.gov/SLTC/ergonomics/index.html*) for ergonomic guidelines and workplace initiatives.

DETECTING USB DRIVES

The Annoyance: How come my Windows XP system won't recognize my new USB DVD-/+RW drive? I connected and reconnected it, but the $@#$ thing doesn't show up.

The Fix: You can usually track external device headaches to a connection or power problem. First, check your blood pressure, and then attach a mouse to the USB port to make sure it works. If you can navigate the mouse, you know the port works. If not, the trouble is with your system's USB port.

> **tip**
>
> Always attach high-speed USB devices such as CD/DVD drives and video-capture devices directly to your system. A USB hub can cause connection and performance problems.

Once you iron out any USB port wrinkles, look at the USB signal cable. Insert the connector firmly and replace any kinked, cut, or scuffed cables. Because external drives need more power than the USB port can provide, make sure you properly connect the AC adapter to the drive. An LED on the drive should light to indicate power.

> **tip**
>
> The system requirements for an external drive can come back to bite you. High-speed USB drives may demand a USB 2.0 port for optimal data transfer speeds. USB 1.1 ports may not always detect the drive properly (or certainly won't handle the drive at the best possible speed). Older USB 1.0 ports will probably not detect a USB 2.0 drive at all.

THE BIG CHILL: STOPPING SYSTEM FREEZE-UPS

The Annoyance: I installed a PCI video capture card and now my system freezes and crashes at the worst possible times. How can I get the card to work without starting from scratch?

Double-Check Connections

The number of setup problems due to poor connections would astonish you. Every connector in your PC should snap, clip, or screw into place—no excuses. Make sure you tighten every connection, and remember to use the little thumbscrews to secure video, serial, and parallel port cables. Don't say I didn't warn you.

The Fix: This setup problem really bites most PC users in the rear, and requires a little more work than the previous annoyance. A bad driver installation or resource conflict almost always causes the trouble. Notice I said "almost always." Before you do anything, remove the device and its drivers, and then check the PC again. Old-time PC technicians call this "last in, first out." In other words, if you remove the last item you installed, it should straighten things out temporarily.

I know manuals offer the perfect cure for insomnia, but stay awake long enough to recheck the installation steps. Sometimes you need to install the drivers and support software *before* you install the hardware. Other times, the PC will simply recognize the new hardware and ask for the drivers after installation. Remove the device and drivers, and then try again in the right order. If you really want to restore the system to a preinstallation condition, use the System Restore wizard.

> **tip**
>
>
> When you install an external device (such as a hard drive), remember to check the signal and power connections.

The driver CD probably includes drivers for a bunch of operating systems, so make sure you install the appropriate driver. Also, new device drivers sometimes ship with bugs or other oversights; check the manufacturer's web site for patches and driver updates.

Windows XP includes a slew of drivers, so you may not even need the driver CD.

If the card still acts up when you reinstall it, check the Device Manager for signs of a conflict. Under Windows XP, open the System control panel, click the Hardware tab, and then click the Device Manager button. Conflicts occur when a card tries to use the same hardware resources (such as an interrupt, DMA line, or memory space) assigned to another device in the PC. If no device problems exist, the particular device may not work with your computer. In this case, remove the card and take it back to the store for a refund, or exchange it for a different make and model. If, however, you see one or more devices marked with errors, right-click the device and select Properties, look at the Device status area for problem details, and click the Troubleshoot button. A troubleshooting wizard will walk you through the issue (see Figure 1-2).

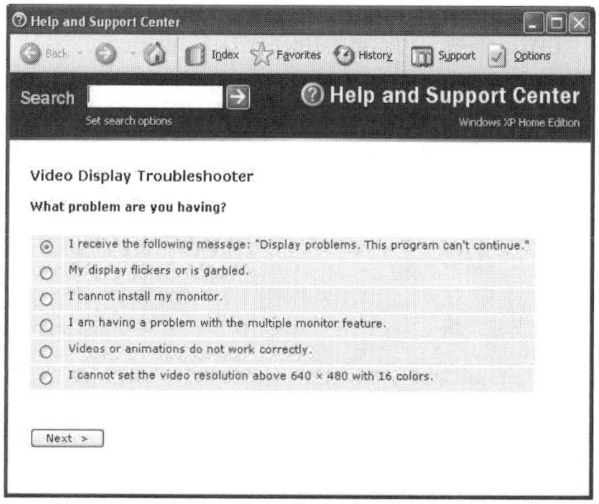

Figure 1-2. Windows provides comprehensive troubleshooting assistance, such as the Video Display Troubleshooter.

Breathe In; Breathe Out

PCs deal with a lot of heat. To keep things running smoothly, the PC must vent warmed air and take in cooler displacement air. Leave ample space around any exhaust fans, and never obstruct intake vents with books, papers, or other objects.

NEW HARD DRIVE JAMS THE SYSTEM

The Annoyance: I purchased a new 80GB hard drive to run Windows XP on an older PC. I want to use the other drive for Linux. I installed the new drive as the master and connected the old drive as the slave. I started to install Windows XP on the newer drive, but the system froze at the BIOS during reboot, and could not detect the drive. Any ideas?

The Fix: Multiple hard drives can be ornery if not configured properly. For example, did you set the master/slave jumpers on each drive to specify their relationship? This is a common oversight when you relegate an old master drive to a secondary position. Do a sanity check of your drive jumpers just to make sure.

Watch the BIOS hardware list at boot time to tell if you installed both drives properly. The BIOS will list a manufacturer's part number for the primary and secondary drives on your first channel. The new drive should be listed as your "Primary Master," and the old drive should appear as your "Primary Slave." If the part designations match your drive positions, you know the BIOS sees each drive at the hardware level. If either entry is marked "None" or "Not Installed," you have a cable problem or jumper mismatch.

A bootable drive in the slave position makes some systems really testy. Disconnect the old drive, but leave the new drive in the master position all by itself. Now install Windows XP on the new drive. Next, power down the system and reconnect the old drive. Copy over any important data files, then repartition the old drive and install Linux at your leisure.

UPS Doesn't Mean Shipping

An *Uninterruptable Power Supply* (or *UPS*) provides cheap insurance for any PC system. When the power fails, the UPS will keep your PC and monitor running for a few minutes. Not long, but long enough to save your important work and shut down safely. Otherwise, a power failure means "crash city"—imagine hours of work lost, and maybe even corrupted system files. A UPS pays for itself with the first crash it averts.

---

t i p

A drive transfer utility such as Symantec Ghost (*http://www.ghost.com*) can efficiently mirror an old drive to a new drive. This eliminates the need to reinstall the OS, applications, and datafiles.

WISDOM OF NEW MOTHERBOARD DRIVERS

The Annoyance: I installed a new motherboard on my Windows XP system, but should I install the motherboard drivers from the accompanying CD, or just let XP handle the hardware?

The Fix: Windows XP offers lots of drivers for all sorts of hardware types. This makes new device installations quick and easy because you don't need to mess around with a driver disc. However, XP isn't perfect (hold your Microsoft jokes) and it doesn't account for every hardware device.

So what the hell does *that* mean? Well, it means there is no hard-and-fast rule to follow. It really depends on the particular motherboard and its hardware features. For example, I saw a Biostar M7NCG motherboard install just fine under Windows XP. The operating system identified many of the hardware devices (such as USB support) without the need for additional drivers. The onboard sound system failed to work, but installing the manufacturer's drivers fixed things straight away. On the other hand, I saw Gigabyte motherboards run perfectly under XP without any manufacturer's drivers.

The real gotcha? You don't want the manufacturer's drivers to overwrite working XP components unless absolutely necessary. I can offer three tests for you to follow:

- Check the motherboard's documentation and the driver disc for any guidance. If the manual specifically says to install the disc under XP (or that XP drivers are included on the CD), then you should install the drivers according to the manufacturer's instructions. You can always email or call the motherboard maker to verify matters.

- If you're still in the dark, try the motherboard without additional drivers. The system will almost certainly boot, but you may find that certain features (such as sound or USB) may not function properly. You should install the minimum number of drivers needed to enable any cripple features.

- If the new motherboard and all its features—sound system, Ethernet (NIC) network port, integrated video port, and USB/FireWire ports—run properly without additional drivers, then don't install the manufacturer's drivers.

KEYBOARD ANNOYANCES

RESURRECTING A DEAD KEYBOARD

The Annoyance: My keyboard absolutely refuses to respond. Did I kill it?

The Fix: A dead keyboard is usually caused by a connection issue or a hardware failure. First, try another keyboard and see if it works. If not, you probably have a keyboard connector problem at the motherboard. Power down and try the suspect keyboard on another system. If the keyboard works on another PC, you know the trouble rests with the original system (not the keyboard). A motherboard replacement may be necessary, or you might be able to use a USB keyboard instead. This may be a cheaper and less time-consuming solution than a motherboard replacement. Clever, eh?

> **t i p**
>
> A quick keyboard check: press the Caps Lock or Num Lock button and see if the corresponding keyboard LEDs light up. If not, the keyboard lacks power.

WAKING NARCOLEPTIC USB KEYBOARDS

The Annoyance: My USB keyboard refuses to bring the PC out of standby mode, and I wind up wiggling the mouse to wake the system.

The Fix: This hassle usually surfaces on older PCs with flaky USB support in the BIOS. To test this premise, turn off your PC and exchange a PS/2 keyboard for the USB keyboard. If it works, you just identified it as a USB port issue. Check with the PC or motherboard manufacturer for a system BIOS upgrade (or take the cheap way out and stick with the PS/2 keyboard).

Sometimes a similar issue pops up on new systems with full USB support. You may discover that neither the keyboard nor the mouse will wake the system from the standby or the hibernate mode. Surprise—this is by design. You need to press the Power button briefly to wake the system. Careful, though—if you hold down the Power button for more than four seconds, you turn off the PC and lose any unsaved data.

So how do you get a USB keyboard to wake a new PC? You need to adjust the power management settings for your Human Interface Device (HID) USB keyboard. Under Windows XP, open the System control panel, click the Hardware tab, and then click the Device Manager button. Now double-click Keyboards and double-click HID Keyboard. In the HID Keyboard Device Properties dialog box, click the Power Management tab and check the "Allow this device to bring the computer out of standby" box.

STOP KEYBOARD S-S-S-STUTTER

The Annoyance: I can hunt and peck pretty well, but when I look up from the keyboard, I notice repeated or missing letters.

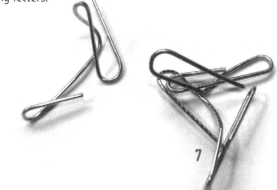

The Fix: It sounds like you have one of the filthiest keyboards in the world, but let's take it one step at a time. Open the Keyboard control panel and look at the typematic rate (see Figure 1-3). A short repeat delay and high repeat rate can spew superfluous characters before you know it. Put your cursor in the blank area labeled "Click here and hold down a key to test repeat rate" and press a key to see how character repeat works.

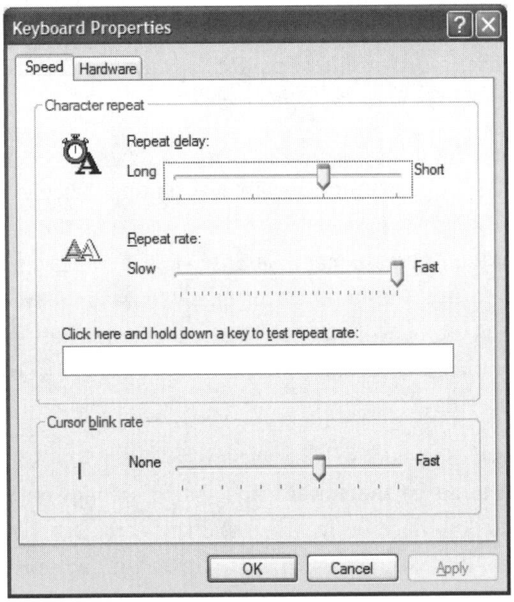

Figure 1-3. A quick look at the keyboard's typematic rate can solve a lot of repeating character headaches.

If your typematic settings seem fine, you probably need to clean the keyboard. Months (and even years) of dust, pet hair, and other debris can jam key mechanisms. This often makes keys hard to press, so a character may not appear until you really poke the key. In other cases, the key may stay down just enough to repeat. Power down the PC, disconnect the keyboard, and take it outside (yes outside—you'll thank me) along with a can of compressed air (available from any Staples or OfficeMax store). Blow air between the keys and watch the crap fly—oh, keep your face clear of the dust cloud. Repeat every 3-4 months or as needed. As a last resort, replace the keyboard.

Wearing Protection

You can use a cheap, plastic keyboard cover to minimize the long-term headaches of dust and debris. For example, Keyboards.com (*http://www.keyboardskins.com/cartexe/disposable.asp*) and ProtecT Computer Products (*http://www.protectcovers.com*) both offer disposable coverings, and a quick search of the Internet reveals dozens more. Don't feel like spending hard-earned cash? Just cover the keyboard with an ordinary towel.

UNSTICKING A STUCK KEYBOARD

The Annoyance: Every time I try to boot my system, an error message says my keyboard is stuck.

The Fix: When the system boots, the BIOS performs the *Power On Self Test* (*POST*). If the test discovers one or more pressed keys, it will report a hardware failure, display a terse "stuck key" error message, and halt the startup process. Look for and remove any object lying across the keyboard—elbows, baby fingers, cat paws, or whatever—and reboot. If the problem persists, some keys may be jammed, so just power down and replace the keyboard.

tip

To get Windows to recognize the special buttons on your keyboard for email, Internet Explorer, Windows Media Player, and the like, you need to install the driver that came with the keyboard. In the unlikely event you already installed the driver, check with the manufacturer for patches or updates.

SYNCHRONIZING A LOST WIRELESS KEYBOARD

The Annoyance: My wireless keyboard acts crazy. Sometimes it works, other times it plays dead. Should I resynchronize my keyboard and receiver?

The Fix: Not so fast, "Sync-Boy." Tired old batteries can cause erratic wireless operation, so check the batteries before you do anything else. Also, wait a few minutes before you insert the new ones. This helps clear any latent macros or other settings stored in the keyboard.

If new batteries don't stop the twitches, consider potential electromagnetic (EM) interference from various electronic devices, such as CRTs, LCDs, speakers, power outlets, network hubs, and so on. If you place the receiver on any type of metal surface, it may cause RF signals to bounce or cancel. Move any potential interference sources at least eight inches away from the receiver, or try a different location for the receiver.

As a last step, give synchronization a shot. The actual synchronization process depends on the particular kit, but you usually press a learn/teach button on both the receiver and the keyboard. For example, to synchronize a Logitech Cordless Access keyboard, hold down the Connect button on the RF receiver for about 15 seconds, and then press the Connect button on the keyboard.

MULTIMEDIA KEYS WON'T LAUNCH PLAYER

The Annoyance: I can't launch WinAmp using the media keys on my wireless Logitech keyboard. I can, however, start WinAmp manually.

The Fix: This problem has reared its ugly head a few times with Logitech cordless keyboards using the company's iTouch software. For example, only iTouch software Versions 2.15 or later can launch WinAmp 3.x. Fortunately, you can download a later iTouch software release and fix this in a jiffy (see *http://www.logitech.com/index.cfm/downloads/categories/US/EN,CRID=1796*).

The Bluetooth Lag

When a PC returns from standby mode, you must wait a few seconds before you can access a Bluetooth wireless keyboard or mouse. This is by design. To save battery power, Bluetooth devices go into a sleep mode after an idle period, and it takes them several seconds to wake up and reconnect. Don't panic.

The manual for your multimedia keyboard will typically list compatible audio players, DVD players, and applications.

KEYBOARD SHUTDOWN SNAGS

The Annoyance: I installed the software for my new multimedia keyboard, and now my system takes forever to shut down.

The Fix: Here's another example of poor software design coming back to bite unsuspecting end users. Windows XP has to exit and unload any software running on the system before it can close. A stubborn application like your keyboard software can snag Windows and prevent a timely shutdown. To nip this problem in the bud, you need to update the keyboard software.

If no software update exists to fix this glitch (wouldn't that be a surprise), quit the keyboard software before you shut down the PC. For example, if you use Logitech's iTouch software, you can just right-click the iTouch icon in the System Tray and choose Exit (PC newbies can find the System Tray icons on the right side of the Windows Taskbar). When the icon disappears, go ahead and shut down.

ENDING WIRELESS CROSSTALK

The Annoyance: A lot of people in my office, myself included, use a wireless keyboard and mouse, and sometimes my colleague's keystrokes or mouse movements show up on my system.

The Fix: This has become a common problem as wireless devices penetrate the workplace and classroom. Wireless RF receivers will respond to any signal on the proper frequency. Most cordless devices have a 6-10 foot range, which means they can easily interfere with each other in a crowded office. Techie-types call this kind of interference "crosstalk," and it happens with both wireless keyboards and mice.

One easy solution is to put 10 feet or more between wireless systems. If workstations are close together, alternate wired and wireless installations to boost the range between wireless devices. Still stuck with nearby devices? Resynchronize each pair of wireless devices to reset their wireless channels.

Surprisingly, timing can play a role in new device separation. Manufacturers such as Logitech suggest you install each new wireless device in 30-minute increments. Even after you connect a wireless receiver, it checks for other devices that it can sync to for another 25 minutes or so. Simultaneously connecting several wireless devices nearby may allow the second device to synchronize with the first receiver. Disconnect all but one of the new wireless devices, and then reconnect each set 30 minutes apart.

MOUSE ANNOYANCES

MAKE MOUSE TRAILS EASIER TO FOLLOW

The Annoyance: I may be getting older, but other people must also find it hard to follow the mouse zipping across the screen. How can I make it easier to see?

The Fix: You can tweak the mouse using a couple of simple tricks. Open the Mouse control panel, and then click the Pointers tab (see Figure 1-4). Use the drop-down menu and select a large or extra-large scheme. A bigger pointer is easier to see, right? If you still need help, click the Pointer Options tab and check the "Display pointer trails" box. Adjust the trail length until you can follow it easily.

Figure 1-4. Larger mouse pointers and trails can make the mouse much easier to see.

MOUSE HELP FOR SOUTHPAWS

The Annoyance: Is there a law against left-handed discrimination? If so, I plan to sue every mouse manufacturer on the planet. How am I supposed to use this right-handed mouse?

The Fix: Work with me here—this is an easy fix. Open the Mouse control panel and click the Buttons tab (see Figure 1-5). Check the "Switch primary and secondary buttons" box to reverse the left and right mouse buttons. This at least gets the buttons right.

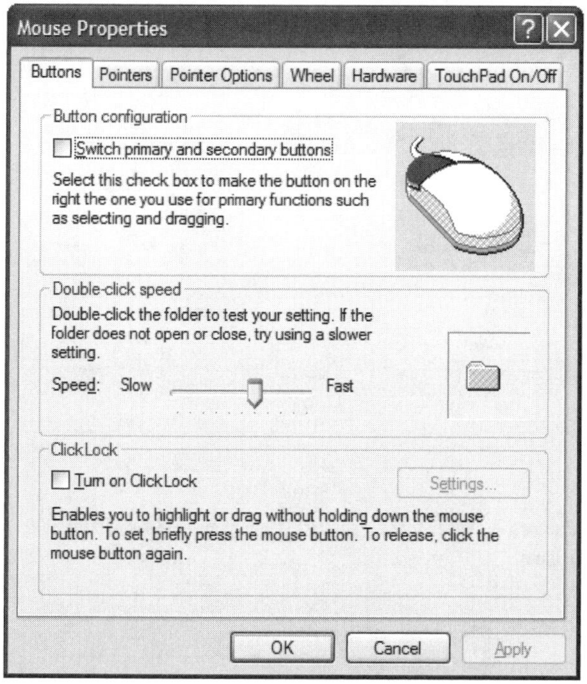

Figure 1-5. Reversing the mouse buttons is a big advantage for southpaw users.

Manufacturers sell a lot of mice in an ergonomic shell tailored to the right hand. You can switch the mouse buttons, but using a right-handed mouse in the left hand stinks. Instead, use an ambidextrous mouse for a more comfortable grip.

STOPPING MOUSE STALLS AND SKIPS

The Annoyance: My cursor seems to jump and stall a lot lately. I need to run the mouse all over my desk just to move the cursor anywhere.

Come Over to My Pad

Optical mice use LEDs and photo sensors (rather than balls and rollers) to distinguish mouse movements. This means the surface and texture of your mouse pad plays a role in cursor sensitivity. Smooth, featureless mouse pads (such as a glassy or shiny surface) can potentially "blind" an optical mouse. Instead, use a mouse pad with a fabric or finely textured surface.

The Fix: Take a second and check your mouse connection. Also, look for any suspicious cuts or kinks in the mouse cable. If the cabling looks all right, it sounds like you need to do a little cleaning. The rubber ball in your mouse picks up all the dust, pet hair, and other general crap from your mouse pad. From there, the debris coats the little rollers inside the mouse and the rollers slip. The ball continues to move, but the X and Y rollers do not, so the cursor just sits there.

The fix is easy, but it takes a minute. Power down the PC and turn the mouse over. Turn the little plastic ring around the ball counter-clockwise to unlock it, and the ring and ball will fall right out. Clean the rubber ball with a paper towel and some light glass cleaner. Use a Q-tip to wipe any gunk from the rollers, and blow out any crap. Now put the ball and ring back in the mouse and lock the ring into place.

Warning. . .

Never use acetone or any other harsh chemical on plastic PC parts. Chemicals will melt the plastic and ruin your parts. Stick with light glass cleaner, such as Windex.

Troublesome Extension Cables

Most keyboard and mouse cables only measure a meter long. Unfortunately, some PC users use extension cables to add extra distance between the PC and the keyboard and mouse. Poorly made extension cables can pick up excess electrical noise and cause flaky keyboard or mouse behavior. Always remove any extension cables and connect input devices directly to your system as part of any troubleshooting process. If you must use extension cables, pony up and buy a well-shielded cable.

STARTUP ANNOYANCES

SHAVING SECONDS OFF STARTUP TIMES

The Annoyance: It takes forever to boot my system. Do I really need to see the memory count or RAID drive check every time the system starts? How can I get to my operating system faster?

The Fix: Most PCs make it through the self-test part of each startup in less than 15 seconds, but you can change several default BIOS settings to shave a few precious seconds off the normal startup. For example, the Phoenix/Award BIOS version used with the Tyan Tomcat i7210 (S5112) Pentium 4 "Northwood" or "Prescott" motherboard provides a Quick Power On Self Test option in the Advanced BIOS Features menu (see Figure 1-6). When enabled, the BIOS skips optional parts of the Power On Self Test (POST), such as the memory check.

You can also disable the Boot Up Floppy Seek option. This prevents the system from looking for a floppy drive at each startup (a test that can take several seconds). Also, check the Boot Sequence, which lets you specify which drives the BIOS checks for bootable media (in other words,

an operating system). Make sure the boot sequence lists the drive you boot from most frequently first (normally the C: drive). If it lists other drives first (like a floppy drive or CD drive), the BIOS will waste precious seconds waiting for each drive to respond. In fact, set any unused drive spots to None (rather than Auto) to prevent the system from checking for nonexistent drives.

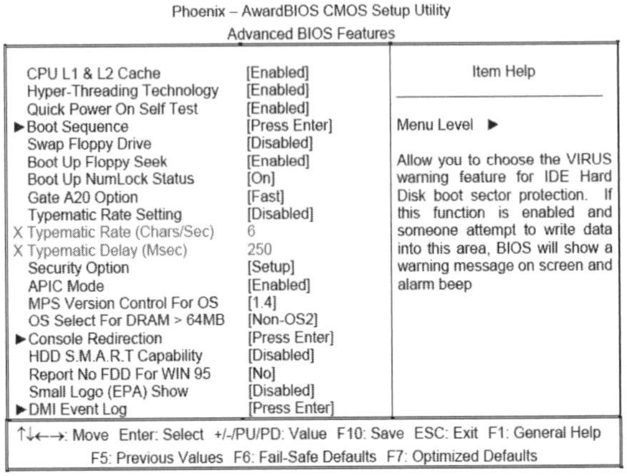

Figure 1-6. Speed your system startup with some carefully selected BIOS options.

> **t i p**
>
> Each BIOS maker often employs unique options and frequently labels them differently. This can make it a bit confusing to find specific BIOS options. Always refer to your motherboard manual for detailed information on each feature.

THAT SON OF A *BEEP* CODE

The Annoyance: When I turn on my PC, it beeps at me and nothing shows up on the LCD monitor. Is my computer trying to communicate using Morse code?

The Fix: Well it's certainly not singing to you. In fact, the blank monitor indicates a very serious problem early on in the self-test startup routine.

PCs perform self tests each time you apply power. When the system discovers errors, it attempts to report the problem as a code or message. Beep codes can vary a lot between BIOS makers. You can see the beep codes for a few popular BIOS makers listed at PC Hell (*http://www.pchell.com/hardware/beepcodes.shtml*) and Computer Hope (*http://www.computerhope.com/beep.htm*). You can usually narrow down most beep problems to three key areas: memory, video, and motherboard. Fortunately, a few quick checks can reveal the most common problems.

Power down the PC and open the case. Check all the expansion boards, especially the AGP video card. Every card should be inserted evenly and completely into its slot. Each card's metal bracket should be secured to the chassis with a single, snug screw. An uneven expansion card may short-circuit one or more metal contacts and cause a signal problem that disables the computer.

A failed graphics adapter could also be the culprit. If you use the motherboard's own onboard video adapter, just insert a graphics card into an available AGP (or PCI) slot and switch over the monitor cable. If, however, you already use an AGP (or PCI) graphics card and the motherboard offers an onboard video circuit, just pop out the graphics card and temporarily switch back to the motherboard's video port.

Still no luck? Open your PC and investigate the memory modules. Make sure you firmly insert and clip each memory module into place. To identify defective modules, insert each module separately and then try to reboot the system. If your system only has one memory module, try a new one. If the system still chirps like a pissed-off parakeet, try another motherboard.

> **Warning...**
>
> Always power down and unplug the computer before you open or perform any work inside the case. Although you run just a small risk of accidental electrocution, best practices dictate safety at all times. Be smart and be safe!

> **BY DEFAULT**
>
> You may be tempted to tinker with the complex (and sometimes arcane) features tucked away in the submenus of your BIOS. However, it takes only one bad setting to stop your system from booting or running in a stable fashion. When disaster strikes, you can restore the troublesome settings *only if* you remember which tweaks caused your system to choke. Fortunately, most systems offer Fail-Safe or Optimized defaults (see **Figure 1-6**) that can automatically restore system-critical settings. You should also load the default settings after you flash a motherboard's BIOS version.

USB BOOT PROBLEMS

The Annoyance: My bootable CD boots fine from my internal CD-RW drive, but how do I get it to work with my new USB DVD-/+RW drive?

The Fix: Well, you probably can't. Most USB drives require a Windows driver to load before you can access the drive. However, hang in there, because an increasing number of BIOS versions and drives support bootable USB. Check for BIOS updates before you throw in the towel. In the meantime, if you need the features offered by your new DVD-/+RW drive, return the external drive for an internal ATAPI version of the same model.

BOOTING FROM A CD DRIVE

The Annoyance: How can I boot my system using the stack of recovery discs the manufacturer threw in the box? Every time I insert a disc, the system just loads the operating system from the hard drive.

The Fix: Every computer has a boot order for its drives, which defines the order in which the system checks for bootable media. In most cases, the boot order starts with the hard drive (the C: drive), the floppy drive (the A: drive), and then the CD drive (perhaps the D: drive). However, the computer will launch an operating system from the first bootable drive in the boot order—even if other drives contain bootable media.

If you forget to insert bootable media in the CD drive, the BIOS will simply go on to the next volume in the boot order. Start the PC normally and insert the bootable disc *before* you attempt the system restoration.

The quick fix: open the System Setup utility (see Figure 1-6) at start time, check the Boot Sequence (or Boot Order) entry, and make sure it lists the CD drive with your system restore disc first. Remember to save your changes when you exit and reboot. The bootable CD should start the restoration process. If not, make sure the disc is indeed bootable. In a few cases, you may need to launch the restoration from a special boot diskette or even the operating system.

HANG-UPS STOP THE OS

The Annoyance: My system starts to boot, but then seems to hang just before the operating system loads.

The Fix: Once the BIOS finishes the self-test process, it tries to pass control to the drive with bootable media. If the POST runs but the operating system fails to load, check your hard drive.

Reboot the system and review the BIOS hardware list that appears a few moments after boot time. Properly connected and powered hard drives should have a manufacturer's part number denoted in the hardware list (such as Figure 1-7). This tells you that the drive is active. If your boot drive does not appear in the hardware list, power down, open the system, and secure the power and signal cables at the hard drive.

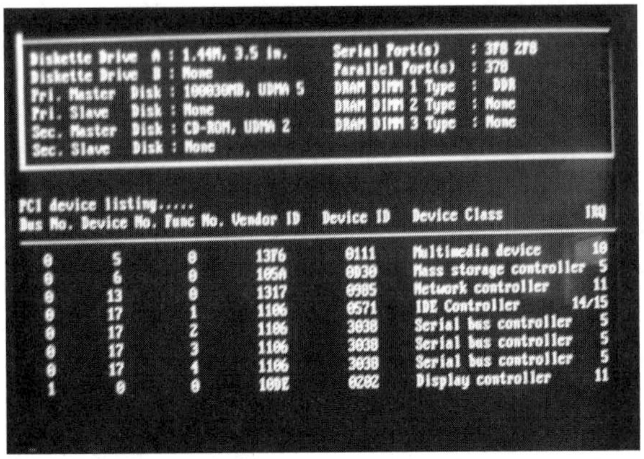

![BIOS hardware list screen]

Figure 1-7. Check the BIOS hardware list to verify that your drive hardware is responding to the POST.

If the boot drive still doesn't appear in your hardware list, open the System Setup utility and check the hard drive entries listed in the Standard CMOS Features menu (see Figure 1-8). Most BIOS support up to four hard drives (two on the primary drive controller channel, and two on the secondary controller channel), though some new systems offer an additional channel for two more drives. Systems typically detect drives automatically, but some demand a certain setting (such as "Auto") in each hard drive entry. An incorrect entry (such as "None") can prevent the BIOS from seeing the attached drives.

What happens when the drive really does appear in the BIOS hardware list and the operating system still refuses to load? This may indicate an issue with the drive partition or critical boot files needed to start the OS. This sometimes happens when viruses or unexpected system crashes strike a computer. Windows XP lets you repair the OS installation using the original CD. Otherwise, you need to repartition and reinstall Windows XP from scratch.

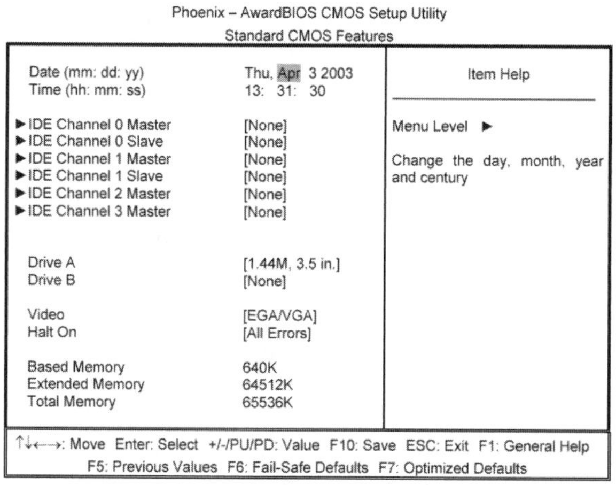

Phoenix – AwardBIOS CMOS Setup Utility
Standard CMOS Features

Date (mm: dd: yy)	Thu, Apr 3 2003	Item Help
Time (hh: mm: ss)	13: 31: 30	
▶ IDE Channel 0 Master	[None]	Menu Level ▶
▶ IDE Channel 0 Slave	[None]	
▶ IDE Channel 1 Master	[None]	Change the day, month, year
▶ IDE Channel 1 Slave	[None]	and century
▶ IDE Channel 2 Master	[None]	
▶ IDE Channel 3 Master	[None]	
Drive A	[1.44M, 3.5 in.]	
Drive B	[None]	
Video	[EGA/VGA]	
Halt On	[All Errors]	
Based Memory	640K	
Extended Memory	64512K	
Total Memory	65536K	

↑↓←→: Move Enter: Select +/-/PU/PD: Value F10: Save ESC: Exit F1: General Help
F5: Previous Values F6: Fail-Safe Defaults F7: Optimized Defaults

Figure 1-8. Verify that each hard drive—especially your boot drive—is enabled in the System Setup.

FIXING A STICKY DRIVE LIGHT

The Annoyance: I upgraded my hard drive, but now the bloody system won't start and the drive LED stays on all the time.

The Fix: It sounds like a cabling snafu. When you installed your new drive and reattached the signal cable, one end of the cable probably went in backwards (upside down). This shorts out important signals and stops the system from booting. It also keeps the drive activity LED on constantly. Power down and unplug the system. Check the signal cabling and pay close attention to the orientation of pin 1. Pin 1 has a red (or blue) stripe on its side. Just reattach the signal cable correctly and try the system again. Easy, right?

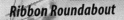

The 40-pin ATAPI ribbon cables are particularly prone to accidental reversal, but more recent cable schemes like Serial-ATA (SATA) are keyed to ensure proper orientation.

More food for thought: most computers use the LED to indicate common activity (like spinning up or normal access), but some drives use an LED for fault reporting. For example, the Seagate Cheetah 36LP drive provides both activity and fault information, so its LED will simply remain dark until the drive or host adapter detects a failure.

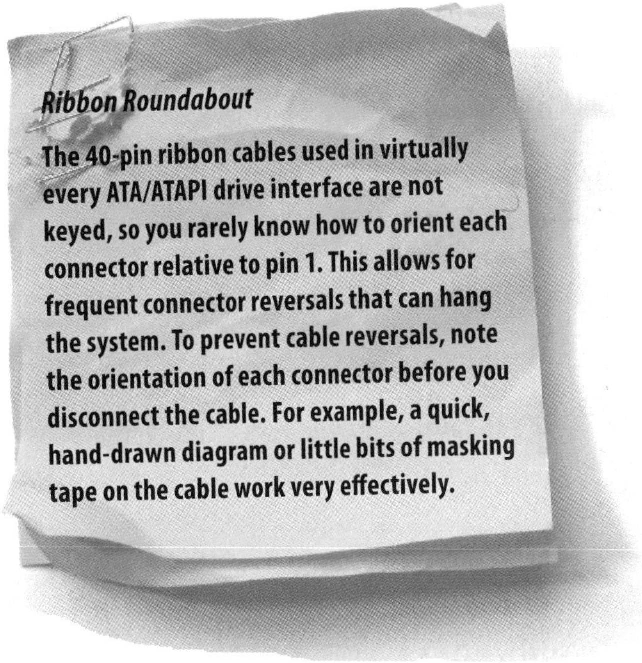

Ribbon Roundabout

The 40-pin ribbon cables used in virtually every ATA/ATAPI drive interface are not keyed, so you rarely know how to orient each connector relative to pin 1. This allows for frequent connector reversals that can hang the system. To prevent cable reversals, note the orientation of each connector before you disconnect the cable. For example, a quick, hand-drawn diagram or little bits of masking tape on the cable work very effectively.

CLEARING A FORGOTTEN CMOS PASSWORD

The Annoyance: I put a password on my computer using the CMOS Setup (rather than Windows), and now I'm completely locked out.

The Fix: Like most password schemes, this one has a back door. Motherboard makers include a handy but little-known jumper that will clear your CMOS password.

> The steps to clear a CMOS password or setup contents can vary a bit between motherboard makers. Always follow the specific directions covered in the motherboard manual.

Look at the motherboard manual and locate the Password Clear jumper (assuming that your motherboard offers that jumper). If you don't have the motherboard manual handy, just download it from the manufacturer's web site. Do *not* bother searching the motherboard itself—you will go blind looking for that obscure little jumper. When you locate the password jumper, power down the system and move the jumper to its "clear" position, then boot the system. You will probably see a BIOS message indicating that the password has been cleared. Shut off the system, return the jumper to its original position, and then boot the system normally (or try another password if you're a glutton for punishment).

Your motherboard may offer a CMOS Clear jumper rather than a password-only jumper. This clears all of the CMOS RAM contents, including the password, and the process is a little different. Power down the system and disconnect any power connectors from the motherboard. This includes unclipping the common 20-pin ATX power connector, along with a smaller 6-pin supplemental power connector. Move the jumper to the "clear" position for 10 seconds, and then move the jumper back to its original position. Reconnect the power connectors and reboot the system.

In some cases, the BIOS reloads default settings automatically. Otherwise, you may need to enter the System Setup and reload your default CMOS settings.

DEALING WITH INVALID MEDIA TYPE ERRORS

The Annoyance: Every time my PC starts, I see an error that says "Invalid Media Type" and the system just halts.

The Fix: This error pops up when the computer tries to boot from non-bootable media, such as a floppy diskette in the drive. Some CD and DVD drives also produce this error when you insert non-bootable discs. Check your drives and remove any media, then reboot the system.

If you prefer to keep non-bootable media in the drive, but want to avoid invalid media errors, configure a boot order through the System Setup (see Figure 1-6). For example, if you disable the Boot Up Floppy Seek, the system will skip the A: drive at start time. Next, adjust the Boot Sequence so the system checks the C: drive first. Save your changes and reboot. The system should jump straight to the master hard drive and start booting.

Password Pushovers

Passwords keep unauthorized users off your computer. To create a secure password, use the maximum number of available characters, employ a mix of upper- and lowercase characters, and include numbers or punctuation. This makes the password much harder to guess or crack. For example, a password like "AlF&afA2" is far more difficult to guess than a simple name like "alfalfa." Avoid obvious passwords such as your spouse's name or children's birthdays.

Things get a bit more complicated if the invalid media error comes from your C: drive when all the other drives are empty. A computer virus, system crash, or even a hardware failure may have damaged or corrupted the boot files on your hard drive. Try to repair Windows XP using the original installation CD. Otherwise, repartition the drive and restore your OS and applications from scratch (or use the recovery CDs included with your system). If the problem persists and the drive seems unrecoverable no matter how much you curse at it, the drive may have failed and should be replaced immediately.

Executive Privilege

If several users share a computer, the main user should establish himself or herself as the system administrator, and select a reasonably secure password. You should also password-protect each new application where allowed. Children discover new system features with remarkable skill. If you don't implement passwords right away, your son or daughter just might, and you can easily find yourself locked out of your own computer.

SYSTEM WON'T WAKE FROM STANDBY

The Annoyance: My system dropped into standby mode and I can't get it to wake up.

The Fix: Normally, any keyboard or mouse activity should bring the idle system out of its power-conservation mode. If neither input device does the trick, press the power button briefly (if you hold down the power button too long, the system will turn off).

A device driver not fully compatible with standby or hibernation power-saving mode can cause the PC to freeze. A *warm reboot* (press the Reset button) will usually resurrect the system, but you will lose any unsaved data.

tip

Older BIOS versions may not support Windows power-saving modes completely. Check with the motherboard manufacturer for a BIOS upgrade.

To find the uncooperative device, you can update the drivers in a hit-or-miss process and hope you nail down the problem. Otherwise, simply disable your power-saving modes. Open the Power Options control panel, click the Power Schemes tab, and set the "System standby" and "System hibernates" options to Never (see Figure 1-9).

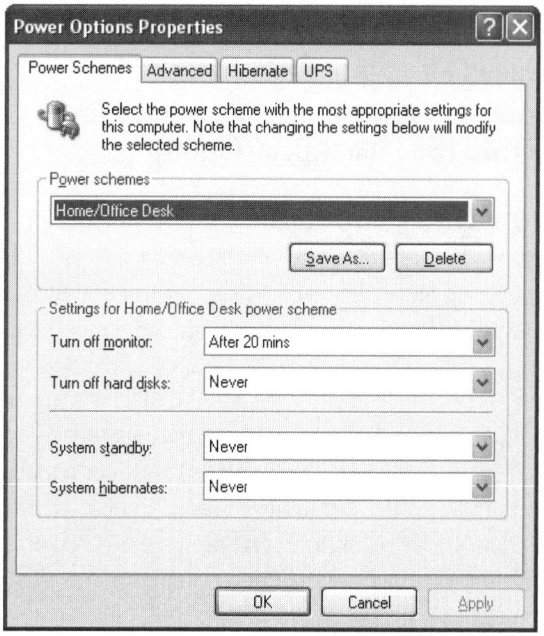

Figure 1-9. To avoid pesky power management troubles, just set the "System standby" and "System hibernates" settings to Never.

Drive Delays

Power management conserves power (and reduces wear) on an idle computer. Even when you prohibit standby and hibernate modes, you can power down the monitor and hard drives. Keep in mind that idle hard drives can take several seconds to spin up again. If you let drives drop into idle mode after short intervals, you may not like the frequent spin-up delays. Select longer hard drive idle mode intervals to make the most efficient use of your time.

BIOS/CMOS ANNOYANCES

GETTING THE TERMINOLOGY RIGHT

The Annoyance: I wish you PC geeks would stop confusing us with so many terms. One book tells me to go to the Setup menu, another tells me to check the BIOS or the CMOS. What magic keys get me into those menus?

The Fix: The computer industry often uses these related terms interchangeably. To set the record straight, the *BIOS* (Basic Input/Output System) is a motherboard chip that stores the instructions needed to boot your PC and transfer control to the operating system. This is often called firmware because the BIOS instructions are recorded on the chip itself.

However, BIOS instructions must adjust for various hardware configurations (such as memory speed and I/O port availability). Part of the BIOS includes a *Setup* (or *System*

Setup) routine that lets you define the hardware particulars (you can see a few example Setup menus in Figures 1-6 and 1-8). A small amount of very low-power *CMOS* (Complementary Metal Oxide Semiconductor) RAM stores each variable. In fact, a little coin cell powers the CMOS RAM when you turn off the PC.

Once you know the trick, you can easily get into the Setup routine. Most BIOS will show you the proper key to press on the screen in the moments following startup. For example, you will see a message like "Press <F2> to enter Setup" (see Table 1-1). You only have a few seconds to start the Setup routine. If you wait too long, the operating system will load.

Table 1-1. **Common keys to access popular Setup routines**

BIOS maker	Key(s)
AMI BIOS (General systems)	<Del>
Award BIOS	<Ctrl>+<Alt>+<Esc>
Compaq PCs	<F10>
DTK BIOS	<Esc>
General systems	<F2>
General systems	<F1>
IBM PS/2 System BIOS	.<Ctrl>+<Alt>+<Ins> after <Ctrl>+<Alt>+<Del>
Phoenix BIOS	<Ctrl>+<Alt>+<Esc> or <Ctrl>+<Alt>+<S>
Sony PCs	<F3> then <F1>

SHORT-TERM CMOS BATTERY LOSS

The Annoyance: I replaced my CMOS backup battery just a few months ago, but I still see occasional CMOS battery errors. How come this battery died so quickly? I thought they lasted years.

The Fix: A fresh lithium coin cell should maintain a PC's CMOS RAM for several years. Unfortunately, batteries can sit on store shelves for quite a while, and the cells you purchased may have already expired. Before you install a fresh battery, make sure you double-check the battery's expiration date.

If this becomes a chronic problem, and fresh coin cells do not last long, there may be an issue with the motherboard's design. Unfortunately, to truly resolve this type of hassle, you need to upgrade the motherboard to a new model. If your system is fairly new, contact the manufacturer and see if this is a known issue. A manufacturer aware of a chronic issue may replace the motherboard for free.

Proactive Replacement

You should replace a CMOS backup battery *before* it goes bad and loses CMOS RAM contents. The CMOS RAM draws so little current that it often retains data for hours (sometimes days) once you remove the battery. This makes it easy to pop out the old battery and insert the new one with very little chance of CMOS RAM data loss. But once the battery fails and CMOS contents disappear, you need to reload the default values (and possibly make other manual tweaks).

CORRECTING SYSTEM SETUP ERRORS

The Annoyance: I experimented with the settings in my System Setup and now my PC acts strangely. Unfortunately, I forgot which settings I changed. Is there any way to undo my changes without having to clear everything and start over?

The Fix: Boy, are you lucky. In the old days, you had to re-enter every setting by hand. Today's BIOS provides default support, so users can quickly restore lost or erroneous settings with a single keystroke. Reboot the system and enter the System Setup according to the manufacturer's instructions (see Table 1-1). Take a look at the Phoenix/Award Standard CMOS Features menu (Figure 1-8). The main menu provides options for loading previous values

(<F5>) from the last time you used Setup, as well as failsafe (<F6>) or optimized (<F7>) defaults. Try to use optimized defaults if possible because this will yield the best system performance. Use the fail-safe option only when absolutely necessary. After loading the defaults, remember to save your changes and reboot the system.

CMOS CHECKSUM CAUSES CONCERN

The Annoyance: My system stops during boot with a CMOS checksum error.

The Fix: A checksum validates data in memory and storage. Basically, an algorithm looks at some amount of data, and then calculates a unique number based on that data. When a system checks the data later, it recalculates the checksum and compares it to the number already stored. If the numbers match, the data is assumed to be valid.

A checksum error means that the CMOS RAM contents are invalid. This happens when the CMOS backup battery fails (and CMOS contents are lost), or after a BIOS upgrade (double-check that you upgraded the correct BIOS version). BIOS will often let you accept default settings and continue booting normally. If the problem continues, just replace the CMOS backup battery and reload the defaults.

FIXING AN INACCURATE PC CLOCK

The Annoyance: My PC keeps the wrong time. I lose, like, 15 minutes a day, and it constantly makes me late for appointments.

The Fix: Although personal computers have a longstanding reputation as precision timepieces (ahem), they often lose (or even gain) time over a matter of months. The CMOS backup battery runs the real time clock (RTC). As the battery drains, time starts to slip, and it gets worse just before the battery fails. Replace the CMOS backup battery and reset your clock.

Windows XP provides an online synchronization feature. Right-click the clock on the right side of the Taskbar and choose Adjust Date/Time. Next, click the Internet Time tab, check the "Automatically synchronize with an Internet time server" box, and select a time server from the drop-down menu (see Figure 1-10). Click the Update Now button to update your clock immediately, or just let the clock synchronize automatically.

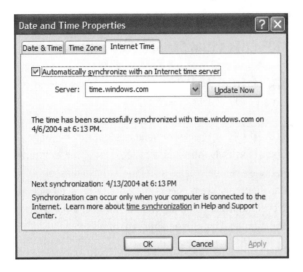

Figure 1-10. You can synchronize the clock with an Internet resource to correct RTC problems.

CLEARING CMOS WITHOUT A JUMPER

The Annoyance: I updated my BIOS and need to clear the CMOS RAM, but my motherboard lacks the proper jumper.

The Fix: Most motherboards provide a jumper to clear the CMOS RAM. This feature comes in handy if you need to clear a password or clean house after a BIOS upgrade (see "Clearing a Forgotten CMOS Password" earlier in this chapter). But not every motherboard supplies this feature, so you may need to fix it the old-fashioned way.

Power down and unplug the PC, then open the case and disconnect the power cables from the motherboard. Now locate the CMOS backup battery and gently remove it from the motherboard. Without power, the CMOS RAM will eventually lose its contents. (This process may take

hours, or even days.) To speed up the process, stop by your local Radio Shack and buy a 10Kohm (kilo-ohm) resistor. Take the resistor and place it across the empty coin cell terminals for one minute. This will safely bleed off any latent charges that might maintain the CMOS RAM.

Reinstall the CMOS backup battery, reconnect the motherboard power cable(s), and turn on the system. If you see a "CMOS Checksum" error, load the default settings (see the earlier annoyance "CMOS Checksum Causes Concern").

Battery Hygiene

A lithium coin cell fits into a small holder on the motherboard. Although this should keep a tight grip on the battery, rough battery replacements can bend the terminals and loosen the battery. Oxides and dust can eventually make the battery contact questionable.

RECOVERING FROM FAULTY BIOS UPDATES

The Annoyance: I updated my BIOS, but my idiot brother rebooted the system in the middle of everything, and now the PC won't boot.

The Fix: You should never interrupt a BIOS flash in progress. This leaves the system without a working BIOS. You can recover from this problem in two ways: boot block recovery or BIOS replacement.

The *boot block* protects a small area of the BIOS from any changes. If you made a backup copy of your original BIOS file before flashing, it may be possible to restore the system again. Power down the system, set the Boot Block jumper on the motherboard, insert a diskette with the flash loader executable (*.EXE*) and original BIOS binary (*.BIN*) file, and fire it up. The protected code should run the diskette and attempt to reload the original BIOS file. You will probably hear several beeps when the recovery finishes. Power down again, remove the diskette, reset the Boot Block jumper, reboot the system to the System Setup, and then reload the CMOS defaults.

Things get a bit more complicated without boot block recovery, because this means you need to replace the entire BIOS chip. Unfortunately, you must send the motherboard (or the entire PC) back to the manufacturer for repair. Bona fide computer geeks may simply find it easier to replace the motherboard outright.

Reducing Battery Guesswork

Ideally, CMOS backup batteries can maintain CMOS RAM contents for years. But how do you know how long the battery has been in service? The next time you replace a coin cell, note the date on a little piece of masking tape and stick it on the bottom of your inner PC case.

MEMORY ANNOYANCES

SHUFFLING RAM IN AN UPGRADE

The Annoyance: I want to increase the RAM in my system (two 256MB DIMMs) to 1GB. I know the system will take the extra memory, but I only see two DIMM slots on the motherboard.

The Fix: When a manufacturer fills the only two DIMM slots in the system, you either learn to live with the existing RAM or dump the old RAM in favor of new modules. In your situation, remove the two old 256MB DIMMs and install two new 512MB DIMMs to get your 1GB RAM total. You can use the old DIMMs in another system (maybe the kids' computer), or sell the old RAM to your friends or neighbors.

Clip It Tight

Little plastic clips lock into notches on either side of the memory module and hold it in place. If the clips loosen, it can cause memory problems. In some cases, the module may actually fall out of its slot.

HANDLING AGGRESSIVE MEMORY TIMING

The Annoyance: I upgraded the memory in my system, and now it just sits there and beeps. I called a technician who says the new memory is "too aggressive" for my system.

The Fix: This type of problem occurs with certain combinations of memory and motherboard chipsets. The memory module itself may be fine. For example, Kingston KHX3200/256 and KHX3200/512 modules won't work in PCs with Intel i865PE, i865G, and i875 chipsets.

So what can you do? Remove the new DIMM first and retest the system (this tells you whether the rest of the system works). Check the DIMM's characteristics against your system's requirements. For example, a high-density memory technology (e.g., a recent SDRAM module with 512MB chips) may not run in a particular motherboard, even though the module's overall size may work perfectly. No problem. Install a different memory module (perhaps from a different manufacturer) and try the system again. Also, check for a BIOS upgrade to fix this little nuisance.

In a few cases, an adjustment to the System Setup might solve the problem. For those cranky Kingston modules, change the "RAS-to-CAS" parameter to 3. Of course, if your particular BIOS doesn't let you tinker with memory timings, exchange the uncooperative module for a more accommodating one. Kingston says that their KHX3200A/256 and KHX3200A/512 modules work with Intel i865 and i875 motherboards.

Static Cling

Memory modules are extremely sensitive to damage from electrostatic discharge (ESD). Keep new memory modules in their anti-static bags until you install them, and always touch the computer's metal chassis first to discharge yourself.

NO MEMORY UPGRADE GOES UNPUNISHED

The Annoyance: I installed some new Rambus memory, but the system just sits there and beeps like an idiot. The PC works fine with the original RAM, and I checked and reinstalled the Rambus already. I also know that my motherboard accepts 256MB modules. What did I miss here?

The Fix: Before you tote those new modules back to the vendor for replacement, take a look at the chip density first. This is the size of the *chips* being used on the module (not the module size). While the overall module size may be just fine, your system might not be compatible with the type of memory chips. For example, Intel's D850EMV2 desktop board can support memory configurations from 128MB (minimum) to 2GB (maximum) utilizing 128Mbit or 256Mbit technology PC600- and PC800-compliant RDRAM RIMMs. Rambus components that fall outside of those specifications will cause problems. This happens a lot when you try newer memory modules in older motherboards. In this case, you need to exchange those modules for lower-density ones.

Always check with the motherboard maker for recommended memory device lists. Also, check for BIOS updates that might sometimes tweak minor memory incompatabilities.

If each Rambus module characteristic checks out, the modules may indeed be defective. Take the modules back to the vendor for replacement.

LATENCY AND MEMORY

The Annoyance: My RAM specs say "CL2," but I noticed that the BIOS is configured for "CL3." If I change this setting to "CL2," will it cause a problem for my system?

The Fix: Before you change anything, it pays to understand the "CL" specification in a little more detail. The *CAS Latency* (*CL*) tells you the number of clock cycles needed between the time your memory receives a read command and the time the system can access the data (usually the first piece of a data burst). CL2 takes two clock cycles for the first data, and CL3 takes three clock cycles. Makes sense so far, right?

CAS Latency affects only the *first* piece of memory data, so the system reads the rest of the data in any given burst at exactly the same speed. For any given burst of data read from memory, a CL2 part only saves you—guess what—one single clock cycle.

The System Setup usually tucks the CAS Latency timing setting in the Advanced Chipset Features menu (see Figure 1-11). If your PC has only CL2 memory installed, you can set the CAS Latency entry to "2," save your changes, and then restart the system. If the system acts funky, change the setting back to "3" immediately. If, on the other hand, your PC has *any* CL3 memory installed, leave CAS Latency set to "3."

```
            Phoenix – AwardBIOS CMOS Setup Utility
                   Advanced Chipset Features

  DRAM Timing Selectable      [By SPD]           Item Help
  CAS Latency Time            [2]
  Active to Precharge Delay   [8]                ───────────
  Tras Max                    [120us]
  DRAM RAS# to CAS# Delay     [4]                Menu Level  ▶
  DRAM RAS# Precharge         [4]
  System BIOS Cacheable       [Enabled]
  Video BIOS Cacheable        [Disabled]
  Delay Prior to Thermal      [16 Min]
  DRAM Data Integrity Mode    [ECC]



  ↑↓←→: Move  Enter: Select  +/-/PU/PD: Value  F10: Save  ESC: Exit  F1: General Help
       F5: Previous Values  F6: Fail-Safe Defaults  F7: Optimized Defaults
```

Figure 1-11. Trimming the CAS Latency has little noticeable affect on system performance.

BIOS UNDERREPORTING RAM

The Annoyance: I know my system has 512MB of RAM, but I only see 448MB listed in the System Properties.

The Fix: This occurs when the motherboard's onboard video chip takes part of the system RAM. Normally, stand-alone AGP video cards supply their own memory (maybe 32MB, 64MB, 128MB, or even 256MB for top-of-the-line graphics cards). However, motherboards with their own video adapter (with or without a separate AGP slot) simply take possession of some portion of the main RAM.

The System Setup may let you select some amount of RAM for video use (termed the *AGP Aperture Size*). For example, the Tyan Tomcat i845GL (S2098) motherboard includes an Intel Extreme Graphics chip. By default, the AGP Aperture Size setting located in the Advanced Chipset Features menu (Figure 1-12) sets aside 64MB of main RAM, but you can opt for 4MB, 8MB, 16MB, 32MB, 64MB, 128MB, or a whopping 256MB. Ultimately, the AGP Aperture Size plus the RAM listed in System Properties should equal the total amount of installed RAM.

```
            Phoenix – AwardBIOS CMOS Setup Utility
                   Advanced Chipset Features

  DRAM Timing Selectable      [By SPD]           Item Help
  CAS Latency Time            [1.5]
  Active to Precharge Delay   [7]                Menu Level  ▶
  DRAM RAS# to CAS# Delay     [3]
  DRAM RAS# Precharge         [3]
  Memory Frequency For        [Auto]
  System BIOS Cacheable       [Enabled]
  Video  BIOS Cacheable       [Disabled]
  Memory Hole At 15M-16M      [Disabled]
  Delayed Transaction         [Enabled]
  Delay Prior to Thermal      [16 Min]
  AGP Aperture Size (MB)      [64]

  ** On-Chip VGA Setting **
  On-Chip VGA                 [Enabled]
  On-Chip Frame Buffer Size   [8MB]
  Boot Display                [Auto]

  ↑↓←→:Move  Enter:Select  +/-/PU/PD:Value  F10:Save  ESC:Exit  F1:General Help
     F5: Previous Values    F6: Fail-Safe Defaults   F7: Optimized Defaults
```

Figure 1-12. The AGP Aperture Size sets aside main system RAM for use by an onboard video system.

NEW MEMORY AND SYSTEM PERFORMANCE

The Annoyance: I installed 256MB of RAM in my system, for a total of 768MB. However, the extra memory seems to have no effect on system performance.

The Fix: Hold on, Sparky. You have two different issues here: detection and performance. First, watch the memory count as your system starts. If the count reaches 768MB, the system detected the memory. If you would rather work through Windows XP, open the System control panel. The System Properties dialog should list the available memory, minus any memory allocated to onboard video use (see the previous annoyance, "BIOS Underreporting RAM").

Now you can think about performance. Additional RAM by itself does not guarantee improved performance. You may notice a snappier response because significant RAM reduces dependence on virtual memory (a swap file on the hard drive). You may also notice other capabilities such as support for larger image files or complex CAD drawings. But to *really* gauge performance differences, you must measure memory performance with a benchmark program like Futuremark's PCMark04 (*http://www.futuremark.com/ products/pcmark04/*).

MEMORY SPEEDS DON'T WORK TOGETHER

The Annoyance: I tried to install DDR333 DIMMs along with my existing DDR400 DIMMs, but ran into problems. I thought the modules were compatible.

The Fix: Be careful here! The memory modules may be physically compatible, but slower 333MHz memory will not magically accelerate to 400MHz. In most cases, the system will not boot. Some newer motherboards may detect the slower RAM and downshift the front side bus (FSB) and multiplier (you can typically run faster RAM at slower speeds). In either case, slower RAM will adversely affect overall system performance. Replace the DDR333 SDRAM with matching DDR400 SDRAM for best results.

DDR: THE NEXT GENERATION

The Annoyance: I need top performance for gaming. Can I use new DDR2 modules in my system, or am I stuck with ordinary DDR modules?

The Fix: Double Data Rate (DDR) memory has emerged as the most popular type of PC memory. Faster DDR2 memory was launched in 2004 and is supported by top-of-the-line desktops, servers, laptops, and other devices. Initial releases of DDR2 used 400/533MHz memory clocks, but DDR2 is expected to handle memory clock speeds to 667MHz and 800MHz and beyond (gulp). However, DDR2 modules will not work with regular DDR systems because of the different pin count, voltage, memory chip technologies, and incompatible keying. What does this mean for us mere mortals? You need a new motherboard with chipsets specifically designed for DDR2 RAM.

Tarnished Reputation

Memory modules and DIMM slots should use the same metal (often gold or tin). Mixing metals can eventually result in oxidization that causes signal contact problems and unreliable memory operation. When memory problems occur, power down the PC, remove the DIMMs, and look at the metal contacts. Clean the contacts with a little alcohol on a cotton swab, and then replace each module carefully.

HANDLING SPD ERRORS

The Annoyance: When I try to boot my PC, I get a Serial Presence Detect error.

The Fix: Old-timers can probably remember the endless headaches configuring a system for new RAM. You had to enter the System Setup and insert the exact total memory size and timings by hand.

Eventually, memory makers wised up and put all the memory size and timing information on a little serial data chip (usually an EEPROM chip) right on the memory module. This is called the *Serial Presence Detect* (*SPD*) chip. The BIOS simply reads the SPD data at boot time, learns everything it needs to know about the RAM, and configures the memory timings accordingly.

A Serial Presence Detect error usually means one of the memory modules has failed. Remove each module one at a time and then retest the system. The last module to be removed before the problem disappears is defective.

PROCESSOR ANNOYANCES

IDENTIFYING A PROCESSOR

The Annoyance: I need some real processing speed to run a CAD program. How can I check the current processor make and model before deciding on an upgrade?

The Fix: Open the System control panel (Figure 1-13). For example, my Toshiba Satellite uses a Pentium 4 2.8GHz processor. However, sometimes the System Properties reports nonsense like "Family 6 Stepping 5." This makes it almost impossible to make heads or tails of the particular processor.

Fortunately, you can download a utility designed to detect hardware, such as SiSoft SANDRA 2004 (*http://www.sisoftware.net*). It will also identify processor details and display comparative test results (see Figure 1-14).

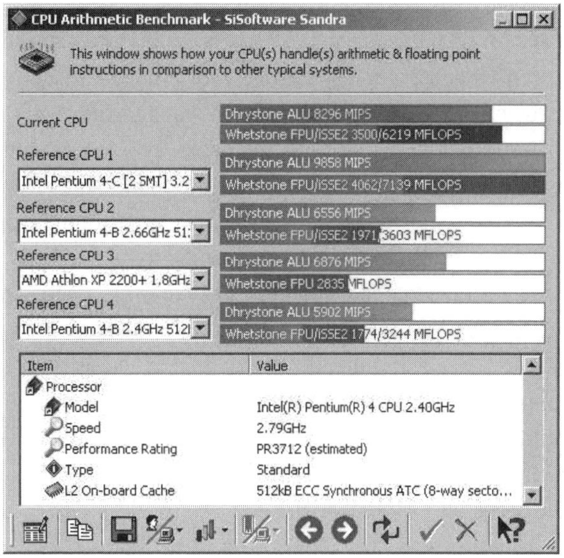

Figure 1-14. SiSoft Sandra identifies processor hardware and other system components.

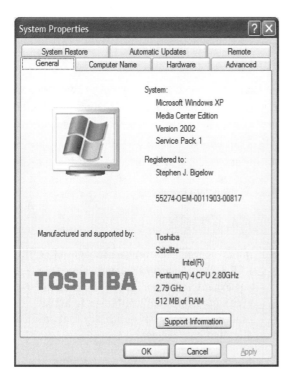

Feeling the Heat

The heat sink/fan assemblies sit atop your system processor and draw heat away from it. If you need to work inside your computer, wait 10–15 minutes for the heat sink to cool *before* you reach inside. If you accidentally grab a hot heat sink, it can easily leave a nasty burn.

Figure 1-13. System Properties often describes hardware information such as processor type and speed.

PICKING A NEW PROCESSOR

The Annoyance: My nephew needs a serious processor upgrade, but I have no idea which processors the motherboard will support.

The Fix: This is one time when the motherboard (or system) manufacturer should be your principal resource. If you have the motherboard manual handy, skim through the introduction or specification pages for a list of compatible processors. Otherwise, look through the manufacturer's web site for the motherboard specifications (you might even get lucky and find a complete table of compatible processors). Companies like Tyan offer a comprehensive table of supported processors for all their motherboards (see Figure 1-15). For example, if you use a Tyan Tomcat i7210 (S5112) motherboard, just skim across the columns to see which processors it supports at 800MHz, 533MHz, and 400MHz bus speeds. At 800MHz, you can use processors up to 3.4GHz.

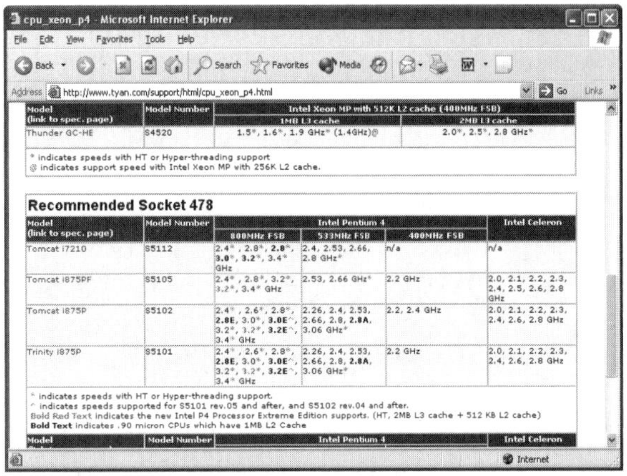

Figure 1-15. Motherboard manufacturers often supply detailed processor compatibility information to help you configure and upgrade a system.

Now you need to decide whether a new processor is worth the investment. Look at the Tyan Tomcat i7210, for example. If the unit already has a 2.4GHz Pentium 4, the cost of a full 1GHz jump in speed to a 3.4GHz Pentium 4 may make sense. But if the system has a 3.0GHz processor onboard, the cost of a 3.4GHz processor may not be worth a mere 400MHz improvement.

PROCESSOR UPGRADES OFFER MEASURED IMPROVEMENT

The Annoyance: I replaced my 2.8GHz CPU with a 3.4GHz model, but the system seems to offer the same performance.

The Fix: Many factors affect computer performance, but here are a few practical pointers. First, moving from 2.8GHz to 3.4GHz will add 600MHz of processing speed to your system (an increase of about 21% for you math whizzes). Unfortunately, increased processor speeds don't necessarily translate into greatly improved performance.

Don't believe me? Just consider some benchmark results for SiSoft SANDRA (see Figure 1-14). The current 2.4GHz Pentium 4 CPU, overclocked to 2.8GHz, yields 8296 MIPS (millions of instructions per second). By comparison, a reference 3.2GHz Pentium 4 CPU yields 9858 MIPS. The 3.2GHz CPU performs better than the overclocked 2.8GHz processor—which you'd expect—but the improvement isn't radical.

Differences in a processor's architecture, die size, cache size, motherboard memory, and chipset account for much of the performance difference between two otherwise identical PCs. To really measure the benefit to your system, benchmark the CPU before *and* after the upgrade.

If you upgrade the processor and notice a 20 percent benchmark improvement, do *not* expect your main applications or favorite games to run 20% faster. In actual practice, you may not notice any real application improvement.

KEEP PROCESSOR FAMILIES SEPARATE

The Annoyance: I want to upgrade my processor from an AMD Athlon XP to an Intel Pentium 4 without buying a new system.

The Fix: Intel and Advanced Micro Devices (AMD) are bitter rivals in the development of leading desktop and laptop processors. They quickly differentiated their products with incompatible pin counts and chipsets. Intel's Pentium 4 ("Northwood" and "Prescott" type processors) use 478-pin sockets, while AMD Athlon XP processors (to 3000+) use 462-pin sockets called Socket A (see Figure 1-16). The companies also tailor motherboard chipsets to each processor family, so a chipset for Pentium 4 processors will not support Athlons, and vice versa. They even use different BIOS code.

Figure 1-16. The differences between the 462-pin AMD Socket A (left) and the 478-pin Pentium 4 socket (right) make these two processor families incompatible.

This basically locks PC users into a particular processor architecture. If you select a Pentium 4 motherboard, you must continue to use Pentium 4 processors. If you want to switch to a similar AMD Athlon, you must swap the entire motherboard along with the processor (though the memory may transfer over to the new motherboard).

SECOND CPU NOT ALWAYS A BENEFIT

The Annoyance: I finally installed a second CPU in my workstation, but the computer runs at the same speed.

The Fix: You need an operating system and applications that can employ multiple processors. For example, multiprocessing operating systems include Windows 2000/XP Professional, Windows NT Server or Workstation, and various types of Unix and Linux. Operating systems such as Windows 95/98/Me and XP Home do not natively support multiprocessing. You also need applications that support multiple processors, such as CAD, animation, scientific, and graphic design programs (e.g., Kinetix 3D Studio MAX, Microsoft's Soft Image, Adobe's Photoshop, and Alias/Wavefront's Maya).

FANNING THE CPU FIRE

The Annoyance: My system keeps halting after just a few minutes. I looked inside and noticed that the CPU fan stopped running.

The Fix: Start with a quick check of the fan cable. Older fans simply used a drive power connector and ran all the time, whereas newer fans use a small connection to the motherboard. In either case, make sure you have a solid connection.

Many newer motherboards like the Tyan Tomcat i7210 include a speed control (or throttle) that automatically adjusts the fan speed based on CPU heat, and can actually stop a fan once the system and processor idle. If the fan starts after a few minutes and increases in speed, it may be throttled (nothing to worry about). To check the fan configuration, start the System Setup and examine the PC Health Status menu (Figure 1-17). If the CPU Fan Speed Control is set to 100%, the fan should run constantly. If not, you many need to replace the fan, along with the entire heat sink assembly. If the speed is set to Auto, the system should adjust the fan speed based on CPU temperature.

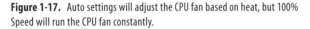

```
                    Phoenix – AwardBIOS CMOS Setup Utility
                              PC Health Status

CPU FAN Speed Control    [100% Speed]           Item Help
Current CPU    Temp.
Current VRM    Temp.
Current System Temp.                         Menu Level   ▶
Current CPU     Fan Speed
Current Chassis Fan Speed
Current Chassis Fan Speed
Current Chassis Fan Speed
Current Chassis Fan Speed
Current Chassis Fan Speed
Current Chassis Fan Speed

VCORE
3VSB
5 VSB
+5V
3.3V
+12V
DDRVTT
2.6VDDR


↑↓←→: Move  Enter: Select  +/-/PU/PD: Value  F10: Save  ESC: Exit  F1: General Help
        F5: Previous Values  F6: Fail-Safe Defaults  F7: Optimized Defaults
```

Figure 1-17. Auto settings will adjust the CPU fan based on heat, but 100% Speed will run the CPU fan constantly.

LOOKING OUT FOR PIN #1

The Annoyance: I want to install my new CPU, but it has hundreds of pins on it. What if I insert it the wrong way and blow up my system?

The Fix: You won't. In fact, the CPU only goes in one way. Look at the processor socket on the motherboard. Notice that there are several pins cut out of one corner (see Figure 1-16). Now look at the pin side of your new processor, find the corresponding corner, and ease it into place. Make sure you completely insert the processor into the socket before you close the Zero Insertion Force (ZIF) lever.

TWO CPUS REPORTED

The Annoyance: My computer has one CPU, but the Device Manager reports two. Am I getting twice the processor performance?

The Fix: This occurs because of hyper-threading (or HT) technology. Hyper-threading supports multitasking, which allows a processor to work on more than one task simultaneously. An operating system (e.g., Windows XP) interprets a hyper-threading processor as two processors and reports each instance in the Device Manager. No

harm done. To test the actual performance of your hyper-threading processor, use a benchmarking utility such as PCMark04 (*http://www.futuremark.com*) or SiSoft SANDRA 2004 (*http://www.sisoftware.net*).

Pin Protection

Intel Pentium 4 and AMD Athlon processors use almost 500 individual metal pins. High-end processors like the AMD Opteron use over 900 pins. Each pin fits evenly and completely into a corresponding socket. To remove a processor from its socket, completely disengage the ZIF lever. Ease the processor from the socket by prying it evenly from all four sides. Be *extremely* careful. If you pull from just one side, you might bend or break the pins still in the socket and possibly ruin the processor.

CPU STUCK IN ITS SOCKET

The Annoyance: I bought a new processor, but I can't get the old one out of its socket.

The Fix: Two common oversights often gum-up the works. First, a Zero Insertion Force (ZIF) lever holds all processor sockets in place (see Figure 1-16). When closed, this lever makes the processor almost impossible to move. A lot of newbies forget about this little lever. Ideally, the processor will lift right out with little (if any) effort.

Still stuck? Check the heat sink/fan assembly mounted over the processor. Some heat sinks fit over the processor and actually attach to the socket (not the processor). This can sometimes hold the processor in place even when you disengage the ZIF lever. In this case, you may need to remove the heat sink/fan unit first, and then remove the processor. Remember to store the old processor in the anti-static packaging from the new processor.

In rare cases, the ZIF mechanism may not disengage completely and leave some tension on the processor pins. Try rocking the ZIF lever to loosen the mechanism if possible. Otherwise, use a wide, flat tool (such as a screwdriver) to *gently* ease each of the processor's four sides from the socket. Do not pop the processor out from one side. This will bend pins on the opposing side and possibly ruin the processor.

> If you have a mini-tower or full tower case with a vertically mounted motherboard, set the case on its side before you lift the ZIF lever. Otherwise, the processor may fall out of its socket and damage expansion cards or other system components.

INCORRECT CLOCK SPEED REPORTS

The Annoyance: The CPU Clock entry in the System Setup only tops out at 132MHz, even though the system supports clock speeds to 233MHz.

The Fix: In virtually every case, the problem lies with your choice of CPU. The BIOS automatically identifies the installed processor and configures the front side bus (FSB) speed accordingly. Some processors use a 100MHz FSB (a 400MHz processor), and this limits the CPU Clock range from 100–132MHz. A processor intended for a 133MHz FSB (a 533MHz processor) should access a CPU Clock range from 133–165MHz. Finally, a processor designed for a 200MHz FSB (an 800MHz processor) unlocks a CPU Clock range from 200–233MHz. However, one processor will not unlock the entire FSB frequency range. If you need a faster FSB speed (for example, to use DDR400 SDRAM), exchange your current processor for a model that handles a correspondingly faster front side bus.

Greasy Goop

A thick, acrid thermal grease helps transfer heat from the CPU to the heat sink (it effectively keeps the processor cooler). Any time you change processors or heat sink/fan units, use a little thermal grease. However, make sure you use latex gloves when you handle this highly toxic cream. Also, watch out for your good clothes because it will stain. Don't say I didn't warn you. You can get thermal grease from electronics stores such as Radio Shack.

PRESERVING BENT CPU PINS

The Annoyance: I yanked out the processor and bent some of the pins. Did I ruin the CPU?

The Fix: You really stepped into a nasty little problem here. If you try to straighten a serious bend, you will likely snap the extremely brittle pins right off and destroy your processor. You can usually fix slight bends (maybe less than 20 degrees or so) with the light touch of some needlenose pliers. Make sure you discharge your hands and the needlenose pliers against the computer's metal chassis before you attempt to straighten any of the processor's pins. Otherwise, you risk damaging the processor from electrostatic discharge (ESD).

ERRATIC OPERATION CAUSED BY CPU HEAT

The Annoyance: I replaced my CPU and the system boots fine, but then it freezes after just a few minutes of operation. I have to wait five minutes before I can restart it.

The Fix: Ah, it sounds like the processor is overheating. Power down and unplug the system, then allow 10–15 minutes for everything to cool completely.

Now start with the obvious stuff. Did you reattach the heat sink/fan? Next, check the heat sink/fan cable. Most current coolers use a three-wire cable that attaches to a CPU Fan port on the motherboard. This lets the motherboard detect the fan, and sometimes even regulate the fan speed (see "Fanning the CPU Fire" earlier in this chapter). Make sure you connected the cable properly (and see that the fan spins when the system fires up). Some modern computers include a Processor Burn-Proof feature that will automatically shut down the system when the CPU fan speed fails, so make sure you connect the cable to the correct fan port. If the fan fails to spin, you may need a new heat sink fan assembly.

> ## Warning. . .
> If you run a processor without an adequate (or properly attached) cooling unit, you can destroy the processor.

Finally, consider the affects of overclocking. Overriding the CPU clock speed or multiplier can sometimes let you wring a few more clock ticks from the processor, but that added speed causes extra heat. Avid overclockers will often upsize the cooling unit to accommodate the added heat. Set the clock speed settings to their native values. If the system stabilizes, you found the problem.

ERROR-PROOF OVERCLOCKING

The Annoyance: I want to overclock my PC, but I fear I may blow something up.

The Fix: Ready to start your journey to the dark side, eh? Overclocking boosts processor performance by slightly increasing the front side bus (FSB) speed and multiplier beyond the values rated for a given processor. Lots of motherboards support a range of FSB speeds (available in increments as small as 5MHz) specifically tailored for overclocking. For example, motherboards such as the Tyan Tomcat i876PF provide default settings of 100/133/166MHz, but let you enter a decimal number for

the desired FSB speed. To overclock most processors, simply tweak the CPU Clock setting in the System Setup (see Figure 1-18).

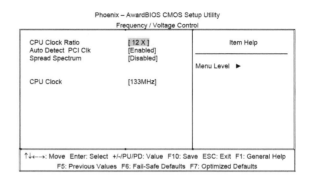

Figure 1-18. Overclocking a processor is often as simple as tweaking the CPU Clock speed, though there are serious drawbacks to consider.

However, overclocking has some very real limitations and drawbacks. First, overclocking forces a processor to run at faster clock speeds. Depending on the processor's design, you may need to tweak the processor voltage to strengthen the faster signal speeds. Faster processors also generate more heat (see the previous annoyance, "Erratic Operation Caused By CPU Heat"), which the heat sink/fan needs to remove. Often, you need a larger heat sink/fan assembly. Hard-core overclockers resort to water-cooled units and even liquid nitrogen cooling (yikes). Other potential problems? Overclocking also increases the memory frequency. Bumping a 133MHz FSB to 143MHz would drive DDR266 SDRAM to 286MHz. The higher processor and memory frequencies can easily cause system instabilities (unexpected crashes and reboots). Ultimately, the added heat and stress of overclocking can potentially cause premature processor failure.

> ## Warning. . .
> Overclocking can damage your system hardware and void your warranty.

Still, overclocking remains a popular pastime for many PC enthusiasts, and you can find lots of dedicated web sites. A Yahoo or Google search for "overclocking" will yield lots of hits, but the following sites will get you started:

- *http://www.overclockers.com/*
- *http://www.extremeoverclocking.com/*
- *http://www.sysopt.com/ocdatabase.html*
- *http://www.anandtech.com/*
- *http://www.helpoverclocking.com/english/*
- *http://www.overclockersclub.com/*

AGGRESSIVE OVERCLOCKING CAUSES SYSTEM PROBLEMS

The Annoyance: I just finished overclocking my PC. The darned thing works fine for a while (it benchmarks higher and everything), but it freezes every now and then.

The Fix: You can usually trace this problem to aggressive overclocking settings. In other words, you jacked up the clock rate too high, or failed to tweak the CPU voltage and cooling scheme. Fortunately, you can fix the problem with a little patience and some basic detective work.

Open the System Setup and locate the CPU Clock speed and CPU Clock Ratio entries (see Figure 1-18). Write them down as your starting point. Now restore the default settings and let the BIOS detect and configure the CPU automatically. Check the clock speed and multiplier again and write them down. This represents your working range. Step up the FSB in small increments and retest the system. Watch your CPU temperature each time you increase the clock speed.

When the system becomes unstable again, you found the maximum clock speed for your CPU voltage and cooling scheme. Try a larger CPU cooler on the processor and see if that makes a difference. If not, increase the CPU voltage (but *not more than 0.1 or 0.2 volts*). If the system remains unstable, just drop the CPU voltage back to its original value and return the system to its last stable clock speed. On the other hand, if the combination of added cooling and/or increased voltage stabilizes the system, try to step up the clock frequency again.

> **t i p**
>
> The amount of overclocking your processor can handle depends on the motherboard, chipset, BIOS version, power supply, and so on.

CARD AND PORT ANNOYANCES

RECOGNIZING UNKNOWN SYSTEM DEVICES

The Annoyance: I see an "unknown" item in my Device Manager marked with a black exclamation mark in a little yellow circle. How do I get rid of it?

The Fix: Windows simply lists devices it can't recognize as "unknown." To resolve this annoyance, you need to identify the problem device, and then get Windows to see it.

Here's a quick tip. If you just installed a device and Windows doesn't see it, then you already identified the problem device. Otherwise, right-click the unknown device and select Remove, then reboot the system and let Windows redetect the device. Windows will probably only identify the device type (such as Wave Audio Device or USB drive).

Next, Windows should launch the Install New Hardware Wizard and ask you for a driver. If not, right-click the unknown device, select Update Driver (see Figure 1-19), and follow the instructions. Check the Device Manager again to make sure Windows properly identified the device.

Figure 1-19. The Device Manager helps identify and troubleshoot a system's diverse devices.

UNDERSTANDING AGP VOLTAGES

The Annoyance: I can't cram this new AGP card into my system no matter how hard I try. I thought all AGP cards were the same.

The Fix: Nope. We usually think of AGP as a single technology, but there are actually three AGP standards: AGP 1.0, AGP 2.0, and AGP 3.0. Each standard uses the same operating voltage, but different signaling voltages.

- AGP 1.0 uses 3.3 volt signaling, and is often termed "AGP 3.3V." AGP 1.0–compliant cards, such as the ATI Rage 128 or ATI Rage Fury Max, will operate up to AGP 2X speed and will fit into AGP 1.0, AGP 2.0, and "Universal AGP" slots. However, AGP 1.0 cards will not install in motherboards where the AGP 2.0 slot is keyed for 1.5V operation (such as Intel i845, i850, or i860 chipsets intended for AGP 4X operation).

- AGP 2.0 uses 1.5 volt signaling, and is often called "AGP 1.5V." AGP 2.0–compliant cards, such as the ATI Radeon 8500 or 9000, will operate at AGP 2X/4X speeds and will fit in AGP 1.0, AGP 2.0, and Universal (2X/4X) AGP slots.

- AGP 3.0 uses 0.8 volt signaling, and will operate at AGP 8X speeds in AGP 2.0 and Universal (4X/8X) AGP slots. However, AGP 3.0 cards, such as the ATI Radeon 9700 or 9800, will not work in AGP 1.0 (2X) slots.

The bottom line: old AGP cards may not fit in new motherboards, and new AGP cards may not fit in old motherboards. Examine the motherboard specifications and determine the AGP slot version, then make sure you select a compatible AGP video card.

NEW AGP PERFORMANCE UNDERUTILIZED

The Annoyance: I installed an ATI Radeon 9800 AGP card in my motherboard, but it provides little improvement over the old Radeon 8500 card. Why even bother replacing the card?

The Fix: You need to make sure you utilize the new video card's full potential. Your Radeon 8500 is an AGP 2.0 card (2X/4X speed), but the Radeon 9800 is an AGP 3.0 card (4X/8X speed). (Confused? Read the previous annoyance.) Your motherboard probably supports AGP 4X, but not AGP 8X. As a result, you don't see the kind of spectacular improvement you might expect. If you want top-notch performance from your new Radeon card, upgrade the motherboard to a model with an AGP 3.0 slot.

A utility such as Futuremark's 3Dmark03 (*http://www.futuremark.com*) lets you benchmark the graphics system performance. If you really want to know how much your new Radeon 9800 boosts the graphics performance, install and run the benchmark on the new card, then reinstall the original Radeon 8500 and benchmark the system again. Note both performance numbers and compare. If you upgrade the motherboard later, run the benchmark again and see how much AGP 8X support boosts the graphics system.

THE INSIDE STORY ON IRQ SHARING

The Annoyance: Will my system crash if two PCI devices share the same IRQ line?

The Fix: A technique called *IRQ steering* (developed in the early 1990s with the PCI bus) lets the PCI system remap the interrupts for each PCI device on demand. This way, devices running under Windows 98 or later can effectively share a limited number of available interrupt signals. However, IRQ steering only works for PCI devices, not legacy modems and COM ports.

As long as Windows properly identifies all the devices, your system will probably not crash. Under Windows XP, open the System control panel, click the Hardware tab, and then click the Device Manager button. Next, look for any unknown or conflicting devices. If everything appears peaceful (see Figure 1-19) and the system runs in a stable manner, your IRQ steering works as intended.

OLD AGP CARD DAMAGES MOTHERBOARD

The Annoyance: I installed an older AGP card on my motherboard, but the system failed to boot (even after I reinstalled the original card).

The Fix: Start with the basics and check all of your internal power cabling. Also check for any loose expansion cards. These little details can mess up any upgrade.

Most likely, you installed an AGP 1.0 card on a motherboard designed for AGP 2.0. But an AGP 1.0 card should work in an AGP 2.0 slot (see "Understanding AGP Voltages"), right? Well it should, but every rule has its exceptions. For example, Intel designed the i845, i850, and i860 motherboard chipsets for AGP 2.0 (1.5 volt) signaling exclusively. When you install an AGP 1.0 (3.3 volt) card, the higher signaling voltages can damage the chipset and smoke your motherboard. Unfortunately, you need to replace the damaged motherboard with one that is compatible with your AGP card. For best graphics, you may want to purchase a newer AGP card to accommodate the motherboard.

CARDS CAN CREEP OUT OF SLOTS

The Annoyance: My system ran fine until the video suddenly cut out.

The Fix: This annoying little glitch occurs when an AGP card eases out of its slot. Like other expansion cards, an AGP card can work its way out of the slot due to vibration and thermal effects. The very fine AGP electrical contacts can short together and shut down the video system with no real warning. This problem crops up much more frequently when you leave the AGP card unbolted to the chassis.

This rarely ever harms the system. Just power down and unplug your PC, then reseat the AGP card (and your other expansion cards). You should fully and evenly insert the card into the slot. Make sure you securely bolt the AGP card's metal bracket to the system chassis and power up the system normally.

Now the bad news: if the problem persists, the AGP card may simply have quit. Power down and unplug the system, then try another compatible AGP card in the slot (see "Old AGP Card Damages Motherboard").

UNDERSTANDING PCI EXPRESS COMPATIBILITY

The Annoyance: Can I use my existing PCI devices with the PCI Express slot on my new motherboard?

The Fix: No. The conventional parallel PCI interface transfers data several bits at a time across a 33MHz bus. By comparison, PCI Express uses a serial interface and passes one bit at a time over a very high-bandwidth connection. Like the Serial ATA (SATA) interface emerging for hard drives, a serial PCI connection can reach speeds that parallel PCI never imagined. PCI Express will eventually replace both PCI and AGP slots, providing increased bandwidth for newer, high-performance graphics boards, FireWire, USB, network adapters, and other devices. Unfortunately, PCI devices (including older PCI-based graphics cards) will not fit in a PCI Express slot.

This incompatibility may seem like a real curse, but PCI Express offers significant benefits. A short (1X) PCI Express slot (ideal for general-purpose devices like network adapters) can handle data rates to 200MB/sec. A full-size (16X) PCI Express slot (intended for high-end graphics adapters) can handle data rates up to 4GB/s.

For the foreseeable future, motherboard makers will continue to provide some conventional PCI slots. You can learn more about PCI Express technology at *http://www.pcisig.com*.

USB DEVICE NOT RECOGNIZED

The Annoyance: Help me out here. I attached a USB printer to the PC, but the system won't even recognize the unit. I thought USB was supposed to automatically detect and install devices?

The Fix: USB has a lot of intelligence and should recognize just about any class of device. First, recheck the USB cable at both the PC and printer. Make sure you use the AC cable or adapter included with the printer and firmly insert both ends of the cable into their respective ports.

No luck? Some manufacturers want you to install the drivers *before* you connect the hardware. Review the installation instructions and make sure you follow the steps closely.

If the printer still refuses to wake up, there may be an issue with the USB port or the printer itself. Try a USB mouse or other USB device you know works and see if Windows recognizes it. If not, try another USB port, or replace the suspicious motherboard. If it detects the USB device normally, try the printer on another PC. If the problem "follows" the printer, exchange it for a new one or get a refund.

USB ONLY PROVIDES LIMITED POWER

The Annoyance: Why do some USB devices need power from an AC cable, but other devices just plug right into the USB port with no power at all?

The Fix: USB was originally designed as a low-speed interface for simple peripheral devices like keyboards, mice, joysticks, web-cams, and other lightweight devices. For example, USB provides +5 volts, and starts a device at just 100mA (milliamps) using just 0.5 watts of power. If the device needs more power, it can negotiate with the USB port for up to 500mA or 2.5 watts of power (one third the power of your child's nightlight). Multiple devices can quickly tax this puny power output, though powered USB hubs can help take some of the load from USB ports.

Printers, scanners, network adapters, and other hardware require far more than 2.5 watts. These high-power devices must take power from an AC cord or adapter, rather than the USB port.

IDENTIFYING THE USB PORT

The Annoyance: I bought a new USB 2.0 device (a DVD+/-RW drive), but I can't remember if my PC has 1.0, 1.1, or 2.0 USB ports.

The Fix: High-speed USB 2.0 supports data transfer rates to 480Mbps (on par with FireWire devices), so you really need a USB 2.0 port on your computer to get the most from your USB 2.0 devices. Full-speed USB ports (USB 1.1) run up to 12Mbps, while low-speed USB ports (USB 1.0) run at only 1.5Mbps. The device may still work on a USB 1.1 port, but even if it does, you won't get top performance. If your computer was manufactured before March 2002 and runs an operating system other than Windows XP, it probably has USB 1.1 ports.

To find out for sure, simply reboot the system and check the BIOS hardware list at start time. Look for a USB port entry such as USB 2.0. Otherwise, enter System Setup, open the Integrated Peripherals menu, and check the Onboard Device entries (see Figure 1-20). If you see an enabled USB 2.0 Controller entry, your ports should be USB 2.0 compliant. You can also use a diagnostic tool such as SiSoft SANDRA (*http://www.sisoftware.net*) to detect and report USB 1.0, 1.1, and 2.0 port types.

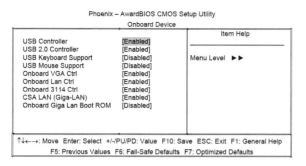

```
                Phoenix – AwardBIOS CMOS Setup Utility
                            Onboard Device
                                                    Item Help
   USB Controller            [Enabled]        ─────────────────
   USB 2.0 Controller        [Enabled]
   USB Keyboard Support      [Disabled]       Menu Level  ▶ ▶
   USB Mouse Support         [Disabled]
   Onboard VGA Ctrl          [Enabled]
   Onboard Lan Ctrl          [Enabled]
   Onboard 3114 Ctrl         [Enabled]
   CSA LAN (Giga-LAN)        [Enabled]
   Onboard Giga Lan Boot ROM [Disabled]

 ─────────────────────────────────────────────────────────────
 ↑↓←→: Move  Enter: Select  +/-/PU/PD: Value  F10: Save  ESC: Exit  F1: General Help
       F5: Previous Values  F6: Fail-Safe Defaults  F7: Optimized Defaults
```

Figure 1-20. Check the Onboard Devices submenu for the presence of USB 2.0 support.

If your system only supports USB 1.1 and you install a USB 2.0 DVD-/+RW drive, it will take considerably more time to move data to the drive. You will also notice a lot of stuttering and dropped frames during DVD playback. If you really want the speed offered with USB 2.0, you can install an inexpensive USB 2.0 PCI adapter available from computer stores like CompUSA.

Even if your motherboard provides USB 2.0-compliant ports, Windows XP requires Service Pack 1A or later to fully support a USB 2.0 port at full speed. The Service Pack is available at *http://www.microsoft.com/windowsxp/pro/downloads/servicepacks/sp1/sp1lang.asp*.

PESKY ZIP DRIVES

The Annoyance: I connected a USB Zip drive to my system, but now the system crashes.

The Fix: Zip drives have a reputation for being cranky, and USB connections don't seem to ease their temperamental nature. Always connect the drive directly to your PC's USB port rather than a hub. Also, check the Iomega web site (*http://www.iomega.com*) for updated drivers, which might help your system stability.

Airborne Maneuvers

Movement and unintended bumps can cause accidental damage to external hard drives and CD/DVD drives. When you connect an external drive, keep it away from desk edges where it might slip and fall. Also, keep all cables out of the way. Otherwise a passerby might trip on a cable and send the drive airborne. You should always unmount, power down, and disconnect an external drive before moving it.

Improper disconnects can affect USB drive media. For example, if you power down or disconnect the Zip drive during a read or write, you can damage the media. Do not power down or disconnect the drive until it comes to a complete stop. In many cases, there will be an icon in the System Tray (such as Safely Remove Hardware), which you can use to disengage the drive logically before you detach the USB cable. Reformat the Zip media and try the drive again. If the problem persists, the Zip drive may indeed be defective. Try the drive on another PC. If the problem "follows" the drive, return it to Iomega for repair or exchange the drive for another model.

USB DEVICES MANAGE POWER DIFFERENTLY

The Annoyance: My USB device has no power management tab.

The Fix: Not every USB device offers its own power management features (separate from the Power Options Properties accessible through Windows' Control Panel). For example, a Linksys LNE100TX PCI network adapter card offers power management options (see Figure 1-21), but a LiteOn DVD-/+RW USB drive does not. Hey, I don't make the rules.

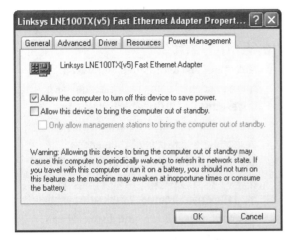

Figure 1-21. Some devices provide a Power Management tab that lets you select device-specific, power-saving options.

Check the documentation that accompanied your USB device to see if it offers a power management feature. If a Power Management tab (or similar) should appear in the device properties, check for a driver upgrade from the manufacturer. Sometimes a motherboard update may be required.

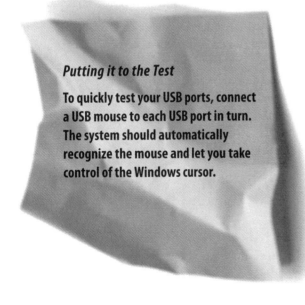

Putting it to the Test

To quickly test your USB ports, connect a USB mouse to each USB port in turn. The system should automatically recognize the mouse and let you take control of the Windows cursor.

NOT ALL USB PORTS WORK

The Annoyance: Why does my USB device work on some USB ports, but not others?

The Fix: Open the System control panel, click the Hardware tab, click the Device Manager button, and then expand the Universal Serial Bus controllers entry (see Figure 1-22). There should be one USB Root Hub and one USB Universal Host Controller entry for every two USB ports on your system. For example, three USB Root Hubs and three USB Universal Host Controllers should support six USB ports.

Figure 1-22. Check your USB resources, such as root hubs and host controllers.

If there are missing entries (or entries marked with an exclamation mark), those ports may be unavailable to your system—usually because the drivers are damaged or improperly installed, or because those USB port resources are damaged on the motherboard. Right-click any Hub or Controller entry and select "Scan for hardware changes."

If all your USB port resources seem properly supported, the trouble may be in the driver for your finicky USB device (such as a USB drive or webcam). Leave the Device Manager open and locate the troublesome USB device. If the device is marked with an exclamation mark, right-click the device and select Remove. A message box says "Warning: You are about to remove this device from your system." Click the OK button and close the Device Manager. Now unplug the USB device, wait a few seconds, then reconnect it to the same USB port. This should launch the New Hardware Detected wizard and walk you through the device installation. If the device is not detected, the port may be defective. Otherwise, the device should install properly and operate normally.

USB DEVICES ONLY WORK BRIEFLY

The Annoyance: My USB devices work for only a few minutes after I boot the system.

The Fix: Windows XP turns off idle USB devices to conserve power. When you access the device again, it should turn on after a few moments. However, certain combinations of motherboards, driver versions, and USB devices may force you to reboot the system.

You can disable Windows XP power management control of the USB hubs to prevent USB devices from powering down. Open the System control panel, click the Hardware tab, click the Device Manager button, and then expand the Universal Serial Bus controllers entry (see Figure 1-22). There should be one USB Root Hub and one USB Universal Host Controller entry for every two USB ports on your system. Right-click the first USB Root Hub, select Properties, click the Power Management tab, and uncheck the "Allow the computer to turn off this device to save power" box. Uncheck the same box for each of your USB Root Hub entries. Click the OK button and exit the Device Manager. Reboot the system if necessary and try the USB devices again.

FIREWIRE DRIVE DISCONNECTS UNEXPECTEDLY

The Annoyance: My FireWire drive seems to disconnect intermittently whenever I try to copy files.

The Fix: First, check the drive's power and signal connections. Like USB, a FireWire port will provide limited power to lightweight devices, but more demanding devices like external CD/DVD drives require their own AC power adapters. Pay particular attention to the FireWire signal cable for any signs of damage. You should replace cut, kinked, crushed, or otherwise damaged cables.

Open the System control panel, click the Hardware tab, click the Device Manager button, and then locate the FireWire drive. An improperly identified device may behave strangely, resulting in problems such as poor performance, lost data, and system crashes. Check with the drive maker for any driver updates or patches.

Finally, the trouble may lie with your FireWire port. Try an alternate port (PCs often provide two or three FireWire ports), or install a PCI FireWire adapter.

BUILD OR BUY

Is it more economical to buy a prefabricated PC or to buy the parts and build the system yourself? This question has plagued computer enthusiasts since the early 1980s. The answer depends on your technical expertise, personal confidence, and budget. Everyday PC users with simple needs would do well to buy a prefabricated system from a major manufacturer. However, PC enthusiasts may prefer the challenges and rewards of building their own custom systems. It will almost certainly cost more than buying a similar system "off the shelf," but it provides more thrills.

NOT ALL EXTERNAL DEVICES USE POWER SWITCHES

The Annoyance: My FireWire hard drive lacks a power switch. How the heck do I turn the drive off?

The Fix: You can certainly leave external FireWire drives (and USB drives) turned on. But environmentally conscious users may not appreciate letting the idle drive run 24/7. Many users opt for a happy medium and remove the drive if it remains idle for an extended period. First, unmount the drive from Windows. For example, Seagate external drives include a little green arrow in the System Tray that will unmount the volume prior to disconnection. Next, power down the computer and unplug the drive power. External hard drives will automatically park their read/write heads when you remove power.

> ### Warning. . .
> *Never* move an external hard drive while it spins. Accidental bumps can cause the read/write heads to crash and damage important data.

MAINTENANCE ANNOYANCES

RECOVERING FROM A VIRUS

The Annoyance: I caught a virus from an email attachment. My anti-virus utility found it and supposedly erased it, but now my system stutters and coughs and crashes left and right. Do I need to wipe the hard drive and reload the operating system from scratch?

The Fix: Even when anti-virus tools manage to locate and eradicate a virus, it can still irreparably damage critical files. This can cause all kinds of system problems and force you to start from scratch. But before you throw in the towel, do a last-minute sanity check.

Start with your anti-virus utility. Older signature definitions may not detect or remove all current virus threats, so update your virus definitions and scan the system again (you might luck out and squash that one last bug hidden somewhere on your PC). On the other hand, if the problems started after a certain date, you might prevail on the System Recovery utility under Windows XP. Select Start → All Programs → Accessories → System Tools → System Restore, choose the "Restore my computer to an earlier time option," and follow the wizard (see Figure 1-23). If the trouble started after you installed a new program, the Add/Remove Programs wizard can remove problem programs.

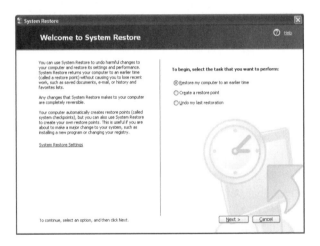

Figure 1-23. The System Restore wizard can often overcome bad software or driver upgrades to fix an unstable system.

You may be able to repair the Windows XP installation if you boot from the Windows XP disc. When the Windows XP Setup appears, press "R" to repair the installation using the recovery console. If all else fails, restore the operating system. Use a bootable diskette to repartition the hard drive, then insert the Windows XP installation disc and restart the computer. When the Windows XP Setup loads, opt to "Setup Windows XP" and follow the instructions.

IMPROVING YOUR ODDS OF UPGRADE SUCCESS

The Annoyance: I want to try some hardware upgrades, but even the thought of mucking with my system scares me half to death.

The Fix: To upgrade a computer successfully, prepare your system beforehand and position yourself for possible problems before you ever open the case. So many folks just jump right into an upgrade and get in a real jam because they wind up missing a Windows CD or boot diskette. The following tips will help you:

RTFM (or Read The...er...Fine Manual). I know this sounds like a cop-out, and most product manuals are about as exciting as a mouth full of Novocaine, but you should at least read the manufacturer's instructions. Do you need to install the software or the hardware first? Are there any known incompatibilities with hardware or software already on your system? The manufacturer will probably know. Walk through the installation steps in your head, and make sure you understand each one. If not, ask for help.

Check the system requirements. How many times have you bought a neat gadget in a pretty box, got it home, and then discovered you couldn't get it to work? To prevent this hassle, compare the system requirements to a system report generated by a utility such as SiSoft SANDRA (*http://www.sisoftware.net*). If you need 512MB of RAM, a 1.5GHz or later processor, or a PCI 2.2 slot for that new video capture card, make sure your system meets or exceeds the specs.

Get updated software. Most hardware devices come with drivers and software on a CD, but the manufacturer may already have patches or upgrades available for download on their web site. Take a quick peek *before* you start and save it to CD-RW or diskette.

Gather the necessary media. Many installations need supplemental media (such as your Windows installation CD) not included with the product you want to install. Cover yourself by finding the Windows CD, motherboard CD, and other driver CDs for your system. If your system comes with recovery discs, keep them handy in case a foul-up forces you to reboot from a CD or diskette.

Check the hard drive. Run ScanDisk and Disk Defragmenter to check the drive for possible file damage and reorganize the drive files. Fix any file problems before you upgrade the system.

Set a System Restore point. The System Restore wizard should do it automatically, but make a manual restore point before you upgrade (see Figure 1-23). If the upgrade causes system problems, you can simply remove the offending device and use the System Restore wizard to recover.

Back up important data. Save the essentials—such as Money, Quicken, and tax software files—in case you need to reinstall the operating system or other applications.

Use anti-static precautions. A quick walk across the rug can kill your expensive new electronic gadget with a shot of static electricity the moment you touch it (which you may not even feel). Discharge yourself against the computer's metal chassis before you handle a processor, memory, or expansion cards.

Tackle one project at a time. Troubleshooters know that the last thing to change before problems occurred is almost certainly the cause of those problems. If you change several items at the same time, it makes it more difficult to locate the culprit.

STOPPING EXCESSIVE FAN NOISE

The Annoyance: The fan in my PC makes a ton of noise.

The Fix: Eventually, a fan will start to fail. In most cases, the crappy little sleeve bearing inside the fan starts to wear out, and the fan's innards start rattling around. (If you've ever lost the wheel bearings on your car, you know what I'm talking about.) Violà, noise!

A full tower PC can employ up to six individual fans. To locate the offending fan, slow each fan in turn by momentarily pressing a pencil eraser gently against the fan's center (be careful the fan doesn't take the pencil out of your hand). A little pressure will usually quiet the fan right away and reveal your troublesome fan. When you locate the noisy fan, check the screws and mounting. Loose mounting screws may let the fan casing vibrate, and this can cause noise even though the fan itself may be fine. Tighten any loose mounting screws and see if that helps.

Screaming Fans

A typical PC has three fans: the power supply, the CPU, and the case exhaust. However, some PCs can have up to six or seven fans for cooling hot components. A fan failure can lead to system stability problems and even damage. How do you identify a failing fan? If it starts to make a lot of racket, replace it at your earliest opportunity.

If the problem persists, replace the fan. Fortunately, computer stores such as CompUSA offer many different fan speeds and mounting hardware options. Most PC fans measure 12 volts and use three-wire connectors to attach to the motherboard (for RPM monitoring and speed control). Once you purchase a suitable replacement, unbolt and exchange the old fan, but make sure to match the airflow direction. For example, if the old fan blew air out of the case, the new fan should do the same.

SURVEYING PC HARDWARE

The Annoyance: Short of cracking open the PC case, how can I tell if my new PC meets the specs as advertised?

The Fix: PC makers are often, err..."optimistic" when quoting a new system's specifications, but performance may not always seem on-par with the specs. Simply run a benchmark like PCMark04 (*http://www.futuremark.com*) or SiSoft SANDRA (*http://www.sisoftware.net*) and check the suspect system's performance against other similar systems or against the specifications provided by the PC maker (see Figure 1-24).

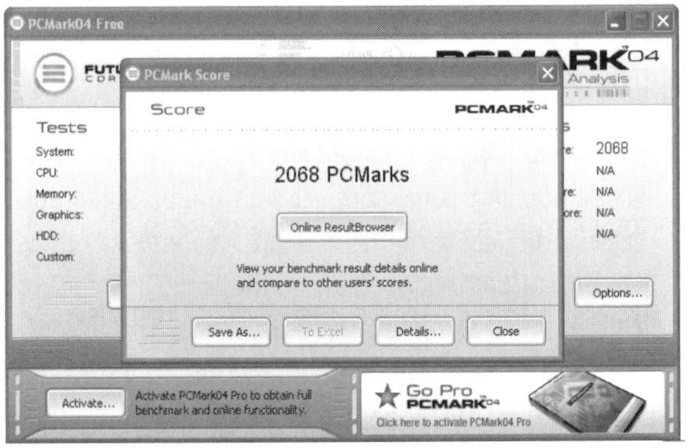

Figure 1-24. Benchmarks like PCMark04 can reveal system characteristics and performance results that mark a powerhouse or a substandard PC.

You can also check any number of PC review sites such as CNET (*http://www.cnet.com*) or PC World (*http://www.pcworld.com*). These folks regularly review new systems using benchmarks such as PCMark or SANDRA.

Sucking It Up

Some folks use their household vacuum cleaners to remove dust and other debris from inside their computers. However, vacuums use cheap plastic tubes and hoses, and the rush of air across those materials can generate static electricity. More than one unsuspecting slob has zapped their video card or motherboard while vacuuming. If you insist on using a vacuum, select a small, battery-powered model rated "static safe."

DON'T BUY UNNECESSARY CLEANING SUPPLIES

The Annoyance: Do I need any of the PC cleaning garbage that stores push?

The Fix: You can do all of your system cleaning with a little paintbrush, a can of compressed air, a bottle of Windex, and a roll of paper towels. Occasionally, a little isopropyl alcohol (ordinary rubbing alcohol) on a Q-tip for contact cleaning does the trick.

Many of the canned or compressed cleaners use ozone-depleting propellants. If you must purchase cleaning products, select ozone-friendly items. CRTs clean off well with even a dry paper towel. Dampen the paper towel a little to remove stubborn marks (never spray onto a CRT or into electronic devices directly). You can loosen dust with a paintbrush and wipe it out with a damp paper towel. For LCDs, use a dry, lint-free cloth to clear dust or pet hair from the screen. You can usually remove stains with a small amount of water on a towel, but always check with the LCD maker for their specific cleaning recommendations. I save the compressed air for keyboard and mouse cleaning, and an occasional squirt into the power supply or other hard-to-reach areas.

TROUBLE CAPTURING THE MOMENT

The Annoyance: I want to capture some vacation videos to my hard drive in order to compile a DVD of family memories, but the capture keeps quitting at the same spot and I get an error.

The Fix: First, make sure your hard drive has enough free space to capture the entire clip length. The amount of space you need depends on the size of your capture window, the bit (color) depth, the frame rate, and any compression (like MPEG) applied during the capture process. For example, products such as the Dazzle Digital Video Creator 80 recommend you set aside a default amount of 4GB for every 20 minutes of video captured (this assumes a 320×240 window at 30 frames per second).

Now, if you clogged your hard drive with games, images, and temporary Internet files and downloads, you may need to clean some space off the drive. Fortunately, Windows provides a Disk Cleanup tool (see Figure 1-25) that can quickly reclaim a lot of wasted space.

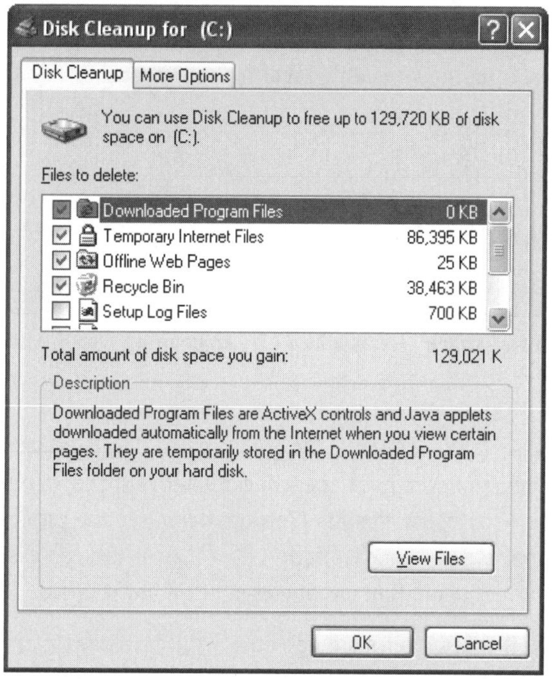

Figure 1-25. Use the Disk Cleanup tool to free additional space on your hard drive.

Select Start → Control Panel → Performance and Maintenance and choose the "Free up space on your hard disk" option. Select the items to clean and click the OK button to free the space.

If you need more space, add a second hard drive for captures. A 120–200GB+ hard drive will probably have ample space, but FAT32 partitions limit file sizes to 4GB (or about 20 minutes of Dazzle video, for example). Instead of capturing one huge file, try to break your captures into smaller segments (you can always edit the segments back together with a video-editing tool later). If you absolutely must capture the entire video event as a single file, convert your FAT32 partition to NTFS. You could also capture directly to DVD if your particular capture software and optical drive hardware support it.

If you want to shrink the capture file size, increase the amount of compression applied to the video data during the capture process. This will save you space, but reduce the image quality. Experiment with different settings to determine the optimum quality level for your needs.

MAKING THE CUT

The Annoyance: My PC seems slow and I get "out of space" errors when I try to save files to my hard drive.

The Fix: Photos, MP3s, games, video clips, application suites, and even leftover email eat up drive space. To clear some space, use the Disk Cleanup utility (see the previous annoyance, "Trouble Capturing the Moment"). It can easily recover hundreds of megabytes in just a few seconds.

But it takes a bit more detective work to *really* clean up the system. Use the Add/Remove Programs wizard to remove any applications that you no longer use. Open the Add or Remove Programs control panel. Scroll down the list of applications, highlight an item to remove, and then click Remove. Dumping those useless old applications can recover several gigabytes of space (and declutter the desktop at the same time). You should also delete outdated or unneeded emails.

Hungry for more? Use the Windows Search tool to locate those beefy multimedia files. Select Start → Search → "Pictures, music, or video"; check the Pictures and Photos, Music, and Video boxes; then click the Search button. After a minute or so, you will see every multimedia file found on your system (see Figure 1-26). You can further sort your findings, or simply right-click unneeded files and select Delete. Hold down the Shift button each time you delete a file, and it will be erased rather than sent to the Recycle Bin. You may free tens of gigabytes in just a few minutes.

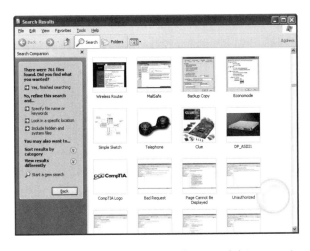

Figure 1-26. Use the Search tool to ferret out large unneeded pictures, music, and video files for deletion.

FIXING FOULED FILES ON THE HARD DRIVE

The Annoyance: I get scary "blue screen of death" messages indicating sector errors on my hard drive. How do I diagnose and fix sector problems?

The Fix: All hard drives occasionally suffer from file problems. Cross-linked files occur when two or more files attempt to use the same *cluster*, a group of sectors allocated by the filesystem. Lost allocation units (industry-speak for lost clusters) can break a file and render it unusable. In other cases, media errors (trouble on the drive platters themselves) can cause file issues. Fortunately, ScanDisk can locate and repair some types of disk file problems: right-click the drive in My Computer, select Properties, and click the Tools tab.

Remember that ScanDisk repairs the disk—not the files—so affected files may no longer be usable. For example, ScanDisk can stop two files from using the same cluster, but you will need to reinstall one of the two competing files. Be ready to replace any damaged files from a backup once ScanDisk repairs the disk.

On the other hand, your drive may be teetering precariously on the brink of failure. If you see more file errors, or additional errors crop up frequently after you fix the drive with ScanDisk, back up your important work and replace the suspicious drive before it dies completely.

FIXING FAULTY CONFIGURATION DATA

The Annoyance: When I try to boot my system, I get an Invalid System Configuration Data error.

The Fix: The Extended System Configuration Data (or ESCD) area of the CMOS RAM stores information about the Plug-and-Play (PnP) devices installed in your computer. The BIOS (as well as the operating system) needs to know the IRQs, memory space, and DMA channels used by each PnP device. When the system boots, it uses the information in the ESCD to assign the same resources to the same devices each time.

This error occurs when the ESCD data has been lost or corrupted. To fix it, clear the CMOS RAM and reload the system default values through the System Setup. This lets the BIOS redetect and resort resources for the PnP devices (see "Clearing a Forgotten CMOS Password," earlier

in this chapter). If the problem occurs right after you install a new PnP device, it usually means the BIOS can't allocate the necessary resources for the new device in your current configuration. You can possibly fix this wrinkle if you shuffle the expansion cards in their slots. If not, you may not be able to use the new device in your particular system.

REGAINING CONTROL FROM A SYSTEM CRASH

The Annoyance: My PC totally froze. How do I regain control of the system?

The Fix: If the mouse responds, click on the current window to make it active, and then try an orderly shutdown. Otherwise, wait a minute or two and see if the condition clears on its own (this can save a lot of lost work).

Next, close disruptive programs. Press Ctrl+Alt+Del to open the Task Manager (Figure 1-27). Highlight the unresponsive program(s) and click the End Task button. Closing programs in this way will dump any unsaved work. See if you can regain control of your desktop. If so, do an orderly shutdown and reboot the system.

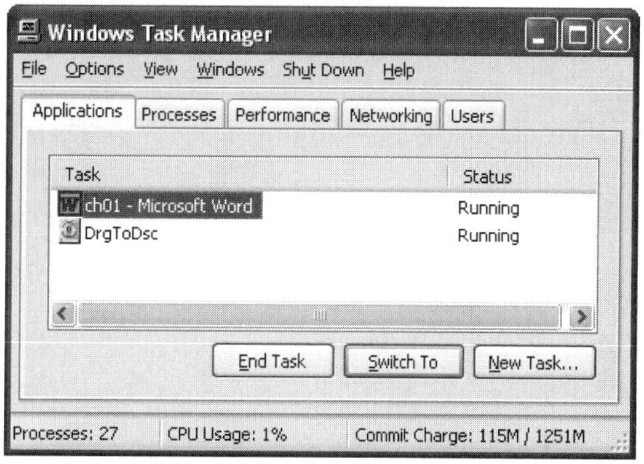

Figure 1-27. The Task Manager can shut down unruly programs, sometimes restoring control of your system.

If the system refuses to respond at all, hit the Reset button on your PC's front panel. Don't be worried if Windows scans the disk before it boots. In a few rare cases, the Reset button may not work, so press and hold the Power button for 5–10 seconds. This will turn off the power supply and shut down the PC. Wait a minute, then reboot.

CREATING A PASSWORD RECOVERY DISK

The Annoyance: I forgot my logon password and now I'm locked out of Windows XP.

The Fix: Passwords provide system and network security. If you forgot your password, contact your system administrator to help you with your account. Of course, if *you're* the administrator...well...you're pretty much screwed.

However, you can create a password recovery disk to protect a new account from forgetful users. Select Start → Control Panel → User Accounts, and then click the account name. Click "Prevent forgotten password" in the Related Tasks area to launch a wizard that will automatically create a password recovery disk. Label the diskette and stash it away for an emergency.

Once you recover from your coma, just click the appropriate user icon at the logon screen and select the little green arrow to proceed without a password. This will prompt you for the password recovery disk and get you into the system.

SQUASHING THE WINDOWS XP BUG REPORT

The Annoyance: Why does Microsoft want to know when my system crashes? How do I stop XP from sending reports?

The Fix: Every time an application crashes, Windows XP tries to send a bug report to the well-meaning but nosey folks in Redmond. Although XP sends the minimum amount of information, this feature disturbs many users. To disable the bug-reporting feature, right-click My Computer, select Properties, click the Advanced tab, and then

click the Error Reporting button. Choose the "Disable error reporting" radio button and click the OK button (see Figure 1-28).

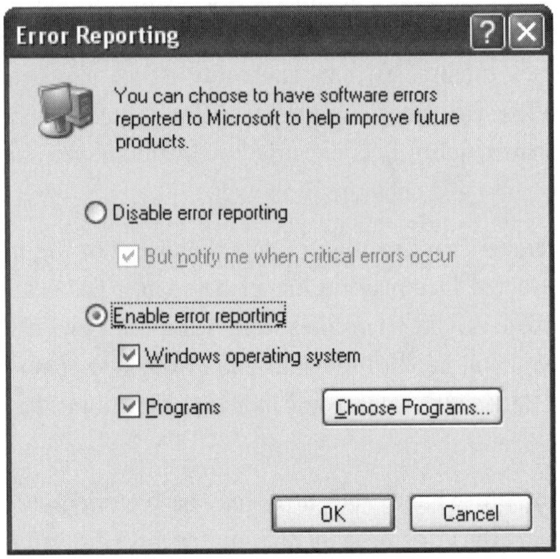

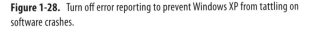

Figure 1-28. Turn off error reporting to prevent Windows XP from tattling on software crashes.

ENABLING AUTOMATIC WINDOWS UPDATES

The Annoyance: With all the security patches and updates available for Windows, it would be a big help to tackle it automatically.

The Fix: Software bug corrections, hardware support improvements, and security vulnerability patches require periodic updates to keep things running smoothly. You can use the Windows Update feature any time you go online. Select Start → All Programs → Windows Update. However, you can also let Windows XP take care of updates for you. Open the System control panel, click the Automatic Updates tab, and choose the "Download the updates automatically and notify me when they are ready to be installed" option (see Figure 1-29).

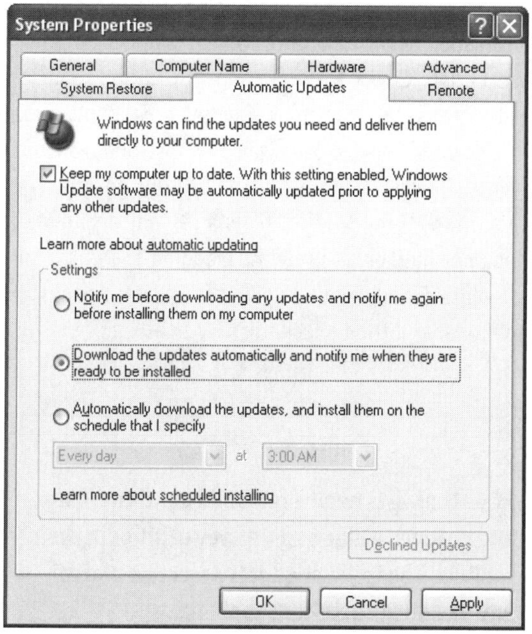

Figure 1-29. Configure Windows XP to download updates and patches automatically.

AVOIDING REDUNDANT PATCH DOWNLOADS

The Annoyance: How can I reinstall Windows XP without spending three days online downloading all the patches?

The Fix: Windows XP stores updates in the *Program Files\Windows Update* folder. You can easily copy this huge folder to a CD-R/RW or DVD disc, but it will take both time and patience to restore each individual patch or update manually.

Instead, use a tool such as Symantec Ghost to image (or duplicate) your system (or at least the operating system) onto a CD-R/RW or DVD disc. This way, if you need to start again from scratch, you can just restore the Ghosted backup, which already has the patches and updates applied.

TURN IT OFF OR LEAVE IT ON

The Annoyance: Do I need to shutdown my PC every night or can I just let it run all the time?

The Fix: PC old-timers like me probably remember classic i286 (yes, I said 286) systems with hundreds of chips in them. All those chips made a lot of heat, and the heat caused expansion of components and connections. When you turned off the system, it cooled, and the chips and connections contracted again. Over time, all this repeated expansion and contraction caused thermal stress breaks that eventually resulted in stability problems and outright failures. To eliminate the alternation between hot and cold, PC gurus just left the PC on all the time.

PCs have gotten a lot simpler since then, and a powerful, full-featured system uses just a small handful of chips. Fewer chips use less power, and so forth. Today, most PCs power down into standby and hibernate modes that use a few watts of power. The traditional worry of thermal stress has largely gone the way of the dodo.

So, turn it off or leave it on? Ultimately, you can leave it running all the time and simply let the normal power-saving modes kick in.

FIXING DLL CACHE ERRORS

The Annoyance: I ran the System File Checker (SFC) for Windows XP and got a DLL cache error.

The Fix: One of your applications probably changed the default source path from *C:\Windows* to some other path (such as *C:\Windows\Options\Install*). To fix this error, you need to tweak your Registry file.

> **Warning. . .**
> Improper registry changes can prevent Windows from booting. Always make a backup copy of your registry files before you make any changes.

Select Start → Run, type `regedit`, and click the OK button to open the Registry Editor (*regedit.exe*). Locate the following key:

MyComputer\HKEY_LOCAL_MACHINE\Software\ Microsoft\Windows\CurrentVersion\Setup

In the main window on the right, locate the SourcePath key (see Figure 1-30). It should read *C:\Windows*. If not, double-click the SourcePath key, set the path to *C:\Windows*, and then click the OK button. Close the Registry Editor and reboot the PC.

Figure 1-30. Use the Registry Editor to tweak incorrect settings, but use caution because improper changes can stop Windows from booting.

PREVENTING PERNICIOUS PC POWER-DOWNS

The Annoyance: My PC suddenly turns off and then I see the power LED flashing.

The Fix: If the system temperature exceeds a preset limit, many new PCs shut down automatically to prevent accidental damage to heat-sensitive components such as the processor.

First, make sure the outer covers are in place. Conventional wisdom suggests you can cool the PC better if you remove its outer cover. Phooey! PC makers carefully design the chassis and fan to achieve optimum processor cooling. If you remove the outer cover, it messes up the airflow, and may actually hinder proper cooling.

Remove the outer covers and make sure every fan runs. Fan failures (such as the CPU fan or power supply fan) can allow heat to build. Check the fan connections and replace any defective fans (see "Stopping Excessive Fan Noise" earlier in this chapter). Also, clear away any obstructions from the air vents. Blocked vents will stop airflow no matter how fast your fans turn. Brush or blow away any accumulations of dust, pet hair, or other debris clogging the intake or exhaust vents. Finally, power down the PC, let it cool for 10–15 minutes, and then check the CPU heat sink/fan.

TOOLS OF THE TRADE

PC enthusiasts need a few solid benchmarking and hardware diagnosis/survey utilities in their toolbox. The following tools deserve a place in any PC do-it-yourselfer's toolbox:

SiSoftware SANDRA (http://www.sisoftware.net).
> **Analyze the latest PC hardware and software setup for your system**

Futuremark PCMark 04 Pro (http://www.futuremark. com/products/pcmark04/).
> **A comprehensive PC benchmark utility to measure a range of performance parameters**

Futuremark 3DMark 03 Pro (http://www.futuremark.com/products/3dmark03/).
> **The industry-standard graphics benchmarking utility for all types of PC video systems**

Futuremark SysMark (http://www.futuremark. com/products/sysmark2004/).
> **The industry-standard office productivity and Internet-content creation benchmark used to characterize the performance of any business-oriented PC**

Laptop and PDA
ANNOYANCES

My old Toshiba 4600 came with a tiny, 12-inch VGA display. I almost went blind from all the squinting and nearly got a hernia carrying that behemoth around. Mobile computing still had a few years before it really caught fire, but I had already caught the bug.

The rest of the world eventually caught on to the advantages of mobile computing. And while desktop systems still rule the roost, their lead shrinks every day. Students, salespeople, estimators, and even everyday PC geeks crave notebooks, sub-notebooks, tablets, PDAs, and all manner of intelligent devices. Of course, this trend will only continue as features improve and wireless access (once a limitation to true mobility) spreads across homes and offices.

However, mobile computers still suffer from some chronic weak spots. This chapter examines some typical startup annoyances and gets into some of the nitty-gritty issues surrounding battery life, display performance, and maintenance.

SETUP/STARTUP ANNOYANCES

USE THE CD/DVD SPINDLE

The Annoyance: When I place a CD in my laptop's DVD-ROM drive, it just flops around in the drive.

The Fix: Hmmmm...okay, I know this may sound a wee bit basic, but the optical drives used in desktop and mobile PCs typically employ different spindles. On desktop drives, you just seat the disc into the drive tray and close it. Laptop drives have a spindle in the tray, so you have to gently (I said *gently*) push the disc onto the spindle until it snaps into place before you close the drive tray. If you just plop the disc on top of that spindle, it will flop around like a fish and the drive won't read it.

LAPTOP STUCK IN HIBERNATION

The Annoyance: When I try to restart my laptop from hibernation mode, I get an error message.

The Fix: This one may take a little explaining. Mobile computers typically provide two power-conservation modes: standby (or suspend) and hibernate. The standby mode simply saves the system's current state to memory, and then idles hardware such as the display, hard drive, and PCMCIA cards. The hibernate mode saves even more power because it saves the entire system's state (including applications, data files, the works) to a disk file, and then almost completely powers down the system. However, any problems with the "save-to-disk" file (like file corruption or a bad drive sector) can prevent the system from resuming properly.

Fortunately, you can work around this hassle. A series of repeated startup failures will usually cause the system to ignore the save-to-disk file and boot directly from the operating system. For example, use the Power button to turn off the laptop for several seconds, and then power it back on for several seconds. Repeat this about five times until the error disappears and the unit boots normally

from its OS. Once you recover the system, use a drive-checking tool such as ScanDisk to check the drive and fix any file problems.

> **t i p**
>
> If you ignore the save-to-disk file, you will lose any unsaved data files. Make sure you save all your important work before you employ any standby or hibernate modes. Also, check the laptop manual for any hibernation troubleshooting notes particular to your system.

NOTEBOOK WON'T HIBERNATE

The Annoyance: I wait forever for hibernation mode to kick in, but it never does.

The Fix: It takes a well-tuned mix of system hardware, drivers, and operating system support to enter the suspend mode (and return successfully).

First, make sure hibernation support is enabled on your system. Open the Power Options control panel, click the Hibernate tab (see Figure 2-1), and check the "Enable hibernation" box. If no Hibernate tab exists, your PC does not support hibernation.

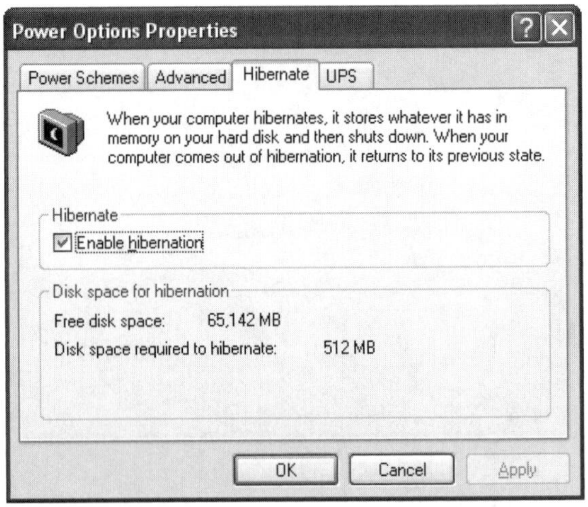

Figure 2-1. Check the Hibernate tab and see that hibernation is enabled.

COMMON-SENSE THEFT PREVENTION

The Annoyance: The laptops in my office seem to grow legs and walk away. How can I keep my laptop from walking off?

The Fix: Physical security is a real headache for all types of mobile devices. Staying mobile (without keeping the unit with you every waking moment) is a serious dilemma. Fortunately, these handy, common sense tips can help reduce theft, protect your valuable work, and possibly even recover lost equipment:

Lock up the unit. Thieves look for the "easy grab." Lock the unit in your desk if you step out for a meeting or luncheon. If on the road, keep the unit covered or out of sight, and lock your car. If the unit must remain on your desk, buy a tether or other security device to deter casual theft. Companies such as Philadelphia Security Products offer a line of Flexguard locking cables (*http://www.flexguard.com/kit_notebook.html*). You can also find a wide selection of security devices at stores such as Staples, OfficeMax, and CompUSA.

Insure the unit. If you use your personal laptop, PDA, or mobile phone for work purposes, remember that your employer is *not* obligated to replace your lost or stolen equipment. Can you say "screwed"? Check with your personal insurance provider about protective loss/theft coverage for your mobile devices. The terms and costs of coverage depend on your provider, the region, and the way you use your equipment.

Brand the equipment. Thieves hate being caught with stolen goods, so mark the unit to thwart sticky fingers. Use a simple engraving tool to mark your name and contact information on the bottom of the unit. Do not include your home address or phone number, though you can use a PO box and email address.

Back up your data. Strangely enough, data is often more valuable than hardware. If push comes to shove, you can always pick up another laptop or PDA, but the data that you spent weeks, months, or even years assembling might be irreplaceable. Regularly back up your important documents, email, Money or Quicken files, or other sensitive information to CD or DVD, and keep those backups stored in a safe place (preferably under lock and key).

Use passwords and include encryption. Most of us avoid the use of passwords on our personal equipment, but that decision may come back to haunt you when some stranger peeks at your checking account, last year's tax returns, or the designs for a new corporate product. Take advantage of passwords and install an encryption product that encrypts email, files, and instant messages—for example, PGP Personal Desktop (*http://www.pgp.com*). This way, your private information stays secure even if the unit is lost or stolen.

Use a recovery service. Products such as Laptrack (*http://www.laptrack.com*) let you install software that communicates with a monitoring service over the Internet. Laptrack uses both passwords and background monitoring to communicate location information to the monitoring service. When it detects an incorrect passcode or unauthorized activity, the service can translate MAC and IP information to a physical address and then relay that information to police or other authorities.

LIGHTEN YOUR LAPTOP LOAD

The Annoyance: I travel several days each week, and lug around 15–20 pounds of laptop and accessories. How can I lighten the load?

The Fix: Cheer up. The more lifting you do, the less time you need to spend at the gym. But if healthy upper-body work scares you, use these tricks to lighten things up:

Dump the documents. My laptop case bulges from all the folders and binders I cram in there. Try to leave the nonessential junk in your car or office.

Adapt or die. Fieldwork means battery power, so leave the AC charger behind. If you spend quality time in your car, use a car charger to keep the battery topped up. Besides, nothing says "loser" like fumbling around your customer's desk looking for an outlet.

Shelve the battery. If you travel to a location where you expect to work for a while (like a library or a remote office space), leave the heavy battery behind and take the AC adapter instead.

Minimize the drain. Extra devices (e.g., PC Cards and USB mice) add weight and drain power, so leave any unnecessary devices at the office.

Ultimately, you need to select a tool appropriate for the task. If you need the mobility and elegance of a smaller, lighter device, you should...well...think about buying a smaller, lighter device. For example, a salesperson who makes frequent face-to-face contacts would probably benefit from a tablet PC and car charger rather than a full-blown laptop with all the bells and whistles.

AN EASIER WAY TO SYNCHRONIZE FILES

The Annoyance: I *constantly* move files between my desktop and notebook PCs using a CD-RW disc. It drives me crazy, but what else can I do?

The Fix: Tired of the "CD shuffle"? Try a USB flash drive instead. These eraser-size flash-memory devices fit on a key chain and plug into a USB 1.1 or 2.0 interface. Windows treats the USB flash drive like a hard drive, floppy drive, or other storage device and even assigns it a drive letter. USB flash drives come in 16MB–2GB capacities.

You could also get a file-synchronization program, such as LapLink Gold 11.5 (*http://www.laplink.com*) or GoTo-MyPC (*http://www.gotomypc.com*), which lets you synchronize files between PCs. Simply connect local PCs with a USB cable, and connect remote PCs via a local area network or the Internet.

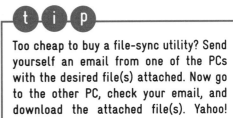

t i p

Too cheap to buy a file-sync utility? Send yourself an email from one of the PCs with the desired file(s) attached. Now go to the other PC, check your email, and download the attached file(s). Yahoo! Briefcase or other web-based file storage services also let you store important files to share between multiple systems.

IGNORING A CUMBERSOME TOUCHPAD

The Annoyance: My thumbs always hit the touchpad while I type. It drives me nuts.

The Fix: Most laptop and notebook users have a love/hate relationship with their touchpads. Either they like the touchpad and always use it, or they hate the touchpad and wish they could physically rip it out of the PC. The easiest solution is to simply use an external USB mouse. They come in all shapes and sizes to fit your specific needs. For example, LapWorks (*http://www.laptopdesk.net*) offers a USB optical mini-scroll mouse.

If you really hate the touchpad and want to disable it altogether, open the Mouse control panel. Click the Touch-Pad On/Off tab and disable the device (see Figure 2-2).

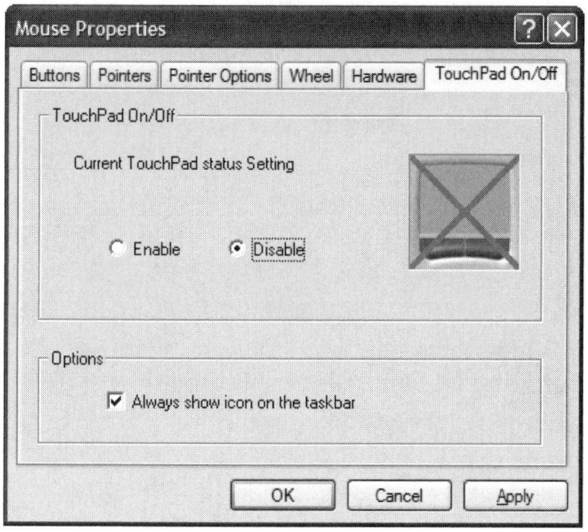

Figure 2-2. Disable pesky touchpads through your Mouse Properties.

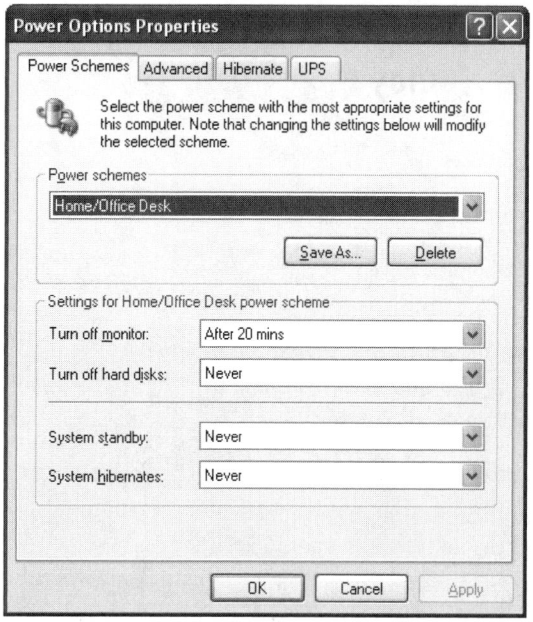

Figure 2-3. Tweak the hard disks so that your system doesn't seem to spin up so often.

SYSTEM HESITATES WHEN DRIVE SPINS UP

The Annoyance: My notebook freezes every few minutes. I hear a whirring noise and then things return to normal after a few seconds.

The Fix: This annoyance crops up a lot with laptops. To save power, the hard drive spins down after a few idle minutes. It can then take several seconds for the drive to spin up again, and the system will seem to pause or freeze.

Open the Power Options control panel and use the "Turn off hard disks" drop-down menu to adjust the spin-down time (see Figure 2-3). Choose a long delay to keep the drives active and avoid the hesitation you experience now. This uses a bit more power, but causes less wear on the drive. Feel free to tinker with different times to see what works best for you.

> **t i p**
>
> Unusual or extreme noises such as repetitive clicking or ratcheting sounds may suggest an impending drive failure.

LIGHTING YOUR DARK KEYBOARD

The Annoyance: I usually take redeye flights to save money, and I like to get some work done during the flight. But when they turn off the cabin lights, I can't see the keyboard.

The Fix: Did you try the small light right over your seat? Just kidding. If you need more light or don't want to disturb your sleeping neighbor, try a USB Light from Lap-Works (*http://www.laptopdesk.net*). It clips onto your LCD and draws power from one of the laptop's USB ports (see Figure 2-4). The light illuminates almost the entire keyboard. In fact, the IBM ThinkPad already comes with its own built-in keyboard light.

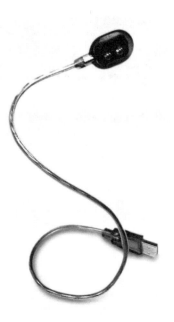

Figure 2-4. The USB Light from LapWorks sheds light on your laptop or notebook keyboard.

ESTABLISHING WI-FI CONNECTIONS

The Annoyance: Why won't my new laptop make a Wi-Fi connection? I can't see any access points.

The Fix: Is your laptop brand-spanking new? Manufacturers such as Toshiba often disable Wi-Fi on new laptops by default to save power. Before you do anything else, check the Wi-Fi configuration and see that it is enabled. In some cases, you need to flip a physical switch (an LED on the laptop body often denotes wireless status). For example, the Toshiba Satellite P25 includes a Wi-Fi antenna on/off switch on the unit's left side. In other cases, you control the laptop's wireless features through an icon in your System Tray. Any available wireless connections should appear in My Network Places once you enable the Wi-Fi feature (such as the "linksys" wireless network in Figure 2-5). Just select an available network and establish your connection.

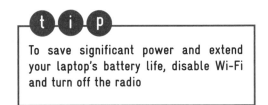

Figure 2-5. Enable your laptop's Wi-Fi features and select an available wireless network to join.

> **t i p**
>
> To save significant power and extend your laptop's battery life, disable Wi-Fi and turn off the radio

NON-STANDARD FEATURES KILL WIRELESS CONNECTIONS

The Annoyance: Why can I connect to some wireless devices with my Dell notebook but not others, such as the wireless router in my home office?

The Fix: This annoying compatibility problem crops up when some wireless manufacturers get "creative" and add features beyond the IEEE 802.11 specification. For example, some manufacturers add security or enhanced performance features. Such features *might* work with some (but not all) access points, routers, or other wireless devices. One known compatibility example occurs with Dell TrueMobile wireless NICs and 3Com Wireless LAN access points. Make sure you configure your access point or router to operate in full compliance with 802.11.

For devices like the 3Com wireless access point, you need to open 3Com's Wireless Infrastructure Device Manager utility on your laptop, select the correct wireless device, and opt to Configure the unit. Under Security, select Open System authentication and disable the 128-bit Dynamic Security Link. Under Radio Settings, select "Long preamble" and disable any Turbo Mode. Of course, not every access point model will offer these same features, but you can look for these common items. Remember to save your changes and reboot the system if necessary.

If you configure dual-band wireless access points (such as 802.11a and 802.11b) to use the same Service Set Identifier (SSID), the laptop's wireless NIC will not function properly

Dump Wireless Defaults

Configure your wireless devices (such as your wireless NIC and wireless access point/router) to use a unique Service Set Identifier (SSID). Otherwise, your next-door neighbor can conceivably access your wireless router and surf the Internet using your high-speed cable connection. Also, Bluetooth connections can often establish and configure themselves with little (if any) direct user intervention.

LOCATION CAUSES POOR WIRELESS PERFORMANCE

The Annoyance: I work in a little cubicle in the rear of the office building, and my wireless network connection seems awfully slow.

The Fix: Don't panic! The interference almost certainly comes from the building, or from other nearby radio frequency sources.

Structural elements such as walls, doors, leaded glass, concrete, water, and other obstacles can weaken wireless signals. The wireless devices will downgrade their data speeds to maintain a connection. Bring your laptop into the same room with the access point and see what happens to the speed. A little empirical testing can easily show you how locations within your particular building will affect data rates. One potential solution is to add more access points to your network.

Nearby electronic devices (e.g., cordless telephones and microwave ovens) can also cause interference. These devices generate signals on the 2.4GHz band (the same band used by 802.11b/g devices). Once your wireless card starts competing with the next-door neighbor's cordless telephone, data rates will drop depending on the level of interference. Manufacturers often suggest you maintain at least 20 feet between wireless devices.

Make sure you configure the wireless access point to ignore connections below a certain minimum bit rate. Why? If a user connects to the access point at a low bit rate, it forces *all* users to operate at the lower rate.

> ### Changing Bands
>
> Ordinary cordless telephones operate on the 2.4GHz radio band, and frequently cause interference with 802.11b/g wireless network devices. One possible solution is to get a 5.8GHz cordless phone. The higher frequency band should alleviate any interference, and possibly coax a little more speed from your nearby wireless devices.

POWER MANAGEMENT BLOCKED AFTER SHARING CONNECTION

The Annoyance: I configured my home network to share an Internet connection through my desktop PC, but now the computer won't go into suspend or hibernate modes.

The Fix: This makes perfect sense if you think about it. You just configured your PC to act as a gateway for other PCs on your home network. This means the other PCs need to access your system to reach the Internet. If your PC powers down, it interrupts Internet access for any other PCs on your network. To re-enable standby or hibernation modes, you must disable the Internet connection on your computer, or disable Internet Connection Sharing (ICS).

However, you could install an Internet router to handle your connection sharing, and then just connect each PC to the router. This takes the pressure off your desktop PC, and you can safely disable ICS.

DVD FRAMES LOST WHEN MOBILE

The Annoyance: When I travel I like to watch DVDs on my laptop, but most movies seem so jerky. Why does this happen? It works fine when I plug the laptop into its AC adapter.

The Fix: Many laptop designs reduce power consumption in any way possible to extend battery life. Since the processor draws a major chunk of power, the very latest laptops automatically "throttle back" the processor speed. The reduced processor speed causes the choppy or "jerky" DVD playback. You need to reconfigure the processor for optimum performance (not optimum battery life).

The manufacturer-specific power applet provided with your laptop typically handles power management. For example, Toshiba laptops use a Toshiba Power Management utility accessible through the Control Panel. Select Start → Control Panel → Performance and Maintenance, and then double-click the Toshiba Power Management icon. When the manager opens, highlight "DVD Mode," click the Apply button, and start your movie (see Figure 2-6). For best battery life, switch back to the "Long Life" mode when the movie ends.

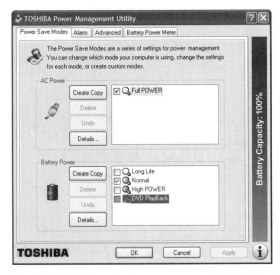

Figure 2-6. Use the laptop's native power management utility to tweak processor operation for performance or battery life.

BATTERY ANNOYANCES

MAXIMIZING BATTERY LIFE

The Annoyance: My laptop battery seems to last about 10 minutes. How can I squeeze more life out of this thing?

The Fix: To get more running time from a battery charge, try these popular tips:

Remove unnecessary devices. For example, PC Cards (PC-MCIA devices) and USB optical mice draw additional power while connected. If you don't really need that PC Card hard drive, NIC, or mouse, remove it from the system.

Dim the display. LCD displays can draw as much as 40% of the laptop's total power budget. Reduce the back-light intensity (usually accomplished through a se-ries of keystrokes defined by the laptop maker). Low-er backlighting will make the display seem a bit washed-out, but it will buy you precious battery time.

Throttle back the processor. Many leading laptops can re-duce the processor speed (and thus its power de-mands) to stretch the battery life (see the previous annoyance, "DVD Frames Lost When Mobile"). Of course, you may need to wait until you plug into AC power before running demanding applications.

Adjust the power management settings. Use the Power Op-tions dialog to adjust the LCD shutdown and hard drive spin-down times for your system. In most cas-es, if you set the Power scheme to Portable/Laptop, it will adjust the display and drive settings to a default value.

Use the suspend mode. Close the LCD lid whenever you step away from the laptop. This puts the laptop into suspend (or standby) mode.

Cycle the battery periodically. If you consistently recharge the battery after every minor use, it can sometimes suffer from shortened charge times. PC old-timers often refer to this as the "memory effect." Let the laptop run until the system shuts down, then re-charge the battery fully. It may take several complete discharge/recharge cycles to properly condition your battery.

Replace the battery. Batteries eventually wear out. If you can't condition the old battery, try a new battery (which you may also need to fully charge and dis-charge several times before use).

Avoid optical drives. CD and DVD drives consume their fair share of power, so copy your work files to the lap-top's hard drive first. This reduces your use of the optical drives.

CREATIVE CHARGING IMPROVES BATTERY LIFE

The Annoyance: I connected my laptop to an AC outlet and fully charged the battery to 100%. However, when I checked the battery meter later, Windows only re-ported a 95% battery charge. How did I lose power?

The Fix: When the battery hits 100%, the laptop's battery charger shuts off the charging circuit and the battery slowly discharges. When the battery hits 95%, a trickle charge starts and slowly tops off the battery. This process starts and stops continuously, but the scheme helps to protect the battery and extend its physical life.

Battery Disposal

You need to dispose of old batteries safely because they employ toxic chemicals. Check with your laptop manufacturer and see if they have a recycling program. If not, check with your local or state government for proper disposal or recycling facilities.

CHECK FOR BAD BATTERY INSERTION

The Annoyance: I installed a new battery, but now the laptop won't work.

The Fix: First, make sure you installed the new battery properly. Battery packs typically slide into place and lock (often with an audible "click"). *Never* jam a battery or any dockable device into a laptop, because you could damage the internal connections. Can you say "repair shop"?

Oh, by the way, you need to charge the new battery before you can use it. Sorry, this is not like buying a package of Eveready Energizers. To fully charge the battery, connect your AC adapter and wait several hours.

If you smell a funky chemical/burning smell or the battery won't take or hold a charge, you may have a defective battery pack. Return it to its place of purchase for a replacement.

To get the best charge time from your new battery, you may need to calibrate it (according to the manufacturer's instructions) during the first few charges. However, this should not affect your ability to charge the battery or operate the laptop from battery power.

IMPROPER AC ADAPTER CAUSES BEEPING

The Annoyance: I always carry an AC adapter because my IBM ThinkPad gets such poor battery life. But one day I had to borrow an adapter and my laptop beeped like mad while running off the charger.

The Fix: You probably grabbed the wrong AC adapter for your particular ThinkPad model. The AC adapter had enough juice to run the laptop (and even charge the battery), but the slightly different specifications caused the laptop to squawk. Try an AC adapter from a colleague using the same ThinkPad model. The beeping should go away.

No Battery Lasts Forever

Laptop batteries used under regular discharge/recharge cycles last about a year (some up to two years). When you purchase a new battery, mark the date on a little piece of masking tape and stick it on the battery to keep track of its longevity.

USING UNIVERSAL AC CHARGERS

The Annoyance: I had to finish a presentation and my notebook died mid-flight at the worst possible time. Short of packing a couple extra batteries, what can I do?

The Fix: You can buy a versatile DC-to-AC adapter for air and auto use, such as APC's $59.99 TravelPower 75 watt air/auto converter (*http://www.apc.com*). The converter translates the low DC voltage from the car or plane into 120 volts AC for small electronic appliances (such as your laptop charger). You just plug the converter into an airliner or automobile power outlet, and then attach the laptop's AC charger to the converter.

LCD ANNOYANCES

IDENTIFYING MANUFACTURER'S PIXEL DEFECTS

The Annoyance: I took a close look at my new laptop's LCD, and I saw more than a few black pixels on my white desktop.

The Fix: A series of microscopic transistors operates each pixel in an LCD display. (Today's LCDs easily incorporate several million transistors.) Obviously, a manufacturer wants each and every one of those transistors to work flawlessly, but a bad transistor can result in a pixel with a fixed color.

LCD manufacturers allow about 9–10 defective pixels in the display. This means you may actually see a few oddly colored pixels on your laptop. On the bright side, you hardly notice a toasted pixel at screen resolutions of 1024×768, 1280×1024, or higher. Still, if you note more than 9–10 locked pixels, the laptop manufacturer may replace the LCD as long as the unit is still under warranty.

IMPROVING A DINGY DISPLAY

The Annoyance: I did a system recovery on my laptop. The recovery went fine, but the LCD image quality looks worse than before.

The Fix: LCD image quality depends on various configuration settings, such as resolution, color depth, refresh rate, and video driver versions. When you restored the system (I assume to its "factory fresh" state), you tossed out all your system updates and tweaks. Try the following tips to improve your view:

Update the drivers. Drivers can profoundly influence your image quality. Download and install any driver updates directly from the manufacturer's web site. You may also want to download and install the latest version of Microsoft's DirectX drivers (available from *http://www.microsoft.com/directx*).

Set the resolution and color depth. Your system restoration probably reset the display to a factory default resolution and color depth. Right-click your desktop, select Properties, and then click the Settings tab (see Figure 2-7). Tweak the "Screen resolution" and "Color quality" settings to your liking. This will improve your display quality a lot.

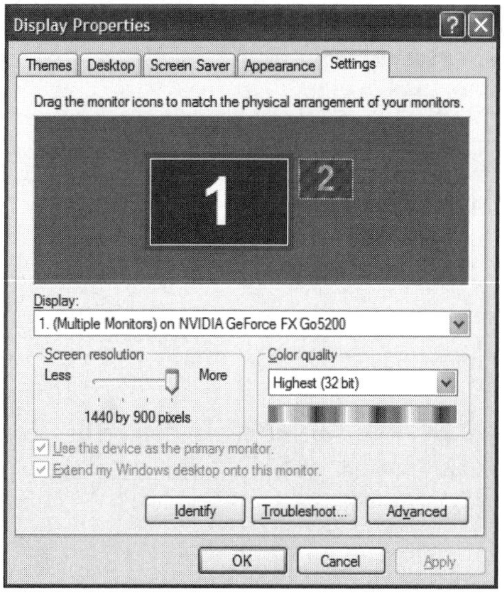

Figure 2-7. Adjust screen resolution and color depth to achieve a clear LCD image.

Check the refresh rate. An improper refresh rate for a particular resolution can cause the image to look a bit dull or out of focus. Click the Advanced button on the Settings tab, and then click the Monitor tab (see Figure 2-8). Select the correct display and try a slightly different refresh rate. You want to pick a refresh rate that provides the clearest image and eliminates visible flicker. (LCDs with manufacturer-specific display drivers may not offer adjustable refresh rates. In this case, opt for the native resolution intended for your LCD, such as 1024×768.)

Figure 2-8. Select the proper monitor type and refresh rate for your specific LCD monitor.

LCD IMAGE CUTS OUT

The Annoyance: Every now and then the whole top half of the display goes dark. If I wiggle the LCD panel, the image pops back.

The Fix: This type of display failure happens with age (and occasional abuse). Unfortunately, you will need to replace the LCD panel.

A hands-on person with an out-of-warranty laptop could try to open the unit and check the LCD connectors that pass through the laptop display hinge. The connectors should be completely and evenly installed. A reasonable sanity check before you drop hard earned cash on a new LCD. Otherwise, contact your laptop manufacturer and arrange to return the unit for service.

Display Cleaning

Laptop displays collect dust, pet hair, and other debris. As a rule, use a soft, dry, lint-free cloth to gently wipe dust from your display. Never use liquid to clean an LCD display.

A CLEARER VIEW OF COMPLEX IMAGES

The Annoyance: I hate scrolling through very large Excel spreadsheets on my notebook's tiny screen.

The Fix: Two tricks may help you. First, increase your display resolution. Right-click your desktop and select Properties, click the Settings tab, and then adjust the Screen resolution slider upwards (as high as your laptop display adapter will allow). A higher resolution will display more Excel cells.

Of course, this also creates smaller cells. Still, you can use the Magnifier feature to enlarge areas of interest on the display. Just click Start → Control Panel → Accessibility

Options → Magnifier. The Magnifier takes a small portion of the display to "zoom in" on your mouse location. Resize the magnifier area to your preferences, and then use the magnifier to see the tiny Excel cells up close.

If your laptop has a separate VGA display port, you can probably attach the laptop to a large 19–21" CRT display when at your desk. A large-screen CRT will make small, fine detail much easier to see at higher resolutions. It also costs less than a 17-inch laptop.

PC CARD ANNOYANCES

FITTING PC CARDS

The Annoyance: I have a Type III PCMCIA drive card that I want to use with my laptop, but it doesn't seem to fit.

The Fix: Easy there, killer. Your laptop probably doesn't offer a Type III card slot. The PCMCIA standards body (*http://www.pcmcia.org*) defines three types of PC Cards. All three card types use the same length and width (and the same 68-pin PC Card connector), but differ in thickness:

Card type	Thickness
Type I	3.3 mm
Type II	5.0 mm
Type II	10.5 mm

You typically use thin Type I cards for memory devices such as RAM, flash, or SRAM cards. Type II cards are usually used for I/O-intensive hardware such as modems, NICs, or USB/FireWire port adapters. Type III cards handle mass-storage devices with large components (such as rotating platters). Since cards differ only in physical thickness, thinner cards can serve in thicker slots, but not vice versa.

However, most current laptops offer two Type II slots together, allowing for either two Type II devices or one Type III (thicker) device. Check the card slots and make sure no plugs or dummy cards occupy the slots (some manufacturers plug these slots to keep out dust). Once you remove the plugs, you may be able to use the Type III drive. If not, you may have an older laptop stuck with Type I or II devices.

SCSI DRIVE IGNORES LAPTOP ADAPTER

The Annoyance: I installed a PCMCIA SCSI adapter, but the SCSI drive refuses to communicate with the laptop.

The Fix: First, open the System control panel, click the Hardware tab, and then click the Device Manager button. Next, check the PC Card SCSI adapter entry for conflicts or any other signs of trouble. If marked with a red "X" or yellow exclamation mark, you may need to re-configure, reinstall, or replace the adapter. The drive will never work properly until you get the SCSI adapter sorted out.

If the SCSI adapter card responds properly, turn your attention to the SCSI drive. Check the basics, such as drive power and the SCSI cable connections between the drive and the adapter. Yes, I know you did this already, but do it again.

Now check the SCSI termination and ID of the drive (by default, the adapter typically ships terminated). Open My Computer, right-click the drive, and choose Properties. Next, click the Hardware tab, highlight the SCSI drive, and click the Properties button. The General tab for the drive should indicate the SCSI ID. If not, check the termination jumper on the drive. (You can also check the SCSI BIOS settings when you start the PC.) Also, make sure the drive uses an acceptable SCSI ID. The adapter usually defaults to ID7, hard drives to ID0 or ID1, and other SCSI drives (like CD/DVD drives) to ID5 or ID6. You typically set termination and IDs with small switches on the drive. The manufacturer's documentation will tell you the exact location and purpose of each setting.

Finally, recheck the manufacturer's instructions one last time and see if you forgot to install any drivers or software applications needed to enable the SCSI drive. This can be a vital step for users running Windows 98 or Me.

Windows XP, on the other hand, usually provides excellent driver support for a wide range of devices.

LAPTOP FAILS TO SEE LAN CARD

The Annoyance: I plugged a PCMCIA LAN card into my notebook, but the system doesn't see it.

The Fix: Start with the obvious and see if the LAN card has been previously installed. If you used the LAN adapter in the past, you won't see any wizards or other installation procedures. The device will be detected automatically and its icon will likely just pop into your System Tray.

> ## t i p
>
> Check the system requirements of a new PC Card LAN adapter against your laptop. Inadequate system requirements may prevent the laptop from properly detecting the adapter.

Another common problem occurs when Windows misidentifies the PC Card adapter or lists it under "Other Devices" in the Device Manager. Open the System control panel, click the Hardware tab, and then click the Device Manager button. Next, check the listings for your PCMCIA ports and devices, as well as any entries under "Other Devices." Right-click any improperly identified PCMCIA device and select Remove, then click the "Scan for hardware changes" button to redetect and reinstall the device.

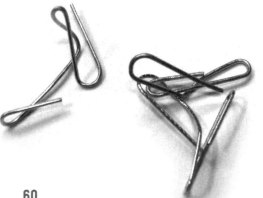

PDA ANNOYANCES

REPLACE WORN STYLUS TIPS

The Annoyance: I wore my stylus tip down to the nub. Do I need to dump this stylus for a new one, or can I just replace the tip?

The Fix: A stylus should slide smoothly and evenly over your PDA display. Still, a slight amount of wear eventually erodes the plastic point. This wear can impact your pen gestures and writing style, so it helps to have a new tip (the same way a sharpened pencil makes for neater writing). Most PDA makers sell inexpensive replacement styluses, but some PDA and tablet PC makers use styluses with replaceable tips. For example, Gateway's Tablet PC series ships with replaceable stylus tips and a replacement tool. Use the tool to grasp the old point and pull. Insert a new point and apply slight pressure to set it in place.

IMPROVE ERRATIC FILE SYNCHRONIZATION

The Annoyance: When I sync my PDA and laptop, I get terribly slow and jumpy file transfers.

The Fix: PDAs and laptop/desktop systems generally sync using infrared (IR) links. However, IR links need to be unobstructed and very close together (no more than a few feet). Excessive distance or dirty IR windows can impair communication and slow the effective data transfer speeds. If the problem persists, synchronize the devices with a USB or serial sync cable. Although less convenient than a wireless IR connection, a hard cable connection will usually offer much better speeds.

You can also configure the speed through the IR port properties. Open the System control panel, click the Hardware tab, and then click the Device Manager button. Next, expand the Infrared Devices entry, right-click the IR port, and select Properties. Click the Advanced tab and adjust the Speed Limit to an optimum setting (see Figure 2-9). For example, you can configure the SMC Fast Infrared Port used with a Toshiba Satellite P25 laptop to 4Mbps.

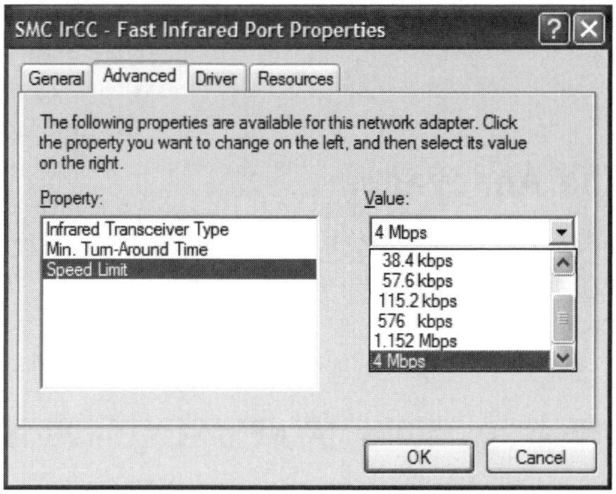

Figure 2-9. Make sure you configure the IR speed setting for fast data transfers.

The process may also seem slow if you sync too much. For example, superfluous programs in the HotSync list can slow down the process. Right-click the HotSync icon and remove unnecessary programs, then try synchronizing the PDA again. The process should go much faster.

SYNCHRONIZING THE PEN AND INK

The Annoyance: How do I get the PDA's display ink to show up under my pen tip? I find it very annoying when the ink shows up a quarter inch away from the tip.

The Fix: Pen stylus input offers a few wrinkles for device designers. Pen contact with the display must be digitized, and then the corresponding position must be matched directly to pixels on the display. The trick is to maintain accuracy between the digitizer and the display. If the digitizer is off just a little, the PDA will think the stylus made contact elsewhere on the display. PDAs and tablet PCs typically offer a calibration feature that lets you set up the computer for one or more users. Calibrate the PDA or tablet the first time you use the unit, or anytime someone else recalibrates it for their own use (such as a left-handed user to a right-handed user).

LOST STYLUS MUST BE REPLACED

The Annoyance: I lost my stylus. Can I use my finger or a ballpoint pen for basic navigation until I get another stylus?

The Fix: A finger tap or stylus from another mobile device will typically not have any effect on the PDA display. And a ballpoint pen is certainly no solution unless you feel like scribbling all over your expensive display (and probably damaging it). Always use the pen or stylus that came with your particular PDA or tablet PC. If you don't have a suitable replacement handy, order another from the manufacturer, or visit your local Staples, Office-Max, or CompUSA. Do yourself a favor and order an extra stylus for emergencies.

PDA DISPLAY GOES WHITE

The Annoyance: My PDA boots to a white screen and I can't get it to do anything.

The Fix: Your PDA may have failed. Manufacturers such as Toshiba often recommend that you remove all extra hardware from the unit (including any compact flash or smart drive cards), and then perform a full reset on your unit according to the manufacturer's specific instructions. If the problem disappears, reinstall your extra hardware one device at a time. If the trouble returns after you install a particular device, you identified the culprit. Otherwise, ship your PDA to the nearest service center for repair.

CALIBRATE YOUR PDA FOR YOUR GESTURES

The Annoyance: I tried to launch an application on my PDA, but when I tapped the icon, nothing happened. The same goes for all the icons.

The Fix: You forgot to calibrate the display to the digitizer pad (see "Synchronizing the Pen and Ink" earlier in this chapter). Use the PDA's calibration feature to adjust the digitizer. For example, for the Toshiba Pocket PC e805, select Settings → System → Screen → Align Screen to make the adjustments. Other PDAs will use different sequences, so check the instructions for your particular PDA or tablet PC. Once you align the digitizer, double-tap the desired icon to launch an application.

If the recalibration fails (or makes no difference), the PDA may have malfunctioned or locked up. Reset or reboot the PDA. If the problem persists, the PDA may require service.

PDA APPLICATIONS SEEM SLOW

The Annoyance: My PDA seems really slow. How can I read email or search my appointment book faster?

The Fix: Your PDA may not have enough memory to run your applications. Close non-essential applications and see if the unit's performance improves. If so, add more memory to the PDA. In a few cases, a software bug may slow down the unit. Quit all your applications and reboot the PDA. If this does the trick, check for software patches and updates for all your favorite applications.

USB DEVICES KILL BATTERY

The Annoyance: I connected a USB device to my PDA, but now I get a battery warning, and the USB device refuses to work.

The Fix: USB devices frequently draw power from the USB port. This power, in turn, comes from the PDA's battery. If the battery charge is too low, the PDA will not enable the USB port, and you will probably see a message like "NOT ENOUGH BATTERY POWER." Connect an AC adapter and charge the battery.

MAKING WIRELESS PDA CONNECTIONS

The Annoyance: I installed a network driver and card in my PDA, but I still can't connect to my wireless network.

The Fix: You need to establish the Ethernet connection yourself. But before you get started, make sure your network has a working wireless access point.

The actual connection process depends on the PDA. For a popular PDA such as the Dell Axim X5, tap Start → Settings → Connections tab → Connections. Tap the Wireless Ethernet icon, select the Wireless tab, and then tap New Settings. Enter the SSID used by the wireless access point, and set your network connection type. Tap the Authentication tab and configure your WEP (Wired Equivalent Privacy) settings to correspond to the wireless access point. The PDA should connect to your wireless access point, and a connection status icon will appear under Wireless Networks.

NEW APPLICATIONS MAY NEED NEW CONDUITS

The Annoyance: I upgraded to Outlook 2003, and now my PDA won't sync with Outlook.

The Fix: Some PDAs (such as PalmOne devices, like the one shown in Figure 2-10) use specially designed software called conduits to synchronize with desktop software applications such as Outlook. However, the PDA conduit software must support the application versions used on your desktop. Otherwise, you will lose synchronization capability with that application.

Figure 2-10. The PalmOne Treo 600 Smartphone can send and receive email wirelessly.

In your case, the PDA's conduit probably lacks support for Outlook 2003 or later. To correct this headache, update the conduit software. For example, PalmOne offers updated conduits for Tungsten T3 and E handheld PCs at *http://www.palmone.com/us/support/downloads/outlookupdate2k3.html*.

OVERCOMING PDA CRASHES

The Annoyance: My PDA crashes when I open an application. How can I stabilize its operation?

The Fix: Software bugs and incompatibilities can strike PDAs just as easily as desktop or laptop systems. Compatibility problems can often result in symptoms such as poor performance, lockups and crashes, poor or distorted displays, and inaccessible PDA features.

First, identify the offending application. Simply exit or unload one application at a time and see how the PDA runs without it. If the unit suddenly stabilizes once you unload a particular application, you found the likely culprit. Check with the PDA maker or software provider for any relevant patches or updates. If you can't patch or update the troublesome application, uninstall it and look for an alternative.

SAVE PDA POWER

The Annoyance: I like to keep my PDA in my pocket or backpack when I travel, but it has an annoying habit of turning itself on.

The Fix: Many PDAs, such as the Tungsten family from PalmOne, come with a Keylock Activation feature. This prevents the unit from being turned on accidentally. To access the Tungsten's Keylock Activation feature, turn the unit on, tap Preferences, tap Keylock (located in the General section), and then tap on either Automatic or Manual to activate the Keylock feature. Other PDA makes and models have similar features, but check your user's manual for specific instructions.

GETTING THE PDA TO CHARGE

The Annoyance: When I put my PalmOne Zire PDA in its cradle, it doesn't seem to charge.

The Fix: Make sure you properly seat the PDA across the cradle contacts. If you leave the unit cockeyed in the cradle, it may not charge. Units like the PalmOne Zire display a small lightning bolt in the application launcher when the unit is charging properly. Also, remember that the cradle itself must be powered (usually from a separate AC adapter). If you still have trouble, try another charging cradle.

HANDLING BIG FILE TRANSFERS

The Annoyance: It takes forever to synchronize huge files between my PDA and laptop.

The Fix: Big file transfers present a real headache for PDA users. It can take time (especially across relatively slow IR ports) to transfer media-intensive video clips or beefy MP3 files.

Some PDA makers offer applications to perk up certain file types. For example, the PalmOne Zire lets you drop AVI, DV, MPEG, and QuickTime files onto a Quick Install icon. This converts the file to the Kinoma Video format, which takes less time to synchronize. For audio files, use an application such as the RealOne Player rather than the HotSync feature. RealOne uses direct file transfers, which can be much faster than using HotSync. Also, a serial or USB link can support faster data transfers than an IR port (helpful for big video or music files).

Finally, swap media cards rather than files. PC users often use diskettes or CDs to transfer files between systems. Why not do the same between desktops and PDAs? If your PC has a card reader compatible with PDA media types, just write your files to media (such as an SD/MMC card) and swap the card to the PDA.

MAINTENANCE ANNOYANCES

EASING A DIFFICULT DOCK

The Annoyance: I really have to fiddle with my laptop to get it to dock properly.

The Fix: Most notebook and laptop PCs provide a rear connection that fits to a compatible docking station or port expander. The connector uses a whole slew of very small contacts and, over time, dust and oils (such as skin moisturizer residue) can accumulate on these contacts.

Laptop makers suggest you clean the contacts with 90% (or better) isopropyl alcohol on a cotton swab. Isopropyl alcohol (aka rubbing alcohol) cleans well and dries quickly without any residue. Clean the contacts on both the laptop and the docking station. Repeat the cleaning two or three times, let the contacts dry completely, then re-connect to the docking station.

SELECTING A RUGGEDIZED PC

The Annoyance: I work with my laptop in construction areas, and I always bump my computer or spill something on it. Is there some way to protect this thing?

The Fix: You really touched on a big dilemma for mobile PCs. How does a device intended for use in the field protect itself from the dangers and foibles of real life? Drops, smacks, and spills are just some of the dangers that await mobile computers on job sites and remote locations—and yet, most laptop, notebook, and tablet PCs are quite fragile. For hardcore Navy SEALS types, Panasonic offers a line of shock, spill, vibration, and dust-resistant Toughbook notebooks that endure MIL-STD-810F testing (the latest and greatest military standards). If you just need to survive the corporate boardroom, you can get a Toughbook for slightly less-demanding field service applications. You can learn more about Panasonic's Toughbook line at *http://www.panasonic.com/computer/toughbook/home.asp*.

COOLING A HOT LAPTOP

The Annoyance: My laptop gets so hot I could fry eggs on it. How can I cool this thing down?

The Fix: A laptop *will* get warm, especially if it houses a fast processor like a Pentium 4 running at 3.2–3.4 GHz. Other things that add heat include running a CPU-intensive application (e.g., gaming, CAD, or image modeling software), configuring the laptop for top performance rather than long battery life (see "DVD Frames Lost When Mobile" earlier in this chapter), and charging the battery. Optional devices like PC Cards and busy internal CD/DVD drives also draw additional energy and add heat.

To cool the laptop, increase the airflow underneath it. The CoolPad (*http://www.roadtools.com*) elevates the laptop enough for air to pass underneath and carry away excess heat (so the laptop won't iron your pants). It's a low-tech solution, but a handy one.

Of course, truly excessive heating may indicate a more serious problem with the laptop. If you actually risk a burn from the heat, contact the laptop manufacturer right away and arrange service for the unit.

TOOLS OF THE TRADE

In addition to the unique utilities and applets that frequently accompany a new laptop or PDA, several other general-purpose applications might enhance your mobile computing experience:

PGP Personal Desktop (http://www.pgp.com)
   Encrypts your files, folders, email, and other system data to protect your work from prying eye.

Laptrack (http://www.laptrack.com)
   An Internet-based utility designed to track a stolen laptop and improve the chances of recovery

Laplink Gold 11.5 (http://www.laplink.com)
   Eases the synchronization of files between laptops, PDAs, and desktop systems

---

Graphics
ANNOYANCES

Processors may get the starring role in any PC, but the graphics subsystem really steals the show. The early days of 16-color palettes and 320×240 pixel resolutions are long-gone. Today, amazingly sophisticated, adrenaline-pumping games such as FarCry and Doom 3 redefine interactive entertainment with their realistic, real-time image-rendering and visceral detail. But graphics go beyond gaming to embrace multimedia tasks such as desktop acceleration, video streaming and capture, and cinema-quality DVD playback. Still, this incredible advancement has come with a hefty price: compatibility and software issues linger long after you install the hardware.

This chapter starts with configuration and driver issues. Next, it looks at important upgrade headaches and desktop snafus under Windows XP. You will also see solutions for CRT/LCD troubles, 3D (rendering-specific) issues, and capture/playback problems. Finally, the chapter covers a range of video-player annoyances.

CONFIGURATION ANNOYANCES

IDENTIFYING UNKNOWN GRAPHICS CARDS

The Annoyance: How can I find out which graphics card my PC currently uses before I drop cash on a new card?

The Fix: Most folks suggest you try the Device Manager to identify your current display system, but I usually recommend the Windows DirectX diagnostic (*dxdiag.exe*) tool. Just select Start → Run, type **dxdiag** in the Run box, and click the OK button. Once *dxdiag* starts, click the Display tab (see Figure 3-1). This identifies the exact display device (e.g., Radeon 9800 Pro), measures the available video memory (e.g., 128MB), and tells you the current driver name, version, and date.

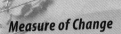

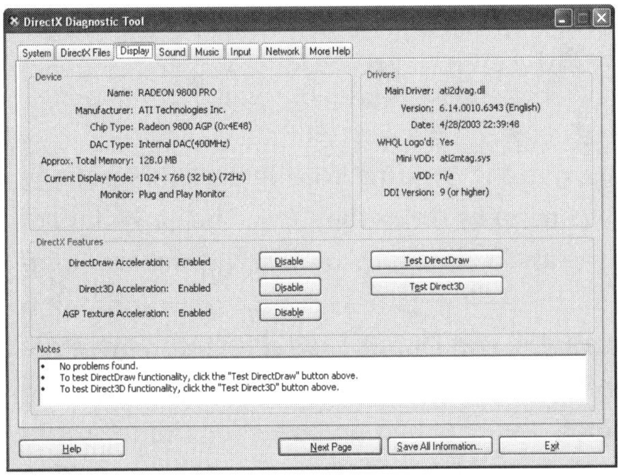

Measure of Change

To see how much a new graphics adapter might help your system, use a graphics benchmark, such as Futuremark 3DMark03 Pro (*http://www.futuremark.com*), to measure your graphics performance before *and* after an upgrade.

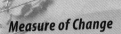

Figure 3-1. Use dxdiag to identify your current display hardware and driver information.

CHECKING VIDEO RAM

The Annoyance: My new game needs a 3D accelerator with 128MB of RAM. How do I check for video RAM and add RAM if necessary?

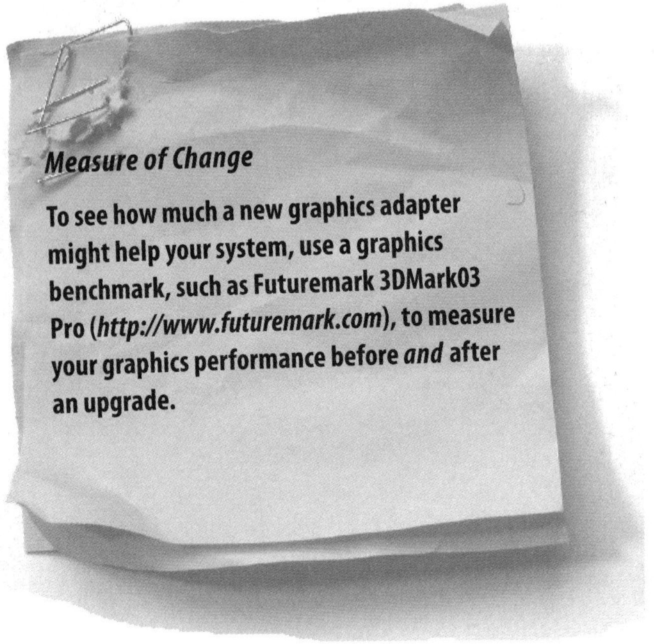

The Fix: First, the good news. Numerous tools will report your video characteristics. Run the *dxdiag* tool (see "Identifying Unknown Graphics Cards") and locate the "Approx. Total Memory" entry under the Display tab (see Figure 3-1). Now the bad news: if your graphics card falls short of the game's system requirements, you must upgrade the graphics card. There is no way to add more RAM to your graphics card.

One small caveat: onboard graphics chips (graphics chips on the motherboard) set aside a portion of the main system RAM for display memory. You can often adjust the amount of memory (also known as the AGP Aperture) through the System Setup (see Figure 1-12). Most recent BIOS versions let you allocate up to 256MB of system RAM for video use. Of course, this reduces the amount of RAM remaining for the operating system and applications.

NO PICTURE WITH DVI CABLING

The Annoyance: I attached my LCD to the DVI port on my graphics card, but there's no picture. What's the problem?

The Fix: You need three items to employ DVI signaling: a video card with a DVI connector, a display (e.g., an LCD) with a DVI connector, and a good-quality DVI cable to connect the two (usually provided with the display). If you make a DVI connection but do not see a picture, make sure that the display is turned on and then recheck the DVI connectors at both the card and display ends. If the trouble persists, try another DVI cable.

What is DVI? *DVI* (Digital Visual Interface) signals correspond to the analog RGB (red, green, and blue) signals used with traditional CRT displays. The DVI standard specifies a single plug and connector scheme that supports both digital signals and legacy analog signals on the same connector. DVI offers some advantages over analog-only display signals. The digital signals are more accurate than analog signals, resulting in truer colors that are more resistant to electrical interference. DVI also handles display bandwidths to 160MHz, supporting high-resolution displays such as UXGA (Ultra Extended Graphics Array) and HDTV.

STABILIZING A FRAME WITH VSYNC

The Annoyance: The display maker says I should turn on the VSYNC signal to get the best possible picture quality. However, I tried the display with the signal turned on and off and the picture seems the same.

The Fix: VSYNC describes how a graphics card renders and sends an image to the display (an LCD or CRT). When you turn on VSYNC, the video card draws one frame of a scene, and waits for the monitor to display it before starting the next frame. With VSYNC turned off, the board draws one image frame, and immediately starts on the next frame.

So, what difference does VSYNC really make in the final image? Well, very little. A display can draw images only as fast as its refresh rate will allow. If you set your monitor for a refresh rate of 72Hz, it will draw 72 screen images per second. So a high-performance graphics adapter pumping out frames at 90–100fps will spin its wheels because the monitor can't keep pace. As a rule, turn on VSYNC. This keeps the monitor and video card synchronized, and usually results in the cleanest display.

Remember that VSYNC has nothing to do with the quality of the image coming from the graphics card (such as resolution or color depth or scene detail), only the way in which the monitor draws the image.

You can typically control VSYNC through the advanced properties of your graphics card. Right-click your desktop and select Properties, click the Advanced button, and click the OpenGL or Direct3D tabs (see Figure 3-2). Look for a VSYNC or "Wait for Vertical Sync" entry.

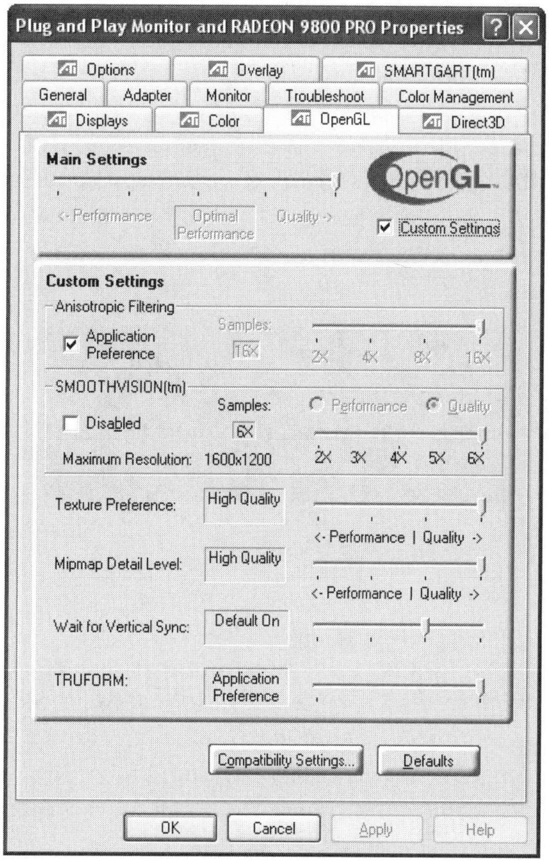

Figure 3-2. For best display quality, configure your graphics card to "Wait for Vertical Sync."

TURBO CHARGING AGP

The Annoyance: What settings can I tweak to max out my AGP card?

The Fix: You can find AGP-related settings in the Chipset Features menu of your System Setup. (Some BIOS makers might not offer these features or might name them differently.)

AGP Turbo or AGP Bus Turbo Mode

Enable the AGP turbo mode to tweak the way your AGP bus handles memory write allocation. Most current BIOS versions probably disable or no longer offer this touchy setting. Don't say I didn't warn you.

Primary Frame Buffer or VGA Frame Buffer

A frame buffer is typically an area of RAM used to hold the finished image sent to the monitor. However, you only need a frame buffer when you use motherboard-based video systems. An AGP video card has its own RAM (and supplies its own frame buffer). If you use an AGP card, turn the frame buffer off to free RAM for the rest of the system.

> **Warning. . .**
> Use caution when altering System Setup values. Incorrect settings may prevent the computer from starting.

AGP Mode

This can really hinder your graphics performance if the speed is set lower than your AGP card and motherboard can handle. Make sure you set the AGP mode to Auto, or select 1X, 2X, 4X, or 8X as appropriate for your AGP card. For example, setting 2X when the card and motherboard will tolerate 4X will cut your potential graphics performance in half.

AGP Aperture or AGP Aperture Size

This entry sets aside an amount of RAM for the graphics system (not to be confused with the frame buffer). If you want better performance from onboard graphics, increase the allocated RAM. If you use an AGP card, shut this feature off. Typical BIOS let you set aside up to 256MB of system RAM for the graphics.

Clip Clap

AGP 8X cards typically employ a small hook to keep the card contacts evenly inserted in the slot. This also prevents the card from shifting in the slot and short-circuiting signals. First, unbolt the card and ease it out of the slot from the chassis-side, and then carefully disengage the card's hook to remove the card completely.

NETMEETING DISABLES AGP

The Annoyance: I started using NetMeeting for corporate meetings, but it disabled my AGP system.

The Fix: This problem strikes Windows 2000–based systems running NetMeeting 3.01. This should not occur under other operating systems or versions of NetMeeting. The desktop-sharing feature of NetMeeting disables Direct3D and AGP to ease compatibility issues with video performance. However, you can easily re-enable Direct3D and AGP.

First, use the Desktop Sharing wizard to enable desktop sharing. Right-click the Desktop Sharing icon (not the NetMeeting icon) in your Taskbar and choose Exit. Now return to the desktop sharing configuration and disable desktop sharing. Finally, reboot the computer. This process should restore Direct3D and AGP. If the desktop palette falls to 16 colors after rebooting, open your Display Properties dialog and click the Effects tab. Uncheck the "Display icons in all possible colors" box, click the Apply button, recheck the "Display icons in all possible colors" box, and then click the Apply button again. This should straighten out your palette.

DRIVER ANNOYANCES

VIDEO PLAYER NEEDS CODECS

The Annoyance: When I try to play a video, the video player cries out for some codec.

The Fix: Multimedia files always employ some kind of compression to make them smaller. Smaller files download faster across the Internet and take up less space on hard drives. Some compression is mild, with very little (if any) loss of the original data, while other compression is very aggressive, with notable loss of the original data. A codec (short for compressor/decompressor) provides the instructions needed for an application (e.g., Windows Media Player or a video-capture program) to compress or decompress the data for a particular file format. Popular codecs include MPEG, Indeo, and Cinepak.

First, reinstall the video player application from scratch. As a rule, suitable codecs are installed along with the drivers and application software on your system. For example, if you install DVD movie-making software, the MPEG-2 codecs (and others) should install with the software. If the trouble persists, check your audio or video codecs for duplicate entries. Open the System control panel, click the Hardware tab, click the Device Manager button, and then expand the "Sound, video, and game controllers" entry.

Right-click the Audio Codecs (see Figure 3-3) or Video Codecs (see Figure 3-4) entry and click Properties to see your codecs. Right-click any duplicates and select Remove.

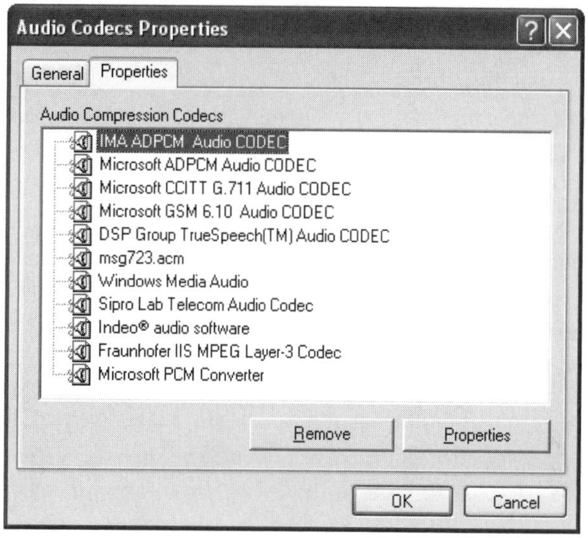

Figure 3-3. Audio codecs include tools for speech, telephony, sound, and music.

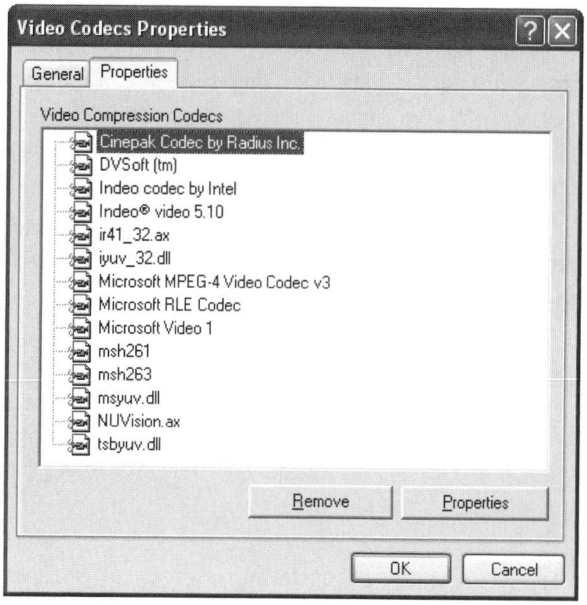

Figure 3-4. Video codecs include tools for video capture and playback of popular formats.

ENSURING A MINIMUM DIRECTX VERSION

The Annoyance: My game installs, but it says it needs DirectX 9 or later. How do I get around this?

The Fix: Some games simply tell you which DirectX version they need, without checking your system first. Use the *dxdiag* tool (see "Identifying Unknown Graphics Cards," earlier in this chapter) to determine your current DirectX version. If you have the current version of DirectX, just ignore the warning and launch the game. If not, the game may not launch at all. If it does start, you may experience problems with colors, textures, scenery complexity, and sound (tip-offs for a DirectX update).

Many games include the required DirectX version right on the game disc, although it may not be the latest version. If necessary, download the latest DirectX version directly from the Microsoft web site (*http://www.microsoft.com/directx*).

FIXING AN EXPIRED MESSAGE FOR DIRECTX 8.1

The Annoyance: A DirectX 8.1 "expired" message pops up on my desktop each time I start the system.

The Fix: This rather obscure error sometimes appears with out-of-date operating system and support files. Make sure you update Internet Explorer (IE), DirectX, and the operating system with any available service packs (including critical security patches). You can obtain Windows and IE updates simply by using the Windows Update feature. You can obtain DirectX updates from *http://www.microsoft.com/directx*.

NEW DRIVERS CAUSE PROTECTION ERRORS

The Annoyance: I upgraded my video driver and now I get Windows Protection Errors every time the system starts.

The Fix: In theory, protection errors occur when an application attempts to use an area of memory reserved by other software. In practice, however, protection errors can crop up from other system configuration problems.

Recheck the video driver. If you installed an older or incorrect driver version (perhaps intended for a similar video card), it can cause profound problems. Install the latest video driver intended for your specific video card make and model. As an alternative, you can undo the last driver installation. Open the System control panel, click the Hardware tab, and then click the Device Manager button. Next, expand the Display Adapter entry, then right-click the video card and click Properties. Select the Driver tab, click the Roll Back Driver button (see Figure 3-5), and follow the wizard. Finally, you can use the System Restore feature to return the system to a previous working state. Select Start → All Programs → Accessories → System Tools → System Restore, and then follow the wizard.

Figure 3-5. Roll back an incorrect or inappropriate driver update to restore system operation.

Check with the system (or motherboard) manufacturer for the latest motherboard drivers. Also, check for the specific motherboard drivers (AGP Driver, AGP Miniport, AGP VXD Driver, Chipset Driver, GART Driver, or VGART) used to enable AGP features in the chipset.

You may also need to turn off the AGP card's FastWrite feature. First, right-click the desktop and select Properties. When the Display Properties dialog opens, click the Settings tab, click the Advanced button, and then select an AGP driver support tab (such as the ATI SMARTGART tab in Figure 3-6). Turn off the FastWrite feature, click the Apply button, and reboot the system.

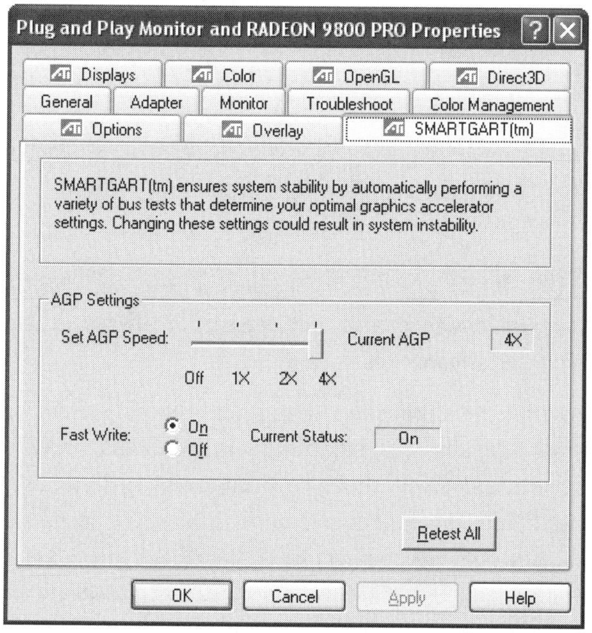

Figure 3-6. Disabling the AGP card's FastWrite feature can sometimes stabilize an unreliable video system.

If the problem persists, check with the system (or motherboard) manufacturer for a BIOS upgrade that may resolve your issue.

FINDING MISSING FEATURE TABS

The Annoyance: The 3D and nView tabs in the Propeties dialog box of my NVIDIA card are missing.

The Fix: You need to reset hardware acceleration for the video card. First, right-click the desktop and select Properties. When the Display Properties dialog box opens, select the Settings tab, click the Advanced button, and

then click the Troubleshoot tab. Set the Hardware Acceleration slider to None, click the Apply button, and reboot the computer. When the computer restarts, return to the Troubleshoot tab and set the Hardware Acceleration slider to Full. Save your changes and reboot the system again. The missing tabs should be restored. If not, reinstall the card's drivers and support software again.

OVERCOMING HARDCODED DIRECTX

The Annoyance: I upgraded DirectX, but now my favorite game won't play.

The Fix: A few games may be hardcoded for a specific version of DirectX. For example, it will check for Version 8.0a, but if DirectX returns anything other than 8.0a, the program flags an error and stops. This type of problem happens most frequently when software is coded hastily, without proper regard for supporting software. Fortunately, some quick recoding can fix this software glitch, so check for software updates or patches that correct this oversight. If the software maker is reluctant to rush out a fix, you should simply return the software for a refund.

NEW DRIVERS DON'T WORK

The Annoyance: I installed the drivers for my video card, but I only see 16 colors at 640×480.

The Fix: First, make sure you downloaded the correct drivers for your specific video card. Yes, I know you already did this, but do it again. One too many Tequila shooters and, well, all those downloads start looking the same.

However, even the "right" driver might not work. For example, the 29.80 driver release for the NVIDIA Quadro card is pure trash. Oddly enough, earlier versions work, as do later versions, such as the 30.82 driver release. See if a later driver for your video card exists. If not, try a recent older driver. It might get you out of trouble until a later driver release becomes available.

GAME STUTTERS IN OPENGL MODE

The Annoyance: My game installs and plays fine in Direct3D mode, but it stutters when I try to play it in OpenGL mode. Why the difference?

The Fix: Games frequently support both Direct3D and OpenGL programming languages. OpenGL sometimes offers a slightly different look and feel to the game, and may support a variety of resolutions and graphic features not offered by Direct3D.

Performance problems in the OpenGL mode occur with certain combinations of video card hardware and driver versions. For example, this problem crops up on ATI Radeon 9500 and 9700 cards under Windows XP when using *wxp-w2k-r9700-7-81-021213a-006924C.exe* drivers. The solution? Download and install the latest drivers and graphic control panel software (such as ATI's Catalyst 3.0 software or better).

FINDING INVISIBLE 3D OBJECTS

The Annoyance: When I play games, I bump into invisible objects (e.g., tables and chairs). I know the objects exist; they just fail to appear on my screen.

The Fix: This happens with older video cards, such as RAGE II and RAGE II+ cards. In addition to missing scenery and some transparent objects, other items may appear as solid colors. Test the issue by disabling hardware Direct3D support in the game (select software emulation instead). Game performance may suffer with software emulation, but the image quality should improve. If so, update the video drivers to their latest version. This should correct the problem and let you use hardware Direct3D support and full 3D hardware acceleration.

DRIVER UPDATES CAUSE WINDOWS ERRORS

The Annoyance: I upgraded my graphics driver, but now I get Windows errors when I try to run my game.

The Fix: New video drivers have minimum system requirements (including minimum DirectX versions). If you use an older DirectX version, a new video driver may cause problems (for example, errors or corrupted displays) when you launch a game. Upgrade to the latest version of DirectX at *http://www.microsoft.com/directx*, and then reinstall the graphics driver if necessary.

NATIVE WINDOWS DRIVERS MIGHT SKIMP ON FEATURES

The Annoyance: I let Windows XP install my new AGP card. It installed fine, but I don't see any anti-aliasing control.

The Fix: Windows XP includes a comprehensive library of device drivers, but they don't always enable high-performance features.

As a rule, trust Windows XP to supply "house" drivers for most device classes, including drives, USB and FireWire devices, and so on. However, video cards usually benefit *most* from manufacturer-specific drivers. If the native Windows XP video drivers work, then leave them. But if you encounter trouble with software compatibility or performance in the future, try the latest drivers directly from the manufacturer.

UPGRADE ANNOYANCES

TROUBLE REMOVING OLD AGP CARD

The Annoyance: I want to upgrade my AGP card with a newer model, but I can't seem get the old card out of the slot.

The Fix: A single screw at the chassis secures every expansion card. You did remove the screw, right? Right. Once you remove the screw, ease the card edge connector from the slot. Remember that a fast AGP card (such as an 8X card) may include a retaining clip at the rear edge of the slot. Lift the front edge of the card until the retaining clip disengages and frees the card, or gently pull the clip aside to free the card.

NEW AGP BREAKS DVD PLAYBACK

The Annoyance: I installed a new AGP card, but now I can't play DVD movies.

The Fix: This happens frequently when new video drivers interfere with existing DVD software (such as PowerDVD or WinDVD). First, use the Add or Remove Programs utility to uninstall the DVD playback software. Reboot the system. Now use the Windows DirectX diagnostic tool (*dxdiag.exe*) to make sure you installed the new video drivers properly. Select Start → Run, then type **dxdiag** in the Run box and click the OK button. Once *dxdiag* starts, click the Display tab and check the video driver version and date (see Figure 3-1). Finally, reinstall your DVD player software. The player should automatically reconfigure for the updated video driver.

ODD SOUNDS AFTER NEW VIDEO INSTALLATION

The Annoyance: I installed a new video card and now I hear a strange crackling sound from my sound card.

The Fix: This annoying little headache usually crops up because of driver or resource glitches in your system. Check the following items:

Mute any unused audio inputs. Computers are notorious for electrical signal interference, and unwanted signals can sometimes carry into unused sound inputs and emerge as amplified crackles or pops. For example, a very noisy AGP card may be cross-talking to the audio system. Overclocking the AGP card commonly causes AGP cross-talk. Check the AGP clock settings in your System Setup and reduce the AGP bus speed to 66MHz (or the closest possible setting). Also, open the Windows Volume Control applet and mute any unused inputs. For example, if there is no Line Input, check the Mute box.

Avoid IRQ sharing. Interrupt (IRQ) sharing—especially between the new video device and sound device—can cause annoying sound problems. Try moving the sound card to another PCI slot. Alternatively, use the Reset PnP or Reset NVRAM options in System Setup to reinitialize the Plug-and-Play device settings.

Adjust your sound card acceleration. Open the Sounds and Audio Devices control panel. Click the Audio tab, click the Advanced button, and click the Performance tab (see Figure 3-7). Adjust the "Hardware acceleration" and "Sample rate conversion quality" sliders to achieve a cleaner sound output. Click the Apply button to save any changes.

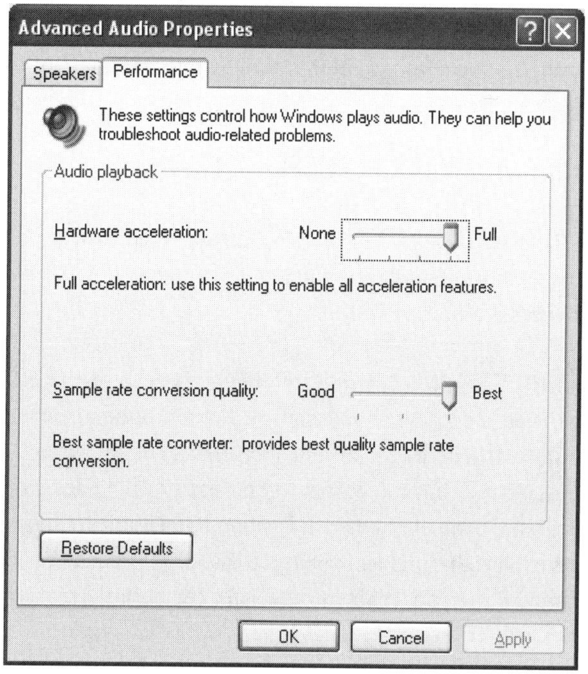

Figure 3-7. Adjust acceleration and conversion quality to clean up unwanted noise.

Update your drivers or BIOS. Older sound or motherboard audio drivers may encounter conflicts with other drivers on the system. Update the sound driver or motherboard audio drivers. Also, update the video drivers. If the sound device is integrated onto the motherboard, and new Windows drivers do not help, check with the motherboard manufacturer for a BIOS update.

OVERCOMING AGP MODE LIMITS

The Annoyance: My 4X AGP card operates at the limited 1X speed.

The Fix: This problem occurs in older motherboards with early (but inadequate) support for faster AGP cards. Check with the motherboard maker for current BIOS and driver versions.

If the trouble persists, you may need to load the System Setup and tweak the AGP Mode setting in the Advanced Chipset Setup menu. In most cases, you can set the AGP Mode to Auto. If not, set 4X manually. Still stuck in 1X mode? Upgrade the AGP driver (such as the AGP Miniport or AGP VXD Driver). In some cases, you may need to reinstall Windows from scratch after you upgrade the motherboard drivers.

NEW VIDEO CARD CAUSES SYSTEM HANG-UPS

The Annoyance: I installed a video card to replace the onboard video adapter, but now the system freezes during boot.

The Fix: Most current motherboards can detect expansion video cards and shut down the onboard video automatically, but some older systems fumble this process. As a result, the system freezes early in the boot process. For example, some HP Pavilion and eMachine models exhibit this problem when you install ATI Radeon 7000 cards. Power down the system and temporarily remove the new video card.

First, check with the system maker for a BIOS update that will correct the problem. Flash the motherboard BIOS according to the manufacturer's specific directions. If no suitable BIOS update exists, boot to System Setup and manually disable the "On-Chip VGA" feature through the Advanced Chipset Features menu (see Figure 3-8). Next, reboot and shut down the PC, then reinstall the new video card and try the system again.

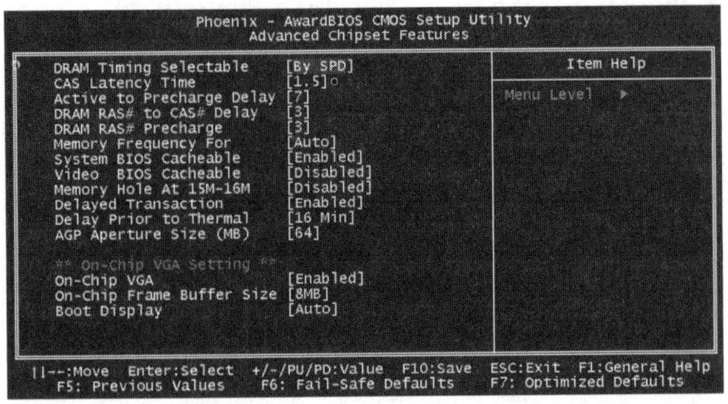

Figure 3-8. If an onboard video system won't disable itself automatically, disable it manually.

RELUCTANT WINDOWS XP DRIVERS

The Annoyance: I installed an ATI All-In-Wonder Radeon card on my i845G motherboard using the native Windows XP drivers, but the system freezes unexpectedly.

The Fix: Even though Windows XP drivers can run many video cards perfectly, motherboards based on Intel i845G chipsets typically do not respond well to the native Windows XP drivers for All-In-Wonder cards. You can avoid this headache if you install the Enhanced Display Drivers provided on the CD accompanying the new video card.

Motherboard drivers (such as the AGP Miniport or AGP VXD Driver) also play an important role in system stability. For example, updated motherboard drivers should also help resolve your symptom with the All-In-Wonder card. When you upgrade the motherboard drivers, you may need to reinstall Windows XP.

DESKTOP ANNOYANCES

LOCATING THE TIMID TASKBAR

The Annoyance: My Taskbar simply vanished. Where did it go?

The Fix: This little annoyance has an easy fix. The Windows XP Taskbar (often just a thin blue line along the bottom of your desktop) may be hidden. Move your mouse over that little blue line; when the cursor turns into a little up/down arrow, left-click and pull the arrow up a bit. The Taskbar should appear.

The Taskbar may also be set to "auto-hide." Move your mouse to the bottom of the desktop. The Taskbar will pop up, and then disappear again when you move the cursor. Go ahead and try it. In this case, right-click the Taskbar, select Properties (see Figure 3-9), uncheck the "Auto-hide the taskbar" box, and click the Apply button. The Taskbar should now stay on your desktop all the time.

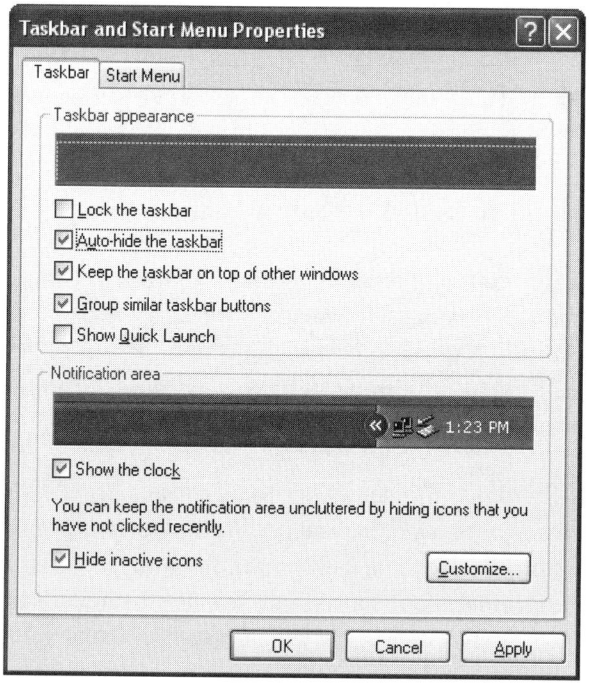

Figure 3-9. Be sure to unhide the Taskbar to keep it on your desktop.

IMPROVING DESKTOP PERFORMANCE

The Annoyance: I run Windows XP on an older PC. It seems OK, but all the fancy little desktop features take time. How can I perk things up without going back to Windows 98?

The Fix: Windows XP comes packed with bells and whistles, which can bog down slower systems. Fortunately, you can shut down these options and light a fire under your desktop response. Select Start → Control Panel → Performance and Maintenance → "Adjust visual effects," click the Visual Effects tab, and select "Adjust for best performance" (see Figure 3-10). This automatically disables most fancy desktop features. If you prefer to keep some features and disable others, use the Custom option and select each desired option yourself. Click the Apply button to save your changes.

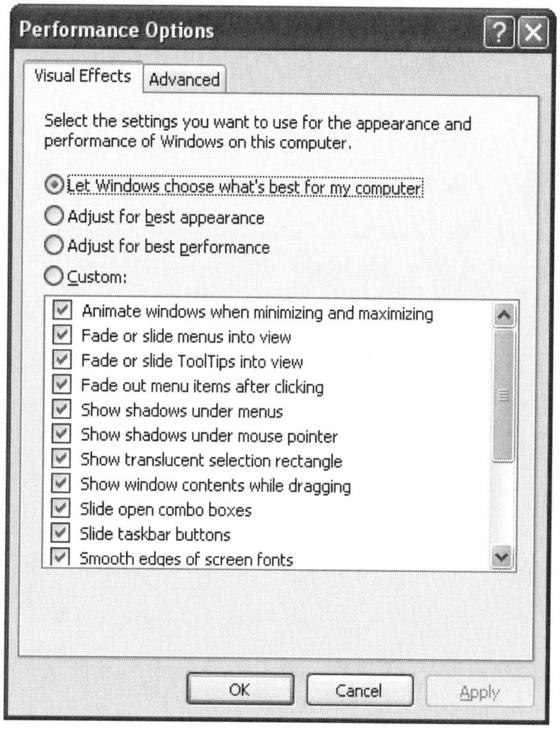

Figure 3-10. Disable unnecessary features to boost desktop performance.

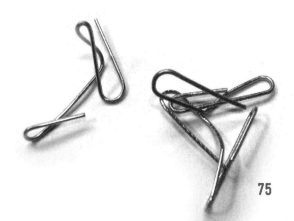

Give your eyes a break with these quick and easy tips:

Turn off the wallpaper. Right-click the desktop, select Properties, click the Desktop tab, and then select None from the list of wallpapers.

Use larger fonts and icons. Click the Appearance tab and select a larger font size from the "Font size" pull-down menu. Try Large Fonts first, but switch to Extra Large Fonts later if necessary. Click the Effects button and check the "Use large icons" box.

Enable larger mouse cursors. Open the Mouse control panel and click the Pointers tab. Now scroll down the list of available schemes and select a large (or extra large) cursor scheme.

Change the color scheme. Open the Accessibility Options control panel, click the Display tab, click the Settings button, and select a high-contrast color scheme (see Figure 3-11).

Use a larger monitor. A 19- to 21-inch monitor makes it much easier to see lots of detail, especially at high resolutions.

Use a high refresh rate. Monitors draw images 60–80+ times per second. This repeated drawing is called *flicker*. Setting the monitor to use its highest allowable refresh rate (such as 72–75Hz or 82–85Hz) reduces flicker, which may reduce headaches and fatigue during long days in front of the PC.

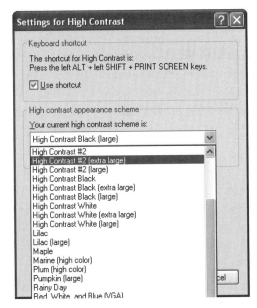

Figure 3-11. Use a high contrast color scheme to make the desktop easier to see.

SHARING A WINDOWS DESKTOP

The Annoyance: I share a PC with my old man, and he keeps messing with all my desktop settings. He says he has trouble seeing all the small icons through my crazy wallpaper displays. Is there a way we can both be happy?

The Fix: Windows XP lets you create a User Profile with your own desktop settings. As the system administrator, just open the User Accounts control panel, click the Add button, and a wizard will walk you through the account creation process. Enter a name for the new account and opt for a limited account type. When you create the new account, you can password protect it and make other changes. From then on, you can switch accounts by simply clicking Start → Log Off → Switch User, and selecting your own account icon. When you return to your own account, your desktop will be exactly as you left it.

BRIGHTENING A DARK IMAGE

The Annoyance: I increased the brightness and contrast on my display, but images still seem a little dark.

The Fix: The problem may be a poor gamma setting for your Windows desktop. Games often provide gamma adjustments and allow you to brighten otherwise dark locations. However, gamma adjustments are also usually included in video cards, such as the ATI Radeon 9800 Pro. Right-click the desktop, select Properties, click the Settings tab, and then click the Advanced button. Click the Color tab (see Figure 3-12) and move the "Desktop brightness" slider to achieve a clear, crisp image. Click the Apply button to save your changes.

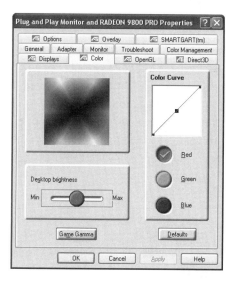

Figure 3-12. Adjust the display gamma to achieve a clear, crisp image quality.

---

t i p

Before you adjust the gamma setting, change the monitor to 80–90% brightness, and then reduce the contrast until the raster (the gray haze around the screen image) disappears.

MONITOR ANNOYANCES

OVERCOMING DISPLAY FLICKER

The Annoyance: My display seems to flicker *a lot.*

The Fix: You can often improve the image quality by increasing the refresh rate. Right-click the desktop, select Properties, click the Settings tab, and then click the Advanced button. The refresh rate adjustment is available on the Monitor tab (see Figure 3-13).

Figure 3-13. A higher refresh rate can sometimes help to stabilize a flickering image.

Select a higher refresh rate from the available options in the drop-down menu. Click the Apply button to save your changes.

Also, check for nearby speakers. They produce vibrations that can translate through to the monitor. For example, I regularly use Real Rhapsody to listen to my favorite tunes. When the volume is turned up, I sometimes see the strong base notes echoed in faint waves across my 21-inch CRT. Move the speakers further away from the monitor, or turn the volume down.

STOPPING THE SHIMMER

The Annoyance: The image on my CRT shimmers or flickers slightly for a few minutes at a time. I tried the CRT on my neighbor's PC and it runs fine.

The Fix: Your household may have a voltage problem. Large appliances such as air conditioners, microwave ovens, refrigerators, and even coffee makers can draw surprising amounts of current. This effectively drops the available voltage on the electrical circuit. If your monitor runs on the same circuit, it may be energy starved.

Use an AC voltmeter to check the voltage level at your monitor's outlet with everything turned off (and the monitor working normally). Test the voltage level again when you turn enough other things on to cause the monitor to shimmer again. If you notice a significant drop in AC voltage, hire a licensed electrician to place your PC's outlet on a separate electrical circuit.

---

t i p

If it would make you feel more comfortable, you can hire a qualified, licensed electrician to test your voltage levels for you.

If no noticeable drop in AC voltage occurs and the monitor image still shimmers when you turn on other devices (e.g., a nearby air conditioner), make sure your AC outlets are properly grounded. You can buy an AC outlet tester from any local hardware or home improvement store. Have a licensed electrician properly ground any ungrounded AC outlets.

WEIRD COLORS IN THE DISPLAY

The Annoyance: When I look at a white desktop on my CRT, the lower right quarter of the desktop seems a bit red, and the text and icon colors appear off.

The Fix: The monitor has been slightly magnetized. Pull up a pillow and let me explain. CRTs accelerate electrons from the rear neck to the front face. When the fast-moving electrons strike colored phosphors on the face, they liberate light (in red, green, or blue). Horizontal and vertical electromagnets direct electron beams around the CRT. However, the electron beams can sometimes strike colored phosphors in adjacent pixels and cause unwanted coloring. To enhance color purity, CRT makers place a mask in front of the phosphors (the pros call this a "shadow mask" or an "aperture grille"). Holes in the mask let the electrons for each corresponding pixel pass through, but block electrons from striking adjacent pixels.

Strong magnetic forces can sometimes magnetize part of the mask. This screws up the electron beams just enough to cause bogus colors in the magnetized area(s). CRTs fight this by wrapping a "degaussing coil" around the bell of a CRT. Each time you turn on the monitor the degaussing coil sends a magnetic surge through the CRT, which scrambles any slight magnetic fields. Still awake?

If the degaussing coil fails, or you expose the CRT to a very strong magnetic field (maybe you placed the monitor on top of an industrial air conditioner), the mask can become magnetized.

To demagnetize the mask, cycle the power to the monitor numerous times. For example, turn off the monitor, wait 30 seconds, then turn on the monitor and wait five minutes. Repeat this process ten times. Repeated firing of the monitor's internal degaussing cable should eventually correct this type of discoloration. If not, return the CRT for service. A professional technician can use a degaussing gun to clear the mask and bring back your color purity.

Staying Cool

CRT-based monitors rely upon simple openings underneath and on top of the unit to prevent overheating. Air heated inside the monitor is vented out the top openings, while the bottom openings draw in new, cooler air. When your cat Fluffy curls up on top of the monitor, it traps in hot air, possibly leading to display problems (and even premature failure). Keep the top openings clear of any obstructions.

IDENTIFYING LINES IN THE CRT

The Annoyance: I just inherited a 21-inch CRT monitor. It works great, except for two thin gray lines across the top and bottom halves of the image.

The Fix: The thin lines are actually wires (called *damper wires*) that stabilize the mask (see "Weird Colors in the Display") and keep it in place. You really *do* need these wires, which may appear faintly against a white background.

Change your desktop color to an off white or light gray to hide the lines. First, right-click the desktop, choose Properties, click the Appearance tab, and then click the Advanced button. Select "Desktop item" from the "Item" drop-down menu and choose a new color from the "Color 1" drop-down palette (perhaps a light gray). Click the OK button and then the Apply button to save your changes.

MY CRT WHINES LIKE A BABY

The Annoyance: My CRT monitor runs fine, but I hear a high-pitched whine coming from the back of it.

The Fix: All CRT monitors produce high frequencies in their everyday operation. Although these frequencies are typically outside the range of human hearing, the frequencies can sometimes create audible vibrations around some of the monitor's internal components. Tilt the monitor up or down, or swivel the unit around its base to quiet it.

If the problem persists, there may be an issue with the CRT's high-voltage circuit. CRT's use extremely high voltages (anywhere from 20,000–45,000 volts) to create the electron beams that illuminate the screen. The high-voltage circuit may be breaking down, or some high voltage may be leaking across old, dry-rotted insulation. In either case, the monitor should be serviced by a professional technician or replaced outright.

SOUND UPSETS SCREEN COLORS

The Annoyance: I put a subwoofer on top of my monitor, and stuck the speakers on either side. Now when I play music, the screen coloring gets all messed up.

The Fix: When speakers are in close proximity to a CRT display, the speakers' magnetic forces can disrupt the electron beams inside the CRT.

Good-quality speakers shield their electromagnetic parts to prevent this type of interference problem, but most cheap speakers do not. You can either relocate the subwoofer to the floor and place the speakers farther away from the monitor, or spend a little more money and exchange the speakers for a high-quality shielded set.

MAINTAINING COLOR PURITY

The Annoyance: Why do I see red and green edges around my fonts and lines? It looks like crap.

The Fix: Okay, time for another boring explanation. Color monitors use separate electron beams for red, green, and blue. The beam strikes corresponding color phosphors on the CRT, thereby making the colors you see. Each beam must converge at its respective hole in the mask (see the earlier annoyance "Weird Colors in the Display"); however, they occassionally fall slightly out of alignment (especially around the edges of the display) and strike incorrect phosphors, which results in color impurities (such as the red or blue "bleeding" you see on your screen).

A few full-featured color monitors include an electronic convergence adjustment as a menu option on the monitor's front-panel controls. A grid or other symbols will appear across the display. You must adjust the red and green beams to make magenta, and then adjust the green beam to make white. When the entire grid turns pure white—free of any color bleeding—you will have properly converged the beams.

If your monitor does not offer a front-panel convergence feature, check the monitor's manual for any auto-convergence options (perhaps a monitor reset will affect convergence). Otherwise, bring the monitor into the shop and let an experienced monitor technician manually adjust the convergence.

DISPLAY LIMITED TO 16 COLORS

The Annoyance: My monitor only displays 16 colors even though I installed the right video adapter driver.

The Fix: A conflict between the video and monitor drivers can cause this problem. For example, this occurs on rare occasions between NVIDIA video drivers and certain manufacturer-specific monitor drivers. Select an alternate monitor driver (such as the generic PnP monitor driver). Right-click the desktop, select Properties, click the Settings tab, and click the Advanced button. Now click the Monitors tab, click the Properties button, click the Driver tab, click the Update Driver button, and then follow the wizard to install an alternate driver. You can also opt to uninstall the monitor device, reboot the system, and select the generic PnP monitor.

In rare cases, the refusal of a video system to operate beyond 640×480×16 may indicate one or more incorrect settings in the System Setup. Reboot the PC to enter the System Setup, and then try the following BIOS settings:

- Plug and Play OS = NO
- Assign IRQ to VGA = ENABLED

Exit (saving your changes), reboot the system normally, and configure the resolution and color depth again.

STOPPING FLICKER IN LCD DISPLAYS

The Annoyance: Why do I see flickering and horizontal lines when I attach my LCD to the DVI port on my graphics card?

The Fix: DVI (Digital Visual Interface) handles display bandwidths up to 160MHz, and supports high-resolution displays such as UXGA (Ultra Extended Graphics Array) and HDTV. LCD displays configured to run at high display resolutions and higher refresh rates may exhibit horizontal lines, flickering, screen glitches, or wavy textures.

As a temporary workaround, reduce the screen resolution and refresh rate (see "Overcoming Display Flicker," earlier in this chapter). For a more permanent fix, see if your video card maker offers a driver with a DVI adjustment feature, which automatically reduces frequencies in high resolutions. For example, the Radeon 9800 Pro drivers provide this feature. If so, you can right-click the desktop, select Properties, click the Settings tab, click the Advanced button, and click the Options tab (see Figure 3-14). Then check the option marked "Reduce DVI frequency on high-resolution displays" and click the Apply button to save your changes.

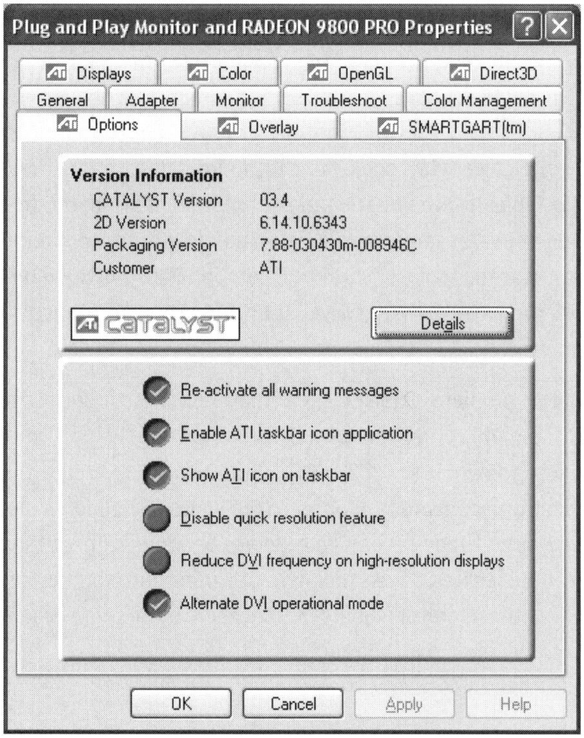

Figure 3-14. Reduce DVI frequencies on high-resolution displays.

MAINTAINING THE RIGHT SCANNING RANGE

The Annoyance: When I changed my monitor's display resolution, I got a message that said "out of scan range."

The Fix: Your monitor supports only a limited range of input frequencies (even if your video card can reach some ungodly resolution or refresh rate). If you exceed the monitor's capabilities, the screen may appear distorted, go blank, or report an error message such as "out of scan range." Windows will normally undo unacceptable video modes within 15 seconds and return the display to its original setting. If not, reboot the PC to Safe Mode and select an acceptable display mode.

> **Warning. . .**
> If you operate a display beyond its scan range, you can eventually cause permanent damage to the monitor.

NO DVD OUTPUT TO AN EXTERNAL MONITOR

The Annoyance: I connected my Windows XP laptop to an external monitor to view a DVD movie, but I only see a black box.

The Fix: You need to properly set the video overlay mode for the external monitor to work. As a rule, this problem occurs because you set up a "clone" monitor rather than a true secondary monitor (such as for an extended desktop). You must configure the clone monitor as an exact duplicate of the original monitor (i.e., your laptop's LCD). Adjust the overlay settings for your video card. For example, right-click the desktop and select Properties, click the Settings tab, click the Advanced button, and then click the Overlay tab (see Figure 3-15). Click the "Clone mode options" button, and select "Same on All."

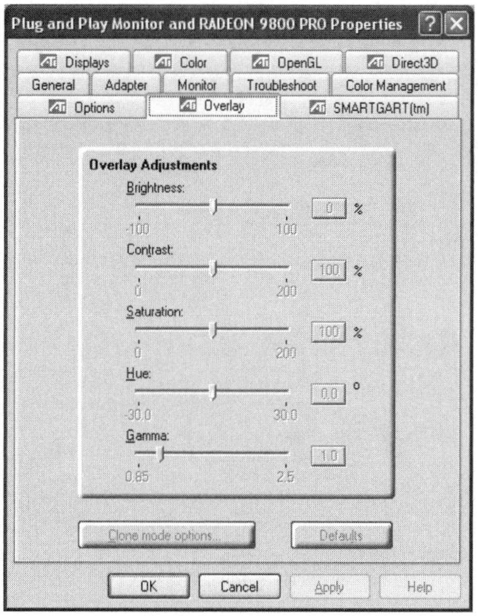

Figure 3-15. Configure clone monitors so that video overlay options are the same on all monitors.

MONITOR IMAGE DISTORTED IN STANDBY MODE

The Annoyance: My monitor completely distorts the screen image when the system enters standby mode.

The Fix: Virtually all monitors manufactured today support at least one common energy-saving mode. However, the energy-saving mode should match the monitor. For example, Display Power Management Signaling (DPMS) powers down a compliant monitor by shutting off a combination of vertical and horizontal synchronization signals from the video card. If the monitor doesn't recognize DPMS, the loss of sync signals from the video card would completely distort the image.

If the monitor does not support energy-saving modes (and you're just too cheap to buy a monitor that does), turn off the monitor's power-conservation feature. Open the Power Options control panel, locate the "Turn off monitor" entry, and choose "Never" from the drop-down list (see Figure 3-16).

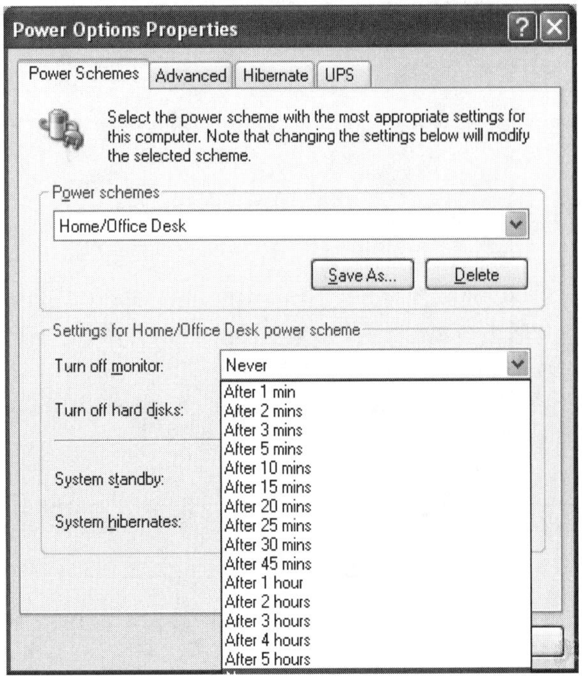

Figure 3-16. Set the monitor delay to Never to prevent power conservation from powering down the monitor.

3D ANNOYANCES

FIXING A POOR FRAME RATE

The Annoyance: When I play games, my video card stutters and the frame rate jumps around.

The Fix: No matter how fast and powerful our graphics cards become, the frame rate always seems to suck. Unfortunately, many factors affect game performance. Here's a whole checklist of items to investigate:

Check the graphics system requirements. Your video card should use the chipset and onboard memory recommended by the game. Underpowered video cards will kill your frame rate (if they work at all).

Check the other game requirements. Your PC should employ the recommended CPU and RAM. Otherwise, the game will not operate at peak performance.

Close other applications. Operating systems can run numerous applications at the same time, but multiple applications siphon off resources (e.g., processor time and memory) from the game. Close all applications and reboot the system if necessary. Press Ctrl+Alt+Del and use the Task Manager to verify that all other applications are exited (see Figure 3-17).

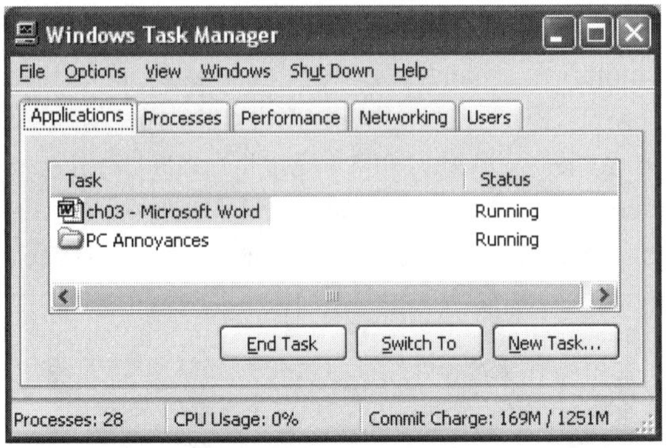

Figure 3-17. Use the Task Manager to see and disable any unwanted applications running in the background.

Consider the game itself. Most modern games offer a wealth of 3D-rendering features, including multiple lighting sources, real-time shadows, long ranges of sight, and other processing-intensive options. If you enable these options, it may bog down your computer and slow down your frame rate.

Install the latest video drivers. Old video drivers may suffer from bugs or inefficient coding that impairs some graphics performance. Check with the video card manufacturer and install the most recent video drivers.

Disable Video BIOS Shadowing. The video BIOS often takes more time to access than RAM. Most motherboards "shadow" the video BIOS (place a copy of the video BIOS in RAM) where it can be accessed faster. However, video BIOS shadowing is not a suitable technique for every system. Reboot, enter the System Setup, and disable the Video BIOS Shadowing option (usually located in the Advanced Chipset Features menu).

Adjust video card properties. The video drivers typically include a wealth of 3D options under the Direct3D and OpenGL tabs. These options include anti-aliasing, anisotropic filtering, texture quality, and so on. To make adjustments, right-click the desktop, select Properties, click the Settings tab, click the Advanced button, and then click the Direct3D tab (see Figure 3-18). Adjust the 3D options downward to reduce image quality, which will improve graphics performance.

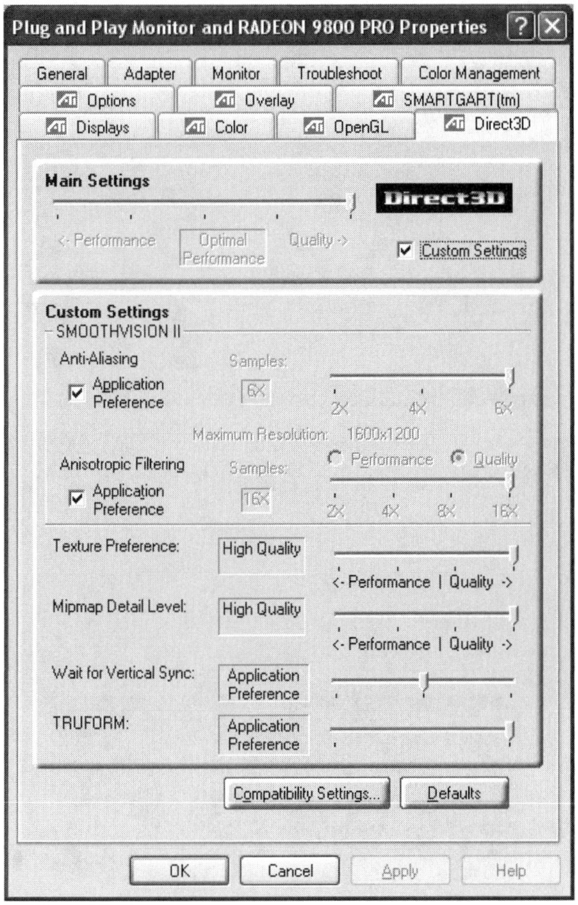

Figure 3-18. Systematically adjust 3D options downward to improve graphics performance.

3D CARD IS RUNNING SLOW

The Annoyance: My 3D-graphics card has plenty of processing power and RAM, but it offers extremely slow and disappointing performance.

The Fix: To gauge graphics performance, use a benchmark such as Futuremark's 3DMarkPro 2003 (*http://www.futuremark.com*). Run the benchmark and get some actual performance numbers, then compare those numbers to reviews published on established sites, such as CNET (*http://www.cnet.com*) or Tom's Hardware (*http://www.tomshardware.com*).

If your video card benchmarks adequately but seems slow when used with real applications (such as FarCry), you might have the game's graphic options (lighting, shadows, texture quality, anti-aliasing, sight range, etc.) set too high.

On the other hand, if the video card benchmarks poorly, you may have a system issue. For example, old AGP motherboard (aka GART) drivers may not support the video card properly or might restrict the AGP speed (such as limiting operation to 2X rather than 4X or 8X). Contact the motherboard manufacturer for the latest motherboard drivers. Also, make sure you use the most recent video card drivers.

THE IMAGE SEEMS TO RIP OR TEAR

The Annoyance: How can I stop my image from tearing when I run 3D software? It seems like the lower half of each frame sticks to the display.

The Fix: An improper refresh rate or VSYNC setting (see Figure 3-2) commonly causes image tearing. Turn on VSYNC to display completed images in-step with the monitor's refresh rate (see "Stabilizing a Frame with VSYNC," earlier in this chapter). If your monitor supports it, lower the refresh rate to 75Hz or 72Hz.

Image swapping can sometimes be a culprit. Games use a basic, old-fashioned animator's trick. The graphics card draws an image in an area of memory (called an *image buffer*) and swaps it to the display while it draws the next image. This technique of constantly swapping finished images to the display creates the optical illusion of smooth motion. You can typically select the image-swapping mode through the application's video options menu. Programmers use several techniques to swap images, but "block transfer mode" causes less image tearing than others.

WRONG 3D COLORS AND TEXTURES

The Annoyance: My 3D game runs fine, but some of the wall and object colors seem way off.

The Fix: Incompatibilities between DirectX and the video driver version can cause some palette issues. For example, most avid gamers update their video card driver, but not DirectX (or vice versa). The two software elements must work together to achieve the best image quality, so make sure you download and install the latest version of DirectX (*http://www.microsoft.com/directx*), and then obtain the latest video card driver for *that* specific version.

UNLOCKING HIDDEN 3D CARD FEATURES

The Annoyance: I heard that programmers hide the most powerful graphics features. How can I access hidden graphics features and tweak my card to run faster?

The Fix: Video card behavior generally corresponds to a variety of Windows Registry entries configured when you install the video card and its drivers (the Registry manages hardware configurations). Drivers normally provide a wealth of software controls such as gamma, VSYNC, anti-aliasing, and so forth (see Figure 3-18). However, programmers intentionally leave some detail features inaccessible. This allows the higher-order options (such as Texture Preference or Anisotropic Filtering) or even the application itself to make detailed selections.

You can get a few utilities to help you squeeze every last frame out of your video card. For example, RivaTuner for NVIDIA GeForce and ATI Radeon–based video cards (see

Figure 3-19) lets you access undocumented features in NVIDIA Detonator (now called ForceWare) and ATI Catalyst drivers. The nVHardPage utility tweaks all NVIDIA TNT and GeForce FX cards, such as the GeForce 4 MX440/Ti 4200 and the GeForce FX 5200/5600 Ultra. You can obtain both tweaking tools through the Guru3D web site (*http://www.guru3d.com*).

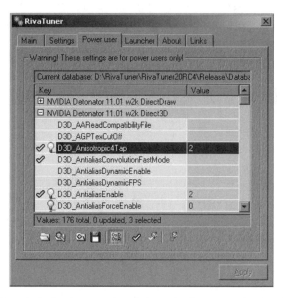

Figure 3-19. RivaTuner is a video tweaking utility for NVIDIA and ATI-based video cards.

In actual practice, a tweaking utility may let you wring a few more frames from your favorite game, or overcome some minor hardware compatibility issues.

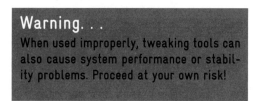

Warning. . .
When used improperly, tweaking tools can also cause system performance or stability problems. Proceed at your own risk!

STREAMLINING GRAPHICS PERFORMANCE

The Annoyance: My game seems to run slower on my system than on other PCs. Is the problem with the graphics card or the PC?

The Fix: Before you condemn a new game, use a system diagnostic tool such as SiSoft's SANDRA (*http://www.sisoftware.net*) to identify the system hardware on your PC and others. Compare the results side-by-side and see where your system may fall short. For example, you can hardly expect a system with an older GeForce video card to pump out frames as fast as a brand new ATI Radon X800. When serious hardware differences appear, you may need a hardware upgrade to bump up the frame rate.

You should also consider configuration options. Video card drivers access a wealth of settings that affect performance (see Figure 3-18). When you increase complexity or quality settings, frame rate typically drops because of the additional workload. For example, top-notch anti-aliasing will create superior images, but the added computational work will slow the frame rate. When using video cards of similar vintage, compare the configuration of both video cards.

Finally, the game itself may be configured differently between multiple systems. Games typically offer a suite of video options, such as particle effects, range of sight, real-time shadows, object density (e.g., showing more trees and grass) and texture quality (see Figure 3-20). Increased video quality will impact the frame rate.

Figure 3-20. Today's games offer a broad range of video options intended to balance frame rate with image quality.

WINDOWS SHOWS TWO VIDEO SYSTEMS

The Annoyance: I installed a new graphics card with a single video port, but when I configure the desktop setup in Windows, I see two displays.

The Fix: Don't you love it when you get more than what you bargained for? Right-click the desktop, select Properties, and click the Settings tab. You probably see two displays marked "1" and "2" (see Figure 3-21).

This is because video card makers sometimes design cards with two available video circuits but only one video port (connector). That way, they can sell single-port and dual-port video cards all using the same basic card design. Pretty slick, eh? Unfortunately, Windows sees the second video port, even though no physical connector for a second monitor exists. Regardless of your connector scheme, this might cause a tussle when you opt for a second (PCI) video card to extend the desktop or to play a multi-monitor game. A second video card will start with display "3" and go from there. Just remember to keep display "2" disabled, and you will be able to configure other video ports as needed.

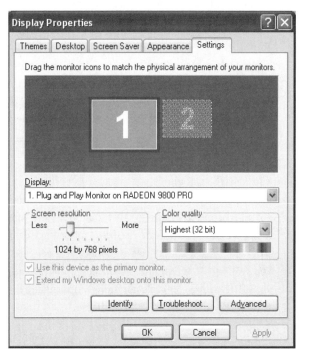

Figure 3-21. Windows will identify the presence of a second video adapter, even when only one monitor connection exists.

VIDEO CAPTURE/ PLAYBACK ANNOYANCES

ELIMINATE DROPPED FRAMES DURING CAPTURES

The Annoyance: At my cousin's wedding, I shot some great footage that I want to edit and drop to DVD. But I can't capture the video without dropping frames all over the place. The capture looks like crap, even though I properly installed everything.

The Fix: Overburdened computers, outdated or conflicting drivers, and inappropriate capture settings can cause lost frames and jumpy, sporadic video. This handy checklist will help you prevent catastrophe:

Use a current capture solution. If you have an antique Intel SVR II card, dump it in favor of a contemporary solution (e.g., a Dazzle 80 external USB capture device, a new internal PCI capture card, or even an integrated video card like the ATI All-In-Wonder AGP). Newer capture devices use far more efficient chips, and often apply on-the-fly compression for smooth captures and small file storage.

Check the system requirements. Even with new capture hardware, the host computer will need adequate processor and RAM support, along with about 1GB of drive space for every 20 minutes of captured video. Old or underpowered PCs will not support video capture properly.

Check for device conflicts. System resource conflicts (e.g., IRQ or memory space contention) can cause the internal video capture device to stutter and hesitate (not really an issue for USB or FireWire capture devices). Use the Device Manager to check for device conflicts. You will need to configure or disable conflicting devices. Often, you can replace internal capture devices with an external USB or FireWire device.

Check the capture settings. Higher frame rates, larger capture windows, and richer color depths all result in additional video data for the PC to process and store. Try lower color depths and smaller capture windows to ease the volume of captured data. You can set these options (and others) in your video capture software.

Defragment the hard drive. A badly fragmented hard drive can impair capture performance because data gets lost waiting for the drive to position itself for writing. Select Start → All Programs → Accessories → System Tools → Disk Defragmenter (see Figure 3-22).

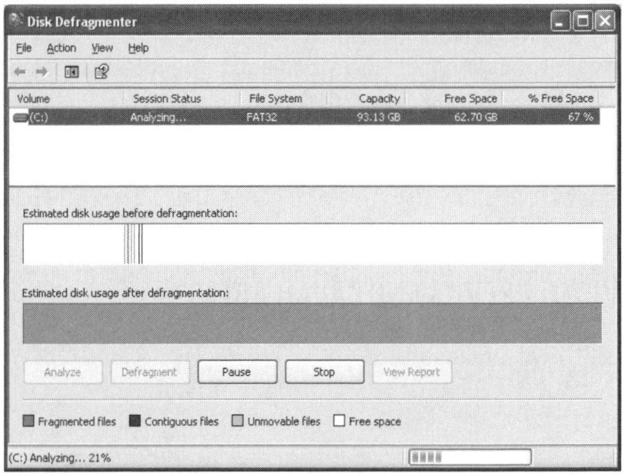

Figure 3-22. File fragmentation can disrupt video capture and cause dropped frames.

Update the capture drivers and software. Outdated or buggy capture drivers can wreak havoc with a capture device. Download and install the latest drivers and capture software directly from the capture device manufacturer.

Turn off the preview. Most capture software will attempt to display the captured video signal in real time. However, this extra work takes processing time away from the capture process. Turn off the preview feature through the capture software (e.g., check "No preview while capturing," as shown in Figure 3-23).

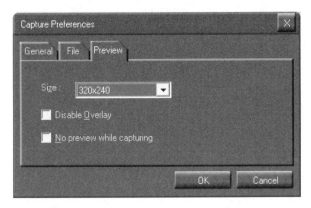

Figure 3-23. Disable the preview feature to conserve the maximum processing power for capture.

Try a faster drive. Older hard drives with slower interfaces (like UDMA/66) may not be fast enough to stream captured video data. If you plan to handle a lot of video, install a new drive controller card (supporting UDMA/133 or SCSI) and a fast hard drive to hold the captures.

VIDEO PREVIEW NOT AVAILABLE

The Annoyance: I want to capture some video, but no image appears in the capture preview window.

The Fix: To see any video in the preview window, you must have a live source *running*. Recheck your audio/video connections, turn on the camera, and take off the lens cover. If you use a VCR as the source, recheck your audio/video connections, put in the tape, and press Play. Once you have an active video signal, it should appear in the preview window. Also, make sure you enable the preview feature in the capture software (see Figure 3-23).

Remember that preview images must travel from the video source, through the capture device, and out of memory before finally arriving at the graphics subsystem. A software incompatibility at any point in the process can prevent the preview feature from working. For example, an older version of DirectX may impair the overlay window (and not necessarily produce an error message).

Check with your capture device manufacturer for incompatibilities with your video card drivers, DirectX version, and capture device drivers/software versions.

TV OUTPUT UNAVAILABLE

The Annoyance: I want to feed my video to a TV, but the "TV Out" button appears grayed out in my video card's desktop-management applet.

The Fix: Typically, a grayed-out feature or function indicates a driver snafu that prevents normal operation. This particular headache occurs because of old or outdated drivers. For example, GeForce3 cards use 21.83 (or later) NVIDIA drivers to support the TV Output feature. GeForce4 cards use the most recent NVIDIA drivers available directly from the card maker or NVIDIA (*http://www.nvidia.com*). Other video cards with TV outputs may experience similar problems with buggy or obsolete drivers.

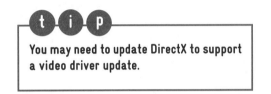

You may need to update DirectX to support a video driver update.

TRANSFERRING VIDEO TO TELEVISION

The Annoyance: I want to get my monitor signal over to a TV for a PowerPoint presentation. However, my video card lacks a TV output. What can I do?

The Fix: First, a TV signal (in the NTSC or PAL format) is not natively compatible with an RGB monitor signal. You need some sort of adapter to attach an RGB cable to a TV because of the different scan and refresh rates. In many cases, you can buy a video card with a complementary S-Video or RCA-type ("composite") video connector built in. Then you just run an S-Video or RCA-type cable between the video card and TV (not all TVs have S-Video connectors), enable the TV output, and select a suitable resolution and color depth for the second monitor (the TV) through the desktop Settings tab (see Figure 3-21).

If you have a conventional video card with an RGB monitor connector, you can get a third-party device to handle the conversion. For example, S-Video.com (*http://www.svideo.com*) sells the PC-to-TV VGA Scan Converter ($149), as well as the high-end ScanMaster ($695) for high-resolution conversions. If you prefer something off-the-shelf, CompUSA (*http://www.compusa.com*) offers the Pinnacle ShowCenter appliance ($270), which lets you watch any digital media file on your TV. If you want to avoid wiring hassles, Grandtec (*http://www.grandtec.com*) offers Wireless Transmitter/Receiver pairs ($52), along with the Ultimate Wireless VGA converter ($150).

Cable Quality

Long video cables, low-quality (or no) shielding, and cut or damaged cabling can all result in poor TV-image quality (even if the monitor image looks great). Keep S-Video and composite cables under six feet and use good-quality, shielded cables with gold-plated connectors. Also, check for nearby sources of electromagnetic interference such as battery chargers, fans, motors, and other high-current devices.

NO TV IMAGE

The Annoyance: I attached a cable from the video card to the TV output signal, but no image appears on the TV.

The Fix: You must turn on and connect the TV *before* you boot the computer (insert smack in the head here). The video card will enable the secondary output only if it detects the TV at boot time. Simply reboot the computer and let the video card redetect the connected TV and enable the secondary output.

Still nothing? Since the video signals come from an outside source rather than the regular tuner, make sure you set the TV to its auxiliary input (such as Line In, Aux In, or some other label). In a few cases, the auxiliary input may default to channels 2 or 3. If the TV has more than one auxiliary input (some large TVs may offer a set of front inputs and a separate set of rear inputs), make sure you select the correct input source (such as Line In 1 or Line In 2).

COPY PROTECTION KILLS DVD PLAYBACK

The Annoyance: When I insert a DVD movie into the computer and try to watch it on my TV, the screen image darkens, then brightens, then darkens, and so on.

The Fix: It sounds like you ran into our old friend Macrovision—a form of copy protection typically used for videotapes and DVDs. I bet you installed a VCR between the video card and TV. Even though you had no intention of taping the DVD (oh no, of *course* not), the video card probably enabled Macrovision copy protection when the movie started. The VCR (or other recording device, such as a DVD recorder) attempts to compensate for the Macrovision-encoded signal and causes the image to alternate between bright and dim playback on your TV. The solution? Connect the video card's output directly to the TV.

TV OUTPUT SEEMS SCRAMBLED

The Annoyance: The image on my TV display looks all scrambled.

The Fix: I bet you tried to use the native Windows XP driver (or an older driver from the manufacturer) for your video/TV card. The TV image looks like a scrambled porn channel, but other features work just fine. The fix? Download and install the latest video drivers from the manufacturer's web site.

NEW DIRECTX KILLS TV TUNER

The Annoyance: My buddy in the UK upgraded to DirectX 9.0b, but now his ATI TV Player won't tune to any channels.

The Fix: Windows 2000, XP, and Server 2003 have a problem supporting PAL and Japanese NTSC ATI All-In-Wonder hardware with DirectX 9.0b. Some of the security fixes in 9.0b cause TV tuner/capture devices using non-U.S. video formats (such as NTSC-J, PAL, and SECAM) to stop initializing properly under Windows. In some cases, if you update to DirectX 9.0b, it will disable the tuner and other software (such as Ulead Video Studio or Pinnacle Studio). In other cases, ATI's TV Initialization Wizard shows no information in the TV Region selector. Fortunately, you can download a DirectX 9.0b hotfix through Microsoft's Knowledge Base article 825116 (available at *http://support.microsoft.com/default.aspx?scid=fh;EN-US;KBJUMP*).

SECONDARY DISPLAY BLANKS TV WINDOW

The Annoyance: My TV window went blank as soon as I enabled my secondary display.

The Fix: Some older TV players malfunction (though you may continue to hear normal audio) if you enable a second monitor. For example, ATI Multimedia Center 7.2 or 7.6 exhibits this problem under Windows XP. ATI suggests you upgrade to Multimedia Center 7.7 or later, but check with your video hardware manufacturer for their latest software releases.

AUDIO MISSING FROM CAPTURES

The Annoyance: I want to piece together a video of my baby's first year, but when I try to capture the video to the PC, I don't hear any sound. I know the tape has sound. What did I miss?

The Fix: Connection and configuration oversights usually cause these problems. In addition to the S-Video and composite video (yellow RCA-type jacks), remember to connect the left and right audio signals (red and white RCA-type jacks) from the video source (such as a camcorder) to the capture device. Once you connect the audio signals, make sure you turn up each channel (see Figure 3-24).

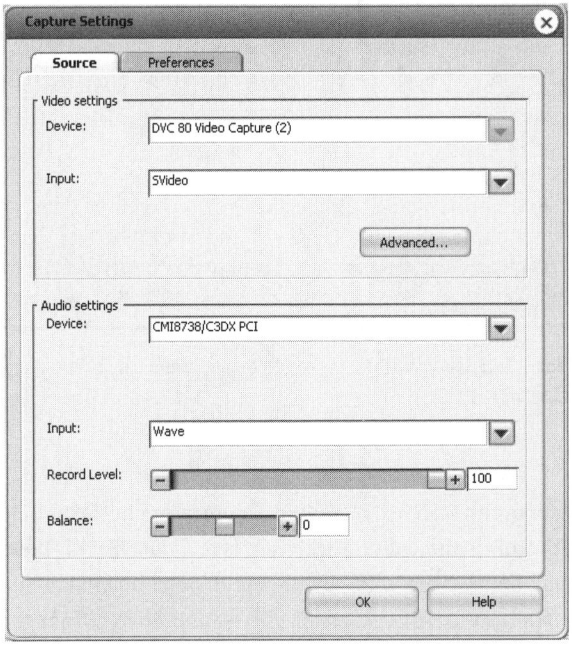

Figure 3-24. Make sure you properly set the audio source, recording level, and balance before you record.

Old or incompatible software may also be the culprit. Make sure you download and install the latest TV player and display driver software.

CAN'T ADJUST THE RECORDING VOLUME

The Annoyance: I want to capture my favorite show, but I can't seem to adjust the recording volume.

The Fix: First, check the recording levels in the system sound mixer. Select Start → All Programs → Accessories → Entertainment → Volume Control. Next, select

Options → Properties, select your Mixer Device, choose the Recording option, and click the OK button. The Volume Control will become a Recording Control panel (see Figure 3-25). Make sure you turn up each volume level. Close the window to save your changes, and try your capture again.

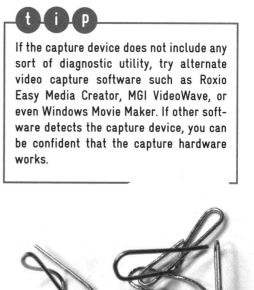

Figure 3-25. Make sure that the basic recording controls are available and adjustable.

If you can't adjust recording volumes in the Recording Control or the capture software (see Figure 3-24), there may be an issue with your sound drivers. Download and install the latest version of your sound drivers from the manufacturer, then reboot the system if necessary. In some cases, you may need to remove the sound devices first, then reboot the system and let Windows redetect and reinstall each sound item using the latest drivers. Open the System control panel, click the Hardware tab, and then click the Device Manager button. Next, expand the "Sound, video, and game controllers" entry, right-click each sound-related item, and select Uninstall. (Some items require you to select Properties, click the Properties tab, and then click the Remove button.) Reboot Windows. When new hardware is detected, make sure you use the latest sound drivers. Now recheck the Recording Control or capture software to verify that the recording volume is available.

CAPTURE DEVICE NOT DETECTED

The Annoyance: I installed a compatible capture device, but my capture software fails to detect it.

The Fix: If the capture device includes its own diagnostic or testing utility, use it to verify that the device responds normally. If not, the capture device may be defective or conflicting with other hardware in the PC (external capture devices may need external power from an AC adapter). Reinstall the capture device using the latest drivers from the manufacturer, or replace the device outright.

Older capture software may experience a software incompatibility. For example, some older capture software supports video captures using the Microsoft Video for Windows (VfW) API, although most current capture software uses the Microsoft DirectShow API. Capture applications intended for use with the VfW API might not run properly (if at all) through DirectShow. Check with the author of your capture application for an updated software version compliant with DirectShow. Otherwise, remove the old capture software and install a DirectShow-compliant application.

> **tip**
>
> If the capture device does not include any sort of diagnostic utility, try alternate video capture software such as Roxio Easy Media Creator, MGI VideoWave, or even Windows Movie Maker. If other software detects the capture device, you can be confident that the capture hardware works.

RECORDING CAPTURES OVER 2GB

The Annoyance: I can only capture video files up to 2GB. This amounts to just a few minutes of footage at a time. What do I do with my two hours of video?

The Fix: The file size limitations of your particular operating system determine the size of your video captures. Older FAT16 disk partitions can only handle file sizes to 2GB, FAT32 file systems can support files to 4GB, and disks partitioned with NTFS can handle files up to 2TB (terabytes) in size. Since your captures quit at 2GB, blame your FAT16 partition.

At a minimum, wipe and repartition your hard drive for FAT32. This means you need to reinstall the OS, applications, and data files from scratch. If you have a small-sized hard drive, you may need to supplement it with a second, larger FAT32 drive to hold your captures.

> **t i p**
>
> Use a utility such as Symantec Ghost to perform a complete backup of your system, and then restore the system image to your new drive formatted for FAT32. Before you begin the backup, make sure you carefully read the manufacturer's instructions to prevent accidental data loss.

However, even 4GB file sizes under FAT32 may be too small for long capture durations. To record TV shows, movies, or extensive video clips, upgrade to an operating system like Windows XP and partition the hard drive(s) for NTFS to gain virtually unlimited file sizes.

LIMITED CAPTURE RESOLUTIONS

The Annoyance: Why is my video capture resolution limited to just 640×240?

The Fix: Check with the manufacturer of the video-capture software for patches or updates that provide higher capture resolutions. If updates don't help, try an alternate capture application. For example, ATI's Multimedia Center 7.1 only supports resolutions to 620×240.

You may also be up against a hardware limitation. To capture video in higher resolutions, you need capture hardware with considerably more processing power. For example, a Dazzle 80 USB capture device only captures resolutions of 320×240, even though the Roxio Capture utility and MGI VideoWave 4 software will support preview windows to 352×288 (see Figure 3-26). To access higher resolutions, you could upgrade to the USB 2.0 Dazzle Digital Video Creator 150, which can capture resolutions to 740×480.

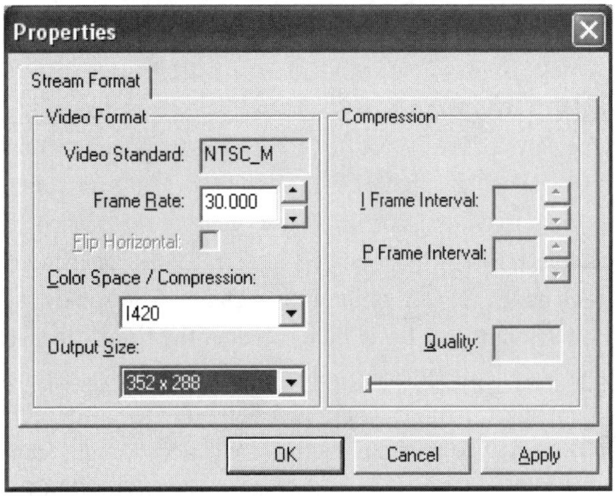

Figure 3-26. Setting a larger Output Size doesn't necessarily mean a larger capture—only a larger preview window.

VIDEO AND AUDIO OUT OF SYNC

The Annoyance: Why do I lose audio synchronization when I capture video in best quality mode? After a while, the capture starts to look like a foreign film or a Sergio Leone spaghetti western.

The Fix: When you capture video and audio simultaneously, it forces the capture software to interleave audio with video frames. This takes additional time and processing power. If the capture demands exceed the host computer's abilities, audio timing may start to shift and fall slightly out of sync with the video (usually worsening as the captured clip drags on).

What can you do? Reduce the capture quality and try the capture again. Perhaps try a smaller capture window, select increased compression during the capture, or reduce the capture bandwidth (depending on how your capture software defines quality). A lower quality capture will generally maintain its A/V sync. For a long-term solution, upgrade the computer's processing and RAM resources (or shift the capture work to a better computer entirely).

RECORDING DEVICES INTERRUPT TV OUTPUT

The Annoyance: If I insert a VCR between my video card and TV, I completely lose all video and audio.

The Fix: Pop a tape in the VCR and press Play. If the tape plays to the TV, you know the VCR-to-TV connection is OK. Remember that VCRs have their own internal tuner, as well as one or more auxiliary inputs, so you need to change the VCR mode until you select the proper input (such as "L1" or "L2" rather than a channel). In some cases, the input switch will be located on the front panel of your VCR. In other cases, you may need the VCR's remote to change the input mode. In a few odd cases, the VCR may need to be recording before it will accept input from an auxiliary source (if this happens, use a different VCR).

TV PLAYBACK SHIFTS MONITOR FREQUENCIES

The Annoyance: When I enable TV Output through my video card's desktop applet software, the monitor falls out of sync. The TV signal looks fine, but my monitor flashes on and off.

The Fix: The frequencies used with common monitor resolutions differ from the frequencies used with TV signals. When you enable TV Output, some video cards shift the horizontal (scan) frequencies used by the card. If the monitor can't adjust to the different frequencies, it can

suffer all sorts of convulsions. For example, some monitors just power down and display a "Frequency Out Of Range" error, but others will flash intensely, flicker badly, or snap between different screen sizes (all really *bad* for the monitor). Most multi-sync monitors offer a very wide range of working frequencies and higher scan rates due to higher resolution support.

This problem has a few easy solutions. You can disconnect the monitor while using the TV Output feature, disable the TV Output feature, or use a new multi-sync type monitor with support for a wide range of horizontal frequencies. You could also install a different video/TV card with an independent TV Output signal that does not shift the monitor frequency.

CLEARING UP BLURRY TEXT ON TV

The Annoyance: Why does my monitor text seem blurry on a TV set?

The Fix: Modern broadcast standards (such as NTSC and PAL) limit video bandwidth to 6–10MHz. Higher bandwidth allows for smaller details in the image (higher resolution). Bandwidth also limits the intensity and color changes in the image. Computer monitors offer much higher bandwidth than TVs; for example, a simple VGA (640×480) monitor clocks in at 30MHz, while high-resolution monitors can exceed 100MHz. Computer images displayed on a TV screen will always appear a bit fuzzy because the TV is simply not able to respond to the high frequencies that form the computer image. As an aside, the dots in a TV tube are much larger than the dots in a monitor, and this contributes to a loss in image detail as well.

A few tricks may help improve the TV image. First, use an S-Video connection instead of a composite (RCA-type) connector (S-Video keeps the color signals separate rather than combining them in a composite signal). Next, increase the size of your fonts and text to 18 points or higher. Strong or contrasting desktop color themes can upset the TV image, so select a softer, more complementary color scheme. Finally, tweak the TV's brightness, contrast, and sharpness settings.

DVD MOVIE COLORS ARE WASHED OUT

The Annoyance: My DVD movies play well, but the colors look washed out. I mean, Barney should look purple, not pink.

The Fix: To tweak the DVD image, adjust the saturation, gamma, brightness, contrast, and hue (color tone) through the advanced Display Properties. Right-click the desktop, select Properties, click the Settings tab, click the Advanced button, and then select your color tab. The exact tab (and the features available on it) will depend on your particular video card, but look for names like Video, S3 Gamma or S3 Gamma Plus, GeForce2Go, or other designations.

PLAYER SOFTWARE ANNOYANCES

PLAYBACK CONTROLS SEEM DISABLED

The Annoyance: I opened Windows Media Player to play back a video, but I found many of the controls—and even some clips—disabled.

The Fix: Ah, this seems like a cache problem. Windows Media Player (WMP for short) stores basic information about each clip you play (such as the clip length). WMP uses this cached information to optimize playback performance the next time you play the clip. It's a slick system when it works, but when you change or replace a clip (perhaps with an updated version), WMP continues to use the old cache information. This can mess up the player controls, or disable the clip entirely.

To work around this problem, give each file iteration its own unique name, or move the edited/altered file to a different folder. However, you may also need to periodically dump the WMP cache file. Select Start → Search → All files and folders. Under "All or part of the file name," type `wmplibrary*.db`. Under "Look in," select Local Hard Drives (C:), and then click the Search button. When Search locates the files, right-click each file and select Delete.

For best results, run a DVD movie in windowed mode while you adjust the color and gamma settings. This keeps the controls from obscuring the movie image.

WMP REQUESTS VIDEO DECELERATION

The Annoyance: Windows Media Player tells me to decrease video acceleration when I try to play a streaming video.

The Fix: With Windows Media Player running, select Tools → Options, and then click the Performance tab (Figure 3-27). Move the Video acceleration slider at the bottom of the dialog to the left, click the Apply button to save your changes, and try the video stream again. This will *not* affect acceleration in other applications, such as games.

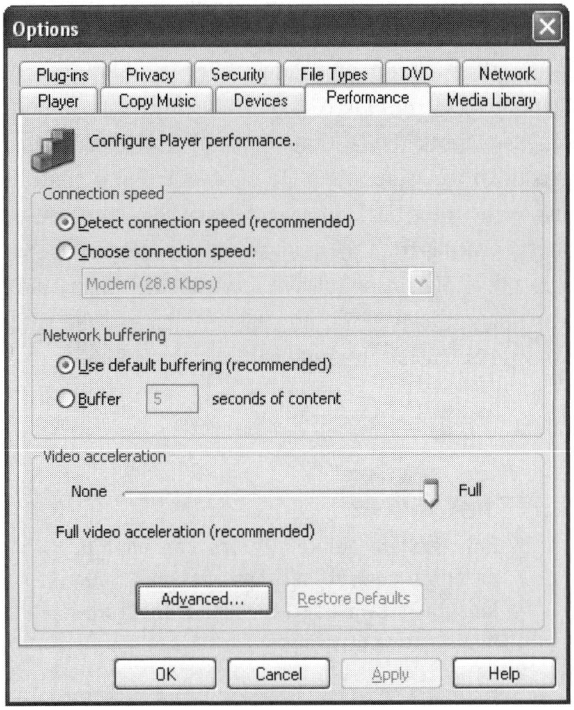

Figure 3-27. Decrease the local video acceleration under Windows Media Player.

WATCHING OVER YOUR PARENTAL CONTROL

The Annoyance: Windows Media Player refuses to play some parts of my DVD.

The Fix: Do you see a message like "Cannot play this portion of the DVD"? Well get that porn out of the drive! Windows Media Player (WMP) includes a Parental Control feature that will refuse to play discs over a selected Motion Picture Association of America (MPAA) movie rating. With WMP running, select Tools → Options, and then click the DVD tab (Figure 3-28). To enable parental controls, check the "Parental control" box and select a maximum viewable rating. To disable parental controls, just uncheck the box. To tweak the viewable rating, select another rating from the pull-down menu. Remember to click the Apply button to save your changes. (Some DVDs won't play at all if the rating is higher than allowed, while other discs may disable only portions of the film.)

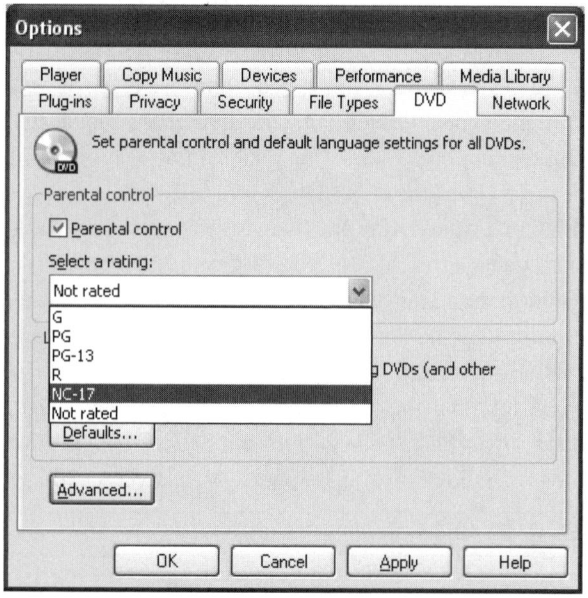

Figure 3-28. Enable Parental controls or adjust the maximum viewable rating for DVD playback.

NO PLAYBACK IN FULL-SCREEN MODE

The Annoyance: Windows Media Player won't let me use the full screen to play videos.

The Fix: Full-screen playback depends on maximum video hardware acceleration. If you have decreased the hardware acceleration due to video performance problems, Windows Media Player (and other players) might restrict full screen playback.

Right-click the desktop, select Properties, click the Settings tab, and click the Advanced button. Next, click the Troubleshoot tab for your graphics card and move the acceleration slider to the Full position. Already at Full? You may need a more powerful video card to handle your video playbacks.

Video cards with less than Full acceleration usually indicate some other performance problem on the system. For example, you may have previously decreased the acceleration in response to another issue, such as erratic crashes. If so, increasing the slider again may resurrect that old problem. When "stuck in the middle" like this, forego full-screen playback (and leave the acceleration slider reduced) or resolve the problem that forced you to decrease the video acceleration in the first place.

FIREWALL CUTS OFF STREAMING PLAYBACK

The Annoyance: I installed a firewall and now my QuickTime movies won't play.

The Fix: QuickTime uses the Real Time Streaming Protocol (RTSP) to send video and audio over the Internet. However, some firewalls (especially corporate firewalls) may restrict RTSP and prevent QuickTime media playback. One easy fix is to reconfigure QuickTime to use HTTP (a web protocol) instead of RTSP. Firewalls typically permit HTTP connections in order to allow browsers to reach the Web.

> **t i p**
>
> According to Apple, playback performance may lag somewhat if you select HTTP streaming instead of RTSP.

Launch the QuickTime player and select Edit → Preferences → QuickTime Preferences. Select the Streaming Transport option from the pull-down menu, then choose the "Use HTTP, Port ID" option (see Figure 3-29). Port 80 is the HTTP default, but you can enter a different port number if necessary. Close the dialog and try streaming QuickTime movies again. As an alternative, use the auto-configuration button to let QuickTime select a transport protocol and port for you.

If you use Windows Media Player (WMP) or another player, you will need to reconfigure your firewall, or opt for an alternate transport protocol allowed by the firewall. For WMP, select Tools → Options and click the Network tab (see Figure 3-30). Use the check boxes to select transport protocols that WMP will accept, such as multicast, TCP, UDP, and HTTP.

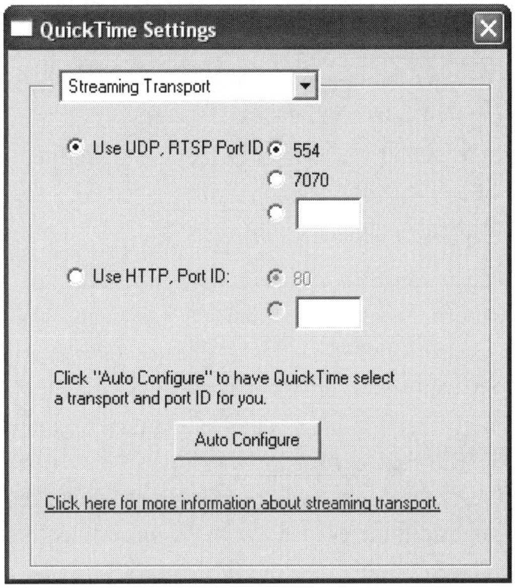

Figure 3-29. To configure QuickTime behind a firewall, select an alternate transport and port ID.

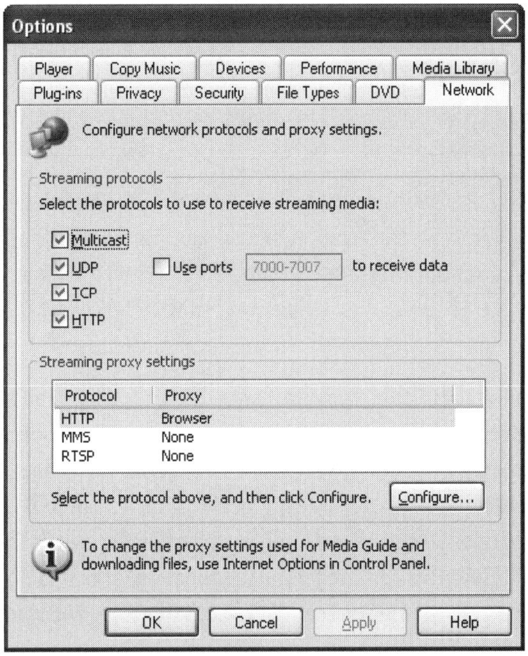

Figure 3-30. To configure WMP behind a firewall, select alternate transports.

TRAFFIC AFFECTS STREAMING PLAYBACK

The Annoyance: Why does my RealPlayer radio sound better during the day than at night?

The Fix: Traffic is often lighter during the day while folks are at work. After supper, the traffic picks up as everyone and his cousin tries to get online. The sheer volume of online traffic can bog down file transfers and decrease streaming quality.

RealPlayer can help you determine the quality of your particular connection. For example, RealPlayer's Play icon changes color based on traffic. Green indicates a good Internet connection, orange indicates some data loss, and red notes a serious loss of data. In addition, a bandwidth meter will report your throughput in Kbps (such as 135Kbps for a good, high-speed Internet connection). If the bandwidth meter sags as the Play icon turns orange (or red), you can blame heavy Internet traffic.

MUSIC DOWNLOADS CAUSE CONNECTION ERRORS

The Annoyance: I get "Cannot connect" errors when I try to download music from my service provider.

The Fix: Can you access web sites or email? If not, the trouble may be with your own Internet connection or ISP (not your music service).

If you can perform other Internet-related activities, the problem is on the remote (server) end. Check the support pages at your music service for server status information. The music server may be overloaded with Internet traffic, or temporarily down for updates or maintenance.

Finally, check the player software. For example, RealPlayer automatically tests online status, but incorrect detection may force the player to work in an offline mode. Always-on connections (e.g., cable or DSL) should not require detection. For example, in RealPlayer select Tools → Preferences → Category → Connection, check the "Assume I am online" option, click the OK button, and restart the player.

t i p

You can check your Internet bandwidth independently using speed testers such as CNET's Bandwidth Meter (available at *http://reviews.cnet.com/7004-7254_7-0.html*).

UNEXPECTED ERRORS IN REALPLAYER

The Annoyance: When I use RealPlayer, I get a message that says "An unexpected error has occurred."

The Fix: Unfortunately, an unexpected error generally has no detailed explanation, but you can usually trace the cause to media file problems or player integrity issues. First, try playing other media files (such as movies or audio clips). Most players include sample files. If other files work, you know only a few damaged or corrupted files caused the unexpected error.

On the other hand, if sample files (or other files) refuse to play normally, there may indeed be an issue with your player software. For example, a virus or cross-linked file may have damaged one of your player's components. Uninstall the player, defragment the hard drive, and then reinstall the player software from scratch.

t i p

Firewalls can cut off access to certain Internet resources, such as music services. Make sure your firewall allows access to the music software (e.g., RealPlayer), or reconfigure the player software to use an alternate transport protocol allowed by the firewall.

4

Sound
ANNOYANCES

It seems like only yesterday that my old Intel 286 system belted out tinny, robotic tones on its internal speaker. Mostly, it sounded like a flock of sick seagulls trapped inside the chassis—or maybe I just have no ear for music. Today, sound hardware goes far beyond the orchestral-quality soundtracks and vibrant noises of popular games. How often have you dropped in your favorite music CD and rattled the windows with the gentle, tasteful strains of Metallica? How would you enjoy your favorite DVD movie without the thrilling sounds of gunfire or the roar of the ocean? Sound also has a place in business, supporting voice in real-time collaboration, speech-to-text conversion, and VoIP telephone calls.

Sound has enjoyed a rapid evolution, but not without its growing pains. This chapter takes you through annoyances ranging from configuration, driver, and setup issues to volume, microphone, and speaker headaches. It also covers the most perplexing CD audio problems and player troubles.

CONFIGURATION ANNOYANCES

FIGURING OUT YOUR SOUND CARD

The Annoyance: I want top-notch sound for my new game. How do I find out what sound card my system currently uses before I splurge on a new one?

The Fix: First, determine whether you use an integrated sound chip or a PCI sound card. Take a look behind the PC and trace the speaker cable to the output jack. If the cable connects to a jack in the rear I/O area of the PC (the cluster of serial, parallel, USB, Ethernet, and other ports commonly found below the power supply), you're using an integrated sound chip on the motherboard.

Now let's get the skinny on your specific sound hardware using the DirectX diagnostic (*dxdiag.exe*). Select Start → Run, enter **dxdiag** in the Run box, and click the OK button. When the dialog box appears, click the Sound tab for a complete breakdown of the sound device and its driver info (see Figure 4-1). Don't let a PCI designation throw you—even a motherboard chip can use a PCI architecture within the system (it's not limited to a card in a slot).

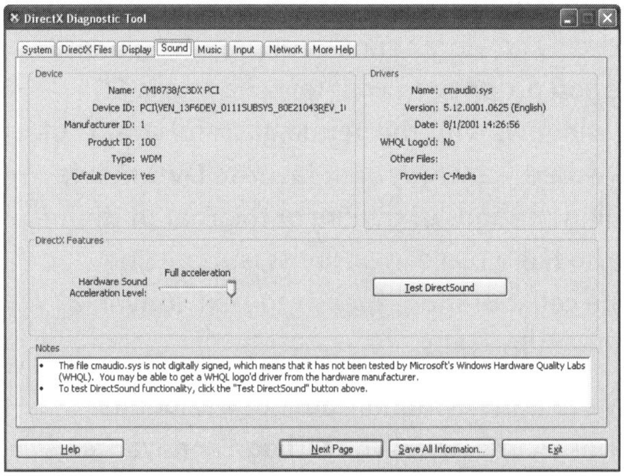

Figure 4-1. Use *dxdiag.exe* to identify your current sound hardware and driver information.

If you decide to add a sound card, it should automatically disable any onboard (motherboard) sound device. However, this does not always happen perfectly. After you install a new sound card, check the System Setup and verify that the integrated sound device is disabled (see the "AC97 Audio" entry in Figure 4-2). If not, disable the sound device and save your changes. Remember to reconnect your speaker cable (along with microphones and line input cables) to the new sound card.

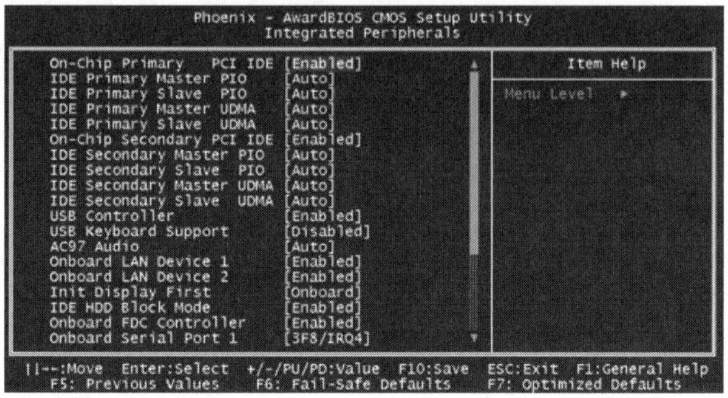

Figure 4-2. When you install a PCI sound card, make sure any onboard sound device is disabled.

AUDIO PORT CONFUSION

The Annoyance: I plugged my PC speakers into the jack with the little music note above it, but I don't hear any sound.

The Fix: Wrong jack, Jack. The little musical note sometimes denotes the Line In connection. The Speaker Out (or Line Out) connection is typically greenish-yellow, and often uses a symbol such as "((o))->" (reminiscent of sound waves with an arrow going outward). The opposite (Line In) jack is often blue, and marked with a reverse symbol, such as "((o))<-" (the same sound waves with an arrow going inward). Recheck your speaker connections and try the speakers in another jack.

Cables and Static

If you hear speaker static—especially when moving your speakers—check your connections at the sound card, and reseat the speaker jack if necessary. If you encounter static when moving the sound cable, you may need to replace the speaker set with a better-quality model.

A3D relies upon a compliant sound device (and drivers), a set of stereo speakers, and a game or other application that can produce 3D sound effects. The specs of your sound system will typically tell you if 3D sound is available. For your game, simply check the Sound tab or submenu of the game's configuration menu. (Refer to the game manual for details.)

To create positional sound, place a speaker on each side of your monitor at a 30–45 degree outward angle.

GETTING THE MOST FROM POSITIONAL SOUND

The Annoyance: What is A3D-I sound and how do I enable it on my sound device?

The Fix: Ah, this is 3D sound. Aureal 3-Dimensional (A3D) sound technology is based on human hearing. In everyday life, you can tell the direction of a sound (front, side, or back) because of slight delays and volume shifts in the sound when it strikes your ears. A3D technology attempts to duplicate these effects through a sound card and only two speakers (rather than the five or more speakers often used with surround-sound systems), by using "positional sound." Positional sound uses slight differences in sound timing and volume to "trick" the listener into hearing sound relative to their location. For example, a listener can hear gunfire off to the left, footsteps creeping up from behind, or any number of interactive sound effects.

ENABLING THE STANDARD JOYSTICK

The Annoyance: My joystick fails to work when I connect it to the sound card's 15-pin port.

The Fix: Start with the basics and check the joystick's connection to its 15-pin port. Also, check with the sound card maker and make sure that the 15-pin port is actually a joystick port (as opposed to some other proprietary feature). You may also need to set the small jumper located on the sound card to joystick mode, rather than MIDI mode.

Next, open the System control panel, click the Hardware tab, and then click the Device Manager button. Expand the "Sound, video, and game controllers" entry, and look for an entry such as Standard Game Port (see Figure 4-3). If the entry is missing, download and install the latest drivers for your sound card. A yellow exclamation or question mark next to the entry indicates a hardware conflict. Power down the computer and remove any other game port devices in the system (look for expansion devices with similar 15-pin ports).

Figure 4-3. Check the Device Manager to ensure that a Standard Game Port is available for the joystick.

If the game port is present with no errors reported, make sure you configured the game to use the joystick. Remember that games often let you select between keyboard, mouse, and joystick input devices. If the problem continues, try another joystick.

ENJOYING SURROUND SOUND

The Annoyance: I've got my speakers connected, but how do I get surround sound to work when playing a DVD movie?

The Fix: You need to configure both Windows XP and your DVD player for 5.1 (6-speaker) sound. To adjust the speaker configuration under Windows, open the Sounds and Audio Devices control panel, click the Advanced button under "Speaker settings," and then select "5.1 surround sound speakers" from the "Speaker setup" drop-down menu (see Figure 4-4). Click the Apply button to save your changes.

Figure 4-4. Configure Windows XP for 6-speaker operation.

Now start a DVD player application, such as WinDVD or Windows Media Player (WMP), and configure the audio for 6-channel (5.1) sound. To do this within WMP, click Tools → Options, click the DVD tab, and then click the Advanced button. Under Audio Interface, select "using 6-speakers" and click the Apply button (see Figure 4-5). Your surround sound should work fine—enjoy the show!

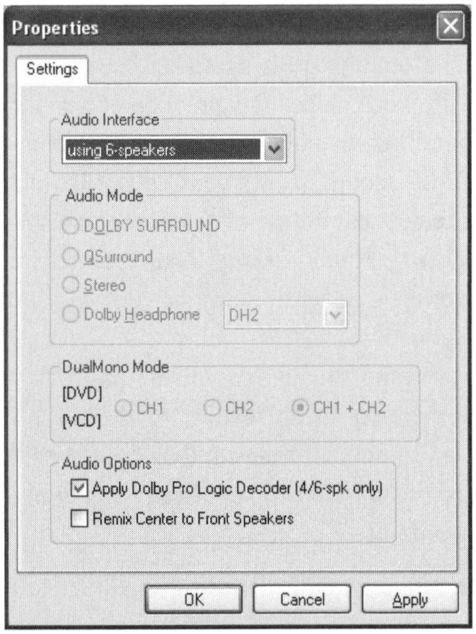

Figure 4-5. Configure the DVD movie player for 6-speaker operation.

Whether in a sound card or in a speaker set, amplifier circuits produce some amount of hum. Since audio signals are amplified at several stages before they reach your ears, excess amplification can bring undesirable noise (like hum) to the forefront and ruin your audio experience. As a rule, increase volume early in the sound process (such as the Windows Volume Control), and keep the speaker volume as low as possible. If you adopt the reverse tactic (keep the Volume Control settings low and force the speakers to amplify things), you'll hear a lot of noise in the signal.

GETTING EAX TO WORK

The Annoyance: How come I can't get my EAX feature to work?

The Fix: Environmental Audio Effects (EAX) bring a wide range of sound effects to a computer's sound playback, including reverb, 3D surround sound, time scaling (to speed up or slow down playback), and so on. EAX can also simulate audio environments, such as theaters or bedrooms, and perform other tasks on sound files. Unfortunately, only certain sound devices support EAX.

With EAX 4.0 drivers now available, make sure you use the most recent sound device drivers from your sound card manufacturer, as well as the latest version of DirectX from Microsoft (*http://www.microsoft.com/directx*). If EAX features work under all but one game, check the game itself (rather than the sound card's EAX support) for problems. Make sure you enable EAX within the game's sound options menu (see Figure 4-6). Also, check for game patches or updates that will enable EAX support within the troublesome game. If no EAX support is available in the game software, you will not be able to access EAX features when you play the game.

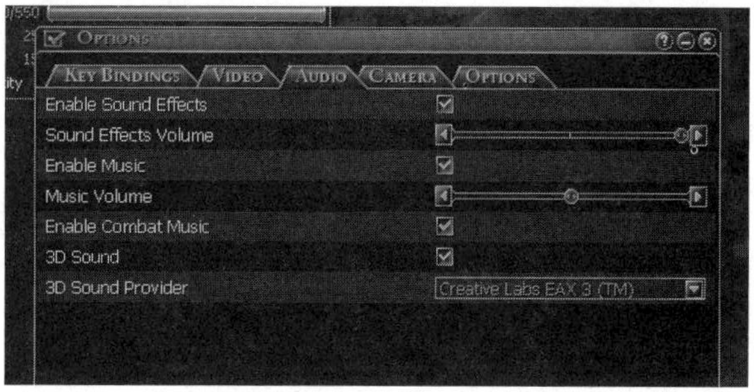

Figure 4-6. Be sure that EAX support is enabled within the game itself.

DEVICE DISAPPEARS AFTER BIOS UPGRADE

The Annoyance: My audio device disappeared after I updated the system BIOS. How do I get it back?

The Fix: BIOS updates have a nasty habit of resetting onboard options to default settings. If you use onboard audio, the BIOS update may have disabled the audio. Windows will no longer see the onboard audio device. Once you complete a BIOS upgrade, make sure you "Load BIOS Defaults" and reboot the system. If the problem continues, reboot to the System Setup and open the Integrated Peripherals menu. Locate the onboard audio device (often labeled something like "AC'97 Audio") and make sure the device is enabled.

If the problem continues to haunt you, download and reinstall the latest motherboard drivers (including the sound drivers) to restore the sound system. However, some motherboard driver updates may call for a complete reinstallation of Windows. If you must reinstall Windows, do it before you install the new motherboard drivers. Finally, restore your other device drivers, applications, and datafiles from backups or original media.

Always perform a complete backup of the system before you attempt a BIOS upgrade or reinstall Windows from scratch.

MULTIMEDIA PLAYER ASKS FOR A CODEC

The Annoyance: When I try to play a sound file, the player stops and asks for a codec. What the %#$@ is a codec and how do I get the right one(s) for my system?

The Fix: Codecs compress and decompress multimedia data and provide the instructions needed for multimedia players (e.g., InterVideo WinDVD 6 or Windows Media Player) to handle a specific file type, such as MPG, MP3, QuickTime, and so on.

Today, common codecs are installed along with the operating system, and additional codecs are installed with their corresponding applications. For example, if you install a music player, you'll likely get MP3 codecs. To inspect your available codecs, open the System control panel, click the Hardware tab, click the Device Manager button, and expand the "Sound, video, and game controllers" entry. Right-click the Audio Codecs entry and choose Properties to see the installed codecs (see Figure 3-3 in Chapter 3).

If a codec goes missing, chances are that the application or its codecs have been damaged or corrupted (or the application was never installed properly in the first place). Uninstall the application and then reinstall it again from scratch. If the trouble persists, check your audio or video codecs for duplicate entries. Duplicates can sometimes occur when you repeatedly install similar programs or hardware devices, and conflicts between duplicate entries can stop that codec from being used. Right-click any duplicate codecs and choose Remove.

HEADPHONES DISABLE INTERNAL SPEAKERS

The Annoyance: I disconnected a pair of headphones from my laptop, and now the internal speakers don't work.

> ### THE COMPLETE CODEC
> **Normally, codecs are installed with media player software (e.g., RealPlayer or Quick-Time). However, software engineers occasionally update codecs to keep pace with bug fixes and compression improvements. Check your player for automatic codec updates from the Internet. To do this in Windows Media Player, click Tools → Options and click the Player tab. In the "Automatic updates" section, make sure you check the "Download codecs automatically" box.**

The Fix: Although this problem may seem like a hardware malfunction, it's really a driver issue. For example, the audio driver recognizes the headphones and disables the internal speakers, but does not re-enable the internal speakers once you disconnect the headphones. Reboot the laptop with the headphones disconnected to restore the internal speakers normally. Also, contact your laptop maker and install the most recent audio drivers.

SETUP ANNOYANCES

CAN'T USE AC-3 AUDIO

The Annoyance: How can I use the Dolby Digital AC-3 audio output when playing DVDs?

The Fix: If your sound card supports Dolby Digital AC-3 audio, it will provide an S/PDIF output jack (it usually looks like a "composite" or RCA-type connector). S/PDIF audio will need a separate Dolby Digital AC-3 (surround sound) amplifier box to process the digital signals and feed your home entertainment speakers. If you don't have a suitable amplifier, stick with the PC speakers and do not enable S/PDIF. If you do have the Dolby Digital AC-3 amplifier, just connect the S/PDIF jack between the sound card and amplifier and plug in your surround sound speakers to the amplifier.

After you set up the hardware, enable S/PDIF in the movie player. The actual setup differs for each movie player application. For Windows Media Player, launch the player, select Tools → Options, click the DVD tab, and click the Advanced button (see Figure 4-7). Choose "using S/PDIF" from the Audio Interface drop-down menu, click the Apply button, and then click the OK button. Now play the movie and enjoy your surround sound.

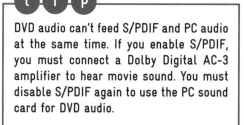

Figure 4-7. Enable S/PDIF for a true surround sound movie experience through the PC.

DVD audio can't feed S/PDIF and PC audio at the same time. If you enable S/PDIF, you must connect a Dolby Digital AC-3 amplifier to hear movie sound. You must disable S/PDIF again to use the PC sound card for DVD audio.

GETTING SOUND WITH TV OUTPUT

The Annoyance: I don't hear any audio when I connect the TV output from my video card to a television.

The Fix: You need to either play the TV audio through your PC speakers, or connect the "Line Out" or "Speaker Out" connections to the audio inputs on your TV (or VCR if you're recording the output). However, some specialized devices, such as Pinnacle's PCTV card, let you connect your TV audio to the sound card's Line In port using a short jumper cable.

Use a cable with a single 1/8-inch mini stereo plug at one and two RCA-type plugs at the other end. You can find these types of cables at electronics stores such as Radio Shack.

DEALING WITH EXCESS EFFECTS

The Annoyance: Why do I get excessive audio effects when I play a sound file?

The Fix: Advanced sound cards generally support EAX, which can apply a wide range of audio effects (see the earlier annoyance, "Getting EAX to Work"). However, EAX controls are not "smart" enough to know whether an effect (or its intensity) is appropriate for a given audio file. This means EAX can vastly improve a sound or completely ruin it. If your audio file doesn't sound right with the selected effects, use the sound card's control software to reduce or disable the EAX effects. For example, the EAX console for a Creative Labs Sound Blaster Audigy 2 ZS Pro (see Figure 4-8) lets you preset environments, such as cathedrals or bathrooms, and also apply customized effects. You can alter the effect, reduce the amount (percentage) of the effect, or disable EAX effects entirely using the software control panel.

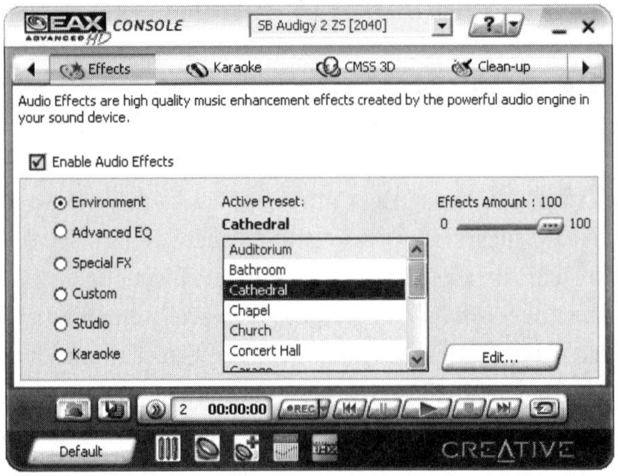

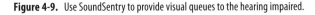

Figure 4-8. Adjust or disable EAX effects when they impair sound playback.

SURROUND SPEAKERS NOT WORKING

The Annoyance: I'm not getting sound from my rear speakers in a 4- or 6-speaker configuration.

The Fix: Multiple speaker modes typically use a series of sound card outputs. I mean, you don't run 4 to 6 speakers off a single stereo jack! First, recheck your speaker connections. Next, try the troublesome speakers in another (working) jack. If the speakers don't work in other live jacks, replace the defective speakers.

Now check the speaker mode in your operating system (see "Enjoying Surround Sound" earlier in this chapter). Finally, make sure your particular application can indeed support 5.1 or 4-speaker mode. For a DVD player, check the audio properties (see "Can't Use AC-3 Audio"). For a game, check the game's audio options menu and select the appropriate speaker mode. If the application does not support your speakers, you won't hear sound as expected.

HELPING THE HEARING IMPAIRED

The Annoyance: My father is hard of hearing. Can I adjust Windows sounds so he will hear them without having to turn the volume way up?

The Fix: One of the easiest methods is to enable the SoundSentry feature under Windows XP. Simply open the Accessibility Options control panel, click the Sound tab, and check the Use SoundSentry box (see Figure 4-9). Select a visual warning to be displayed when the system makes a sound and click the Apply button. SoundSentry essentially disables sounds in favor of visual queues. For example, when Windows makes a sound, the active caption bar, the active window, or the entire desktop flashes. Now your Dad can work without turning up the volume.

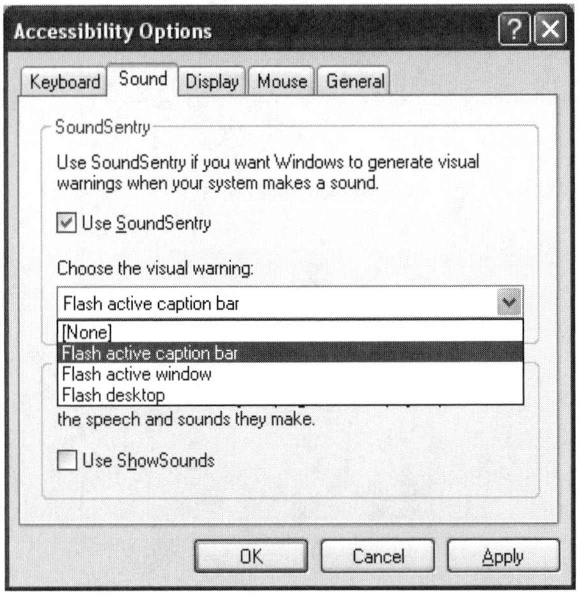

Figure 4-9. Use SoundSentry to provide visual queues to the hearing impaired.

ELIMINATING AUDIO DISTORTION

The Annoyance: I want to rock the house, but my speakers produce a distorted sound.

The Fix: Well, turn the damn thing down! Distortion occurs when the signal overwhelms the amplifier circuit or speakers. The excessive signal causes the distortion. First, check your mixer signals. Select Start → All Programs → Accessories → Entertainment → Volume Control (see Figure 4-10), then set each of the inputs to your main sound mixer at about 75% and the mixed signal output between 75–100%. You should mute any unused inputs. If certain inputs seem prone to distortion (such as voice clips recorded through your microphone), turn the input down until the distortion disappears.

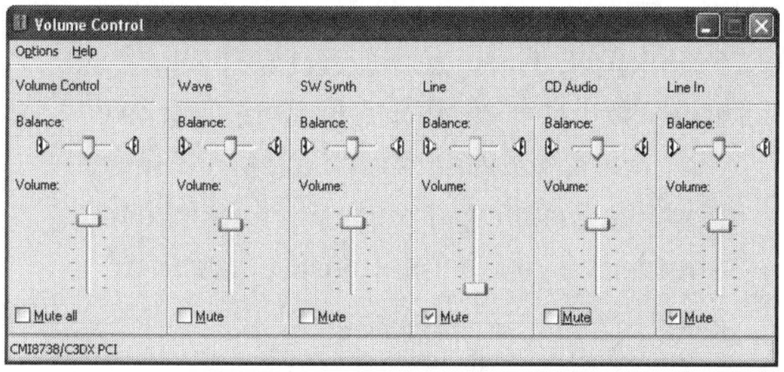

Figure 4-10. Adjust excessively loud inputs and mute unused inputs.

Another common oversight is the speaker volume setting. As a rule, a set of simple powered speakers should not need to go over 25–30% volume. If you cranked the speakers, turn down their volume knob until the sound clears up. If you still feel the need to shake paint from the walls, buy a good quality Harman Karden or Bose speaker set designed to deliver serious audio power.

Sound and Color

In most cases, your TV or VCR uses color-coded connections to match your patch cable. Remember: the red RCA-type connector is the right channel and the white RCA-type connector is the left channel.

TAKING STATIC OUT OF THE SOUND

The Annoyance: I adjusted the volume to play a QuickTime file, but now I hear static.

The Fix: If you turn down the volume too low and turn up the amplified speaker volume to compensate, you will likely hear static in the output. In this case, turn down the speaker volume knob, then open the Windows Volume Control (see Figure 4-10) and adjust the volume levels to achieve an acceptable signal. If you reduced the QuickTime volume too low (below 20%), turn up the QuickTime volume again and adjust the WAV volume setting in the Windows Volume Control accordingly.

Some hardware platforms (such as laptops or notebooks) may cause static when you adjust player volume through the keyboard. This static continues even when you finish adjusting the player volume. Quit QuickTime (or whatever player you use) and restart the application to clear the static. In the future, pause the QuickTime file before you make any volume adjustments, and then continue the playback.

> **t i p**
> Reduce static by using the Windows Volume Control to mute any unused audio inputs.

REDUCING MICROPHONE SENSITIVITY

The Annoyance: My microphone is very sensitive to background noise, such as my kids playing in the other room. How can I reduce its sensitivity?

The Fix: Before you mess around with volume controls, make sure you use the appropriate microphone for the job. You can record with two kinds of microphones: omni-directional and unidirectional. Most run-of-the-mill microphones are omni directional, which means they pick up sounds from all parts of the microphone. A unidirectional microphone only picks up sound from the top of the microphone. If you need to reduce background noise, then you should use a unidirectional microphone or tape your kids' mouths shut (not recommended). If you absolutely must use an omni-direction microphone, try to get your subject closer to the microphone. Also, use one of those little foam windbreaks (or pop filters) around your microphone to ease the harsh "pah" sounds in words like "picnic" or "Peter."

If the problem persists, just turn down your recording volume. Open the "Sounds and Audio Devices" control panel, click the Audio tab, and click the Volume button in the "Sound recording" area (see Figure 4-11) to open a Recording Control mixer where you can lower the Microphone volume. Try lowering the volume in small increments and rerecording until the background noise fades out.

Figure 4-11. Reduce the microphone recording volume to ease undesirable background noise.

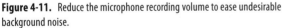

> **THE PHANTOM**
>
> **To create audio signals you can amplify and record, microphones require a source of power. There are three basic microphone types: condenser, dynamic, and electret. Dynamic and electret microphones produce their own internal signal voltages and offer good signal quality. The cheaper condenser microphones need a source of power from the sound card (usually called _phantom power_). If your sound card provides constant phantom power, you must use a condenser microphone. If you can switch phantom power off (usually through a jumper on the sound card), you can also use dynamic or electret microphones.**

ENABLING A TROUBLESOME MICROPHONE

The Annoyance: I want to record some personal research notes as voice messages on my PC, but my microphone doesn't seem to work.

The Fix: Start with the obvious things, such as your microphone connection. If the microphone has an on/off switch, make sure you flip on the switch. Also, check the microphone type and set your phantom power on or off as required (see the sidebar "The Phantom"). For example, you should turn off phantom power when you use a dynamic microphone, and turn on phantom power when you use a condenser microphone. Now make sure you selected the correct recording source, and set the recording volume to an appropriate level under Windows (see the previous annoyance "Reducing Microphone Sensitivity").

Try a simple recording application, such as Windows Sound Recorder. Select Start → All Programs → Accessories → Entertainment → Sound Recorder (see Figure 4-12). Click the Record button, speak into the microphone, and click Stop. Now click Play to hear your words played back. Adjust the Microphone recording and WAV playback volume controls to achieve the clearest sound. As an alternative, use the Sound Hardware Test Wizard to test your recording and playback setup (see the next annoyance, "Clearing Up Garbled Voice").

Figure 4-13. Use the Sound Hardware Test Wizard to test your recording and playback setup.

Figure 4-12. Use the Windows Sound Recorder to test your microphone setup.

CLEARING UP GARBLED VOICE

The Annoyance: My recordings sound OK, but the voice seems just a bit garbled.

The Fix: Lots of folks get too close to the microphone and speak too loud. This practice overwhelms the microphone and causes awful distortion during playback. Try recording a bit further back from the microphone, and use a foam windbreak (pop filter) to help smooth out fricative sounds during speech. Also, make sure you set the phantom power to match the microphone (see the sidebar "The Phantom").

Another possible problem is incorrect audio properties. Open the Sounds and Audio Devices control panel, click the Voice tab, and select the proper recording device from the "Default device" drop-down menu. Now click the "Test hardware" button to launch the Sound Hardware Test Wizard and follow the wizard to test your recording and playback setup (see Figure 4-13).

SPEAKER ANNOYANCES

MANAGING SPEAKER HUM

The Annoyance: Why does so much hum and buzz come from my speakers?

The Fix: Symptoms like hum and buzz indicate a power grounding issue, but start with the basics (e.g., checking for tight speaker connections). Remember that high volumes on your amplified speakers can really bring out any unwanted noise in your audio, so turn up the mixer signals in the Windows Volume Control, and turn down the speaker volume to the lowest acceptable level (see "Eliminating Audio Distortion" earlier in this chapter). This minor adjustment often goes a long way toward cleaning up a noisy signal. Of course, there may be damage to the speaker's amplifier circuit, so try another set of powered speakers.

Also, check for low-frequency noise on the AC power line. For example, high-energy devices such as air conditioners, motors, coffee makers, and even a low-quality computer power supply can sometimes place noise on the AC circuit. Turn off any high-energy devices in the house, or power the speakers from a different circuit in the house.

Another common hum problem occurs when you attempt to wire your PC speaker output to your home stereo's auxiliary input. When you connect two separate systems in this way, a ground loop sometimes occurs because of the different voltages at both ends of the "ground" wire. Use a ground loop isolator—such as the $29.95 unit from Xitel Pty., Ltd. (*http://www.xiteldirect.com*)—to isolate the PC speaker output from the stereo's auxiliary input and decouple the electrical connection between the two devices.

> **t i p**
>
> Use a basic AC receptacle tester (from any hardware or appliance store) to check for proper grounding. You may need a licensed electrician to properly ground any faulty outlets. If the outlet passes the test, try another AC adapter.

WRONG JACK IMPAIRS SOUND QUALITY

The Annoyance: I connected my speakers to the headphone output jack and now the sound seems distorted.

The Fix: Because headphones don't typically include an onboard amplifier, designers amplify the headphone outputs instead. If you connect powered speakers to an already powered headphone output, the sound level can easily seem "overdriven" or distorted. The easiest fix is to reconnect your speaker output to the regular speaker output jack. If you must connect your powered speakers to the headphone output, reduce the speaker volume, and then ease back on the headphone volume slider (if present) in the Windows Volume Control until the distortion disappears (see Figure 4-10).

REDUCING UNWANTED SOUND INTERFERENCE

The Annoyance: My speakers pick up a radio station even though the PC has no radio tuner.

The Fix: One of your audio inputs probably picked up unintentional interference from a nearby RF source, which it amplified and sent to your speakers. First, use the Windows Volume Control and mute each channel in turn to see which input actually picked up the unwanted signal (see Figure 4-10). Once you identify the offending input, route the wiring differently (for example, wrap it up or make it as short as possible). If the problem persists, purchase a small ferrite doughnut core from an electronics store (such as Radio Shack) and pass several wraps of the input cable through the core. This fix will change the induction in that signal wire and eliminate the unwanted signal.

> **t i p**
>
> Power cabling can cause hum and other signal interference. You should keep audio cables and power cables separate—if they do cross, they should cross at a 90-degree angle.

> **HUMMING ALONG TO USB**
>
> A grounding problem between your speakers and your PC, or other interference, can cause hum. Many sound cards have very little shielding against the radio interference and hum caused by your computer's power supply. You may need to move to a USB audio interface. This interface takes the audio signal outside of the PC for conversion from digital to analog. If you can't get a USB audio interface, then move your sound card as far away as possible from the PC power supply. Also, make sure you plug your speakers and computer into the same power strip or AC outlet.

SPEAKER APPLET INTERRUPTS OTHER PROGRAMS

The Annoyance: My USB speaker applet pops up and interrupts other applications.

The Fix: This simple-sounding problem actually has a simple solution—just disable the pop-up mode in your speaker management applet. For example, Altec Lansing speakers include speaker management software that will pop up on the desktop if you adjust any of the controls on the speaker (see Figure 4-14). Although the pop-up will disappear if you don't make any adjustments for three seconds, it can still be a pain in the rump. Simply uncheck the Popup box in the software's View menu to disable it.

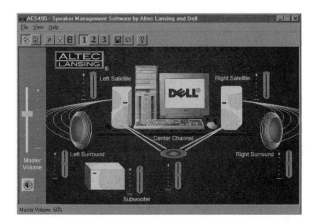

Figure 4-14. Use the View menu to stop pop-up behavior in Altec Lansing speaker management software.

If your speaker software does not offer a pop-up control option, check with the speaker manufacturer for updated drivers or control software that may provide a pop-up blocking feature.

SOUND AT ONLY THE FRONT CHANNELS

The Annoyance: I connected the digital output from my SoundBlaster sound card to the digital input on a multichannel home theater receiver, but I can only hear sound from the front channels.

The Fix: Home theater receivers typically use coaxial connections. When it receives compressed audio data (e.g., AC3 or DVD audio) from a sound card's digital output, it decodes the audio and drives the proper speakers to produce "surround sound." However, coaxial connectors will not handle multichannel audio already in analog form from the sound card. If you feed analog signals to the receiver, only the front channels will operate (as if you played sound through your stereo PC speakers). Check your sound card's specifications to make sure it can produce multichannel digital audio (not all can). Next, enable multichannel digital audio through the sound card's setup or operating applet (usually visible in the System Tray). Also, refer to the sound card's manual for the proper audio connection schemes.

Finally, remember that not all sources produce multichannel audio. For example, DVD movies or standalone AC3 files offer native multichannel support, but ordinary MP3 files and games in stereo mode will only produce stereo sound. In other words, you will not get surround sound from garden-variety stereo sources.

NO SOUND FROM CENTER SPEAKER

The Annoyance: I use a SoundBlaster Audigy sound card, but the center speaker in my 5.1 setup refuses to work.

The Fix: Does your audio source include a discrete center channel? To answer this question, check the characteristics of the audio source itself. For example, DVD movies will use 5.1 sound (with a center channel), but a self-recorded DVD video may not. In other words, if the audio source lacks a center channel, the center speaker will not produce any signal.

However, Creative Labs products offer a feature called the Creative Multi Speaker System (CMSS), which enables the center speaker when no center channel is otherwise available. First, enable CMSS in the Creative Play Center. For example, click Start → All Programs → Creative → Creative Play Center, then click the CMSS button and select Movie mode. Now open the Creative Surround Mixer and select 5.1 speakers. In this case, click Start → All Programs → Creative → SoundBlaster Audigy → Surround Mixer, and then choose 5.1 speakers (see Figure 4-15). The center speaker should now work.

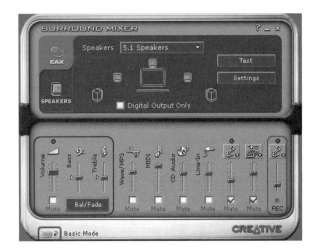

Figure 4-15. With the SoundBlaster Audigy, enable CMSS to simulate a center channel in surround sound playback.

Of course, not every speaker set will output to a center channel from the digital connector. For example, Creative Labs' DTT2500 speaker set will not drive the center speaker when connected to the SoundBlaster Audigy digital connector. The DTT3500, on the other hand, does support 5.1 multichannel sound through the digital connector. Go figure! To make sure the speaker set supports your digital output, check the specifications or visit the manufacturer's web site.

DIGITAL SPEAKERS DON'T WORK AT HIGH SAMPLING RATES

The Annoyance: I just attached digital speakers to my Creative Labs Audigy sound card, but they don't produce any output at high sampling rates.

The Fix: Not all digital speakers will reproduce sound at every possible sampling rate of the audio card. If your speakers fail at a high sampling rate (such as 96kHz), reconfigure the sound card for a lower sampling rate (such as 44.1kHz or 48kHz). For an Audigy sound card, open the Creative Labs Audio HQ control panel, click Device Controls, click the Sampling Rate tab, and choose a lower sampling rate.

CD AUDIO ANNOYANCES

GETTING CD MUSIC TO WORK

The Annoyance: I can hear my game just fine, but not CD music. What gives?

The Fix: Select Start → All Programs → Accessories → Entertainment → Volume Control, and make sure the CD Audio input channel is turned up and not muted (see Figure 4-10). Next, check your audio player software (such as Windows Media Player) and turn up the playback volume (see Figure 4-11). Also, make sure that the disk is actually playing (the time slider will advance from left to right).

Still no sound? Power down and open the PC. Check for a thin, 4-wire cable between the CD drive and sound card. Reconnect any loose ends, or install a new CD audio cable (available from any computer store, such as CompUSA) if missing. If you have more than one optical drive in the system, check for a CD audio cable between other drives and the sound card. For example, the system manufacturer may have thrown you a curve and connected the CD audio cable to the DVD-ROM drive instead of the CD-RW drive.

CONFIGURING DRIVES FOR DIGITAL AUDIO

The Annoyance: I don't have an audio cable between the CD drive and sound card. Is there still a way for me to play audio CDs?

The Fix: Playback software such as Windows Media Player can play music in digital form. It passes the Red Book–standard audio across the drive's signal cable (rather than the 4-wire analog cable). Don't believe me? Disconnect the 4-wire analog audio cable and pop in a music CD. Your player should start and violá—music! If you're still doubtful, select Start → All Programs → Accessories → Entertainment → Volume Control and adjust the CD audio channel volume (see Figure 4-10). No luck, huh? Now adjust the WAV channel volume. This channel works because Windows Media Player takes the music from the disc digitally.

GETTING ERROR-TOLERANT PLAYBACK

The Annoyance: Can I still play audio CDs with occasional errors in the recording?

The Fix: Generally speaking, player software will continue to play Red Book–standard audio tracks in the face of errors, but you may notice pops, static, or other audible anomalies. Players such as Windows Media Player (WMP) provide an error correction feature to hide small data errors. With WMP running, select Tools → Options, click the Devices tab, choose the CD-ROM drive, and then click the Properties button. Next, click the Audio tab and check the "Use error correction" box in the Playback area (see Figure 4-16).

> While error correction may prevent small errors in the audio data from becoming obnoxious audio anomalies, the feature can cause brief skips on the disc.

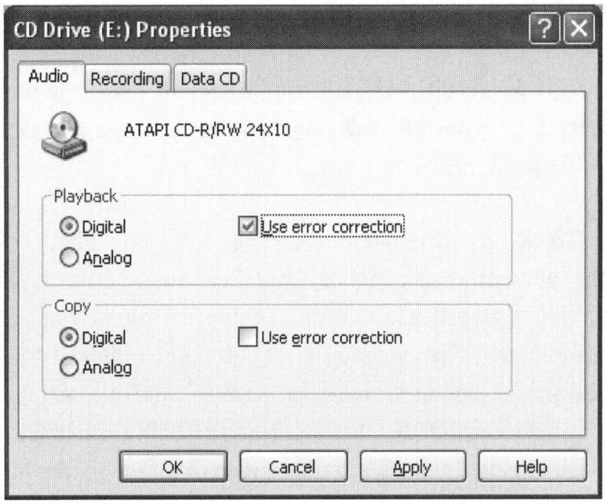

Figure 4-16. Use error correction to ease slight audio anomalies in your music discs.

MUSIC PLAYER ANNOYANCES

CAN'T INSTALL MULTIPLE MUSIC PLAYERS

The Annoyance: Why do I have trouble installing more than one music player on my PC?

The Fix: Two words: software incompatibilities. For example, if you install Musicmatch (*http://www.musicmatch.com*) after Liquid Audio Player 6.01 (*http://www.liquidaudio.com*) under Windows XP, a known CD drive compatibility issue can wreak havoc. What can you do? Check for upgrades from the music software vendors. Often a quick patch will ease compatibility problems. In some cases, however, it may be necessary to uninstall all of your player applications and then reinstall only one.

Also check with your CD drive manufacturer for a CD drive firmware update. For example, Plextor CD-R drive owners can download a bootable patch directly from the Plextor web site (*http://www.plextor.com*) to resolve the conflict between Musicmatch and Liquid Audio Player.

REVENGE OF THE CODECS

The Annoyance: When I try to play common MP3 files, I get an error saying Windows Media Player cannot support the file type.

The Fix: Do you remember the importance of codecs for your multimedia applications? (See "Multimedia Player Asks for a Codec" earlier in this chapter). If you attempt to play an MP3 file and the player software stops and tells you that it cannot support the file type, your file was not created as a *true* MP3. In fact, it was probably ripped with a nonstandard or incompatible codec that renders the file unreadable on other "standard" player applications.

> **tip**
>
> Subscription-based music download services such as Rhapsody (*http://www.listen.com*) typically distribute nonstandard file types you can play only in their *own* player software. These are not true MP3 files. True MP3 files can be played in any multimedia player that supports the original Fraunhoffer MP3 codec.

Try playing the file in other players (such as iTunes for Windows). If the file plays on one application but not others, the file is likely intact, but you probably have a nonstandard music file. Go back and download (or re-rip) a true MP3 version of the music track. If, however, the file won't play on *any* player (and you're sure that it's a real MP3 file), either the file might be damaged or you don't have an MP3 codec on your system. Check with the music software maker for software/codec updates, or uninstall and reinstall the player software from scratch.

MP3 PLAYER NOT RECOGNIZED

The Annoyance: I connected my Nomad Jukebox 3 MP3 player to my PC via USB, but I see a big yellow exclamation mark next to it in the Device Manager.

The Fix: Open the System control panel, click the Hardware tab, and then click the Device Manager button. Make sure no yellow exclamation marks appear next to the USB Root Hub entry and the corresponding USB Universal Host Controller entry. You need to resolve any problems with your USB ports for your USB devices to operate properly (see "Detecting USB Drives" in Chapter 1 and similar USB annoyances from that chapter).

If only the MP3 player has a yellow exclamation mark, reinstall the drivers. Double-click the player to open its Properties dialog box, click the Drivers tab, and then click the Update Driver button to launch the "Found New Hardware Wizard." Choose the "Install the software automatically (Recommended)" option, and use the driver CD that accompanied the player. Once properly installed, the system should recognize the player.

MP3 PLAYER DOESN'T SEE ALL MUSIC FILES

The Annoyance: My Creative Labs PlayCenter software sees only some of the tunes on my MP3 player. Is it trying to tell me I have bad taste in music?

The Fix: First, clear the MP3 player software's cache on your PC. For Creative's PlayCenter under Windows XP, delete the *.NJB* file from the following folder:

C:\Documents and Settings\All Users\Application Data\Creative\PlayCenter2\Cache

Once you clear the cache folder, search the drive and delete any other instances of *.NJB* files.

> **tip**
>
> Once you delete the cache file, it may take several minutes for Creative's PlayCenter to create a new list of available tunes.

A software conflict between PlayCenter and other audio player software installed on your computer could also cause this problem. Uninstall PlayCenter, along with any other audio players on your system, such as RealPlayer, WinAmp, Musicmatch, and so on. Reboot the computer and reinstall only PlayCenter.

CAN'T SEARCH LARGE MUSIC COLLECTIONS

The Annoyance: I can't navigate large collections of music files using my Nomad MuVo MP3 player.

The Fix: This annoyance strikes the MuVo, but you may see similar issues with other MP3 players. It seems that older firmware versions ("BIOS" for the device) make it difficult to browse MP3, WAV, and WMA files. To correct the problem, download a firmware upgrade (Version 1.40.12 or later) for the MuVo at *http://www.nomadworld. com/downloads/firmware/*.

Next, connect the MuVo in "recovery" mode (press and hold the Play button for 10 seconds while inserting the unit into a USB port). Then just double-click the firmware upgrade file to launch the installer and follow the instructions. When finished, close the installer and remove the MuVo. Of course, refer to the specific instructions for your particular device whenever updating firmware on your music player.

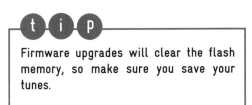

tip

Firmware upgrades will clear the flash memory, so make sure you save your tunes.

MP3 PLAYER ABSENT FROM MY COMPUTER

The Annoyance: My Nomad MuVo shows up in the Device Manager, but not in My Computer.

The Fix: Players like the MuVo will appear as a "Removable Disk" or "USB Mass Storage Device" in Windows Explorer or My Computer. If Windows XP does not map the USB device to a proper drive letter, you may need to tackle this manually. This problem occurs with the MuVo and other USB flash drive type devices.

First, connect the player to an available USB port and close any network connections. Next, reboot the system and make sure you log on with an Administrator account (or another user account with full administrative privileges). The MuVo should appear as a Removable Disk in My Computer. If not, try the unit in another USB port.

Once you see the Removable Disk listed, open the Administrative Tools control panel, then double-click the Computer Management icon. Browse the Storage → Disk Management area, right-click the MuVo's drive letter, and choose "Change Drive Letter and Paths" (see Figure 4-17). Select the MuVo's drive letter, click the Change button, and change the letter to one not currently used on the system (e.g., change E to H). Now restart the computer and log onto the network if necessary. The MuVo should appear as a Removable Disk with the new letter in My Computer.

Figure 4-17. Use the Computer Management panel to change the drive letter for your removable disk device.

PC WON'T SEE MP3 PLAYER

The Annoyance: I connected my Nomad MuVo MP3 player to my PC's USB port, but the PC failed to recognize it.

The Fix: First, plug a USB mouse in the port. If the mouse works, you know the USB port is active. If not, the trouble is in the port, not the MP3 player. Also, make sure you installed the latest drivers for your player. Windows XP does not need additional drivers because it treats players such as the MuVo as Removable Disk storage devices (just like a regular disk drive); however, older versions of Windows will require supporting drivers.

If the system still refuses to recognize the MP3 player, Creative Labs suggests you reformat the drive. Simply insert the MuVo into a USB port, select Start → All Programs → Creative → Nomad MuVo → Format, and then click the Start button to begin the formatting process. After formatting, the device should be detected normally. If the problem persists, reformat the drive again using the Creative Labs formatter with the "recover" option.

> **tip**
>
> If you use the regular Windows formatter on your MP3 player, you will reformat the player as a disk drive, rendering it useless as an MP3 player.

FILE TRANSFERS SLOW AFTER FORMATTING MP3 PLAYER

The Annoyance: I formatted my Nomad MuVo MP3 player, but now it transfers files very slowly.

The Fix: You probably reformatted the MP3 player using the native Windows formatter utility instead of the formatter included with the Creative Labs software. The player continues to work fine as a data storage unit, but no longer serves as an MP3 player. In this case, you need to recover the player.

For the MuVo, press and hold the Play button while you insert the player into a USB port. Hold the Play button for another 10 seconds or so to activate recovery mode. Now click Start → All Programs → Creative → Nomad MuVo → Format. The formatter will detect the unit in recovery mode, and a warning will tell you to wait until the device LED turns red. Reopen the formatter, click the Media Recovery tab, and click the Start button (see Figure 4-18). When the recovery finishes, click the Media Format tab and click the Start button to format the unit.

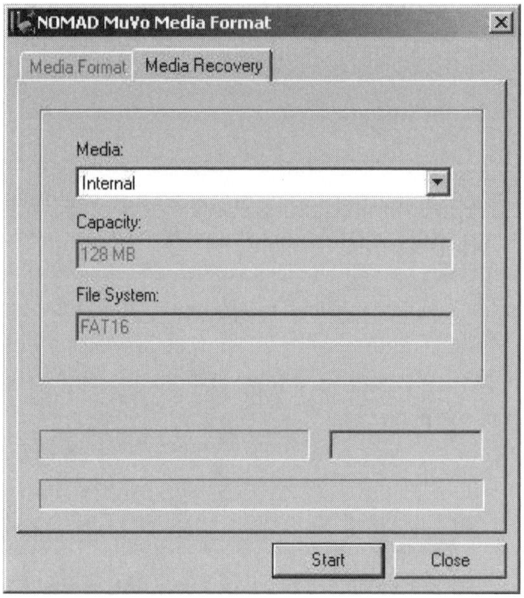

Figure 4-18. Use the Media Recovery feature to restore an improperly formatted Nomad MuVo.

> **tip**
>
> If your software does not offer an Emergency Media Recovery mode, uninstall the latest drivers and reinstall the original (older) drivers.

MP3 players are basically a block of flash memory with some firmware used to operate controls, manage music files, and handle playback of MP3 files. Windows treats MP3 players such as Creative Labs' MuVo and other USB flash storage devices as removable drives. Drives must be formatted before the operating system can access files on the device. However, players such as the MuVo might not accept the generic Windows format process—formatting a device under Windows might overwrite the firmware (also recorded on the flash memory) and disable the player capability. In effect, a Windows format might turn the player into a simple flash drive, forcing you to recover the firmware to restore the player's operation. Always opt to use the player's "format" feature provided through its software application.

Note that later versions of the MuVo firmware *will* support the native Windows formatter (FAT16/FAT32, not NTFS). Check with the player manufacturer for their current firmware version—just make sure it addresses the Windows formatting issue before you install it.

GETTING MORE BATTERY LIFE

The Annoyance: My music player sounds great, but I have to constantly replace the batteries.

The Fix: A typical player will usually provide 4–6 hours of music from a set of batteries (a bit less if you recharge the unit or crank the volume). However, a flash memory–type player typically draws power only when you play tunes. In this case, check your music files. For example, WMA files produce superior sound quality but drain the batteries faster. See if you get better battery life with MP3 versions of the same tunes.

A firmware upgrade for your music player may correct the battery problem. Contact the player manufacturer for firmware updates and a list of corrections.

HANDLING IPOD FILE EXCLAMATIONS

The Annoyance: When I turn on my iPod music player, I see a folder with an exclamation mark.

The Fix: If you use an Apple iPod on a Windows-based PC, make sure you install the latest iPod Windows software for your specific model. Otherwise, Windows may not recognize the iPod. For example, a 10GB iPod can use software to Version 1.3, while a later 10GB iPod with a Dock Connector can only use Versions 2.1 and above. If you're not sure exactly which iPod model you have, use the latest iPod Updater software from Apple to install the latest software for your particular iPod model (available at *http://www.apple.com/support/downloads/ipodupdater.html*).

The unit may also be short of power. A discharged iPod may not identify itself to the host PC. Charge the iPod or connect the external power adapter. Finally, the iPod's internal hard disk may have been improperly formatted. As

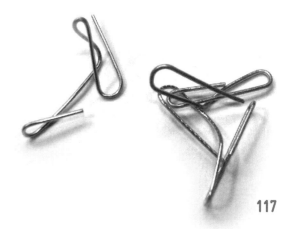

a rule, you should never format the iPod. If you do, use the iPod Software Updater utility to recover the unit. If the problem persists, return the unit to Apple for service.

TOOLS OF THE TRADE

Most audio utilities are installed with Windows or provided with your sound device. Still, several services might attract the interest of any audiophile:

Musicmatch Jukebox 8.2 (http://www.musicmatch.com)

> **A premium download service for music enthusiasts.**

RealOne Rhapsody (http://www.rhapsody.com)

> **Another premium download service for music enthusiasts.**

CNET's Bandwidth Meter (http://reviews.cnet.com/7004-7254_7-0.html)

> **Allows you to measure the performance of your Internet connection to get the most from your streaming media.**

5

Hard Drive
ANNOYANCES

I love flashy sound and video as much as the next geek, but hard drive technology has always impressed me. Those little electromechanical marvels can spin tiny steel platters at thousands of revolutions per minute, while delicate read-write heads skim the surface on a microscopic cushion of air. Yet the drives store hundreds of gigabytes of data error-free, access that data in a matter of moments, and (at least theoretically) run for up to 30 years without breaking down. Heck, I have to jiggle the handle just to get my toilet to stop gurgling.

But like most other PC components, hard drives can be finicky, and because today's computers absolutely rely on proper drive operation, any trouble can result in system performance problems and file loss—trashing days (even weeks) of your hard work. This chapter covers a multitude of hard drive annoyances. It starts by addressing a bevy of configuration annoyances (ones you'll likely encounter when adding or replacing a drive), and then looks at ways to perk up drive performance. It also includes a series of maintenance fixes that will keep your drive error-free, and finally examines a range of backup and restoration issues to protect your important work.

CONFIGURATION ANNOYANCES

DRIVE GOES MISSING

The Annoyance: I can't access my internal hard drive and it no longer appears in the list of hardware detected by the BIOS at boot time.

The Fix: Power down and open the PC, and make sure the 4-pin power connector is securely attached to the drive. Also, secure the nearby ribbon or serial data cable at both ends (the drive end and the motherboard end).

If the system won't detect a newly installed hard drive, check the drive ID jumpers. ATA-type drives use "master" and "slave" (and "cable select") jumper designations to assign the drive ID. A single hard drive should always be set to "master." A secondary hard drive should be jumpered as a "slave." Refer to the drive documentation (or markings on the drive itself) for specific jumper locations. SCSI drives are a little different. SCSI hard drives typically use ID0 for the boot drive, but subsequent drives can use higher IDs, such as ID1, ID2, and so on.

DRIVE SPACE SHORTFALL

The Annoyance: Why does my system only see 137GB of a 200GB drive? Otherwise, the drive seems to format and operate fine.

The Fix: You run into this common capacity barrier with huge hard drives. Ideally, the system BIOS should query and configure the drive, allowing you to utilize the whole drive. If not, the BIOS or operating system effectively "cuts off" any unrecognized drive capacity. Fortunately, this annoyance has several possible remedies:

Upgrade your BIOS, especially if the motherboard is more than two years old. Since most drive capacity limits are BIOS-related, a motherboard BIOS upgrade will often ease the problem. However, always check the README files associated with any new BIOS. If the update does not specifically address capacity limits, don't bother with a BIOS upgrade.

Update the operating system. Older operating systems (such as Windows 98) have problems creating and operating huge partitions. Drive manufacturers, such as Maxtor (*http://www.maxtor.com*), recommend you upgrade to Windows 2000 with Service Pack 3 (or later) or Windows XP with Service Pack 1 (or later). Once updated, you may also need a specific patch from the drive manufacturer. For example, the Maxtor Big Drive Enabler (with the clever filename *big_drive_enabler.exe*) will automatically update the Windows registry for huge drive support.

Use a new drive controller. Consider a new PCI drive controller card with 48-bit logical block addressing (LBA) support. For example, both the Maxtor Ultra ATA/133 PCI card and Promise Technology Ultra133 TX2 PCI card (*http://www.promise.com*) support huge drives. They bypass the system BIOS and OS drivers and provide their own onboard firmware and drivers.

MAKING A DRIVE IDENTIFICATION

The Annoyance: I need to repartition and reformat the PC I inherited (and probably reinstall the correct drive overlay software). How do I figure out the hard drive make and manufacturer?

The Fix: Locate the drive ID in the BIOS hardware list at boot time. The BIOS queries the drive hardware and lists the model for you (such as in Figure 1-7 in Chapter 1). However, you need to be quick because the hardware list appears for only a few moments before the operating system starts to load.

You can also open the System control panel, click the Hardware tab, click the Device Manager button, and expand the "Disk drives" entry (see Figure 5-1). Western Digital (*http://www.wdc.com*) drive models use

"WD" prefixes (e.g., WD1000BB drive); Seagate (*http://www.seagate.com*) uses "ST" prefixes; and Maxtor drives (*http://www.maxtor.com*) use alphanumerical designations (e.g., 6Y120L0). Of course, to be completely sure, open the PC and locate the drive label listing the manufacturer and part number. Next, visit the manufacturer's web site and download the corresponding overlay software (such as MaxBlast or Data Lifeguard Tools).

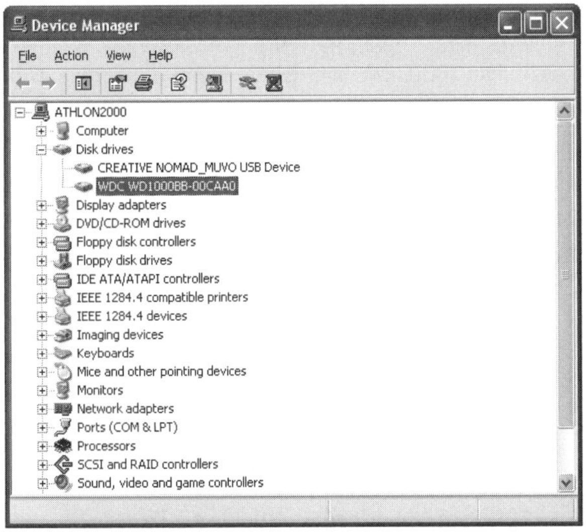

Figure 5-1. The Device Manager is often a good source for drive manufacturer and model information.

> **t i p**
>
> If you open the PC and there is *no* label—sometimes it happens—take the FCC ID number off the drive (every electronic device has one), go to the FCC web site (*http://www.fcc.gov/oet/fccid*), punch in the code, and find the product model and maker.

Overlay Software

Most hard drives ship with "overlay" (or Dynamic Drive Overlay) software, which augments the system BIOS and allows the operating system to overcome some drive space limitations. Of course, you should use the DDO software only as a last resort because it adds yet another potential drive problem should the DDO software become corrupt.

NEW DRIVE HANGS THE SYSTEM

The Annoyance: I installed a new UDMA hard drive to replace the old one, but now my system hangs.

The Fix: When two or more devices on a cable share the same jumper setting, it can cause serious stability problems. For example, two "master" devices (HDD, CD-RW, or DVD drive) on the same ATA cable, or two or more SCSI devices using the same SCSI ID can result in conflicts. Make sure each device uses unique jumper settings (see the first annoyance in this chapter, "Drive Goes Missing").

Drive capacity limits can also cause system hang-ups. Check for motherboard BIOS updates specifically intended to overcome drive size limits. Otherwise, you may need a new drive controller to support the larger hard drive (see "Drive Space Shortfall" earlier in this chapter).

If your hard drive includes a cylinder (or capacity) limitation jumper (CLJ), enable the CLJ pin on your drive and reboot the system. If the BIOS now detects the drive automatically without hanging the system, continue partitioning and formatting the drive using the manufacturer's overlay software (e.g., MaxBlast Plus II for Maxtor drives). If the system still hangs, power down the system and return the CLJ to its original position.

In a few cases, the BIOS may not be able to detect the drive automatically. If problems persist, you may need to configure the drive parameters manually. Power down the PC and remove the new drive. Now reboot the system into the System Setup and locate the drive setup entries (opt to configure the corresponding drive manually instead of automatically). Select a User Definable drive type with 1,024 cylinders, heads, and 63 sectors. Set LBA to normal or standard, and set the Write Pre Comp (WpCom) and Landing Zone (LZ) entries to zero. Save your settings, power down and reconnect the drive, then boot the system.

FDISK REPORTS WRONG DISK SPACE

The Annoyance: I'm resurrecting an older PC and installing a used 100GB hard drive for more space, but FDISK only sees 36GB of the drive during partitioning.

The Fix: This problem occurs with older versions of FDISK (available under Windows 95 and Windows 98/SE). Older versions only recognize hard drive partitions up to 64GB. When FDISK encounters a larger drive, it subtracts 64GB from the total size. For example, an 80GB hard drive would be reported as 16GB and a 100GB drive would be reported as 36GB. One solution is simply to upgrade Windows to a newer version, such as Windows XP. However, you can download a patch from Microsoft to correct this particular problem in Windows 95 and 98/SE. Search the Knowledge Base (*http://support.microsoft.com/default.aspx?scid=fh;EN-US;KBJUMP*) for article 263044.

---

40 VERSUS 80

While early hard drives used 40-pin/40-wire cables, today's hard drives rely on 40-pin/80-wire cables. The additional 40 wires help eliminate unwanted electrical noise that might affect data signals going to and from high-speed UDMA/66, UDMA/100, and UDMA/133 drives. Whenever you use UDMA/66 or faster drives, use good-quality 40-pin/80-wire ribbon cables. Otherwise, the drive interface will "downshift" to lower UDMA/33 performance.

FIDDLING WITH FDISK

FDISK is a DOS-based partitioning utility (available under Windows 95, 98, and Me). You can use it to prepare (partition) a new hard drive for formatting as well as to delete and check the current partitions on a disk. Today, more advanced partition management utilities, such as Symantec's Partition Magic (*http://www.partitionmagic.com/partitionmagic/*), offer additional features and better user interfaces. Remember to use extreme caution when you work with disk partitions, or you could render your data inaccessible. Before you start, always create a backup of your important work.

DISK SHOWS LESS SPACE IN SYSTEM

The Annoyance: I installed a 200GB hard drive, but Windows Explorer reports slightly less space than marked on the box. Did I get ripped off?

The Fix: The PC industry uses two slightly different yardsticks to measure drive space: decimal and binary. Hard drive manufacturers market their products in terms of decimal capacity. In decimal notation, one Megabyte (MB) is equal to 1,000,000 bytes, and one Gigabyte (GB) is equal to 1,000,000,000 bytes. However, programs such as FDISK, system BIOS, and Windows (see the Drive Properties dialog in Figure 5-2) use the binary (or base 2) numbering system.

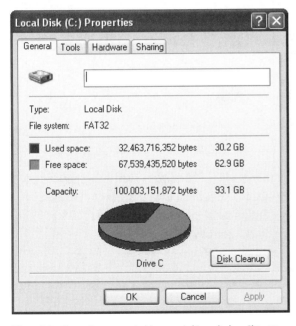

Figure 5-2. Most software reports drive space in binary (or base 2) terms.

In the binary numbering system, one Megabyte is equal to 1,048,576 bytes, and one Gigabyte is equal to 1,073,741,824 bytes. As a result, the programs just mentioned calculate the storage space a bit lower. For example, a tool like FDISK

will report 186.26GB (200,000,000,000/1,073,742,824) rather than the 200GB claimed by the manufacturer. Neither measure is really "wrong," but the difference between the two can throw you off.

DRIVES WON'T PLAY NICE TOGETHER

The Annoyance: I installed a second hard drive, but they won't work together. I reversed the drives, but they still misbehave.

The Fix: Drives that strictly adhere to ATA standards should operate together on the same cable (channel) without interfering with each other. Unfortunately, not every drive model and vintage implements the ATA standard perfectly, so some drives simply do not work well together.

If you reverse the primary/secondary (or "master/slave") relationship of the drives, it usually clears the trouble. But if two drives do not work well regardless of their primary/secondary relationship, separate the drives onto different ATA channels. For example, keep the main drive as the "master" device on the first channel, and place the new drive on the secondary channel (perhaps keep the unit as a "slave" device along with an existing master CD-RW or DVD drive). No space on the secondary channel? Install a UDMA PCI controller card, such as the Maxtor Ultra ATA/133 PCI card or the Promise Technology Ultra133 TX2 PCI card, and then simply cable the new drive to the PCI card. Adding a PCI-based drive controller should not interfere with the drive controllers currently on your motherboard—you can usually run drives from both controllers—but it may be easier to just disable the motherboard controller (through the System Setup) and use the PCI controller card exclusively. Be sure to check the documentation for your new controller card for any caveats.

USING CABLE SELECT

The Annoyance: My brother uses something called CSEL to distinguish his hard drives automatically. Why am I stuck using drive jumpers instead?

The Fix: You're not stuck, but using Cable Select (CS or CSEL) is a bit more involved than you might think. CSEL is an optional feature in the ATA specification. Rather than using drive jumpers to determine the "master/slave" relationship of your drives, you set the drives to their CSEL jumper positions, and a special cable makes the choice for you. In practice, it always considers the "master" drive to be the one connected to the end of the cable and the "slave" drive to the one attached to the middle connector. You need three items to support CSEL:

- Drives with CSEL jumper options
- A CSEL-compliant ribbon cable
- A drive controller with CSEL support

> **t i p**
>
> Always double-check the drive jumpers and make sure each drive uses a unique designation. Do not use the "cable select" designation unless you use a cable specially designed for that purpose.

CSEL may seem easier, but you need a specialized and more expensive cable than the typical 40-pin/80-wire cable. Even drive manufacturers such as Maxtor recommend you stick with your conventional "master/slave" settings unless your computer is cabled for CSEL already. But if you insist on experimenting with Cable Select, you can purchase CSEL cables from vendors such as Stonewall Cable (*http://www.stonewallcable.com*).

PIO MODE REPORT IS FALSE

The Annoyance: I know that my drive is in UDMA mode, but why does Windows 2000 report it as PIO mode? Does this mean that my drive is performing poorly?

The Fix: Without Service Pack 2 (or later), all UDMA devices default to UDMA/66 or a PIO mode under Windows 2000. Simply use the Update Windows wizard, or visit the Microsoft Support Site (*http://support.microsoft.com*) and

search for "service packs." You can download Service Pack 4 from *http://www.microsoft.com/downloads/*.

ATA PERFORMANCE

The venerable IDE (ATA) interface just keeps getting faster and faster. Each generation of interface has a higher maximum (burst) performance level:

Interface	Maximum speed (in MB/s)
PIO 0	3.3
PIO 1	5.2
PIO 2	8.3
PIO 3	11.1
PIO 4	16.6
UDMA/33 (Mode 3)	33
UDMA/66 (Mode 4)	66
UDMA/100 (Mode 5)	100
UDMA/133 (Mode 6)	133
SATA/150	150

Serial ATA (SATA) delivers even faster performance, with burst data transfers to 150MB/s. Future serial interfaces will reach 300MB/s bursts and beyond.

SILENCING THE LOW DISK SPACE ALARM

The Annoyance: How do I disable the annoying low disk space warning that pops up on my screen?

The Fix: Windows will automatically offer to run the Disk Cleanup utility whenever your disk runs short of free space. While this feature protects the system from unexpected crashes or data loss, it annoys the heck out of a lot of people. If you can't stand Windows telling you what to do, you can edit the Registry to turn off the low space warning. Select Start → Run, enter `regedit`, and click the OK button. When the Registry Editor starts, browse to the following key (see Figure 5-3):

*HKEY_CURRENT_USER\Software\Microsoft\Windows\
CurrentVersion\Policies\Explorer*

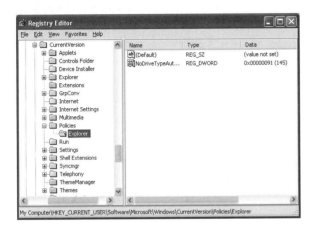

Figure 5-3. Use the Registry Editor to stop those pesky low disk warnings, but do so at your own peril.

After you browse to this key, create a new DWORD value and name it **NoLowDiskSpaceChecks**. (Use the Registry Editor's Help feature if you're not sure how to create a new DWORD value.) Double-click this new item, enter a value of **1**, click the OK button, and exit the Registry Editor.

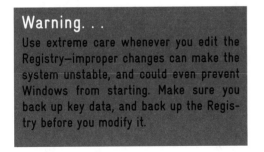

Warning. . .
Use extreme care whenever you edit the Registry—improper changes can make the system unstable, and could even prevent Windows from starting. Make sure you back up key data, and back up the Registry before you modify it.

Too timid to tinker with the Registry? You can use a low disk space notification utility such as Space Patrol from JD Design (*http://www.jddesign.co.uk*). Suitable for any

version of Windows, Space Patrol lets you tweak the threshold levels (see Figure 5-4), and easily enable or disable the notification on any of your disk drives. Of course, you could also just upgrade the hard drive to a larger model, or add a second hard drive to hold your files and applications.

Figure 5-4. Third-party tools such as Space Patrol automate the control of your system's low space warnings.

ADDING SERIAL ATA DRIVES

The Annoyance: Can I add a serial ATA drive to my computer without ripping out the existing UDMA drives?

The Fix: You *can* employ serial ATA drives and ordinary UDMA drives in the same computer, but you need two separate drive controllers. For example, simply add a serial ATA (or SATA) PCI adapter card, such as the SATA150 TX4 from Promise Technology (*http://www.promise.com*). In this situation, the system will continue to boot from the original UDMA drive(s) connected to the motherboard controller; the SATA drives will simply provide you with additional storage space for programs and multimedia. However, some motherboards (such as the Tyan Thunder

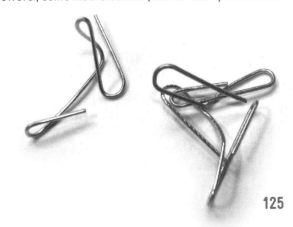

8KW) offer both SATA and UDMA interfaces, which eliminates the need for the extra card. Before you buy any motherboard, carefully review the specifications to determine the available onboard drive interfaces.

SCSI PERFORMANCE

SCSI drives are still a popular choice for file servers and other "performance-computing" platforms. As with ATA, SCSI speeds have evolved to keep pace with advances in technology. The performance of the most popular SCSI standards can be broken down as follows:

SCSI standard	Speed (in MB/s)
SCSI-1	5
Fast SCSI (SCSI-2)	10
Wide SCSI (SCSI-2/3)	20
UltraSCSI (SCSI-3)	20
UltraWide SCSI (SCSI-3)	40
Ultra2 SCSI (SCSI-4)	40
Ultra2 Wide SCSI (SCSI-4)	80
Ultra3 SCSI (Ultra 160)	80
Ultra3 Wide SCSI (Ultra 160)	160
Ultra4 SCSI (Ultra 320)	160
Ultra4 Wide SCSI (Ultra320)	320

RECOGNIZING SCSI DRIVES

The Annoyance: My system fails to recognize my new SCSI drive.

The Fix: SCSI devices need a SCSI adapter (called a Host Bus Adapter or HBA), such as the Adaptec 39320A Ultra320 SCSI adapter (*http://www.adaptec.com*). Open the System control panel, click the Hardware tab, click the Device Manager button, and look under the "SCSI and RAID controllers" entry. If you don't see your SCSI controller, review your documentation for the SCSI adapter and make sure you installed it properly. If the system won't recognize the SCSI adapter, remove (or disable) the SCSI adapter and install a different make and model.

If your system does see the adapter, check the SCSI cabling and termination between the adapter and drive. By default, the SCSI adapter is terminated; make sure you terminate the last SCSI device on your ribbon cable (often by setting a jumper on the SCSI drive as per the manufacturer's instructions). When you install a new SCSI drive, you may need to rearrange the order of the drives on your SCSI ribbon cable. (Remember: only the *last* device should be terminated).

SCSI devices also employ a unique ID (from 0 to 6). Hard drives use ID0 and ID1, CD/DVD drives and scanners use ID2 through ID6, and the SCSI controller is assigned to ID7. Check the SCSI ID on your drive and make sure it does not conflict with any other SCSI devices on the ribbon cable.

PERFORMANCE ANNOYANCES

GETTING PEAK PERFORMANCE

The Annoyance: My hard drive seems slower than molasses in January. What can I do to get the most from my drive?

The Fix: Before you go off on a fool's errand, use a benchmark such as PCMark04 Pro from Futuremark (*http://www.futuremark.com*) to measure your hard drive performance before and after you make some changes. When you compare the numbers, you will know just how much things improved, instead of saying "gee, it seems faster." Here are some tactics to improve your drive's performance:

Clean up the drive. Use Disk Cleanup to empty your Recycle Bin, clear away cookies, remove temporary files, and erase other unneeded junk from your drive.

Select Start → Control Panel → Performance and Maintenance → Free up space on your hard disk. Select the categories to clean and click the OK button (see Figure 5-5). You'd be amazed how clearing a cache can perk up a system.

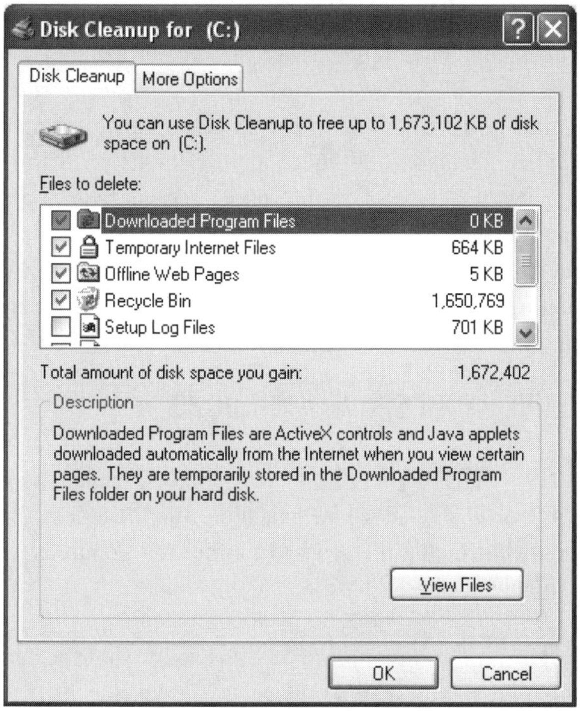

Figure 5-5. Clean up unnecessary files from the drive.

Defragment the drive. Files can become broken up and scattered across your hard drive, forcing the drive to seek out all of the file's parts when loading and saving. This extra work reduces performance and can shorten the drive's working life. Defragmenting the drive rearranges the files so that each part of every file is contiguous. To make programs run faster, select Start → Control Panel → Performance and Maintenance → "Rearrange items on your hard disk." Analyze the disk first, and then defragment the volume (see Figure 5-6).

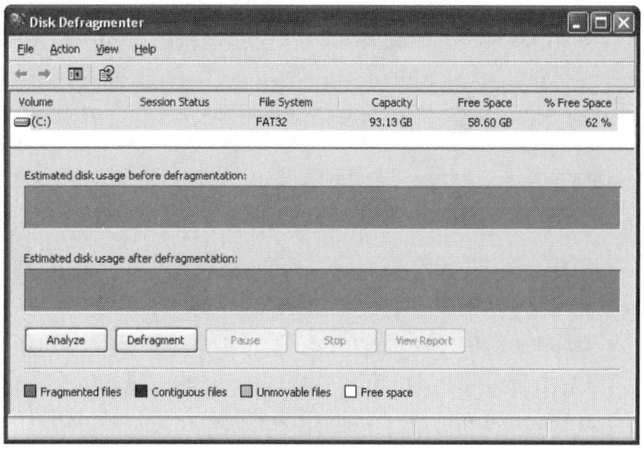

Figure 5-6. Defragment the drive to rearrange and organize scattered file clusters.

Check the data transfer mode. Data is transferred using a PIO or UDMA mode (such as UDMA/100 or UDMA/133). You get best performance by using the fastest possible interface supported by your drive and controller. For example, if you have a UDMA/133 drive and controller in the system, make sure Windows operates in the UDMA/133 mode. Open the System control panel, click the Hardware tab, and then click the Device Manager button. Expand the "IDE ATA/ATAPI controllers" entry, right-click the Primary IDE Channel entry, select Properties, and click the Advanced Settings tab (see Figure 5-7).

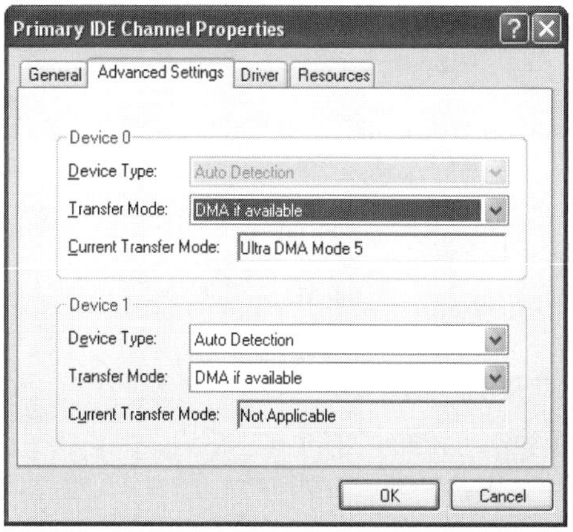

Figure 5-7. Utilize the optimum data transfer mode for your drives and controllers.

Make sure you set the Transfer Mode to "DMA if available." PIO modes are too old and slow to take advantage of today's hard drives. Repeat these steps for the second IDE channel.

Enable write caching. Write caching puts the data to be written to disk into RAM; the system writes to the drive when time is available. This feature will not make the drive run any faster, but it lets applications regain control faster (rather than waiting for the drive to finish writing). With the Device Manager still open, expand the "Disk drives" entry, right-click the hard drive, select Properties, and then click the Policies tab. Check the "Enable write caching on this disk" box and click the OK button.

Check your cables. Drive cabling can sometimes cause poor performance. Open the system and examine the cabling between the drives and controller ports. Securely attach each cable and replace any cut, scuffed, crimped, or otherwise damaged ribbon cable. If you work with UDMA/66 to UDMA/133 drives, make sure you use a 40-pin/80-wire cable.

Update Windows. A service pack can sometimes boost your storage speed. Check the Windows Update feature to load any Service Packs or patches that enhance your operating system. Also make sure you install the correct motherboard drivers from the manufacturer. For example, Via and Intel both have specific IDE drivers to configure the motherboard chipset for high-performance IDE operation.

After you work through these steps, remember to run the benchmark utility again and measure any difference in performance.

RECOVERING DRIVE PARAMETERS

The Annoyance: My CMOS battery failed and I lost my setup parameters. I replaced the battery and reloaded the BIOS defaults, but now the drive seems a little slow. Maybe it's just my imagination, but can I tweak drive performance by adjusting the translation mode or parameters in the System Setup?

The Fix: It's not worth the trouble. If you're an "old timer" like me, you remember the days when you needed to specify cylinders, sectors, heads, and landing zones, and write pre-compensation parameters manually (from the drive maker's documentation). Today's hard drives are "intelligent" enough to inform the BIOS of their parameters and capacities automatically.

You should, however, consider the type of defaults you load. Most BIOS provide for basic (called *failsafe* or *compatibility*) defaults and improved performance-oriented (*optimal*) defaults. Although both defaults have little impact on drive performance directly, using failsafe defaults may slow other aspects of the system (such as memory timing). Load the optimal defaults and see if you notice a difference; otherwise, try the tips in "Getting Peak Performance" earlier in this chapter.

DRIVE WON'T SHOW IN WINDOWS

The Annoyance: I installed a second hard drive on my Windows XP machine. The BIOS sees the drive, but it doesn't appear in either My Computer or Windows Explorer.

The Fix: You forgot to partition and format the new drive (duh). Fortunately, Windows XP makes it easy to prepare a secondary hard drive for service. Open the Administrative Tools control panel, double-click the Computer Management icon, and click the Disk Management entry (see Figure 5-8).

The Initialize and Convert Disk Wizard should start to initialize the new drive. Once initialized, the drive will appear with an "Unallocated" designation back in the Disk Management panel. Right-click the "Unallocated" region and select the New Partition or Create Partition option from the pop-up menu. There are three steps to creating a partition. First, select a type (such as primary), select a size (usually the entire volume), assign a drive letter, and choose a format (such as NTFS or FAT32). Second, click the Finish button to complete the partition. Third, go back to the drive and select the Format option to prepare the drive volume.

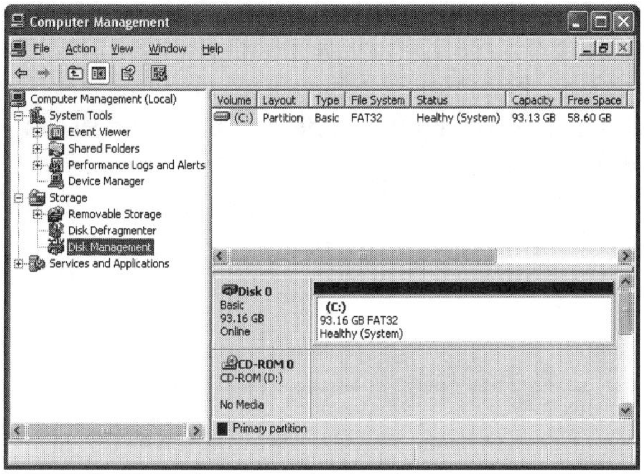

Figure 5-8. Use the Computer Management panel to partition and format new hard drives.

A FIX FOR SLOW DRIVES

The Annoyance: My Maxtor UDMA drive seems to write very slowly.

The Fix: If the cabling and data transfer modes seem fine (see the earlier annoyance "Getting Peak Performance"), the trouble may lie in your drive's "Write Verify" mode. When a manufacturer ships a new hard drive, some particles on the media may shift and cause reliability problems. Maxtor includes a "Write Verify" feature that carefully rereads the data written to a new drive. This additional work slows down the drive's performance, but the feature should be disabled automatically after 10 power (on/off) cycles.

NEAT CABLING CAUSES PROBLEMS

The Annoyance: Right after I tried to sort out the mess of cables inside my PC, I started to get drive errors. What did I do wrong?

The Fix: When electronic signals pass down a wire, they create a small amount of interference in the form of electromagnetic waves (the same principle behind radio).

The fast signals used in today's PCs create even more interference from cables and expansion cards. You probably bundled cables together in close proximity, allowing signals from one wire to efficiently couple to another. Electromagnetic noise effects can include slow system performance, device detection problems, and unexpected error codes or messages. Unfortunately, you need to open your PC and separate your neatly organized cabling. You can always use the case to hide the mess, right?

UNMOUNT EXTERNAL DRIVES FIRST

The Annoyance: Why do I lose files when I disconnect my external hard drive from the USB port?

The Fix: External hard drives or CD/DVD rewriters offer some terrific mobility benefits for PC users, but they *do* impose a few rules when it comes to disconnection. A USB port will automatically detect and mount an external drive. However, you should unmount the drive before you disconnect it from the USB port. You certainly *could* just yank the cable, but you risk losing any unsaved (perhaps cached) data. Unmounting the drive ensures that all open files are saved and closed, and that the system is ready for a disconnect once the drive is idle.

Click the "Safely remove hardware" icon in the Windows System Tray. A list of possible devices will appear. Click the device you want to unmount. Once the system tells you that the device is ready to be disconnected, just remove the USB cable and power down the drive.

FAST EXTERNAL DRIVES SEEM SLOW

The Annoyance: I connected my external hard drive to a USB 2.0 port, but it still seems slow.

The Fix: Even a new motherboard and its USB 2.0 port won't run at top speed under early versions of Windows 2000 and XP. Windows 2000 has a patch to support USB 2.0, but you should probably upgrade to Service Pack 4. Windows XP requires Service Pack 1 or later for optimum USB 2.0 operation. You can obtain Service

Packs through the Update Windows feature, or by visiting Microsoft's support site (*http://support.microsoft.com*).

Windows 98/SE and Me do not include native support for USB 2.0, so make sure you install the drivers that accompany your USB 2.0 device.

POOR OPERATION FROM INTERNAL DRIVES

The Annoyance: I installed and connected an internal ATA/133 drive, but it delivers terrible performance. I also get constant disk errors.

The Fix: Any time you use a UDMA/66 or faster drive, you must use a short, good-quality, 40-pin/80-wire ribbon cable. If you try to slip by with an old 40-pin cable (or a cable your dog uses as a chew-toy), the drive simply will not work. A fast ATA cable should also measure 18 inches or less (preferably 12).

Always verify that the drive and controller both support optimum speed. For example, using a UDMA/133 drive with a UDMA/100 controller port will limit the drive to UDMA/100 performance levels.

Next, check with the motherboard manufacturer for any BIOS upgrades that address fast ATA drive stability or performance problems. Some systems do not handle optimum speed equally on both ATA channels. For example, the primary channel may support ATA/133, but the secondary channel may only support UDMA/100 (or worse, UDMA/66). In this case, try the drive on the fully compliant UDMA/133 channel. Again, a BIOS upgrade can sometimes correct a difference in speed support.

Mixing speeds can also be problematic. For example, if you use a UDMA/133 and UDMA/66 device on the same channel, the controller is "supposed" to switch speeds to accommodate the different devices, but that doesn't always work properly. Try the UDMA/133 drive by itself on the UDMA/133 controller channel. You may need to relegate the slower device to the secondary controller channel.

Some drives will ship set to a lower operating speed and need a "mode switching" utility to unlock the fastest operating mode. Check the manufacturer's installation instructions and see if you need to run a mode switching utility to enable UDMA/133 operation.

MAINTENANCE ANNOYANCES

DRIVE PERFORMANCE AND VIRTUAL MEMORY

The Annoyance: Can I reduce or disable virtual memory to minimize drive access and increase my system performance?

The Fix: You're treading on some tricky ground here. The operating system sets aside hard drive space and essentially treats it like RAM. This virtual memory (VM) prevents your PC from crashing when real memory runs short. On the downside, VM is a lot slower than true RAM.

If you eliminate VM, you can prevent the operating system from using the drive space as RAM and improve your system performance. But you will not supercharge your system. For example, you may only gain an average of five seconds per minute, the time it takes your system to access VM. Without VM, you will also need to install enough physical RAM to accomodate the applications and their data files. As a rule, do not disable VM without a minimum of 1GB of RAM in the system.

Windows XP lets you control the amount of drive space allocated for VM. Select Start → Control Panel → Performance and Maintenance → "See basic information about your computer." Click the Advanced tab and click the Settings button in the Performance area. In the Performance Options dialog box, click the Advanced tab. Note the amount of space set aside for virtual memory (such as 768MB). To disable VM, choose the "No paging file" option and click the Set button. Otherwise, click the Change button and set a custom size or let Windows manage the VM size automatically (see Figure 5-9).

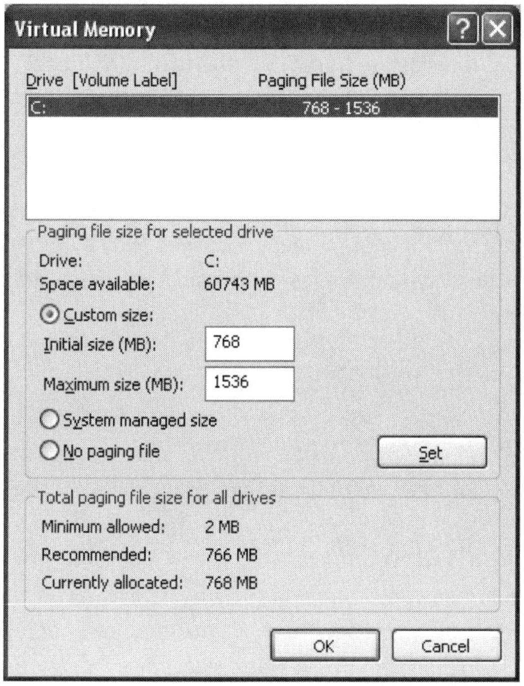

Figure 5-9. Use the Virtual Memory dialog to disable VM or tailor VM to your particular needs.

HANDLING HARD DRIVE NOISE

The Annoyance: My hard drive makes a lot of noise. It sounds like my old rock tumbling kit.

The Fix: Are you sure it's the hard drive? Cooling fans often make far more noise than hard drives. If the drive is indeed the culprit, check the four screws holding the drive in place. Loose screws can allow the drive to vibrate in the chassis (and make a surprising racket).

Remember, too, that all hard drives make some amount of noise. Faster 7,200–10,000 RPM drives tend to run louder than 5,400 RPM drives. Drives from some manufacturers may just be louder than similar drives from other manufacturers.

t i p

Some hard drives support a "quiet mode," which you can set with a utility from the manufacturer. While "quiet mode" reduces the drive noise, it can also reduce the overall performance.

CHECKING AND CORRECTING CORRUPTED FILES

The Annoyance: I'm seeing an increasing number of corrupted files (they won't open, or I get errors when I try to read them), which makes me think there's trouble with my hard drive. How do I see what's going on?

The Fix: ScanDisk will test your drive for file and media problems (and lets you correct many of the errors). Select Start → My Computer, right-click your drive, and choose Properties. Click the Tools tab and then click the Check Now button in the "Error-checking" area. When the Check Disk dialog box opens (Figure 5-10), click the Start button to run the test without checking any options. If ScanDisk returns errors, rerun the test with both disk options selected.

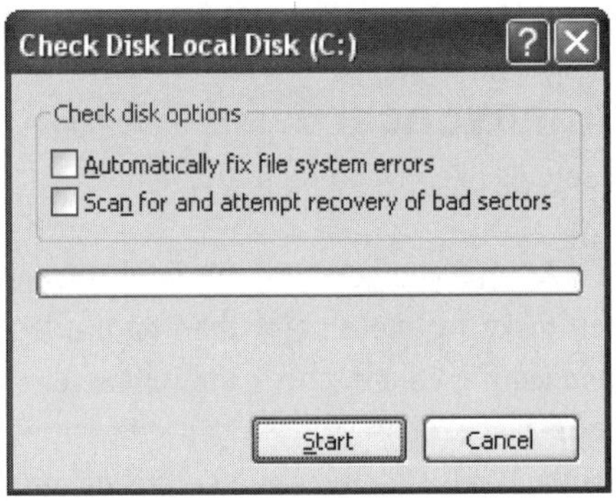

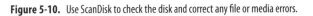
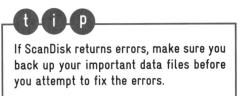

Figure 5-10. Use ScanDisk to check the disk and correct any file or media errors.

> **tip**
>
> If ScanDisk returns errors, make sure you back up your important data files before you attempt to fix the errors.

Make sure you rescan the drive every few days for new errors. If the drive remains error-free, it probably works fine. If, however, you find new errors with increasing frequency, the drive may be headed for failure. Back up and replace the drive at your earliest opportunity.

Two other respected third-party tools ideally suited for detailed diagnostics and file repair or recovery are Symantec's Disk Doctor (*http://www.symantec.com*) and SpinRite 6.0 from Gibson Research (*http://grc.com/spinrite*).

NEW INSTALLATION MAKES DRIVE DISAPPEAR

The Annoyance: I installed a new hard drive, but now my CD-ROM drive has disappeared.

The Fix: Remember that each device on a ribbon cable requires a unique designation (see "Drive Goes Missing"). ATA drives use a "master/slave" relationship, while SCSI drives use ID0 through ID6 (ID7 is for the SCSI controller). When more than one drive uses the same designation, it causes a conflict that prevents one or both of the drives from working.

It may also be a matter of timing. Fast drives (like UDMA/133) don't always reside comfortably with slower devices (like CD/DVD drives) on the same channel. Today's UDMA interface should adjust its speed for slower devices, but it doesn't always accommodate every combination of hardware. This incompatibility can cause slower drives on the same channel to be ignored. The best fix here is to try the optical drive on the secondary drive controller channel.

NEW BIOS BOUNCES ATA DRIVES

The Annoyance: My IDE drives disappeared as soon as I updated my BIOS.

The Fix: You forgot to clear the CMOS RAM and reload your BIOS defaults. Simply set the CMOS Clear jumper on your motherboard (refer to the motherboard manual for the jumper's exact location), cycle power to the PC if necessary (turn it off and then turn it back on—don't just hit the Reset button), then return the CMOS Clear jumper to its original position. Next, boot the PC to the System Setup, load the "optimum" BIOS defaults, and make sure you set all the drive entries to Auto. Save your changes and reboot normally. The BIOS should automatically identify your drives again and load the operating system.

STOPPING USB DRIVE AUTOPLAY

The Annoyance: AutoPlay starts every time I attach my external USB hard drive.

The Fix: When you attach new media or insert a new disc into an external USB CD/DVD drive, Windows XP typically asks you how to deal with the newly detected media. To turn off this feature, select Start → My Computer, right-click the external drive, choose Properties, and then click the AutoPlay tab (Figure 5-11). Choose "Select an action to perform," and then select the "Take no action" option.

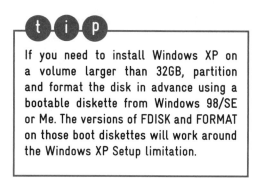

If you need to install Windows XP on a volume larger than 32GB, partition and format the disk in advance using a bootable diskette from Windows 98/SE or Me. The versions of FDISK and FORMAT on those boot diskettes will work around the Windows XP Setup limitation.

Figure 5-11. Tell Windows XP to take no action when your external hard drive is detected.

XP VOLUME IS TOO BIG

The Annoyance: I'm installing Windows XP on my new drive, but a formatting error tells me that the volume is too big.

The Fix: This annoying little Setup issue with Windows XP prevents you from formatting a partition larger than 32GB under the FAT32 file system. Now don't misunderstand me—Windows XP can certainly mount and support volumes larger than 32GB. You just can't format a volume larger than 32GB during Windows XP Setup (blah). If you need to format a partition larger than 32GB, use the NTFS filesystem. Microsoft actually explains this problem thoroughly in KnowledgeBase article Q314463 (*http://support.microsoft.com/default.aspx?scid=fh;EN-US;KBJUMP*).

BETTER TOOLS THAN DEFRAG

The Annoyance: Can I use the Disk Defragmenter utility to defragment critical system files?

The Fix: Disk Defragmenter (lovingly referred to simply as "Defrag") will *not* defragment or relocate critical system files, such as the master file table (MFT) or the swap file (used for virtual memory). You need an industrial-strength tool such as Diskeeper 8.0 from Executive Software International (*http://consumer.execsoft.com*), which quickly handles ordinary defragmentation tasks and also defragments critical system files such as the MFT and swap file (see Figure 5-12).

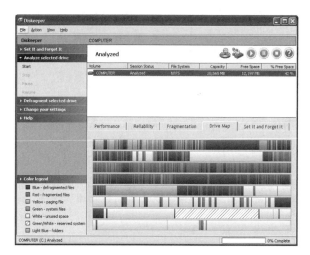

Figure 5-12. Third-party tools such as Diskeeper 8.0 are often superior to standard Windows utilities like Disk Defragmenter.

DEFRAG RESTARTS UNEXPECTEDLY

The Annoyance: Why does Disk Defragmenter report activity and then restart itself?

The Fix: Are you running other applications in the background? Any read/write activity can cause fragmentation. Because Defrag must keep track of the file clusters it moves, any activity can cause a difference between the way Defrag sees clusters and the actual layout of clusters on the drive. Obviously (or not so obviously), this discrepancy can present some serious file problems. To prevent these types of errors, Defrag restarts whenever another application causes disk activity. Before you run Defrag, make sure you close all applications (such as anti-virus checkers and system diagnostic tools), log off of the network, and turn off power-management and screen-saving features.

> **tip**
>
> Run Defrag at night or during other idle periods, such as the weekend. The Windows Task Scheduler is an ideal tool for configuring automatic defragmentation.

FULL DRIVES WON'T DEFRAGMENT

The Annoyance: I want to defragment a partition on my hard drive, but the volume refuses to defragment completely.

The Fix: Defragmentation tools such as Defrag or Diskeeper need some free space (usually up to 15% of the drive's capacity) to sort out and reorganize the file clusters. Extremely full drive volumes may simply run out of room and prevent files (especially large files) from defragmenting properly. Move a few large files to a second hard drive (or CD or DVD media) and defragment the drive again.

Inadequate access privileges can also impact the defragmentation process. Tools such as Diskeeper require an Administrator account. Otherwise, the utility will quit when it encounters a file that cannot be accessed for security reasons.

EMPTIED FILES MIGHT BE UNRECOVERABLE

The Annoyance: I deleted a bunch of files from my PC a few weeks ago, and then I emptied the Recycle Bin. Now I need those files back. I bought a utility that promised to recover those "emptied" files, but it failed to find everything.

The Fix: There's probably nothing you can do at this point. When you "delete" a file to the Recycle Bin, the file still exists on your disk (Windows just put in a different folder). If you need the file later, simply move the file from the Recycle Bin folder to its original location. Easy, right?

But when you "empty" the Recycle Bin, you make those file clusters available to newly created or altered files (though the actual file data remains on the drive platters). In other words, once you "delete" a file and mark its clusters as free, you can still use a utility such as Symantec's Norton Disk Doctor (*http://www.symantec.com*) to locate and reconnect the clusters involved in the file.

Over time, however, the newly created or altered files will use the free clusters and overwrite the old data. At this point, you can no longer recover (at least not fully) the old data. Because you emptied your Recycle Bin a few weeks ago, you will probably not be able to recover all your files. Instead, restore the missing files from a recent backup. (You do have a backup, right?)

BACKUP AND RESTORE ANNOYANCES

BACKUP TOOLS SHOULD SPAN DISCS

The Annoyance: Why does it take only one blank CD to back up my system?

The Fix: This little gotcha bites you at the worst possible time (when you need it most). Not all backup utilities can back up your data across multiple discs (called *spanning*). Because most system backups today easily total 10–20GB or more, make sure you purchase a backup tool that will support spanning (such as Symantec Ghost and DriveImage 7.0). Ideally, the backup tool should also be able to create bootable media that you can use to recover your system (and launch the recovery process) in the event of a hard drive disaster.

Make sure you store your backup media in a secure location along with your other important installation media and system documentation. Remember to mark the backup discs clearly.

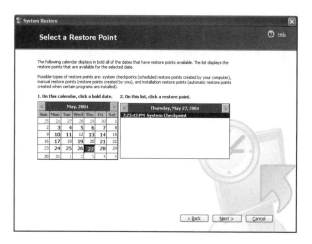

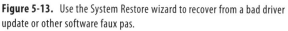

Figure 5-13. Use the System Restore wizard to recover from a bad driver update or other software faux pas.

RECOVERING FROM NEW DRIVERS

The Annoyance: I upgraded a device driver and now my favorite game crashes. Can I remove the new driver and start again?

The Fix: You could simply reinstall the older driver version for your particular device. However, finding the older driver on the original installation CD (or on the manufacturer's web site) can be a real pain. Fortunately, the System Restore feature under Windows XP can return a system to a recent working state. Select Start → All Programs → Accessories → System Tools → System Restore and choose the "Restore my computer to an earlier time" option. Click the Next button, and then follow the wizard to select a recent date prior to your driver installation (see Figure 5-13). You'll need to restart your PC once the selected point is restored.

REMEMBER YOUR BACKUP MEDIA

CD-R discs store 700MB and DVD-R discs hold 4.7GB. Divide the amount of data you have to back up by the capacity of your media (and round up to the next whole number) to determine the number of discs you need for backup. For example, if you're backing up 10GB using CD-R discs, you need (10GB/0.684GB) 14.61 (or 15) discs. If you opt for DVD backups, plan on (10GB/4.7GB) 2.12 (or 3) discs. Backup software will often tell you how many discs you need after you select the files/folders to back up.

DISABLING SYSTEM RESTORE

The Annoyance: I get a lot of prompts from System Restore. How can I turn off this annoying feature?

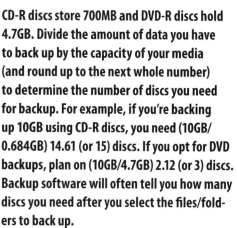

The Fix: If System Restore makes you crazy (or you just want the maximum available space on your drive), open the System control panel and click the System Restore tab (Figure 5-14).

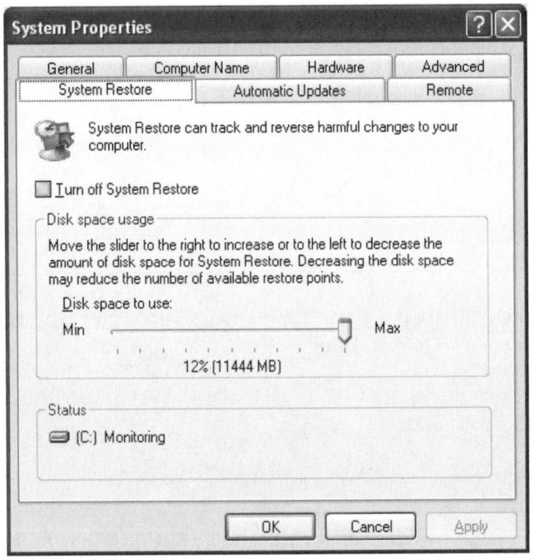

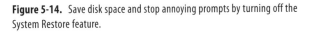

Figure 5-14. Save disk space and stop annoying prompts by turning off the System Restore feature.

If tight drive space is your real demon, ease back on the "Disk space usage" slider. You can pick up a few gigabytes just by dropping the slider to 50% or so. But if you really have it in for System Restore, check the "Turn off System Restore" box, click the Apply button, and then click the OK button.

OVERCOMING A BAD RESTORE POINT

The Annoyance: The Windows XP System Restore tool returned the PC to a really bad point. Can I undo my restoration?

The Fix: You sure can! System Restore lets you undo a restoration if you happen to pick a bad point. Actually, you just need to select a new restore point. Select Start → All Programs → Accessories → System Tools → System Restore and choose the "Restore my computer to an earlier time" option. Click the Next button, and then follow the wizard to select an earlier restore point.

Creating a Restore Point On Demand

System Restore normally creates a restore point each day the system runs successfully, or whenever you install new hardware and software. However, you can always create restore points manually before you make any significant changes to the system. After all, why trust Windows to make a restore point for you? Just launch the System Restore wizard and choose the "Create a restore point" option, then follow the wizard.

MIGRATING TO A NEW DRIVE

The Annoyance: I need more space, so I'm replacing my hard drive with a larger model. Do I have to reinstall the OS and every single bloody application from scratch, or is there a way to transfer things to the new drive?

The Fix: The process of migrating to a new hard drive has always had a little bit of "black magic" associated to it. For most PC users, a new hard drive has meant reinstalling the operating system, drivers, and applications, and copying over their data files from other media. It's a time-consuming and error-prone process. In most cases, you never get the system back to its original glory. However, utilities like Symantec Ghost let you "mirror" the original drive to a new drive, and then simply exchange the new drive in place of the old one.

For example, install the new drive as the secondary (or "slave") hard drive along with your current bootable (or "master") hard drive. (Note: if you already have a secondary hard drive installed, you can temporarily remove it). Install Ghost and use the application to copy the entire contents of your first hard drive, byte by byte, to the second drive. Now remove the old drive and rejumper the new drive as the first ("master") device. When you power on the system, the new drive should look and feel exactly like the one you replaced, with all of your data and system settings in place.

> Some PC experts avoid "true" drive imaging utilities because they transfer any configuration defects, viruses, spyware, and other unwanted things to the new drive. If you feel uncomfortable with imaging, try a "migration" product such as AlohaBob PC-Relocator (*http://www.eisenworld.com/PCRelocator.asp?sub=1*).

LOW SPACE SUSPENDS SYSTEM RESTORE

The Annoyance: I got a message that says System Restore is suspended. How do I get it back?

The Fix: The System Restore feature demands at least 200MB of free space on your boot partition (the drive letter that holds your operating system). When drive space runs low, System Restore is suspended, and you'll see the status change for each hard drive in the Status area of your System Restore tab (see Figure 5-14). To get the System Restore feature back, free up at least 200MB of disk space. Use Disk Cleanup to clear unneeded or temporary files, or use the Add or Remove Programs control panel to uninstall unused programs. Of course, deleting old multimedia images and MP3s (or offloading them to CD/DVD disc) can free a substantial amount of space very quickly.

GHOST WON'T IMAGE TO USB DRIVES

The Annoyance: Why can't I get Symantec Ghost to save or load a drive image from my USB hard drive?

The Fix: How about a sanity check? Try to read and write files to the drive through My Computer. If the drive responds normally, you know that the drive (and your USB port) work properly.

Next, check the drive make and model against Symantec's latest drive compatibility information (*http://www.symantec.com/techsupp*). If your drive is not on the list of compatible devices, check directly with Symantec technical support for their advice. Otherwise, you may have an issue with the software itself. You may need to update software versions older than Symantec Ghost 8.0 or Norton Ghost 2003. Check the Symantec web site for the latest Ghost patches and upgrades.

> As a rule, do not connect a USB drive through a hub or daisy chain it through another device. Always connect the USB drive directly to a USB port on your computer. USB 1.1 ports should use the USB 1.1 drivers with Ghost.

GHOST IS FINICKY WITH CD-RW MEDIA

The Annoyance: I'm trying to ghost my hard drive to my CD-RW drive, but I keep getting errors and the process quits. What can I do to get this going?

The Fix: Ghost writes to unformatted CD-RW discs only. A formatted CD-RW disc will cause errors. You can use a CD-RW utility (such as the Erase feature in Roxio's

Drag-To-Disk) to wipe a formatted disc clean (including the file system), and then try Ghost again.

This is another case where drive hardware compatibility and software versions can wreak havoc with otherwise normal CD-RW writing. Always start by checking the drive make and model against Symantec's latest drive compatibility information (*http://www.symantec.com/ techsupp*). If your drive is not on the list of compatible devices, check directly with Symantec technical support for their suggestions and corrective actions.

Check your software versions as well. You need Symantec Ghost 7.0 (or later), or Norton Ghost 2001 (or later) to save image files to supported CD-RW drives. Check the Symantec web site for the latest Ghost patches and upgrades.

FRAGMENTATION STOPS GHOST DEAD

The Annoyance: I'm using Symantec Ghost to back up my hard drive, but the program crashes as soon as it tries to copy the MFT.

The Fix: File fragmentation in the Master File Table (or MFT) causes this oddball problem. Before you run Ghost, defragment the drive using a utility that will handle the MFT and swap file, such as Diskeeper 8.0 from Executive Software International (*http://consumer.execsoft.com*).

TOOLS OF THE TRADE

Hard drive support and management are important tasks for any PC do-it-yourselfer. The following "must have" tools deserve a place in your toolbox:

Space Patrol (http://www.jddesign.co.uk)
> Adjusts or disables low disk space warnings under Windows

PCMark04 Pro (http://www.futuremark.com)
> Benchmarks your PC performance (including hard drive system performance)

Symantec Ghost (http://www.symantec.com)
> Can mirror one hard drive to another or back up the drive to other media, such as CD/DVD discs

SpinRite 6.0 (http://www.grc.com)
> Diagnoses and corrects a wide range of drive ills

Diskeeper 8.0 (http://consumer.execsoft.com/ diskeeper/)
> Defragments your hard drives quickly and efficiently, including MFT and swap files

6

CD/DVD Drive
ANNOYANCES

Multimedia has really come of age. The slow, old CD-ROM drives that played music and muddled through new software installations have long since been replaced by high-speed CD-recordable and -rewritable drives (CD-R/RW). Today's drives can burn family photo albums, record favorite tunes, and back up your system in a surprisingly short time. DVD drives have also found a permanent home in today's computers. Not only can you enjoy feature-length Hollywood blockbusters on your desktop, but you can also create your own feature-length movies and archive massive amounts of data with the new generation of recordable and rewritable DVD drives.

Even as optical drives play a greater role on our desktops, everyday users face ongoing problems with hardware and burning/rewriting software compatibility and performance. This chapter starts with CD/DVD configuration annoyances, and then covers a series of performance issues. It also examines a wide range of playback, recording, and rewriting problems. Finally, you'll see some of my favorite fixes for writing/rewriting and DVD playback software headaches.

CONFIGURATION ANNOYANCES

IDENTIFYING UNKNOWN DISCS

The Annoyance: I inherit all kinds of unidentified blank media and it drives me crazy. For example, how do I know if I have an 8X CD-RW disc or a 16X CD-R disc?

The Fix: Download and install Erik Deppe's Nero InfoTool 2.21 (*http://www.cdspeed2000.com*). This powerful utility reveals an extensive array of information about your optical drives and media. Simply insert your blank disc in the drive, launch the program, and then click the Disc tab to see everything you need to know about the disc (see Figure 6-1). The utility also helps you identify information about the optical drive hardware and software.

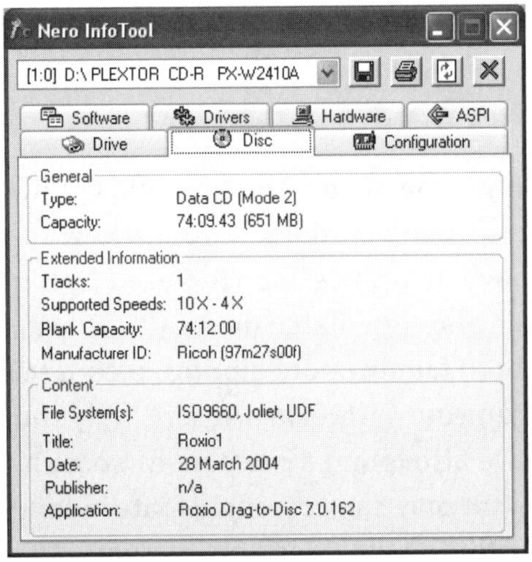

Figure 6-1. Tools like Nero InfoTool 2.21 can reveal a great deal of practical information about optical media.

MASTERING THE DVD REGION CODE

The Annoyance: I love obscure movies and order DVDs from all over the world. The problem is that I sometimes have to fiddle with the DVD region code before I can sit back with a bucket of popcorn. Is there any way to master these silly codes?

The Fix: The entertainment industry (a.k.a. Hollywood) releases DVD movies in different parts of the world at different times. For example, Warner Bros. released *The Matrix* in the U.S. in September 1999. They then released it two months later in the U.K. To control the release of movies and prevent you from playing a disc from, say, the U.S. in Europe, they encode the DVD with a region code. This means that a DVD from one region typically only plays in a DVD player from the same region. The six major regions are:

1. North America
2. Japan, Europe, Middle East, South Africa
3. Southeast Asia (plus Hong Kong)
4. Australia, New Zealand, Central & South America
5. Northwest Asia, North Africa
6. China

The region code for the DVD player is set when you *first* play a DVD. So when a user in North America puts a disc into their drive, it's set for region 1. You can easily determine the region code just by looking at the drive properties. Open the System control panel, click the Hardware tab, and then click the Device Manager button. Expand the DVD/CD-ROM drives entry, right-click your DVD drive and choose Properties, and then click the DVD Region tab (see Figure 6-2).

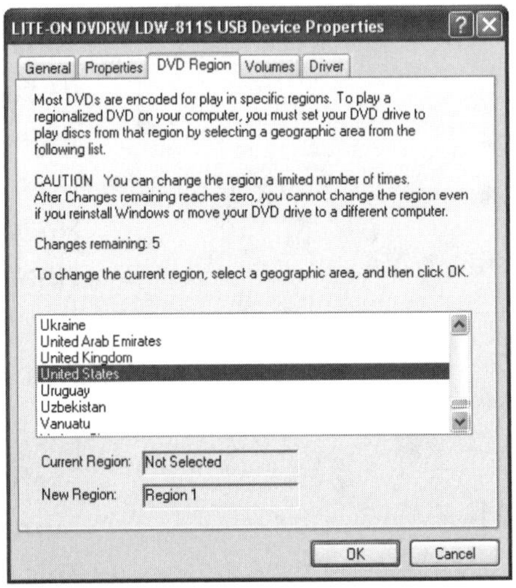

Figure 6-2. Check the DVD drive properties dialog to determine the current region code.

You can change the region code setting on most DVD drives. Simply insert a DVD disc for a different region, select the corresponding region from the DVD Region tab, and click the OK button. However, you can only change the region code a few times. Once you reach the limit, the drive will remain permanently locked into the last region code you selected.

> **t i p**
>
> The DVD drive manufacturer typically will *not* reset the region code for you once you reach the change limit.

READY LED VERSUS BUSY LED

The Annoyance: The LED indicators on my drive always stay lit. The drive works fine, but those lights really bug me.

The Fix: Most optical drives use an LED to indicate a "busy" (or working) condition while the drive reads and writes discs. However, the LED should turn off when the drive is idle. Sometimes an LED indicator serves as a "ready" light, which will illuminate whenever you load a disc in the drive (regardless of whether you access the drive). You can then simply look at the LED to tell if you have a disc loaded. You can often reconfigure this LED with a jumper on the drive mechanism itself.

DRIVE FIRMWARE FLASH FAILS

The Annoyance: I've tried to flash the firmware on my Plextor CD-RW SCSI drive, but I keep getting errors from the flash utility. Thankfully, the drive still works.

The Fix: The problem is with your Advanced SCSI Programming Interface (ASPI) drivers, which allow SCSI devices to talk with host adapters. Your ASPI driver layer must be complete in order for Plextor's flash utility to work. Otherwise, the drive may function, but the flashing utility will fail. Try downloading Adaptec's ASPI Driver For Windows 4.71 (*http://www.adaptec.com/worldwide/support/driverdetail.jsp ?cat=%2fProduct%2fASPI-4.70&filekey=aspi_v471. exe&sess=no*). This fix should update your ASPI layer to the latest drivers for Windows 2000/XP. It also includes the *ASPI-CHK.EXE* utility, which will check your ASPI layer for integrity. Run ASPICHK. If it indicates trouble with the ASPI layer, run *ASPIINST.EXE* to reinstall the complete ASPI driver set. Now reboot the system and run ASPICHK again to verify the ASPI drivers. If everything checks out, try the flash upgrade again.

> **t i p**
>
> If the ASPI layer checks correctly, but the flash utility does not work, contact the manufacturer's technical support department.

NEW FIRMWARE IMPROVES PERFORMANCE

The Annoyance: I've got a Plextor PX-712A DVD+/-R/RW drive in my system. The drive works all right, but it seems awfully slow.

The Fix: Well, don't expect blistering speed from a DVD-rewritable drive. For example, the Plextor PX-712A only boasts a 4X write/4X rewrite speed. That's just 600KB/s, so a 1GB file takes 1,667 seconds (or 27.8 minutes) to write. Get it?

To test the drive, run a benchmarking program, such as DVD Speed (*http://www.cdspeed2000.com*). If the write speed falls below the expectations, it may be time for a firmware upgrade. For example, Plextor released firmware version 1.01 for the PX-712 family on May 24, 2004. The upgrade specifically improves write performance for all types of media. Simply download and install the firmware upgrade, and then run the benchmark again to determine any improvements in performance.

NEW FIRMWARE NIXES DRIVE

The Annoyance: I just updated my optical drive firmware. The upgrade process seemed to go fine, but now the drive refuses to write.

The Fix: You can often trace this annoyance to the Windows Registry. In some cases, changing the drive firmware alters the way your system identifies the drive. The drive no longer corresponds to its entry in the Registry, effectively "blinding" Windows to the drive (even though you haven't made a single change to the hardware). Open the System control panel, click the Hardware tab, and then click the Device Manager button. Expand the DVD/CD-ROM drives entry, right-click the suspect drive, and then click the Uninstall button. Now reboot and allow Windows to redetect the drive.

> **Warning. . .**
> If you install the wrong firmware or interrupt the flash update process (due to a power failure, for example), you can render your optical drive unusable. In this case, you'll probably need to return the drive to the manufacturer for replacement.

STOP DISC THEFT

The Annoyance: I've had CDs disappear from my office on more than one occasion. Is it possible to secure my CD drive to stop sticky fingers from walking off with my CDs?

The Fix: That's an interesting question from several different angles. First, you don't want anyone making off with your expensive Microsoft Office XP CD, and you sure don't want disgruntled employees walking away with the corporate database backup CD. One way to protect your physical disc is to "lock" the drive tray by rendering the Eject button inoperative. Some optical drives, such as the LG Electronics CRD-8240B CD-ROM drive, include "lock/unlock" utilities with the driver media.

However, you might also consider a "virtual CD" utility. In effect, a virtual CD creates a complete image of a disc on the hard drive, and then makes the disc available from the hard drive directly. Space on the hard drive is set aside to emulate a CD/DVD drive. Once the original CD is imaged to the hard drive, you can remove and secure the CD media (lock it up in your desk or briefcase). For example, Virtual CD v6 from H+H Software, GmbH (*http://www.virtualcd-online.com*) provides single, network, and server editions of their virtual CD product. Of course, a quick search of the Internet will locate other virtual CD emulators from Linksys (*http://www.linksys.com*) and others.

> **GOING VERTICAL**
>
> You generally mount CD/DVD drives horizontally (left-to-right the long way, wise guy). In this case, you just plop the disc on the drive, close the tray, and away you go. A few PC cases, however, will let you mount the CD/DVD drive vertically. While the drive itself should work fine vertically, you'll need to do something about the disc tray—a vertical disc will jitter around in the tray like an epileptic fish on caffeine. If you intend to mount an optical drive vertically, make sure the drive tray includes small clips you can turn inward to secure the disc.

NEW DRIVE NOT RECOGNIZED

The Annoyance: I installed a new CD/DVD drive, but I don't see it in Windows Explorer or My Computer. Where'd it go?

The Fix: Take another look at your installation and make sure you securely attached the power and signal cables. Also, double-check the drive jumper and see that other devices on the same channel don't duplicate the drive ID (see "Drive Goes Missing" in Chapter 5 for more information on drive jumpers). For example, you don't want two "master" drives on the same ATA cable (or two drives with ID4 on the same SCSI cable). If you've installed a SCSI drive, make sure you only terminate the last device on the SCSI cable. If the problem persists, try the drive on another PC to ensure that the drive itself works (if not, replace the defective drive).

LONG TIME TO AUTO START

The Annoyance: Why does my optical drive take so long to AutoPlay a CD?

The Fix: Ordinarily, you expect a newly inserted disc to "AutoPlay" in a matter of seconds, but some drives require a few moments to set the optimum read speed for the particular disc. Plextor drives basically compare a disc's TOC (table of contents) to the last track on the disc and check data integrity at the outside of the disc. The drive will then set a read speed based on the test (usually resulting in better read performance). However, the process delays disc initialization and auto-run execution. You can't really prevent this behavior unless you replace the drive with a different manufacturer's model.

DISABLING AUTOPLAY

The Annoyance: I hate it when a disc automatically starts up in the drive. How can I turn off this annoying AutoPlay feature?

The Fix: Open My Computer, right-click your optical drive, select Properties, and click the AutoPlay tab (see Figure 6-3). Use the drop-down menu to select the disc type you want to disable, and then choose the "Select an action to perform" option and select "Take no action."

Repeat this for various media types, and then click the Apply button to save your changes.

Figure 6-3. Use the AutoPlay tab to adjust the drive behavior for each disc type.

USB DRIVE DOESN'T SEE DISC

The Annoyance: I can see the drive letter for my USB CD-RW drive, but I keep getting errors telling me there's no disc in the drive.

The Fix: Each time you insert a disc, you probably see an error message such as "No disc in drive." This error appears when the drive uses the native OS drivers (prior to Windows XP) in place of the manufacturer-specific drivers. For example, this annoyance plagues the Archos MiniCDRW drive (often used with notebook computers like WinBook systems). In this case, you must use the ISD (manufacturer) drivers rather than the native Microsoft drivers. Open the System control panel, click the Hardware tab, and then click the Device Manager button. Expand the USB entry, double-click the storage unit, and click the Driver tab. If it shows Microsoft as the Driver Provider, click the Update Driver button and use the manufacturer's drivers that accompanied the device. Reboot the system and try inserting the disc again.

PERFORMANCE ANNOYANCES

NO SPACE AFTER FORMATTING

The Annoyance: Why do I see 0MB of usable space after I format a CD-RW disc?

The Fix: The trouble is often in the writing software itself. For example, this issue occurs with Nero's InCD Version 4.0.3.2 and some AOpen CD-RW drives (DRW2412Pro) under Windows XP (SP1). Check with the writing software maker for a patch or update. For InCD, update to 4.0.1.11 or later to resolve the problem (*http://www.nero.com/en/nero-up.php*). If no suitable patch or upgrade exists, try an alternate RW utility, such as Roxio's Drag-to-Disc (*http://www.roxio.com*).

MOVING TO 80 MINUTES AND BEYOND

The Annoyance: Why can't I burn 80 minute CDs with my drive? Do I need an upgrade? Can I upgrade the drive I have?

The Fix: Ordinary CD-R discs can fit 74 minutes (650MB) of music onto a single disc. CD manufacturers normally leave the last six minutes blank to prevent fingerprints and other goop along the edge of the disc from interfering with reading or writing. If you want to use all 80 minutes (700MB), you'll need a disc specifically marked for 80-minute use. You'll also need a drive and writing software (such as Nero 6) capable of burning 80 minute discs (check the specifications of your drive and software).

However, that only gets you an extra six minutes (50MB). What about those funky discs that promise 90 or 99 minutes? To pack even more data on a CD, you can use a

technique called "overburning," which ignores the stated storage limit of the CD. As with oversized writing, your drive and writing software must support overburning. Recording software such as Nero will tell you whether the drive can overburn a CD.

You can enable overburning through the writing software, which lets you enter the total write time (usually up to 99 minutes and 99 seconds) for the disc. Then you must confirm the decision to burn (write) before the process starts.

Before you overburn a CD, most software programs let you perform a write test. If any errors occur during the test, reduce the write time and try again

So what happens if your drive doesn't support overburning? You may be able to upgrade the drive firmware to enable support. For example, the Plextor PX-W4824TA/TU CD-R/RW drive requires firmware Version 1.04 or later. The PX-W4012TA/TU requires firmware Version 1.05 or later. Always check with the drive maker for firmware updates before you attempt to overburn a CD.

MIXING AND MATCHING DISC FORMATS

The Annoyance: I sent my grandparents a Video CD (VCD) of my wedding, but they said their CD-ROM couldn't read the disc. I know the disc works because I tested it on my own computer before I mailed it.

The Fix: To read a Video CD, you need a "multi-read" (or "multiplay") compliant drive. Early CD-ROM drives only read CD-ROM Mode 1 discs. As new formats were introduced, emerging CD drives had to support additional formats. Today, mulit-read CD-ROM and CD-RW drives (along with more recent DVD-ROM and DVD-RW drives) support a wealth of different formats.

For example, Plextor's PlexWriter 40/12/40 drive handles CD-DA, CD-Extra, CD-ROM Mode 1, Mix CD-ROM XA, Photo CD, Video CD, CD-I Multisession, CD-Text, CD+G, UDF, and MRW (Mt. Rainer) ready discs. It really covers a lot of ground. Obviously, this particular drive would handle your Video CD. To find out which formats your grandparents' drive supports, check the specifications page in the manual (or look on the drive manufacturer's web site). They might need to upgrade to a more recent model.

QUASHING NOISY DRIVES

The Annoyance: My optical drive makes a lot of noise when a disc spins. It really gives me a headache.

The Fix: There are several possible culprits here, but it all comes down to speed and balance. Have you ever felt your car shake when you drive above a certain speed? It often happens because unbalanced wheels create a vibration. The same principle applies to optical discs—an unbalanced disc spinning at today's 40X–52X read speeds can shake enough to cause vibrations that you actually hear.

Small, credit card sized CDs are notorious for causing drive noise. Avoid the use of undersized CDs whenever possible.

Start by inspecting the disc itself. Look for adhesive labels that only occupy a portion of the disc, or circular "CD" labels not centered on the spindle. Try several un-labeled (blank) discs. If the noise persists, the drive mechanism may be damaged, so consider replacing the drive outright. If the noise stops, you know the problem is with the disc. Remove the label, or rewrite the data to a CD without a label. The problem may not even be a label—the thickness of the disc itself may not be even across the entire media. For example, some driver discs included with the older Plextor 1210A, 2410A, and 4012A drives had an uneven thickness, resulting in a wobble at high speeds. Try media from a different manufacturer.

If you're stuck using oddly labeled CDs and the noise is enough to give you headaches, you may be able to limit the drive speed artificially using a tool such as Nero DriveSpeed (part of the Nero 6 Toolkit). You can also download it from *http://www.cdspeed2000.com*. Simply set the maximum speed for the drive while the utility runs in the Windows System Tray (see Figure 6-4). Of course, you will limit your drive's top performance, but it beats peeling sticky labels off your important discs.

Figure 6-4. Nero DriveSpeed lets you slow a noisy CD drive artificially.

PERKING UP A SLOW DRIVE

The Annoyance: My optical drive runs dog slow. How can I speed it up without breaking the bank?

The Fix: First, use a tool such as CD Speed (*http://www.cdspeed2000.com*) to evaluate your drive's performance (see Figure 6-5). If the drive's actual speed meets its stated specifications (e.g., 40X read/16X write/12X rewrite), then you really have nothing to complain about. In fact, most CD drives only hit their peak speeds in the latter half of the disc. For example, a 32X drive may start at 15X near the spindle, and then ramp up to 32X by the time it reaches the end of the disc. (Note that the speed profile shown in Figure 6-5 will vary based on the make and model of your drive.)

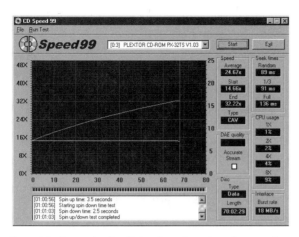

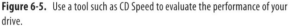

Figure 6-5. Use a tool such as CD Speed to evaluate the performance of your drive.

> **t i p**
>
> Remember that other system factors, such as background virus protection, a misconfigured IDE interface (perhaps set for PIO data transfers rather than DMA transfers), background file downloads, excess hard drive activity (e.g., accessing virtual memory), and even a slow CPU can sometimes affect the drive's speed profile.

You can also use the following tips to perk up your drive's performance:

Make sure you clean the disc. Scratches and fingerprints sometimes force the drive to slow down and re-read corrupted data.

Close background tasks. CPU-intensive tasks can interfere with reading and writing processes. Shut down any unnecessary programs on the Taskbar before you read or write a disc.

Check the drive's data transfer mode. Open the System control panel, click the Hardware tab, and then click the Device Manager button. Expand the "IDE ATA/ATAPI controllers" entry, right-click the Primary or Secondary IDE channel (whichever channel your optical

drive is on), and choose Properties. Click the Advanced Settings tab and check the Transfer Mode for each device. Make sure you select "DMA if available" (see Figure 6-6) and click the OK button.

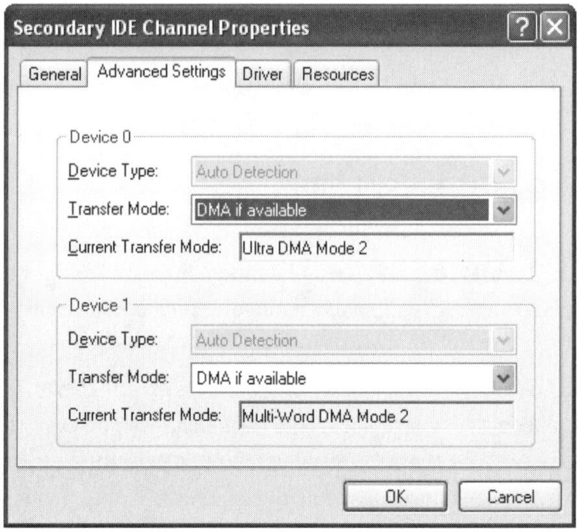

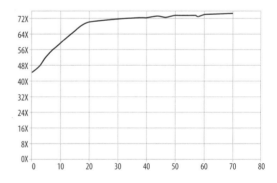

Figure 6-6. Make sure that the Transfer Mode for your optical drives is set to DMA if available.

Replace the drive with a more recent model that offers faster speeds and better performance. For example, the Kenwood TrueX 72X drive starts off at 44X, and then climbs to 68X just 20 minutes into the disc (see Figure 6-7).

Figure 6-7. The Kenwood TrueX 72X drive offers far better data speeds for quick reading.

Optical discs and hard drives spin their media in different ways. Hard drives spin their platters at a constant number of revolutions per minute (RPM), resulting in a constant angular velocity (CAV) for the media. This method poses a challenge for the read/write mechanism because the data actually moves "faster" at the edges of the platter than at the point nearest the spindle. By comparison, optical drives adjust the spindle speed to maintain a constant flow of data, resulting in a constant linear velocity (CLV). This technique slows the spindle as the optical reader moves farther out along the disc, and speeds the disc as it reads data closer to the spindle.

CABLING FOR CD AUDIO

The Annoyance: I put an audio CD in the drive and opened Windows Media Player (WMP). I can see a track playing, but there's no sound.

The Fix: Select Start → All Programs → Accessories → Entertainment → Volume Control. Make sure that the CD Audio channel is not muted and that the volume is turned up to an appropriate level.

Now check the CD drive configuration. Open the System control panel, click the Hardware tab, and then click the Device Manager button. Expand the "DVD/CD-ROM drives" entry, right-click the troublesome drive, select Properties, and then click the Properties tab (see Figure 6-8). See that the CD Player Volume slider is turned up and check the box labeled "Enable digital CD audio for this CD-ROM device." If the checkbox is grayed out or unavailable (perhaps your CD-ROM or Windows version is too old to support the feature),

you will need to connect a thin, 4-wire CD audio cable between the CD drive and a mixer port on your sound card. You can obtain CD audio cables from any computer store. If the audio cable is connected to another drive (maybe you have two optical drives in your PC), you can play the audio through the connected drive, enable digital CD audio, or upgrade the drive/OS to support digital CD audio.

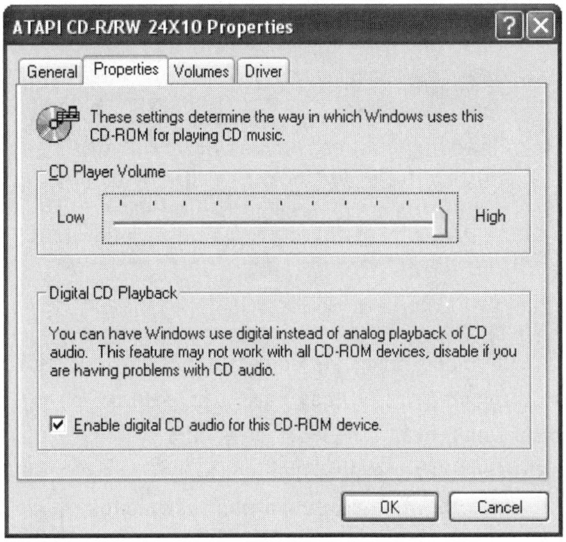

Figure 6-8. Turn up the drive volume, and enable digital CD audio if possible.

TEMPERAMENTAL DRIVE TRAY

The Annoyance: My CD-RW drive refuses to eject my audio CD. I can think of one way to get the disc out, but it involves a hammer.

The Fix: Don't panic—we'll rescue your disc. First, put the hammer down and try the Eject button again. Yes, I know you've already tried it about two hundred times, but do it again. The button itself may be failing. This time, hold the button firmly and evenly for a second. If that still doesn't work, open My Computer, right-click the drive and choose Eject.

Now here's the rub. If the drive doesn't appear in My Computer, it probably lost power (that's why the system can't see it). For example, this can happen if you don't firmly plug in the 4-wire power cable during a new drive installation or replacement. Power down the PC, open the chassis, and recheck the power cable. Power up the system again, make sure that the drive appears in My Computer, and then try ejecting the disc again.

> Rewriting utilities, such as Roxio's Drag-to-Disc, typically "lock in" a CD-RW disc until you eject it through the utility.

If the drive appears in My Computer, but still refuses to give up your disc, you may have a failed drive on your hands. Don't fret, just power down the system. Find a large-gauge paper clip, straighten it, and then carefully insert one end into the Emergency Eject Hole (usually located just below the drive tray). This manually operates the tray motor and moves it out just enough for you to grab it with your fingers and gently ease out the tray.

If the tray is jammed and refuses to open, the disc may be stuck. If you yank out the tray, you can ruin the disc, the drive tray, or both. If you can't open the tray after disengaging the emergency eject latch, you may need to remove the drive from the system, open its outer cover, and physically un-jam the disc. Of course, if the tray *still* refuses to track in and out once you removed the disc, replace the drive.

OVERCOMING CRC ERRORS IN DISC WRITING

The Annoyance: Why do I get CRC errors when I write to disc?

The Fix: You're experiencing cyclic redundancy check (CRC) errors because of data corruption. File data is divided into segments, and processed through an algorithm that calculates a CRC value for each segment. When the data arrives at its destination, a new CRC value is calculated and compared against the original CRC sent with the data. If the two CRC values match, the data is good. Otherwise, the data is toast.

Interference inside the PC is the most common cause of CRC errors. For example, signals from one cable cause false signals on a nearby cable. If the interference is intense enough, data bits may change (precipitating the CRC errors). Manufacturers (and many PC do-it-yourselfers) tend to bundle and route any internal cabling to present a neater appearance. Please *stop* that! Unbundle any cabling and let it hang freely, replace any obviously damaged cables, and then try the writing again.

Before you get too comfortable celebrating a victory, make sure you recheck the data transfer modes for your optical drives. For example, CRC errors may cause the operating system to step down the data transfer mode from DMA to PIO mode. PIO is slower, and does not use the CRC technique. Make sure you maintain the DMA mode to continue CRC testing and get best performance from the drive (see Figure 6-6).

CLEARING UNNEEDED DISCS

The Annoyance: I need to erase a bunch of CD-RW discs, but the Format feature in Roxio's Drag-to-Disk takes forever. Is there a quicker way?

The Fix: Well, you could just *erase* the disc rather than format it. Rewriting utilities such as Roxio's Drag-to-Disc typically provide a straightforward Erase feature, and Nero 6 offers a Quick Erase option. Erasing an RW disc is a lot like deleting a file from a diskette or hard drive—the actual data remains intact, but the space is simply marked as "free." This can present a potential security issue for sensitive personal or business files because files can be recovered just as easily from an RW disc as from a hard drive. If you need the disc "wiped," use the Full Erase feature under Nero 6, or stick with the lengthy Format feature in Drag-to-Disc.

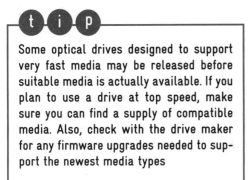

Some optical drives designed to support very fast media may be released before suitable media is actually available. If you plan to use a drive at top speed, make sure you can find a supply of compatible media. Also, check with the drive maker for any firmware upgrades needed to support the newest media types

WRITING AND REWRITING IN HIGH SPEED

The Annoyance: Why can't I use high-speed (or ultra-speed) media in my CD drive? How do I know what's compatible and what isn't?

The Fix: Modern drives (such as Plextor's PlexWriter 52/24/52A) can write discs at full CD-ROM speeds (52X), and rewrite at speeds up to 24X. The trick is to find media that takes full advantage of the drive's available speeds. Here's the rub—there are slight differences in media design between normal speed (1X–4X) discs, high-speed (4X to 10X or 12X) discs, and ultra-speed (24X) discs. The problem is further complicated with 32X and faster writers/rewriters. You typically can't use older (1X–4X) discs with newer, "high-speed" drives (over 4X), and you can't use faster (4X–10X) discs with older drives. The bottom line: match the drive speed range to the media speed for best results.

So how do you get optimum writing speed? Make sure you use the fastest media your drive can handle. For example, Plextor's 52/24/52 CD-R/RW drive can use CD-R discs rated for 52X writing (though you're hard-pressed to find CD-R discs faster than 32X today), and CD-RW discs rated for 24X. And what about the discs themselves? Knowing the speed of a blank disc can be tricky unless the disc is labeled specifically. If there are no markings on the disc, use a utility such as Nero InfoTool to identify the disc and its speed range (see Figure 6-9).

Figure 6-9. Nero InfoTool can reveal detailed information about the drive as well as the disc.

INSIDE CD SPEED MULTIPLIERS

You may be confused by all of those "X" numbers relating to optical drives. While it's easy to tell that a 54X drive is faster then a 24X drive, getting to real data transfers can be a chore for the uninitiated. All CDs are based on the floppy drive transfer rate of 150KB/s (the 1X or CD audio data rate). CD music is meant to run at 150KB/s, and all drives drop back to that level when playing a disc from your favorite artist. However, it didn't take long for engineers to figure out that programs and data can run at a faster rate. For example, a 4X drive can handle data at 600KB/s (4×150KB/s). On the other end, a 54X drive can pass data at 8.1MB/s (54×150KB/s).

HANDLING SOFTWARE EJECTION

The Annoyance: Why do I have to use the Eject option in my packet writing software to eject an RW disc? Why can't I just hit the Eject button on the drive?

The Fix: Packet writing software such as Roxio's Drag-to-Disc and Ahead Software's InCD must "prepare" an RW disc before ejecting it—that is, the software must ensure that the data and TOC info are written to the disc. The software prevents this premature...er...ejection by locking out the drive's hardware Eject button. The important thing to remember here is that the packet software is working normally. When you're finished with a disc, simply use the software's Eject feature. Select how the disc should be prepared and click the Eject button (see Figure 6-10). It may take a few moments to prepare the disc, but it will eject normally.

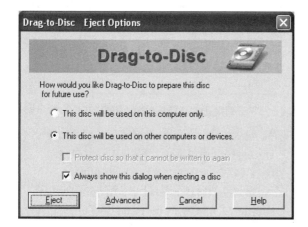

Figure 6-10. Use the packet writing software to close and eject a rewritable disc.

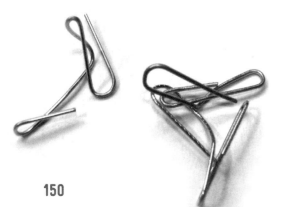

PLAYBACK ANNOYANCES

DIRTY DISCS DISTORT VIDEO

The Annoyance: I spent 50 cents at a yard sale for a DVD of my favorite western, "The Good, The Bad, and The Ugly." But when I popped the movie into my laptop, it played for about 10 minutes and then started to hesitate and break up into weird colored blocks.

The Fix: Your disc is simply dirty. What do you expect for fifty cents? Remove the disc and use a lint-free eyeglass-cleaning cloth to gently wipe fingerprints and other debris off the disc. Now you can watch Clint, Lee, and Eli in all their wide-screen, spaghetti western glory.

REMOVING POPS AND CLICKS

The Annoyance: Why are there pops and clicks in music I burned to CD?

The Fix: Audiophiles often "rip" tracks from music CDs for MP3 conversion or CD-R compilations of their favorite tunes. The trick is to "rip" the audio data as cleanly as possible. Simply ripping audio at top speed from any old CD-ROM will not give you the best results. Instead, rip from a CD/DVD drive that supports Digital Audio Extraction (DAE)—virtually all modern optical drives support DAE, but check the specifications to make sure.

Although many personal audio players support WMA files, you can rip to MP3 with Windows Media Player by using a plug-in such as CyberLink's MP3 Power-Encoder (*http://www.gocyberlink.com*) or InterVideo's MP3 Xpack (*http://www.inter-video.com*).

If your drive does not support DAE (or DAE still doesn't give you the best results), try ripping from another drive. Alternatively, rip the tracks at a higher quality. For example, Windows Media Player (WMP) can rip CD tracks to Windows Media Audio (WMA) files on your hard drive. With WMP running, select Tools → Options, and click the Copy Music tab (see Figure 6-11). Move the "Audio quality" slider towards the "Best Quality" side—you can see the resulting space required for the recording. For even better quality, you can opt for lossless WMA conversion (though that takes considerably more space).

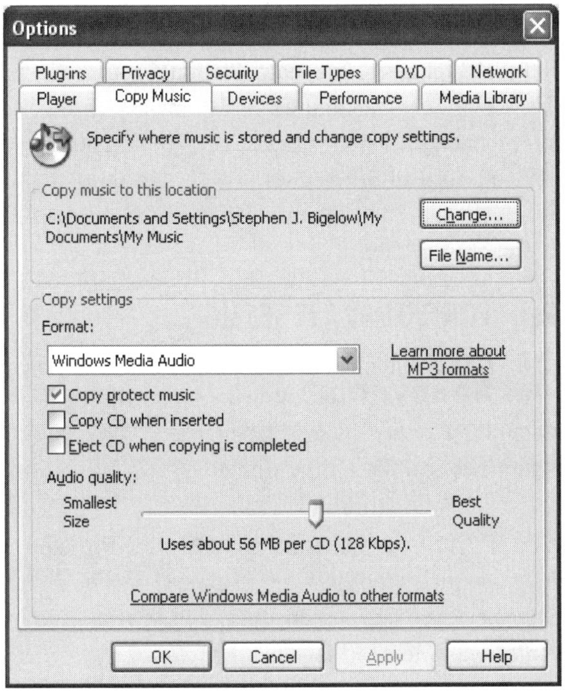

Figure 6-11. Select a recording format and quality level before ripping CD audio tracks.

HANDLING DISC READ ERRORS

The Annoyance: When I try to read a CD, I get obnoxious read errors. What can I do to whip this disc into shape?

The Fix: There are two possible sources of read errors: the disc and the drive. First, clean the drive (especially if it has been in service for several years). Sending some compressed air through the opened drive tray or playing a CD cleaning disc intended for delicate CD-R/RW drives will probably do the trick. After cleaning, try several other discs. If the problem persists, the drive may be failing and should be replaced.

If the trouble seems limited to just one disc, check the disc and look for fingerprints, smudges, scratches, or other defects. Try to clean the disc. You can often remove mild scratches using a repair device, such as the Memorex OptiFix Pro CD/DVD repair kit (*http://www.memorex.com/products/category_display.php?cid=72*). However, serious scratches, cracks, and chemical damage (such as acetone from nail polish remover) can render the disc unusable. Also, don't leave your favorite CD on the car dashboard in the hot August sun for a week and expect it to work.

Always keep your expensive CDs in their plastic jewel cases, and make backups in the event your originals get lost or damaged. Use CD/DVD duplication and emulation software such as Alcohol 120% (*http://www.alcohol-soft.com*) to make personal backups of your own discs.

Careful Cleaning

Ordinary CD/DVD handling can leave scratches and smudges on the data surface, resulting in read errors and lost information. Fortunately, you can gently clean discs with a dry, lint-free cloth (such as an eyeglass-cleaning cloth). To remove stubborn stains, moisten the cloth with a little isopropyl alcohol (never use ammonia or harsh cleaners). Wipe from the spindle to the edge as if you were drawing spokes on a wagon wheel. Do *not* wipe in a circular motion.

DISABLED HEADPHONE JACK

The Annoyance: Why doesn't the headphone jack work on my optical drive? I can play music through the PC speakers just fine.

The Fix: Remember that today's optical drives can output audio in digital form (rather than relying on those little, 4-wire audio cables to the sound card). However, drives don't provide audio and digital outputs simultaneously. When you enable digital CD audio on the drive, analog audio (from the 4-pin rear jack and front headphone jack) is disabled. If you need to use headphones, switch the drive back to analog audio. To do this, open the System control panel, click the Hardware tab, and then click the Device Manager button. Expand the "DVD/CD-ROM drives" entry, right-click the desired drive and choose Properties. Click the Properties tab, uncheck the "Enable digital CD audio for this CD-ROM device" box, and click the OK button (see Figure 6-8).

USING HYBRID DISCS

The Annoyance: When I try to read my CD on a PC, it tells me that there are no files on the disc. The CD works fine on a Mac.

The Fix: Well, start with the obvious reasons. First, PCs can't read native Mac discs. Apple systems use the HFS file system, which is incompatible with Windows file systems, such as FAT or NTFS. If you insert a Mac CD into a PC, the PC simply won't read the disc. However, a number of utilities such as Robert Leslie's HFS Utilities tool (*http://www.mars.org/home/rob/proj/hfs/#related*) allow HFS volumes to be manipulated from UNIX and Windows. To read a CD on both PCs and Macs, you need to create a hybrid disc. Writing tools such as Nero 6 can create non-shared hybrid CDs. Basically, a non-shared hybrid CD creates two copies of the data: one copy using FAT for the PC, and another copy using HFS for the Mac. Of course, duplicating data in this way means that you can only use half the disc's capacity for either operating system.

READING NEW DISCS ON OLD DRIVES

The Annoyance: My cousin's old CD-ROM drive can't read the CD I burned. However, the disc reads fine in other drives.

The Fix: Hardware manufactured before the age of writable discs may not be capable of reading burned media. Since the disc works on other drives, you know that the disc is not the issue, so check the specs for the CD-ROM drive. It's probably not multi-read compliant with your disc type (see "Mixing and Matching Disc Formats" earlier in this chapter). So how do you get around this problem? Well there are two solutions. You can check with the drive manufacturer for a firmware update, but they probably no longer support any CD-ROM drive that is too old to read R/RW discs. The second solution is to replace the old CD-ROM with a current, entry-level CD-ROM or CD-RW drive.

SEEING ONLY THE LAST SESSION

The Annoyance: When I try to read a multi-session CD-R disc, Windows Explorer only shows the last session. How can I see the entire disc?

The Fix: In Windows 95 and 98, Windows Explorer often only shows the last track of a multi-session disc. To access selected sessions on the disc, try a CD-R utility such as MultiMounter (included with Nero).

Windows XP should show you the entire disc, but if you have any trouble, open the System control panel, click the Hardware tab, and then click the Device Manager button. Expand the "DVD/CD-ROM drives" entry, right-click the desired drive, and choose Properties. Click the Volumes tab and then click the Populate button to show the disc characteristics and various sessions (if any) on the disc (see Figure 6-12).

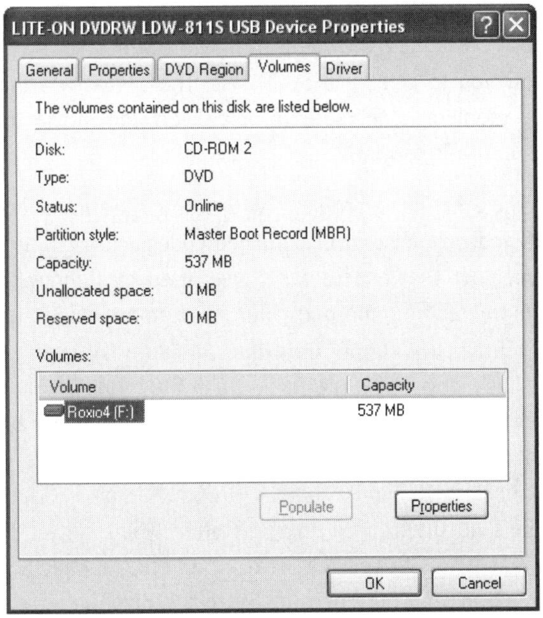

Figure 6-12. Use the Volumes tab to identify and select multiple sessions on a CD-R disc.

FILLING A BLANK DVD WINDOW

The Annoyance: When I try to play a DVD movie, the player window just goes blank. I can, however, hear the audio.

The Fix: In virtually every case, the trouble is with your screen resolution or color depth. As a rule, play DVD movies on a display with a resolution of 1,280x768 (or higher) and a 32-bit color depth. To change your display's resolution, first right-click the desktop and select Properties. Then click the Settings tab and adjust the "Screen resolution" and "Color quality" settings to at least the minimum requirements of your DVD player software.

> **t i p**
>
> DVD players often employ video overlay modes for real-time video playback. Make sure you update your video card driver and DirectX version to accommodate the requirements of your DVD player.

ALTERNATIVE AUDIO CABLING

The Annoyance: I want to play CD audio, but I don't have one of those little 4-wire cables, and my drive doesn't handle digital audio. What's a PC geek to do?

The Fix: Fortunately, you can use a stereo patch cable to connect the headphone jack output on the drive to the sound card's Line In jack. You can buy the cable for a few dollars from a local Radio Shack (much cheaper than a new drive). Select Start → All Programs → Accessories → Entertainment → Volume Control and make sure that the Line In channel isn't muted and that it's turned up to a reasonable level. Now just play the audio CD and turn up the headphone volume knob on the drive to achieve a comfortable sound.

READING REWRITABLE DISCS

The Annoyance: I formatted an RW disc and copied data to it, but my Windows 98 PC won't read it.

The Fix: You need a Universal Disk Format (UDF) driver for Windows 98 to support the file format for rewritable CDs. A packet writing utility such as Roxio's Drag-to-Disc gives you complete RW support and should read the disc. Windows XP includes UDF support for CD-RW discs, but only for reading. If you want to write or rewrite RW discs, you need a packet writing utility.

RECORDING ANNOYANCES

LOST DVD SPACE

The Annoyance: I'm writing to a 4.7GB DVD-R, but I only see 4.38GB of free space. What gives?

The Fix: Ever work with hard drives? Well, hard drive vendors often use "decimal" gigabytes (1,000,000,000 bytes) to denote capacity, while software makers apply "binary" gigabytes (1,073,741,824 bytes). So, when you examine the disc with a typical software utility, a 4.7GB DVD disc may actually appear to have just 4.38GB (4.7/1.073) of space available. There is no "missing" space—it's simply a different way of expressing the disc's capacity.

Remember that a small percentage of the recordable DVD is set aside for overhead, such as link blocks, track information, video title areas, and so on. It typically consumes about 1MB of disc space.

OVERCOMING PMA ERRORS

The Annoyance: Why do I get "Cannot recover from PMA" errors with my new media?

The Fix: Each time you insert a disc into the drive, it checks and calibrates the laser power in the disc's Power Management Area (PMA). If the drive can't discern the appropriate laser power settings, it returns a PMA error. In many cases, the media is defective or unsuitable for the drive. Rewritable discs may simply be worn out (from being rewritten so many times). In either case, try a fresh, brand-name disc that meets the drive manufacturer's recommendations.

If the problem persists, the drive may have trouble calibrating power for a particular brand of media. Check with the drive manufacturer for any firmware upgrades that may address media compatibility with the drive. Otherwise, the drive itself may be defective, so consider replacing the drive (or have the drive repaired under warranty).

VIDEO FORMAT NOT SUPPORTED

The Annoyance: I want to burn a video to CD, but when I place the clip into the compilation window, Nero says that the file format isn't supported.

The Fix: You can usually trace this annoying little issue to codecs, but check the file format first. Nero should certainly support the standard file formats, including *.AVI*, *.MOV*, *.WMV*, *.ASF*, and *.MPG*. If you're using

other formats, however, the burning software probably doesn't recognize the file as a "movie" format, so it won't allow you to create an SVCD disc. The best way around this problem is to recreate or convert the movie to a standard file format.

On the other hand, problems with standard formats probably indicate missing or damaged codecs on the system. Remember that codecs are drivers used by Windows to interpret and handle particular file formats (such as an MPEG-2 codec for DVD playback, or an MOV codec for Apple QuickTime file playback). Each file format demands a corresponding codec. Problems with the codec can prevent the burning software from recognizing the file. For example, if you try to burn a DivX movie as SVCD, but there's no DivX codec on the system, you'll get a "File Format Is Not Supported" error. To check the codecs installed on your PC, open the System control panel, click the Hardware tab, and then click the Device Manager button. Expand the "Sound, video and game controllers" entry, right-click the Video Codecs entry, and select Properties. The list of available codecs appears on the Properties tab (see Figure 6-13).

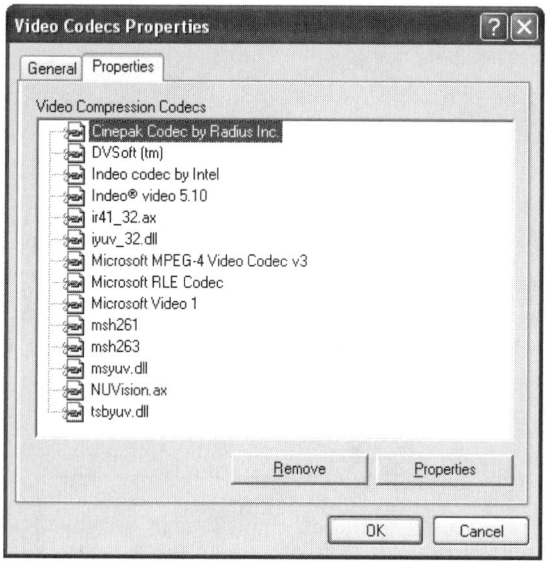

Figure 6-13. Check SVCD burning support by verifying codecs on the system.

If the necessary codec is missing, install it. If the codec is present (but the error persists), uninstall and reinstall the codec. In most cases, the codec installs with the related application (for example, suitable MPEG-2 codecs should install with a DVD player such as WinDVD). Reinstall the related program from scratch, or check the web site for a self-installing patch that will update the codecs for you.

REDUCING DISC USE

The Annoyance: Easy CD Creator tells me that I need 23 CDs to back up my hard drive. That'll take me all day! Is there any way to backup with fewer discs?

The Fix: The easiest way to reduce your media demands is to use the compression feature available in your backup software. For example, Nero's BackItUp software offers a compression option (see Figure 6-14). It's impossible to say just how much media compression will save you because the amount of compression depends on the data that you're trying to compress. For example, Word documents may compress very well, while other file types (such as movie clips) may compress little (if at all).

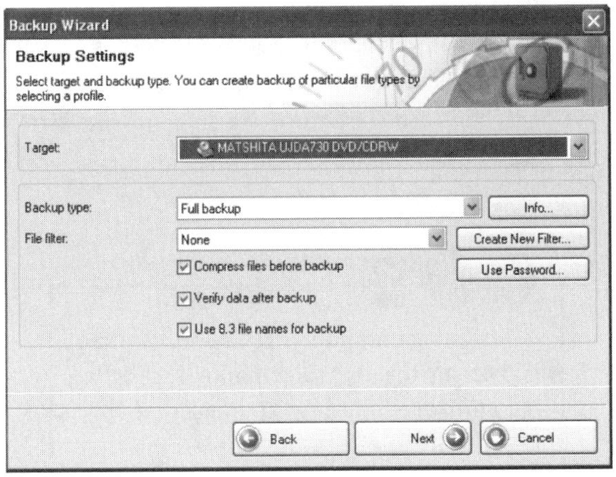

Figure 6-14. Compression can significantly reduce the number of CDs needed to backup a system.

Another tip is to use CD-R discs rather than CD-RW discs. You can fit 650MB on a CD-R, but only about 530MB on a formatted CD-RW. If you *really* want to reduce the media count, opt for DVD+-R/RW discs rather than CDs. A DVD holds up to 4.7GB, which can reduce your media needs to just 2 or 3 DVDs.

FINALIZING AND CLOSING

The Annoyance: My software asks me to finalize the disc. Should I do this or not?

The Fix: Finalizing (or "closing") the disc prevents any additional data from being written, so your choice really depends on your future plans for that CD-R disc. If you have written a complete disc, and you never intend to add more data to the disc, then opt to finalize the disc. This is a good idea if you're creating discs that you don't want anyone else messing around with later. If you plan to add more data to the disc in future sessions, leave the disc open (older burning programs may ask you to "close a session" rather than "finalize the disc"). Keep in mind that a few older drives may have trouble reading discs that are not finalized.

DEALING WITH BUFFER UNDERRUNS

The Annoyance: I tried to burn some MP3s, but I got a buffer underrun error, which ruined my disc. I know blank CD-Rs are cheap, but I've already gone through 10 discs.

The Fix: Every CD drive has a buffer—a small portion of memory that holds the data being written to the disc. The drive reads this buffered data and moves the writing laser accordingly. However, a "buffer underrun" can occur if the buffer empties during the writing process and the laser turns off. This stoppage results in a data gap that will render the file (and the disc) unreadable. To prevent buffer underrun errors, follow these simple steps:

- First, close any unneeded background applications. I mean, if you're trying to download music from the Internet while making a complete backup of your system, you may well run into problems.

- Another trick is to record at a slower speed. Fast drives can empty a buffer in a matter of moments, so slowing the recording process buys a little time for the system to catch up (though it will take longer to record the disc).

- A third tip is to create an ISO image file first, rather than writing "on the fly." Writing "on-the-fly" simply tells the system which files to copy, then lets the hard drive locate each file. Conversely, making an image file organizes all of your data in advance, which puts less stress on the hard drive.

- Finally, opt for a drive (and writing software) that supports "burn-proof" technology. When a drive buffer does empty, burn-proof drives will turn off the laser and keep track of the last valid writing location. When the buffer refills, the laser will turn on again and pick up where it left off. For example, the Plextor PlexWriter 52/24/52A offers burn-proof technology, which you can read about at *http://www.plextor.com/english/news/burnproof.html*.

CAN'T RECORD ON-THE-FLY

The Annoyance: Windows XP records my CDs just fine, but it doesn't seem to write CDs on-the-fly. Why? Is there some feature that I'm missing?

The Fix: Windows XP doesn't natively support CD recording "on-the-fly." Instead, it creates a temporary image of the disc before the recording process starts. Writing on-the-fly requires more processing power, and frequently leads to buffer underrun errors that can waste CD media. Creating a disc image first ensures that all of the files destined for the CD are available and organized in advance. Plan on at least 1.5GB of free space on your hard drive before you start a CD writing project under Windows XP. If you have processing power to spare, and would rather avoid the commitment of hard drive space, use a third-party burning program such as Roxio's Easy Media Creator or Nero 6.

FINDING THE RECORDING SIDE

The Annoyance: How do you know which side of a CD-RW disc to write on? I bought some discs in bulk and both sides look the same.

The Fix: Check the printed alphanumeric code that circles the hole in the center of the disc. The side where you can read the letters and numbers "forward" goes up (that is the "printed" side). This is the side you write on or label. The side where those same letters and numbers are "reversed" goes down (that is the "data" side).

BURNED MUSIC WON'T PLAY

The Annoyance: I just burned a music CD, but my stereo refuses to play it. I know the disc works because I played it on my PC.

The Fix: The problem is almost certainly a compatibility issue between your newly minted audio CD and the stereo player. Remember that your garden-variety CD players are designed to play Red Book audio at 1X speeds. Today's electronic music formats such as MP3 and WMA are *not* Red Book compatible. A growing variety of home entertainment equipment *does* support other music formats, but check the specs to make sure the player supports your file types.

If you encounter any problems writing a disc on-the-fly, reconfigure the burning software to create an image file first (see "Dealing with Buffer Underruns")

If your home stereo refuses to play your burned Red Book music, the trouble may be in your recording speed. Fast recording may impair the quality of the music data; prevent playback; or cause skipping, static, and other sound quality problems. Re-burn the music disc at the slowest speed possible for the CD-RW drive (try 1X if available). Sure, it'll take longer, but it might fix this little playback annoyance.

DVD WON'T WRITE CDS

The Annoyance: Why do I have trouble writing CDs on my DVD-R/RW drive? I can write DVD discs just fine.

The Fix: DVD recorders/rewriters operate in either a CD or DVD mode. It's easy enough to write CDs with your DVD drive, but you'll need to switch the drive's mode in order to support CD writing/rewriting. First, open My Computer, right-click the DVD drive, choose Properties, and click the Recording tab. Check the "Enable CD recording on this drive" box (see Figure 6-15).

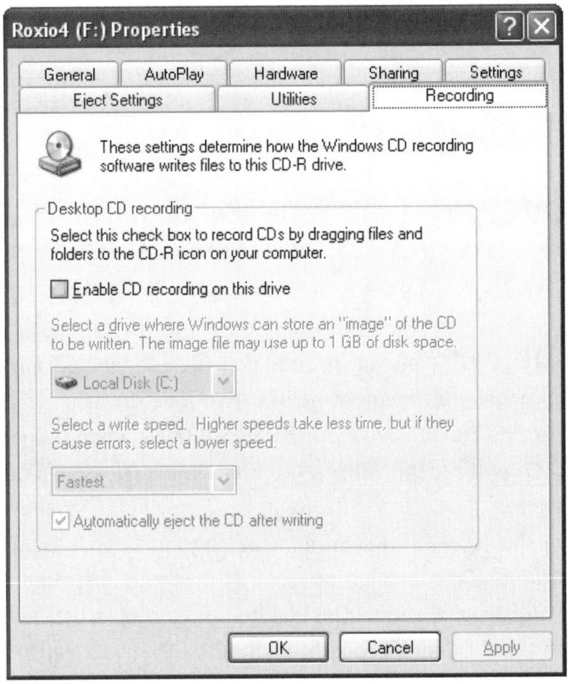

Figure 6-15. Enable/disable CD recording to switch between DVD and CD recording modes.

REWRITING ANNOYANCES

INTERCHANGING "+" AND "-" MEDIA

The Annoyance: Why can't I use a DVD-R/RW disc in a DVD+R/RW drive?

The Fix: It's really all about the compatibility. DVD+ and DVD- are two similar (but different) DVD standards. Both –R/RW and +R/RW technologies are generally based on CD rewritable (CD-RW) hardware. Pioneer actually developed –R/RW, which adheres very closely to established CD-RW drive hardware and media. The –R/RW standard is so popular that it is supported by the DVD Forum industry group (*http://www.dvdforum.com*). By comparison, +R/RW technology resulted from the combined effort of industry leaders such as Sony, Philips, HP, Dell, Ricoh, Yamaha, and others, and has recently been endorsed by Microsoft. Although +R/RW is not supported by the DVD Forum, both standards exist in the marketplace today.

So, what the hell does all of this mean for you? Many contemporary DVD drives now support both –R/RW and +R/RW. For example, the Plextor PX-712A drive supports both formats, and can write +R DVDs at 8X speeds (-R discs at 4X speeds). However, the support is not universal. The trick is to check your media against the drive's particular specification.

DISC LIFESPAN

The Annoyance: I've been using some CD-RW discs to backup my daily work, but I've been getting some flaky behavior from a couple of the discs lately. Are the discs failing?

The Fix: In an ideal world, rewritable discs should last up to 1,000 rewrites. In the real world, however, things don't always work so well. Rewritable technology is sound enough, but the real-life drives and media that we rely on can easily become compromised due to poor construction, poor-quality materials, and environmental factors (such as excess dust in the air).

Address flaky CD-RW discs the same way you would any commercial CD: check for dust and stains that might interfere with reading and writing. Also, clean your drive periodically.

Next, quality can have a profound influence on the life of your RW media. A quality name-brand disc in its own jewel case will last longer than a generic disc sold in bulk rods.

Fortunately, packet writers include diagnostic tools for testing and repairing rewritable discs suffering from damaged or lost files (see Figure 6-16). Discs that demonstrate frequent problems are unreliable, and should certainly be replaced immediately.

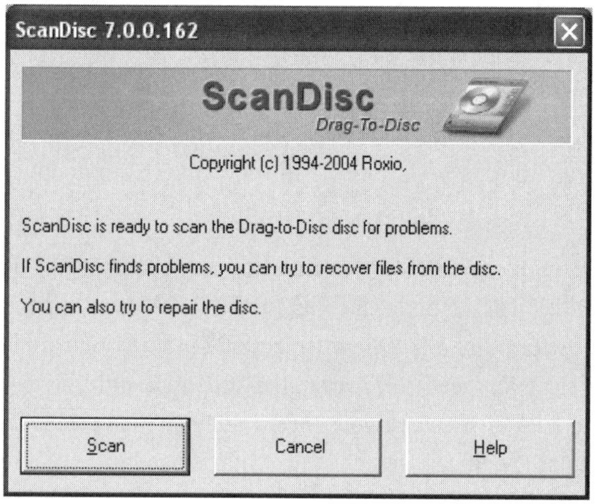

Figure 6-16. Use ScanDisc (or your own packet writer's diagnostic) to check an RW disc for serious file problems.

REWRITABLE DISC SHORT ON SPACE

The Annoyance: My CD-RW disc is supposed to hold 650MB, but I only see about 530MB available after formatting. Where did the space go?

The Fix: This is a perfectly normal side effect of Roxio's DirectCD packet writing technology. You did indeed buy a 650MB rewritable disc, but about 120MB of the disc is set aside for packet writing purposes. This leaves you with just around 530MB of actual storage space. That's still plenty of space for documents, photographs, and even your favorite music.

SOFTWARE INCORRECTLY REPORTS MEDIA

The Annoyance: Why are Easy CD and DVD Creator reporting my DVD+R media as +RW media?

The Fix: If your drive does not fully support DVD+R, the software will report a +R disc as a +RW disc. For example, the Ricoh DVD+RW RW5120 drive incorrectly reports +R media. Check with the drive manufacturer for any available firmware updates. Otherwise, you should consider a drive upgrade to a more recent DVD+/-R/RW model that offers better compatibility.

REWRITING AT 32X

The Annoyance: My new CD-RW drive is supposed to rewrite at 32X, but I can't find any media for the drive. How do I get the best speed from this drive?

The Fix: You may need to do a little shopping to find 32X media. Although some of the newest drives (such as Plextor's PlexWriter External USB 52/32/52 drive) support 32X rewriting, the drives are actually being released in advance of available media. In other words, you're stuck using slower 24X media until media companies such as Verbatim and Ricoh catch up (see "Writing and Rewriting in High Speed" earlier in this chapter). Even after a thorough search of CompUSA and Staples, 32X RW media can't be had for love or money. Fortunately, the newest RW drives also frequently support slower "high-speed" (4X–10X) drive media, which is much more readily available (and far less expensive).

Check with the drive manufacturer and verify the compatibility of any 32X media before you actually buy it. Also, check for firmware upgrades to streamline any potential 32X compatibility or performance issues with the drive before you start recording.

XP DOESN'T ERASE RW FILES

The Annoyance: Why can't Windows XP erase files from my CD-RW disc?

The Fix: You'd think that Microsoft could beg, borrow, or steal some decent rewritable support for Windows XP, but that's one feature that really fell through. Windows XP doesn't incorporate UDF packet writing, so it can't format CD-RW discs. When you insert an unformatted CD-RW disc, Windows XP treats the disc as a CD-R. You can certainly copy files or folders to the CD-RW disc, but you can only erase the entire disc (you don't get the individual file control that rewriteable media promises). Maybe Windows XP Service Pack 2 (or even Longhorn) will fill in this gap. In the mean time, you'll need to use a packet writing utility such as Roxio's Drag-to-Disc in order to enable UDF and format the CD-RW disc. With a packet writer in place, it's a simple matter to treat the RW disc like a big floppy—adding and erasing individual files as needed.

DVD FILE SIZE LIMITS

The Annoyance: Why can't I write files larger than 2GB to my DVD?

The Fix: You've probably selected the ISO format rather than the DVD-ROM (UDF) format. Since the ISO standard does not allow files larger than 2GB, you'll need to select an appropriate UDF format instead. Go back into your software (such as Nero Burning ROM) and recreate your video project, but be sure to select the "DVD-ROM (UDF)" format (see Figure 6-17).

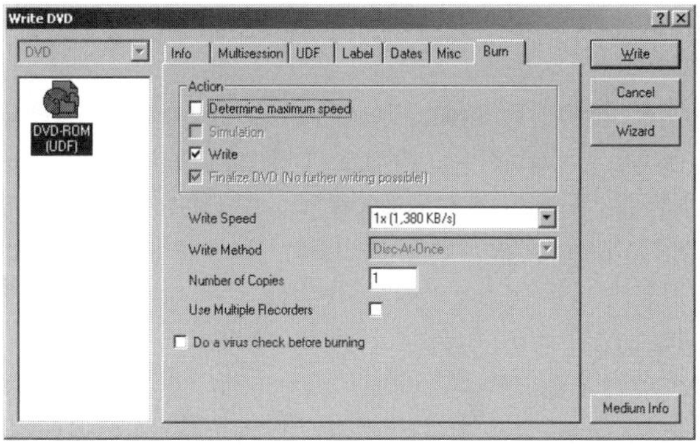

Figure 6-17. For large DVD video projects, be sure to select the DVD-ROM (UDF) format type.

BURNING SOFTWARE ANNOYANCES

ELIMINATING MUSIC GAPS

The Annoyance: I want to burn some music, but I hate the gaps between each track. How can I get rid of those aggravating gaps?

The Fix: So you want to run one song into another, right? Well, okay. To reduce or eliminate the inter-track gap, insert a fresh CD, open your burning software (such as Nero 6), and then open your project (your selected songs will appear in the compilation window). Highlight each song where you want to eliminate the pause. Right-click in the compilation window and choose Properties. Enter "0" as the new pause length (or enter a small number to keep a brief pause). Now click OK to save your changes and burn the new CD.

HANDLING PARAMETER ERRORS WHILE BURNING

The Annoyance: I get parameter errors when I try to burn audio CDs using MP3 files. What should I do?

The Fix: Parameter errors often occur because the burning program (e.g., Easy CD Creator) can't convert MP3 files into Red Book audio (CD-DA) data. Most burning software requires an MP3 data bit rate of at least 128Kb/s. Check the characteristics of your source MP3 files—if the bit rate (quality) is too low, the burner can't recreate accurate CD audio data. Remember that music CDs use a bit rate of 192Kb/s, so rip your CD-quality MP3s at 192Kb/s.

You may also need to acquire better quality MP3 files. In other cases, the source MP3 file may not contain enough information for proper validation. Again, try a good-quality MP3 file. As a rule, use the burning software's Test feature before writing. This should identify any troublesome MP3 files for you without wasting media on poor burns. Once you've identified the file(s) that are causing the parameter errors, you can delete them from the project or obtain good-quality versions of those files.

TRACK ORDER CHANGES

The Annoyance: Why does the file order of my MP3 tracks change when I burn an MP3 CD?

The Fix: An audio CD uses the Red Book (CD-DA) audio format, which keeps track names in their physical order on the disc. However, a disc containing MP3 files is basically a CD-ROM Yellow Book data disc. As with any data disc, the CD-ROM Yellow Book standard forces all data files into alphabetical order, regardless of their location on the disc. In other words, an MP3 file is just a regular data file. Burning a CD full of 11 hours of digital music files is the same as creating a disc full of documents.

For example, suppose you burned four tunes to the disc in this order: Giant Steps, Cousin Mary, Spiral, and Naima. If the tracks were pure Red Book audio, they'd appear in exactly that order. But if you burned them as MP3 tracks, My Computer or other browsing utilities would show them in their alphabetical order ("Cousin Mary," "Giant Steps," "Naima," and "Spiral").

To work around this little annoyance, re-burn the disc after renaming the files using prefixes that will place the tracks into your desired order (such as *01_Naima.MP3*, *02_Spiral.MP3*, *03_Giant Steps.MP3*, and *04_Cousin Mary.MP3*). The files will still be sorted alphabetically, but the prefixes will cause the files to appear in the desired order.

PLUG-INS EXTEND BURNING FEATURES

The Annoyance: Why does NeroVision Express only offer support for Video CD projects? How do I record Super VCD or DVD projects?

The Fix: The basic versions of NeroVision Express do not support SVCD or DVD burning. For example, the DVD-Video Plug-In is not included with the OEM version of NeroVision Express 2 SE (OEM) bundled with typical computer systems. Function-limited software generally requires an upgrade or registration purchase in order to unlock advanced features. To enable SVCD and DVD projects with Nero, you'll need to purchase the plug-in for NeroVision ($24.99), or upgrade to the Nero 6 Ultra edition ($69.99). Once installed, the DVD plug-in provides unlimited MPEG-2 encoding. Of course, you can opt for an entirely different burning program that includes SVCD and DVD recording right out of the box (such as Easy Media Creator). So, open up your wallet, because either way it's going to cost you in the end.

WINASPI DRIVER ERRORS IN NERO

The Annoyance: When I launch the latest version of Nero, I get WinASPI driver errors.

The Fix: The burning software can't initialize and access your CD-RW drive. Burning software such as Nero relies on ASPI (Advanced SCSI Programming Interface) drivers to carry commands and data between the SCSI host adapter and drives. If the burning software can't find its required drivers, it either means the software didn't install properly, or the ASPI drivers were removed. For example, Nero uses the *WNASPI32.DLL* driver. You can download the driver from Nero's Website (*http://nero.com/us/631940733573829.html*) or copy it from the Windows XP installation disc and put it in the *C:/Windows/System/* folder. Otherwise, uninstall your burning software using the Add or Remove Programs wizard, and then reinstall the software from scratch.

DRIVE SPEED DROPS

The Annoyance: Why does my selected recording speed drop down after I insert a disc?

The Fix: Well we'd all like to record our discs at 100X, but that's just not going to happen, is it? The drive speed and the media you use will limit the top recording speed for your system. For example, your 24X CD-RW drive will only record at 12X if you insert a 12X disc. The recording software will typically detect the drive and media speeds before burning. If you attempt to select a burning speed faster than the drive (or media), the burning utility will generally reduce the speed during the burn process.

If you're looking for additional burning speed, check your media speed against the drive's recording speed. Try faster media (or a different brand) if the drive will support it. For example, try 24X media in your 24X CD-R drive. Also, check with the drive maker for any available firmware upgrades that might improve burning performance. Sometimes a firmware upgrade improves performance by easing compatibility issues with certain brands of media. (See also "Writing and Rewriting in High Speed" earlier in this chapter.)

HANDLING SCSI TARGET ERRORS

The Annoyance: When I try to burn a disc with Nero, I get "SCSI Target" errors. What can I do?

The Fix: This little annoyance is really more of a SCSI communication issue than a software problem. Before you whip out your screwdriver and start taking the system apart, check your media—poor-quality, incompatible, or defective media can cause this type of error with your SCSI recorder. Try a disc recommended by the drive manufacturer.

Software conflicts are another common issue. When multiple burning programs are installed, their drivers may load and poll the drive, causing SCSI communication problems. Uninstall any other CD recording applications. If the problem persists, uninstall *all* of your recording programs, and then reinstall the recording software again from scratch.

If you're still stuck, there may be a more serious problem with the CD-RW drive or its connections to the computer. Power down the computer, open the chassis, and examine the drive's signal cable. Make sure that the cable is secured at the drive and the controller ends. Make sure that your SCSI devices are terminated properly. For example, if your SCSI CD-RW drive is the last physical device on your SCSI cable, its termination should be enabled. Finally, the drive itself may be defective. Try a different drive or burning application. If other applications fail to write, replace the drive.

CAN'T READ CDS ON ANY SYSTEM

The Annoyance: I installed Nero under Windows XP, but I can't read the mastered CDs on any system.

The Fix: It turns out that older releases of Windows XP are rather finicky when it comes to CD-R/RW recording and playback support. Fortunately, the fine folks in Redmond have identified the trouble. Search Microsoft's Knowledge Base (*http://support.microsoft.com/default.aspx?scid=fh;EN-US;KBJUMP*) for article Q320174 and download the patch. Alternatively, use the Windows Update feature to download and install all of the updates for Windows XP.

KEEP SNOOPERS OUT OF DISCS

The Annoyance: I burn many discs with sensitive company information. Is there any way to prevent the data on my CDs from being read by others?

The Fix: It sounds like you'd be an ideal candidate for encryption and an industrial-strength shredder. Burning software such as Roxio's Easy CD Creator provides an encryption feature that will protect your valuable data from prying eyes. For example, just create a new CD project and add your data files. Then click the button with the little white piece of paper and a red padlock on it (three buttons left of the Burn button). Check the "Enable file encryption (128 bit)" box, then enter a password and confirm it. If you'd also prefer to obscure the file names, check the "Hide file names on this disc" box and click OK. Now burn the disc as usual. No one will be able to open your encrypted files without the correct password.

Retrieving encrypted files is easy using a corresponding utility such as Roxio Retrieve. This application is automatically added to every encrypted disc so that you can recover files on any computer (even systems that do not have Easy CD Creator installed). The Retrieve application should start automatically once you place an encrypted disc in the drive. Otherwise, just use My Computer to locate and start *Launch_Retrieve.EXE* on the CD. Enter the password and click OK. A list of files will appear. Check the files you want to copy to the host PC—decrypting the files in the process.

This is an important point. Unlike ordinary CD-R discs, which can be read directly (their contents do not need to be transferred to a host PC), encrypted CD-R discs can't decrypt their files on-the-fly. Instead, the encrypted files must be moved back to the PC to be decrypted. Consequently, reading an encrypted CD will demand hard drive space and time to decrypt the files.

Keep your password in a safe place—you can't decrypt the data without the correct password.

TROUBLE COPYING DVD MOVIES

The Annoyance: Why can't I copy the movie I bought? I just want to create my own personal backup.

The Fix: You're probably using the wrong software. Burning tools such as Roxio's Easy Media Creator will certainly duplicate your own personal CD or DVD movies (such as footage from your family vacations), but it will not copy any media with protective encryption technologies, such as CSS (Content Scrambling System).

By the way, you should remember that there are legal implications involved in any commercial DVD or CD copying. Look, I'm no lawyer, but even I can read the copyright statement at the beginning of any motion picture. Many legal-eagles might argue that the "fair use" clause of today's copyright law allows duplication for the purpose of personal archival backup, but it's clearly illegal to sell (or even give away) copies of movies, games, or other copyrighted works.

DISC SCRATCHES IMPAIR COPYING

The Annoyance: How come I get read errors when I try to copy my movie?

The Fix: Copying utilities attempt to make exact duplicates of discs. This means the software expects to see every bit and byte on the disc in order to transfer it to the new disc (or disc image to be burned later). A read error typically means that there's a scratch, smudge, dust, fingerprint, or other gunk that the drive can't read through. Little scratches won't cause a problem during playback, but a duplicator may pick them up. Find a soft, dry, lint-free cloth, and gently wipe the disc from the spindle to the edge (as if you were drawing the spokes of a wagon wheel). Now try the disc again.

If read errors persist on a movie disc, you can typically accept the error and continue—there will likely be little (if any) real data loss. However, the matter is a bit more critical for data CDs (e.g., games) where read errors may interrupt important files and render the copied disc defective or unusable.

HANDLING DIRECTCD ERRORS

The Annoyance: Why do I get an error telling me that the drive is in use by DirectCD? Why would the program lock out my drive?

The Fix: In most cases, DirectCD has locked a formatted disc, so other software (such as Easy CD Creator, Sound Stream, and CD Copier) can't access the formatted disc for writing (they expect to see blank, unformatted media). Remove the formatted media and insert a blank disc instead. That's the *easy* solution.

In other cases, there may be trouble with the burning software's installation. Try removing the burning application using the Add or Remove Programs wizard, and then reinstall the application from scratch (don't forget to check with the burning software maker for patches or updates).

There may also be a conflict with other software running in the background. For example, Norton System Works is known to occasionally cause this frustrating little glitch. Try disabling or removing any of your major background applications one at a time and try the burning software again. If you discover an application (such as System Works) causing the trouble, you can check for patches or upgrades that might ease the compatibility problem (or remove the conflicting software outright).

SOFTWARE DOESN'T RECOGNIZE DRIVES

The Annoyance: I just installed Easy CD Creator 6, but my CD and DVD drives don't show up under Windows.

The Fix: You've stumbled across a perplexing Registry error. Burning software (such as Easy CD Creator) depends on particular registry entries in order to recognize and access the optical drives on your system. If these entries become damaged or corrupted during software installation (or removal), the drives may no longer appear as part of your system. If you have more than one burning program on your system, try uninstalling all but the desired program. If the problem persists (or there's no other burning software on the system) there may be a registry glitch. Check with the software maker for patches or updates that will correct this problem. Roxio has a patch for Easy CD Creator available at *http://softwareupdates.roxio.com/gm/support/tools/DriveFixEZ_Installed.exe*.

RECOVERING LOST RW FILES

The Annoyance: I lost power while copying some files to my CD-RW disc, and I can't find those files even though now there's less free space on the disc. Can I recover those lost files, or do I need to rewrite the disc again?

The Fix: It might be possible to recover your files, though I wouldn't bet your next mortgage payment on it. Roxio's Drag-to-Disc includes the ScanDisc utility, which can often recover files not seen in Windows Explorer. This problem typically occurs because the writing process was interrupted before the file directory information was completed (though most or all of the files were actually written). ScanDisc can also recover damaged or lost files (see "Disc Lifespan"). For example, start ScanDisc from the Drag-to-Disc menu, select the RW drive, and click Scan. The utility will get disc information, find lost files, repair the disc, and check file integrity (see Figure 6-18).

Of course, file recovery is not a perfect process. If ScanDisc fails to recover the data, it's a simple matter to erase and rewrite the disc. (If you do not use Roxio, check your burning software for a recovery tool similar to Scan Disc.)

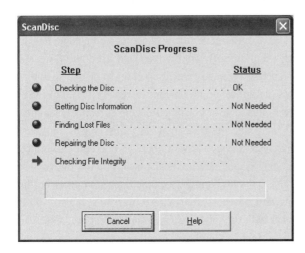

Figure 6-18. Roxio's ScanDisc utility can find lost files, repair damaged files, and often recover lost information.

DVD PLAYER ANNOYANCES

MP3 PLAYBACK FROM DVD

The Annoyance: My set top DVD player will play music CDs, but not MP3s burned to DVD-R or written to DVD-RW. Why not?

The Fix: Your commercial DVD player probably supports Red Book CD audio, but may be too old to handle MP3 file playback. The best way to approach this problem is to check the manufacturer's specifications of your player. If it doesn't support MP3 file playback, you're pretty much screwed. If the player does handle MP3 file playback, then chances are that it doesn't support the DVD-R or DVD-RW media. Again, check the manufacturer's specifications for compatible media. If the player only handles DVD-ROM media, you are out of luck.

DRIVER UPDATES BREAK DVD PLAYER

The Annoyance: I updated my video device driver, but now I can't start my DVD playback software. Any ideas?

The Fix: You probably broke the link between the DVD player and the video driver. When you install a DVD player (such as WinDVD), the software depends on the video driver and DirectX to access the video hardware. When you change the video driver, you can "break" the dependency between the player and driver. The player now fails to launch because it can't find the video driver. Launch the System Restore wizard to roll the system back to an earlier state (or use the Roll Back Driver button in the display adapter's Properties dialog to reinstate the earlier driver). If this fix works, you know the updated driver is the culprit. Update the driver again, and then uninstall and reinstall the DVD player software to reestablish the link between the player and driver.

MACROVISION WARNING

The Annoyance: When I try to play a DVD, I get a Macrovision warning from WinDVD. What's the problem?

The Fix: Macrovision, an anti-pirating technique, prevents you from recording movies during playback. For example, if you try to record from a DVD movie to a VCR, the tape becomes bright, and then dark, with very low sound. This makes the taped copy virtually unviewable. DVD Playback software such as InterVideo's WinDVD will not play a DVD through any video card with a TV output (unless the TV output supports Macrovision). If you receive Macrovision warnings (see Figure 6-19), you'll need to disable the TV output as directed by the video card manufacturer.

Figure 6-19. DVD movies might not play on video cards with TV output jacks.

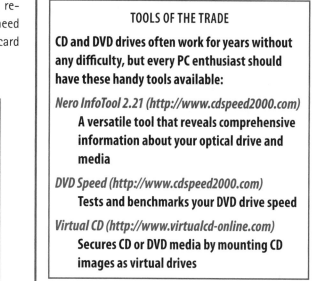

TOOLS OF THE TRADE

CD and DVD drives often work for years without any difficulty, but every PC enthusiast should have these handy tools available:

Nero InfoTool 2.21 (http://www.cdspeed2000.com)
    A versatile tool that reveals comprehensive information about your optical drive and media

DVD Speed (http://www.cdspeed2000.com)
    Tests and benchmarks your DVD drive speed

Virtual CD (http://www.virtualcd-online.com)
    Secures CD or DVD media by mounting CD images as virtual drives

Network
ANNOYANCES

When I started tinkering with PCs, the only way to share files between PCs was through the "sneakernet," which involved carrying floppy disks from one PC to another. Of course networks existed long before the PC, but only in the realm of high-end mainframe installations. The broad adoption of Ethernet networking transformed the way that computers exchanged information, which in turn enabled dramatic growth in Local Area Network (LAN) sizes, while lowering the cost. Then the Internet evolved, linking individual PCs and entire LANs into the single global information resource that we can't live without today.

Still, connecting diverse PCs to each other and the Internet is rarely a simple proposition. This chapter examines network hardware configuration and driver issues, and then looks at particular headaches related to ordinary dial-up modems and high-speed cable/DSL connections. You'll also find solutions to common wireless problems, along with some practical remedies for resource sharing and firewall annoyances.

CONFIGURATION ANNOYANCES

FINDING DETAILED NIC INFORMATION

The Annoyance: The Device Manager under Windows XP doesn't tell me very much about my Network Interface Card. How do I probe deeper into this device and find its gory details?

The Fix: Don't give up on Device Manager so hastily. Granted, you won't find anything other than basic identification information on the General tab or common driver version details on the Driver tab of the NIC Properties dialog. But if you move on to the Advanced tab (see Figure 7-1), you'll find lots of information about the device's current settings (such as Flow Control, Link Wakeup settings, Media Type, MAC address, I/O resources, and so on), though the exact options can vary dramatically between models and manufacturers.

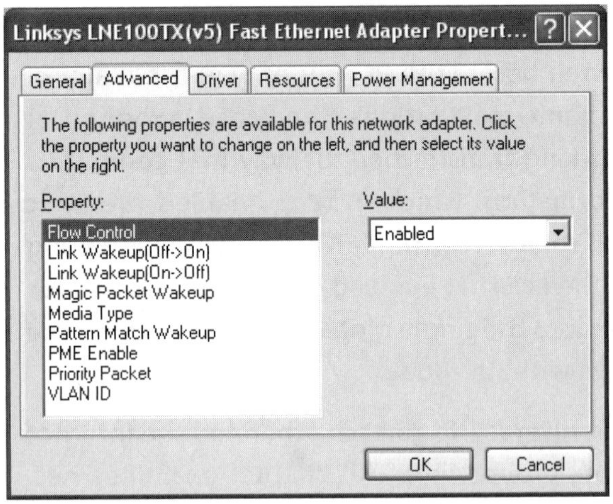

If you need further information about the adapter (the current firmware version, for example), other resources are available that can help you. For example, Windows XP provides a detailed System Information utility that outlines most aspects of your system's hardware and software. Just click Start → All Programs → Accessories → System Tools → System Information. Browse to Components → Network → Adapter, and the complete details of your NIC will appear (see Figure 7-2). Don't forget third-party tools, either. System diagnostic tools such as SiSoft SANDRA (*http://www.sisoftware.net*) will give you a slew of technical information about your NIC (see Figure 7-3), including power management settings.

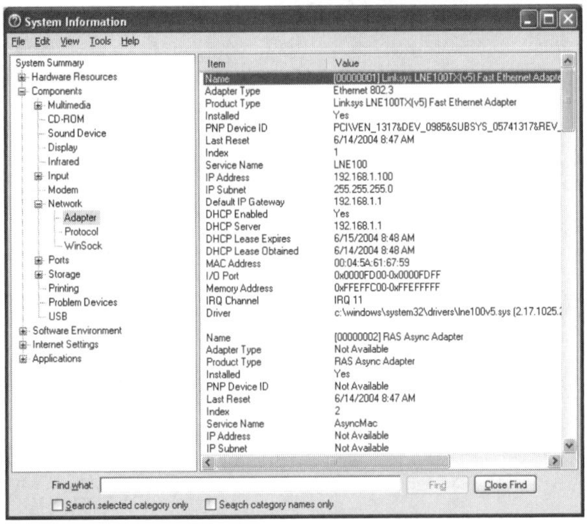

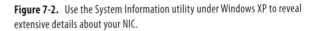

Figure 7-2. Use the System Information utility under Windows XP to reveal extensive details about your NIC.

In some cases, the NIC manufacturer may also provide a special utility that will provide the working details of your device. Check for utilities on the driver CD that accompanied the NIC or on the vendor's web site.

Figure 7-1. The Device Manager can offer a wealth of information about your NIC under Windows XP.

Figure 7-3. Utilities such as SiSoft SANDRA can reveal obscure and sometimes undocumented technical details about NICs and other devices.

UNDERSTANDING NETWORK NUMBERS

The Annoyance: When I went shopping for a router the other day, I was overwhelmed by all the choices. How am I supposed to make sense of 802.11b, 802.11a, and 802.11g? What do the numbers mean? What kind of speeds can I expect?

The Fix: Ah, the numbers can certainly be confusing, so here's what you need to know before you go shopping again. Home and small office wireless devices are all based on variations of the Institute of Electrical and Electronics Engineers (IEEE) 802.11 wireless standard. The 802.11b standard is the oldest and most widely adopted standard. It uses the popular 2.4GHz frequency band, and provides data rates to 11Mbps (megabits per second) at ranges of 100 to 150 feet indoors. The 802.11a standard is a bit more recent, using the relatively open (and otherwise unused) 5GHz band to achieve data rates to 54Mbps at ranges of only 25 to 75 feet. Typically, 802.11a devices are more expensive than 802.11b devices, but can coexist with 802.11b wireless network devices in the same area. The newest IEEE wireless standard is 802.11g, which tops out at to 54Mbps and uses the more common 2.4GHz band. It operates at ranges of 100 to 150 feet, and is backward compatible with 802.11b devices.

Data rates vary depending on real-life radio transmission factors, such as range and interference. As a wireless device ranges farther from its access point, radio signals weaken and data rates fall. You may notice that you get better data rates at your desk (closer to the access point) than in the coffee room (located further away from the access point). Interference also plays a part, especially on the popular 2.4GHz band, which is also used by cordless phones, microwaves, and other commercial electronic devices. For example, you may notice data rates fall dramatically whenever your neighbor talks on his cordless phone. That's because the phone's interference forces your wireless devices to resend any data lost due to interference, which reduces the effective data rate.

t i p

If you're configuring a new home or SOHO network today, opt for 802.11g devices because of their lower cost and greater range (compared to similar 802.11a devices), higher speed, and backward compatibility with existing 802.11b devices.

LOOK FOR FIRMWARE UPDATES

The Annoyance: What's all this talk about firmware updates for my Internet router? Am I going to have to buy new networking equipment?

The Fix: Put your wallet away. You don't need to buy new equipment just to change the firmware. First, determine your current firmware version. For example, you can locate the firmware version for an Internet router just by accessing the unit through a web browser and checking the Status or other configuration page (see Figure 7-4). Now you'll need to determine if a firmware upgrade is needed. That's usually as simple as a quick visit to the hardware maker's web site. Check the product support pages and see what's available. In most cases, upgrading firmware involves little more than downloading and executing a file, then rebooting the network hardware so that the new firmware takes effect. Bear in mind that vendors sometimes issue frequent updates, especially for products based on new standards like 802.11g, where fixes are needed to eliminate bugs and improve compatibility.

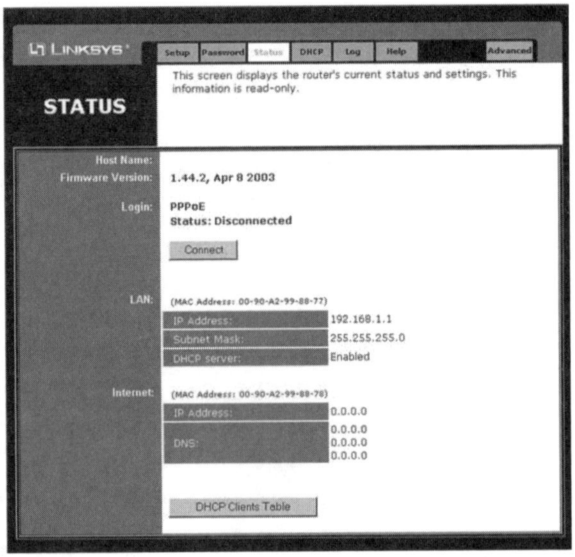

Always be sure to download the exact firmware version for your particular device, and follow the manufacturer's installation instructions closely. Because a firmware upgrade usually wipes out your existing wireless configuration, take note of your current channel, WEP/WPA keys, and other specific details before starting the upgrade.

BE CAREFUL WITH CROSSOVER CABLES

The Annoyance: Why can't I use a crossover cable to connect the PC to my hub? What difference does it make?

The Fix: A little knowledge is a dangerous thing. There are two types of Ethernet cables: straight-through and crossover. A straight-through cable is just as the name implies—each wire is connected to the same pin at each end of the wire (e.g., pin 1 at one end is connected to pin 1 at the other). A crossover cable reverses a pair of wires, connecting pins 1 and 2 at one end to pins 3 and 6 at the other end (and vice versa). For most Ethernet connections between devices (such as a PC NIC to a hub, or a router's WAN port to a cable modem), you need to use a straight-through cable. If a crossover cable is required—for example, to connect two switches or routers—you'll usually see an "X" next to the port.

The general rule is to use a straight-through cable for NIC-to-hub connections, but a crossover cable for NIC-to-NIC, PC-to-PC (peer-to-peer), or hub-to-hub connections.

Figure 7-4. Check the current firmware version of your networking devices before looking at upgrades.

Take a moment to check your connection. You can tell if the cable is correct by checking whether the link lights at both ends of the cable are illuminated. If you use the wrong cable (or the cable is damaged), the link LED will remain dark—showing that you have a cable problem.

CAN'T KEEP THE SAME IP ADDRESS

The Annoyance: Why the $#%@ do I get a different IP address every time I boot the PC? Can I keep the same IP address by leaving the PC on?

The Fix: This one takes a bit of explaining. Today's networks commonly use a technique called Dynamic Host Configuration Protocol (DHCP) to distribute configuration data (such as the IP address, subnet mask, and other settings) automatically to the PCs on a network. This process eliminates the need for you to reconfigure PCs manually every time you move one or add a new one to the network. DHCP doesn't permanently assign settings. Instead, it uses a short-term DHCP "lease" that ranges from a few hours to a few days. And you guessed right—leaving the PC on and active (not in standby or hibernate modes) is one way to renew the same IP address, since the lease is renewed periodically. When you log off the PC, its assigned IP address is released, and may be reallocated to another device on the network. This also explains why you can have more devices on the network than available IP addresses.

If you get a different IP address each time you start your system, that's a clue that your network is probably too congested. In other words, many PCs are probably vying for a limited number of IP addresses. Less congested networks (such as home networks with just a few users) often have no need to reassign IP addresses, because there are more addresses than PCs. In either case, DHCP should do the work for you.

As a rule, dynamic IP addresses are nothing to fear. The DHCP server (which could simply be your Internet router) keeps track of your PCs' IP and MAC addresses so that you can maintain access to your email and the Web regardless of how often your IP address changes. Dynamic IP addresses are, in fact, beneficial to PC security because they hinder hackers and other intruders from finding your particular IP address. The only time that dynamically assigned IP addresses may turn around and bite you is when you use them for a resource that requires a static IP address, such as a web server. A web server's IP address needs to remain static so that DNS lookup services across the Internet can consistently find it.

WRONG TIMESTAMP ON EMAIL

The Annoyance: The timestamp on my email is always wrong. Why does the Internet think I sent my mail before I actually did?

The Fix: Anytime you send an email or post to a newsgroup, the time setting from your PC is used to timestamp the transmission. If your PC clock is inaccurate, the timestamp will also be off, which can cause confusion if you try to track your email by time. Fortunately, it's easy to keep your clock on track.

Because PC clocks typically lose several seconds each week, you cannot consider them to be precision timepieces. In fact, as the PC ages, the CMOS backup battery weakens, and the timekeeping tends to slide even more. If you're losing several seconds a day or more, try replacing the CMOS backup battery on your motherboard (see Chapter 1 for more details).

You should enable automatic adjustments for daylight saving time (if you live in a time zone that uses it). First, double-click the clock icon in the Taskbar, then use the Date & Time tab to adjust your time on a regular basis (or whenever you see the time slipping). Next, select the Time Zone tab and check the "Automatically adjust clock for daylight saving changes" box.

In addition, you can synchronize your PC clock automatically over the Internet using the Internet Time tab (Figure 7-5). Select an available time server and click the Update Now button. Check the "Automatically synchronize with an Internet time server" box to have your clock updated for you. Remember to apply your changes before you close the dialog box.

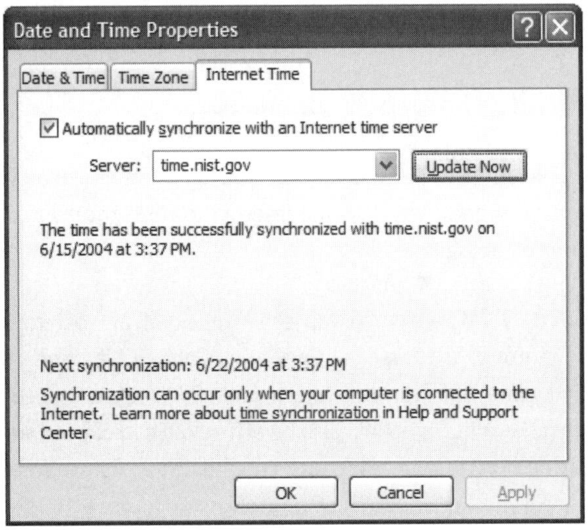

Date and Time Properties

Date & Time | Time Zone | Internet Time

☑ Automatically synchronize with an Internet time server

Server: time.nist.gov ▼ | Update Now

The time has been successfully synchronized with time.nist.gov on 6/15/2004 at 3:37 PM.

Next synchronization: 6/22/2004 at 3:37 PM

Synchronization can occur only when your computer is connected to the Internet. Learn more about time synchronization in Help and Support Center.

OK | Cancel | Apply

Figure 7-5. Avoid timestamp problems by keeping your PC clock automatically synchronized with Internet time sites.

If you notice a large difference between the timestamp and the actual time you sent the message (say, five to eight hours), it's probably because your ISP applies their timestamp to your email. Many ISPs with servers in multiple time zones will set their entire network to UTC/GMT time to use a common time standard. For example, Hotmail always uses GMT stamps, regardless of where the sender or recipient accesses the Net.

MODEM ISN'T RECOGNIZED

The Annoyance: I installed a modem in my home-brewed PC, but the system doesn't seem to recognize it. Any suggestions on how I can wake it up?

The Fix: Today's PCI-based Plug-and-Play systems are very adept at recognizing devices like modems, so it's pretty unusual to find an uncooperative system. Still, it does happen. Start by checking the modem installation. Make sure that the PCI card is evenly and completely inserted into its slot and secured to the chassis with a single screw.

Recheck the modem's installation instructions. Some devices require you to install software before connecting the hardware device. If you install the modem card before the software, the system may not recognize it or it may identify the device improperly. Fortunately, you can easily remedy this annoying little glitch by removing any entries for the device from your Device Manager (including any "other" or "unknown" device categories). Next, power down the PC and remove the modem. Finally, install the modem software and reinstall the device as recommended by the manufacturer.

Still having trouble? In that case, a hardware conflict might be the culprit. Internal modems traditionally use the same resources applied to COM (serial) ports, so start by disabling your PC's COM ports through the System Setup routine. Unless you're using serial ports for some other purpose (like syncing your PDA), you won't need those ports for anything. Reboot the system and see if it recognizes the modem.

You can also try using a third-party diagnostic utility like Hank Volpe's Modem Doctor (*http://www.modemdoctor.com*) to confirm that the modem is installed and available. If all else fails, it's time to call tech support.

CONFIGURING MULTIPLE DIAL-UP CONNECTIONS

The Annoyance: I have a second ISP as a backup. Can I set up more than one dial-up connection in Windows?

The Fix: Windows allows you to set up as many dial-up-networking (DUN) connections as you'd like, though you can only use one at a time. Open the Network Connections control panel and choose "Create a new connection." The New Connection Wizard appears (see Figure 7-6). Follow the wizard to establish your new dial-up connection. To do this, you'll need to assign a name to the new connection, and have on hand a local POP number for your ISP and information about the type of connection. When you finish the wizard, the Dial-up Connections Settings dialog will accept your username and password, domain information, and any other details needed by your ISP. Then it's just a matter of double-clicking the connection icon on your desktop to test the new connection.

Fiure 7-6. Use the New Connection Wizard to establish additional dial-up network connections.

Modem. After a few seconds, a series of queries and replies should appear (see Figure 7-7). Locate the ATI11 entry, and make sure the response includes V.92. If not, you may need to contact the modem (or PC) manufacturer for assistance in either forcing the V.92 mode or replacing the modem with a true V.92 device.

Figure 7-7. Query the modem to confirm its V.92 operating status.

CONFIRMING V.92 MODE

The Annoyance: Is there a quick and easy way for me to ensure that my modem is actually working in V.92 mode?

The Fix: Yes, there is. The ATI11 response in your modem's diagnostic display will tell you exactly which operating mode the modem is in. So, where is it? Open the Phone and Modem Options control panel, click the Modems tab, highlight your modem device, and click the Properties button. When the Modem Properties dialog opens, click the Diagnostics tab and then click Query

MODEM CHANGES COM PORTS

The Annoyance: Why does my dial-up modem seem to change COM ports spontaneously?

The Fix: This happens with some Zoom V.92 PCI modems using Agere chipsets—the modem keeps jumping between COM3 and COM4. Basically, this changes the modem's hardware resource assignments, meaning that software that relies on the modem (such as AOL) has to search for the modem again. You can often fix this problem by updating the driver, which you can usually download from the manufacturer's web site. If the problem persists or no updated drivers are available, replace the modem with another make and model.

INSIDE ERROR CORRECTION

Modems use error-correction techniques to verify that information remains intact during a data exchange. A checksum is calculated and attached to each frame of data being sent. The receiving modem calculates a new checksum for the data frame and compares it to the checksum received with the data. If the two checksum figures match, the frame is good—if not, the frame is resent. Error correction is an essential part of large file transfers such as downloads. The two popular error-correcting protocols used by modems today are MNP2-4 and V.42. Remember that both modems must support the error correction protocol in order for it to be used. Otherwise, the modems will "negotiate down" to the lowest common protocol, which will slow down their data exchange rate.

QUIETING A NOISY MODEM SPEAKER

The Annoyance: How do I turn off the modem speaker? Its squealing is driving me nuts.

The Fix: This is an easy one—you can control the modem's speaker volume directly through the modem's Properties dialog. Open the Phone and Modem Options control panel, click the Modems tab, highlight your modem device, and click the Properties button. When the modem Properties dialog opens, click the Modem tab (see Figure 7-8). Lower the "Speaker volume" slider to off, and

click OK to save your changes. If your modem doesn't provide this slider, click the Advanced tab instead and type the following command in the Extra Settings line:

    M0L0

The M0 command will turn off the speaker each time the modem initializes.

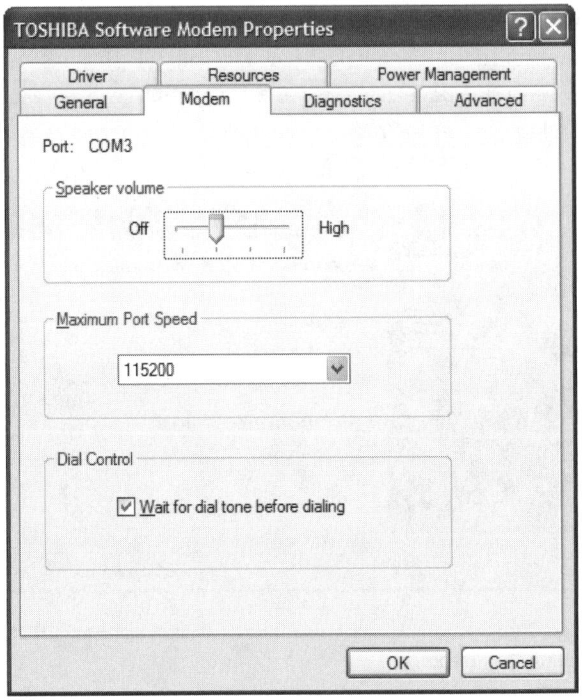

Figure 7-8. Use the slider to lower (or disable) the modem's internal speaker.

NEW CABLE MODEM ISN'T WORKING

The Annoyance: I bought a new cable modem and set it up according to the instructions, but I can't get it to work. What am I doing wrong?

The Fix: Start by rechecking the cable modem installation. Make sure that the cable modem is properly powered on and securely attached to the cable provider's coaxial connector. Next, make sure that you're using the proper Ethernet cabling for your network. You normally need to use a straight-through cable rather than a crossover cable, though some cable modem models may require a crossover cable to a router—it really depends on the specific cable modem device. You may need to give your cable provider the Media Access Control (MAC) address of your new cable modem so that they can configure your account to service the new device. The MAC address is usually located on a label underneath or behind the device.

> **tip**
>
> Not all cable providers will support every retail cable modem. Some providers favor their own "preferred" model(s). Obtain a list of compatible cable modems from your cable provider.

DUN PASSWORD ISN'T SAVED

The Annoyance: Why doesn't my dial-up networking service save my password?

The Fix: Normally, your dial-up networking feature is supposed to save your password along with other logon credentials (like your username). Make sure the "Save password" box is checked when entering the logon credentials. If you close and reopen the connection dialog, a password entry should appear. However, if a password entry does not appear (forcing you to re-enter the password each time you attempt a connection), chances are that your password file is corrupt. Locate every .PWL file in the C:\Windows folder. Rename the file(s) and then reboot Windows. This should force Windows to create new PWL files for you. Try the connection again. You'll need to re-enter the password once again, but it should be saved this time. You may also be able to locate a patch for this issue directly from Microsoft (*http://support.microsoft.com/*).

CONNECTION FAULT PAUSES PC

The Annoyance: Ever since I installed a NIC on my system, it seems to pause periodically.

The Fix: The system pauses because the NIC can't communicate with the network. I'd suspect a faulty network connection. Perhaps you haven't connected your NIC to other PCs through a hub yet, or perhaps you're using a crossover cable rather than a straight-through cable (see the earlier annoyance "Be Careful With Crossover Cables").

As soon as you attach your PC to the network and see the link light illuminate, I bet that the system hesitation goes away. If not, the NIC itself may be defective. Try disabling the NIC through the Device Manager. To do this, simply right-click the NIC and select Disable, then reboot the system so that Windows completely disables the NIC. If that solves your unexpected pauses, recheck the NIC configuration, update the NIC driver, or replace the NIC with another make and model.

NEW DEVICE DISABLES NIC

The Annoyance: I installed a new device in my PC, but now the NIC isn't working.

The Fix: Hmmm...you may have created a hardware resource conflict by adding the new device. Conflicts are rare today because the PCI expansion bus allows for interrupt sharing between devices, but if your system is heavily loaded, the odds that you'll have a conflict increase. To check, open the System control panel, click the Hardware tab, and then click the Device Manager button. If the NIC is marked with an exclamation mark icon, expand the "Network adapters" entry, right-click the NIC, and select Properties. Examine the "Device status" area of the General tab (see Figure 7-9)—any conflict information will be displayed for you. The easiest way to correct this type of problem is simply to remove the new device (which follows the troubleshooting rule of thumb "last in, first out"). If the problem clears up, you've confirmed that the new device is indeed the culprit. If so, you'll need to reconfigure the new device (try swapping PCI slots with another device) or opt for an external (USB or FireWire) version of the device.

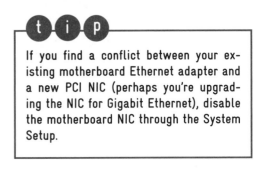

Figure 7-9. Use the Device Manager to check for hardware conflicts that might interfere with your NIC.

If the NIC stops working but there's no conflict, there may be an issue with the NIC drivers. Perhaps the new device drivers are interfering with your NIC drivers. Download the latest NIC drivers from the manufacturer, highlight the NIC in your Device Manager, click Delete, then reboot

the system. As Windows reboots, it should re-detect the NIC and allow you to install the latest drivers.

POWER LOSS STOPS INTERNET ACCESS

The Annoyance: Ugh, I just lost power. When the power came back, I no longer had Internet access from my PCs. What's the deal?

The Fix: Power failures may cause the Internet router to stop working properly. First, you'll need to see whether the Internet router is the problem. Test this by connecting the NIC from one of your PCs directly to the LAN port on your cable/DSL modem. If you can get to the Internet from that PC, you know the router is at fault. If not, contact your high-speed ISP for further assistance in testing your service (and possibly replacing your cable/DSL modem).

If you determine that the router is the problem, try pressing the router's Reset button or cycling power to the router once your PCs are running. Disconnect the AC adapter, count to 10, then reconnect the AC adapter. These steps may allow the router to redetect the networked PCs and restore Internet access. If that fails, reset the modem according to the manufacturer's instructions. This usually involves cycling power to the unit while you hold down the Reset button, which forces the router to restore its factory defaults. After that, you may need to reconfigure the router for your network.

Of course, if you cannot access the router (directly or through its web configuration utility), or if its indicators suggest an internal fault, the router itself may be damaged and need to be replaced. While an everyday power failure shouldn't toast a router, I've lost several network devices (including a router) in a particularly nasty New England lightning storm, so it can and does happen.

REDUCE NETWORK DELAY

The Annoyance: I've got some Windows 2000 PCs on my network that stay busy and cause annoying delays. How can I speed things along without making a huge investment in gigabit Ethernet?

The Fix: You may have a latency problem. Latency indicates how long it takes for a packet of data to get from one point to another. Busy networks might experience heavy latency because of excess traffic. Although you'd ultimately do better to segregate the network architecture and connect the different segments with a switch (rather than just a hub), a cheap alternative might be to increase the size of the request buffer in the system Registry. The SizReqBuf value ranges from 1024 to 65535 bytes, with 4356 being the default. If you have more than 512MB of RAM, increase this value to 16384. To make this change, follow these steps:

1. Select Start → Run, type **regedit**, and click OK.

2. Browse to the following entry (see Figure 7-10):

   HKEY_LOCAL_MACHINE\System\CurrentControlSet\ Services\LanmanServer\Parameters

3. Select Edit → New → DWORD Value, use the name SizReqBuf and select REG_DWORD, then enter a decimal value of 16384.

4. Save your changes and restart the computer.

You should notice better performance, especially when browsing large file folders.

t i p

Microsoft tells you how to modify the default SizReqBuf value in Article Q320829 (*http://support.microsoft.com/default.aspx ?scid=fh;[LN];kbjump*).

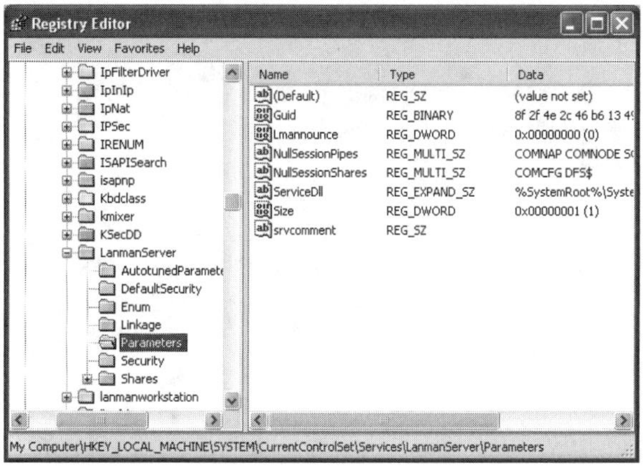

Figure 7-10. Use the Registry Editor to increase the size of the request buffer.

Warning. . .
Always make a backup copy of the Registry before making any changes. If you make Registry changes incorrectly, your PC may not boot.

LOCATING AN ELUSIVE MAC ADDRESS

The Annoyance: My ISP wants something called my NIC MAC address before it'll let me set up a broadband connection. Where do I find that?

The Fix: The Media Access Control (or MAC) address is a unique identifier that is assigned to each device on the network. This address is encoded into the firmware of each device by the manufacturer, and must be unique so that no two devices in the world use the same address. The MAC address is typically printed on the underside of major components (e.g., routers), but is harder to find on internal network devices such as NICs. Fortunately, the Windows utility *ipconfig* will show you the MAC address without you ever having to lift a screwdriver. Simply open a command prompt, type **ipconfig /all**, and press Enter. You'll see the MAC address listed as the "Physical Address" (see Figure 7-11).

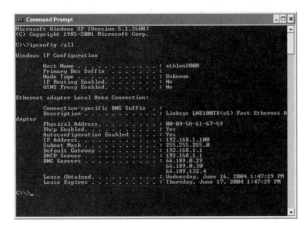

Figure 7-11. The ipconfig utility will reveal your local PC's MAC address, along with many other operating details.

MODEM ANNOYANCES

MODEM WON'T DIAL OUT

The Annoyance: I can't get my modem to dial out. I hear a click followed by the number tones, but I don't hear a dial tone. I don't see anything wrong in the Device Manager.

The Fix: You've probably got a problem with the telephone line. First, plug a telephone into the wall jack using the same phone cord that you plugged into the modem. Verify that you get a dial tone. If not, then there's a problem with the telephone cord, the phone line, or the jack. Try another telephone cord first. If that doesn't work, contact your local phone company and report the problem.

Examine the little metal fingers on your modem's phone jacks; look for any bent or damaged contacts that might prevent a good connection. If you find damage, you'll have to replace the modem. Otherwise, reconnect the telephone cord and ensure that you attach the cord to the modem port (not the daisy-chained telephone port). If the problem persists, the modem's internal phone interface circuit may be damaged, so try another modem instead.

MODEM DROPS CONNECTION AFTER SEVERAL MINUTES

The Annoyance: My modem connects for just a few minutes over a dial-up connection, then disconnects.

The Fix: Disconnect problems are very common with dial-up connections, and can usually be traced to one of several areas. Before you simply assume that there's a problem with your hardware, consider your phone line. Keep in mind that a telephone connection between two points is established through a hodgepodge of telephone cables, switching stations, and analog-to-digital-to-analog telephone company infrastructure. Chances are that you'll occasionally encounter noisy connections. Poor line quality (especially in rural areas or when you dial into distant POPs) is a frequent culprit. Try selecting a different access number for your ISP, ideally a local number so that you can avoid racking up long distance charges.

Old or bug-ridden modem drivers can be another source of problems. Since the driver operates your modem hardware and tells the modem how to respond to line events, it's always a good idea to make sure you've got the latest modem driver. Check the vendor's technical support or web resources for any driver updates.

If your ISP is still using a V.90 modem (which is usually listed in the access number list on its web site), you may need to extend the negotiation time during your dialing process or force your modem into V.90 mode by adding the following initialization string to the modem's Properties:

```
S7=150+MS=V90
```

Open the Phone and Modem Options control panel, click the Modem tab, highlight your modem, and click the Properties button. Next, click the Advanced tab, enter the string in the Extra Settings field, and click OK. Now reboot the system and try the modem again.

BROWSING PROBLEMS WITH EARTHLINK

The Annoyance: Why can't I display web pages when using Internet Explorer with EarthLink?

The Fix: The problem is that EarthLink Accelerator and its companion Fast Lane utility interfere with Internet Explorer (IE), forcing proxy server settings that prevent IE from accessing web pages normally. If you want to browse the Web with IE, the solution here is to uninstall both EarthLink Accelerator and Fast Lane using the Add or Remove Programs wizard. (Of course, by doing this, you're disabling the accelerated service for which you're paying a premium. Instead, you may want to switch to a different web browser, shop for a new ISP, upgrade to broadband, or subscribe to EarthLink's non-accelerated service.)

Once you've removed EarthLink Accelerator and Fast Lane, adjust your Internet Explorer properties to disable any proxy server selection. For example, Start Internet Explorer and select Tools → Internet Options, and click the Connections tab (see Figure 7-12).

Figure 7-12. Remove any proxy server selections to restore normal IE operation.

Highlight the EarthLink connection, click Settings, uncheck any proxy server options in the dialog, and click OK. Back in the Connection tab, select "Always dial my default connection." Now click the LAN Settings button, uncheck any proxy server options there as well, and click OK. Apply your changes and click OK. Close and reopen Internet Explorer or reboot your PC. This should restore IE to normal operation.

ISSUES WITH MOH AND ID

The Annoyance: I'm having trouble with the modem's advanced features, such as modem-on-hold and caller ID. Any advice?

The Fix: Modem-on-hold (or MOH) is an interesting feature of V.92 technology. Prior to V.92, an incoming call would simply knock a modem offline. You'd need to disable call waiting by adding a command prefix like *70 to your dialing sequence. Of course, you'd then miss any calls that came in while you were online. With MOH, a modem alerts you to an incoming call. If you answer, the modem suspends its communication with the ISP for several minutes (long enough for a brief conversation), then re-establishes communication so that you can pick up where you left off.

> **tip**
>
> Your Internet service provider or online service will determine the maximum on-hold time for your modem. It is often limited to less than 10 minutes.

Of course, you'll need to subscribe to call waiting in order to use MOH. Also, both ends of your modem connection (you and your ISP) must use V.92-compliant modems with MOH enabled. Check with your ISP to confirm that they're using these settings. In some cases, you may need to use a different phone number to access V.92 hardware at the ISP. Also, check your phone bill to ensure that Caller ID (or Caller ID Plus) is part of your service.

179

USB MODEM SHOWS NO LIT LEDS

The Annoyance: I installed a USB modem, but I don't see any LEDs lit up on the device.

The Fix: Because many external USB modems draw power from the USB port itself, be sure to connect the modem directly to a USB port or to a powered USB hub. If you don't see any lit indicators on the connected modem, you're probably dealing with an installation issue.

> **tip**
>
> Once the modem is installed, use the Diagnostic tab of the modem's Properties dialog to query the device (see Figure 7-7).

Highlight the modem in your Device Manager. Remove it, and then remove any modem software using the Add or Remove Programs wizard. Now unplug the modem from its USB port and reboot the computer. Download the latest modem driver directly from the manufacturer's web site. Once the new drivers are in place, try reconnecting the modem to a different USB port, if possible. You should see one or more indicators lit up on the modem, which tells you that the modem is ready for use. If not, recheck the power connections and installation instructions once again, or contact the modem manufacturer for specific assistance.

PC UPGRADE DISABLES MODEM

The Annoyance: I upgraded my PC's operating system, but now the modem won't respond. Why do I see only generic modem drivers now?

The Fix: Although I can't say for sure just what happened to your particular system, it seems that the upgrade interfered with the existing modem, and forced the system to use generic "Hayes-compatible" drivers. Though

frustrating, this is hardly fatal. Just reinstall the modem using the latest drivers.

Highlight the modem in the Device Manager. Remove it, delete any entries listed under your Device Manager's "Other devices" category, and then remove any related modem software from the Add or Remove Programs wizard. Now shut down the computer and physically disconnect the modem. Restart the system, then download and install the latest modem driver directly from the manufacturer. Once the newest drivers are in place, power down again and reinstall the modem. The next time your system starts, it should detect and install the modem properly.

DATA COMPRESSION BASICS

Modems transmit data over telephone lines using analog sounds. By increasing the complexity of those sounds, a modem can transmit more bits in a given time. Still, the process can be quite slow. Modems commonly employ data compression to repackage data in smaller chunks prior to transmission, and then use the same compression scheme on the receiving end to restore the data to its original format. Modems negotiate their compression scheme during the initial dial-up, and agree on the highest common scheme supported at both ends. Two common compression protocols are MNP-5 (with a compression ratio of 2:1) and v.42bis (which has a 4:1 compression ratio). Some file types (such as files already compressed with ZIP) cannot be further compressed. V.42bis can sense if compression is unnecessary, and can speed up transfer of precompressed files as well. Today's V.92 modems employ V.44 compression, which specializes in speeding up web page downloads.

INCOMPATIBLE AT COMMANDS

The Annoyance: Some AT commands won't work with my modem. I can't configure the modem the way I want.

The Fix: Modem features can vary dramatically from model to model, and not every modem supports every AT command. For example, a voice-over-data modem (often used by gamers) uses AT commands that a generic fax/modem doesn't support. As a more specific example, a modem that doesn't support modem-on-hold lacks the functionality to recognize a +PHMR (Initiate MOH) command.

Bottom line: if you feel the need to tinker with your modem, be sure to have its user guide or command reference guide handy. Guides typically include the complete suite of commands supported by your particular modem model, so check for compatible commands before wasting your time fiddling with commands that won't work. If your modem doesn't support the features you want, be prepared to shop for a new one.

V.44 DOESN'T IMPROVE ALL TRANSFERS

The Annoyance: I installed a V.92/V.44 modem to make my FTP download speed faster, but see absolutely no change. What's the problem?

The Fix: I hate to disappoint you, but there's probably no problem at all. V.44 compression is optimized for common file types normally associated with Internet use—e.g., web pages, GIF graphics, and documents such as Adobe Acrobat PDFs. As a result, you'll see the greatest improvement when you're browsing the Web, rather than using the Internet for other things, such as FTP, Telnet, and gopher. You'll also notice that web searches are faster, especially searches of web stores or pages that have large amounts of text and lots of small images. Email and text files show a noticeable (but modest) improvement. You're unlikely to see any detectible improvement when downloading files (usually program, text, or zipped files) from an FTP site. As always, your mileage may vary.

CABLE ANNOYANCES

STREAMING DATA GETS CHOPPY

The Annoyance: Why is my streaming video choppy now that my son is sharing the cable connection?

The Fix: This happens because average bandwidth drops as you add more PCs to the network. You're only buying a certain amount of bandwidth from your cable provider, regardless of how many PCs are networked to your Internet connection. When your PC was the only system using that connection, you had enough bandwidth to play streaming video without any difficulty. But when your son connected his PC to the home network, it reduced the amount of bandwidth available for you. So if he's downloading a file on his PC while you're playing streaming media, your streaming video will probably appear choppy or erratic. If it's any consolation, your son is probably wondering why he's getting such crappy download speeds.

The easiest solution is to increase the buffer size for your streaming video, or "time share" your download-intensive tasks. For example, if you watch streaming videos from 8pm to 9pm, your son can start downloading after 9pm when you're done. This takes a little cooperation, but it's free. Otherwise, you may need to increase your Internet bandwidth by purchasing a faster service plan. Fortunately, broadband costs are falling, so see what alternative plans are available.

SPEEDING UP THE BROADBAND CONNECTION

The Annoyance: Can I wring any more speed from my broadband connection by making changes in the Registry? I've heard that there are settings that can help, but I don't know what they are.

The Fix: While it is possible to tinker with individual Registry settings, why bother? Instead, use an automated tool such as SpeedGuide's TCP Optimizer utility (*http://www.speedguide.net/downloads.php*). This free program supports Windows 9x through XP, and does not require installation—just download and run. The utility finds your best MaxMTU setting, tests latency, and automatically tweaks all of the important broadband-related Registry settings (see Figure 7-13).

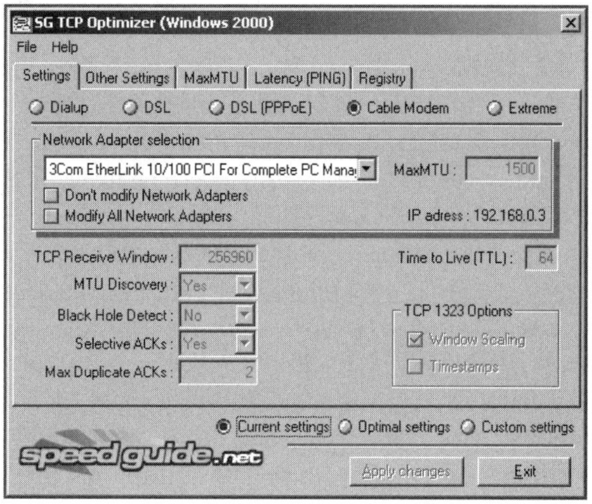

Figure 7-13. SpeedGuide's TCP Optimizer automatically tweaks the broadband-related entries in the Wndows Registry.

Before you tinker with the innermost workings of your operating system, run a few quick tests to gauge the system's current speed. First, try SpeedGuide's online TCP/IP Analyzer to check current settings such as MTU, MSS, RWIN, bandwidth, and other parameters. The information returned by this utility will not only show you the current settings, but also flag potential areas for improvement (see Figure 7-14). Another popular resource is CNET's Bandwidth Meter (*http://reviews.cnet.com/7004-7254_7-0.html?tag=cnetfd.dir*), which measures the bandwidth of your broadband connection at any given time.

If you're still tempted to mess with the Registry yourself, bear in mind that you're courting disaster if you don't know what you're doing. Always make a backup of your Registry before you touch it. There are many cryptic and arcane entries in the Registry; by changing the settings incorrectly, you can easily render your system unbootable. My advice? If you've never heard of *regedit*, put the mouse down and slowly step away from the computer.

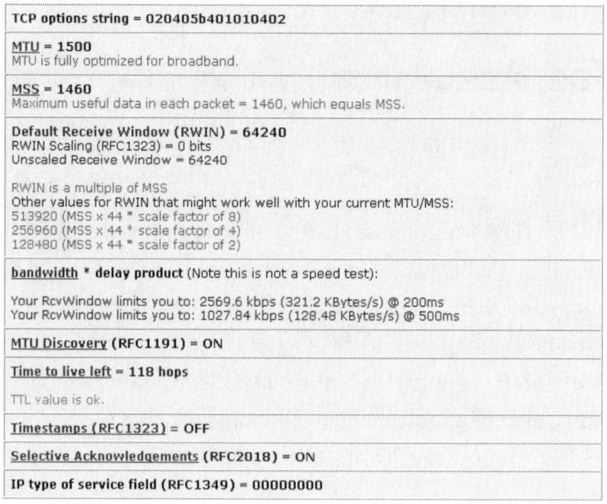

Figure 7-14. Online tools like SpeedGuide's TCP/IP Analyzer can reveal connection details before you even get started.

CHECKING BROADBAND SECURITY

The Annoyance: I just moved to a broadband connection, but all these recent security problems have me spooked. Is there an easy way to check how secure my PC is before I drop more cold, hard cash on security software?

The Fix: Don't underestimate the power of decent security software. Always-on connections, such as cable and DSL connections, can easily leave your PC exposed to hackers. If you do nothing else, be sure to invest in firewall software for your PC. A firewall prevents unauthorized communication between your PC and other systems (from the Internet, for example), and warns you when someone attempts to poke around. McAfee Personal Firewall Plus (*http://www.mcafee.com*), Symantec's Norton Personal Firewall (*http://www.symantec.com*), and Zone Labs' ZoneAlarm (*http://www.zonelabs.com*) are all well-recognized firewall products to consider. If you have several PCs networked together and sharing an Internet connection, use a NAT-enabled router for even greater security. NAT (Network Address Translation) works by "hiding" your PCs safely behind a single router.

So, how vulnerable is your PC? Online tools like Security Scan at SpeedGuide.Net (*http://www.speedguide.net/scan.php*) will scan your PC and look at the information that your PC is sharing. It then provides a detailed listing of your port status, showing potential entry points into your system and offering suggestions to improve each port's security (see Figure 7-15). Alternatively, Steve Gibson's Shields Up site (available from *http://www.grc.com*) provides detailed feedback on all your system's ports (see Figure 7-16). Once you identify the possible entry points into your computer, you can apply a firewall to systematically close any unneeded ports. It's not a perfect system, but it's effective for most everyday PC users.

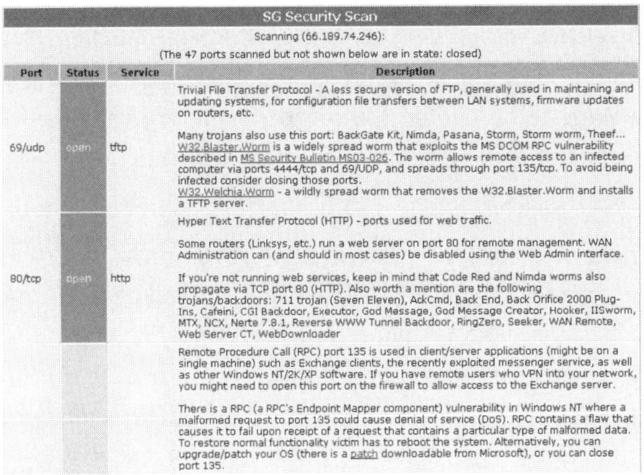

Figure 7-15. Online tools like SpeedGuide's Security Scan can quickly highlight the vulnerability of your system's ports.

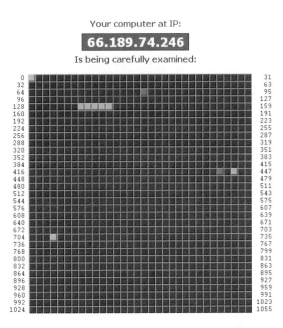
Your computer at IP:
66.189.74.246
Is being carefully examined:

Figure 7-16. Steve Gibson's Shields Up site provides comprehensive testing for hardware ports.

BI-DIRECTIONAL DATA RATES IMPAIRED

The Annoyance: Why does my download speed slow to a crawl when I try to upload data at the same time? I'm well below the bandwidth limit for my ISP.

The Fix: The problem you're experiencing is a common complaint. It's caused by the way TCP acknowledgements are handled in a network connection. It's a matter of traffic rather than bandwidth.

During an upload (or download), your PC communicates the RWIN (the TCP Receive Window) value to the remote server. When an RWIN's worth of data is transmitted, the receiving side must send an ACK (acknowledgement). This flow of acknowledgement packets is the means by which the sender paces the delivery of data to the recipient. To exchange data quickly, the data packets must arrive quickly, and the acknowledgements must be received promptly. It works the same way whether you're sending or receiving. Sounds simple, right? However, cable modems typically implement rate caps for uploads and downloads, so the combination of upload and download demands cause acknowledgement packets to queue up, waiting for a gap. The receiving end will see this as a slow link and reduce transmission speed accordingly, which cripples your upload or download speed.

One way you can get around this is to increase the RWIN value. This allows the sending PC to send a larger amount of data before it stops to wait for an acknowledgement. Windows 98 typically sets RWIN to 8192, which is so small that it always impacts simultaneous uploads and downloads. Windows Me typically uses 16384, but that's still a bit small. Windows 2000/XP generally adjusts to the prevailing line conditions, though you can still tweak the RWIN value by using a tool like SpeedGuide's TCP Optimizer (see Figure 7-13 and "Speeding Up the Broadband Connection," earlier in this chapter).

You can also use a smart download/upload management utility (such as P2P file sharing utilities), which can internally regulate the data rate demands on your network connection. By configuring the smart manager just below the rate caps of your cable modem, you can ensure that gaps are always available for acknowledgement packets. Ideally, you'll end up optimizing the data rate in both directions simultaneously.

FORBIDDEN WEB SITES

The Annoyance: My two XP computers use a router to share a cable line. Sometimes it works fine, but other times I get a "Forbidden. Access denied by access control list" message when I try to visit certain web sites.

The Fix: Since both of your networked PCs appear to access the Internet just fine, it isn't a network or PC problem. You'll see forbidden (or 403) errors in your browser window whenever the web server understands a URL but refuses to allow you access. You'll run into this error when a web page is restricted to personal or "in-house" use, and you don't have the password. You'll also see it if the webmaster for the site has configured the desired page incorrectly. For example, he may not have assigned "read permission" for all users. Finally, the web server

may be congested or down for maintenance, thereby prohibiting you from accessing it.

Start with the basics. Check the URL again; you may have copied or typed it incorrectly. If the URL is correct but you need a password to get in, recheck the password as you type it. Many passwords are case sensitive, so make sure you don't have Caps Lock on by accident. Since congestion can tie up a web site, try reloading or refreshing the page with the browser's Refresh button (or try again later). If the problem persists for more than a day or two, alert the webmaster.

CABLE MODEM GOES MUTE

The Annoyance: I can see other PCs on the network through my router, but I can't access the Internet through my cable modem. What's up with that?

The Fix: Since the router's internal hub is letting your PCs talk to one another, you've proven that the NICs and cabling to the router are fine. This eliminates a lot of troubleshooting. The problem has to be with the cabling from the router to the coax, or with your ISP. Start by checking the Ethernet cable between the router's Wide Area Network (WAN) port and the cable modem. You should see a link LED lit up on the cable modem port and a WAN LED lit up on the router. If not, the cable is detached or damaged.

Next, check the coaxial cable to the cable modem. First, make sure that the cable is tight. Power down the cable modem for at least 10 seconds, then power it up again and watch the indicator light sequence. It may take up to 30 seconds for the cable modem to synchronize with the ISP. You should see some kind of activity indicator telling you that data is moving at the cable line. If not, you may need to reboot the router, too. If you still don't see activity, then it probably means there's a problem with the cable line itself. Perhaps there's a line down somewhere, and your service is affected. Or perhaps there's an issue with your ISP or account. You do have to pay your bill, you know.

SLOW CABLE MODEM COMMUNICATION

The Annoyance: Why does my cable Internet connection seem so slow? I got broadband because it was supposed to be a lot faster than dial-up.

The Fix: Slow Internet access can be caused by several issues that you may or may not be able to control. The first thing that you should do is to measure the speed of your Internet communication using an online tool such as CNET's Bandwidth Meter (*http://reviews.cnet.com/7004-7254_7-0.html?tag=cnetfd.dir*) or SpeedGuide's TCP/IP Analyzer (*http://www.speedguide.net*). Once you've measured the bandwidth, compare it to the service level listed on your monthly cable bill. If the figures are relatively close, you're getting the speed that you've paid for, so it's not an issue with your ISP. Chances are that you're just visiting a high traffic or overly complex web site. If your bandwidth is significantly below the service level you're paying for, there may be interference from other PCs or other hardware (such as hubs, switches, and routers), all of which share bandwidth with your system. Try connecting your PC's NIC directly to the cable modem and try your speed tests again. If you notice a dramatic increase in performance, disconnect unneeded hardware from your network to lessen the load, or consider a faster service.

If there's no difference in bandwidth when your PC is connected directly to the cable modem, there may be a problem with your service. Try using your service at different times. If you use your service during peak traffic periods (such as 6pm to 9pm), you'll often see a slowdown in service because you're one of many users vying for access at the same time. If you notice a slowdown during non-peak hours (8am to 11am, for example), your ISP may be experiencing technical difficulties. Contact your local service provider and discuss the problem with them. Don't be afraid to make a stink; you're entitled to receive the service that you pay for each month.

ROUTER NOT DISTRIBUTING IP ADDRESSES

The Annoyance: I can't get an Internet connection because my router doesn't have an IP address. I thought it was supposed to get an IP address from the ISP automatically. What's the problem?

The Fix: The Internet router normally receives its IP address from the service provider, then uses DHCP to distribute dynamic IP addresses to any connected PCs. First, verify that the router is properly connected to the cable modem. Check to see whether the link LED is lit on the cable modem, and a WAN LED is lit on the router. That'll tell you whether the two devices can communicate with each other. If one or both LEDs are not lit, then you probably have a loose or damaged cable—or perhaps the wrong type of cable. You might need the opposite cable type (e.g., a straight-through cable rather than a crossover cable).

When the LED on both the router and the cable modem is illuminated, open your web browser and access the router. Using the manufacturer's instructions, load the router's Setup page and locate the WAN settings (the Internet Connection Type). Many cable providers use DHCP, so make sure that it is selected. However, if your ISP uses a static IP address or PPPoE WAN connection, be sure to select the appropriate connection type. Next, check the router's Status page to see the IP address assigned by the ISP (see Figure 7-17). If you see an address such as 0.0.0.0, that means the router is not properly communicating with the ISP and can't receive an IP address.

Try cycling power to the cable modem and rebooting the router, then recheck the router's Status page to check the IP address. Once the router receives a valid IP address, it will distribute suitable IP addresses to the client PCs, thereby giving them Internet access. If your router still doesn't have a valid IP address, check the status of your service with your cable provider. A line may be down, or they may be experiencing technical difficulties. If that's the case, wait until your ISP service returns to normal and check the router again.

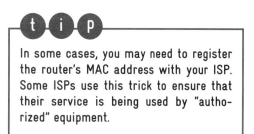

Figure 7-17. Make sure that the router receives a valid IP address from the ISP. If not, PCs on the network won't be able to access the Internet.

In some cases, you may need to register the router's MAC address with your ISP. Some ISPs use this trick to ensure that their service is being used by "authorized" equipment.

TURNING OFF A HOT MODEM

The Annoyance: My cable modem feels hot enough to fry an egg. Should I make breakfast, or just turn it off when I'm done using it?

The Fix: Hungry or not, there's no need to turn off the cable or DSL modem. Broadband connections are "always on," so it's normal to leave the modem on all the time. However, lightning can sometimes damage electronic equipment through energy spikes induced along power and communication lines. To be prudent, protect your cable modem during a thunderstorm or electrical storm by turning it off and disconnecting it from AC power (along with your PC and router), and detaching the coaxial cable.

Uninterruptible power supply (UPS) units like the APC Back-UPS family (*http://www.apcc.com*) provide PC battery back-up and device surge protection, as well as Ethernet, telco, and coaxial cable surge protection. This type of protection keeps your hardware running during a power loss, and reduces the risk of damage to your equipment from spikes and surges.

DSL ANNOYANCES

USING A SPLITTER

The Annoyance: My home alarm started behaving strangely after I had DSL installed. Is there a way to fix this?

The Fix: Simply put, DSL is broadband Internet access that runs over your existing telephone line. DSL service can coexist on your telephone line because it uses a different range of frequencies than conventional phone and fax equipment. However, other telco devices in your home can sometimes affect (and be affected by) the DSL service. To eliminate the interference, install a filter at each telephone jack in your home. Inexpensive filters prevent most telephones, fax machines, and other gadgets from interfering with your data service. You can buy inexpensive DSL filters from any computer store, including CompUSA, Staples, or OfficeMax.

However, filters are not a universal cure for device interference. If you can't overcome interference with filters, you may have to install a splitter to completely separate data from voice signals. Homes with alarm systems or TDD systems (devices for the deaf) often require a splitter at the point where telephone wiring enters the home, and separate cabling to a phone jack set aside for data use. Contact your DSL service provider. They may be able to test your home wiring, install the splitter for you (if necessary), and even install the additional wiring and jack for your data access.

> Remember that telephone companies typically charge for any in-home wiring work, so be sure to understand any additional charges before authorizing the work. You may get better deals from a local private telephone installer.

HANDLING DSL DISCONNECTIONS

The Annoyance: My DSL modem sometimes disconnects when my kids are on the phone. Is there an easy way to solve this problem?

The Fix: Since DSL service operates using a set of frequencies above the voice band, a good-quality telephone line will support simultaneous voice and data. This allows you to surf the Web or download files while your teens are chatting away with their friends. However, the electrical load of common electronic devices in the home (such as multiple telephones, a DSL modem, an answering device, and perhaps a fax machine) could interfere with your DSL service, which could in turn cause occasional disconnections.

Because DSL modems are sensitive to line conditions, try detaching your auxiliary telephones and other equipment from the line. (Of course, you'll need a crowbar to pry the phone from your teenager's ear as well.) If the DSL connection improves, you or your DSL provider may need to install a splitter on the line entering your home, then run a separate line from the splitter to your data jack. This leaves the

other jacks in your home exclusively dedicated to telephone devices. On the down side, the DSL signal strength can be significantly reduced if you install multiple splitters. In that case, remove unnecessary ones to avoid sapping the strength of the signal to your DSL modem.

> Contact your DSL provider (often your local telephone company) to have a technician check for adequate signal strength. Check ahead of time to see whether having your DSL provider perform the wiring work inside your home carries additional charges or fees.

PREVENTING DISCONNECTS WITH PPPOE

The Annoyance: Why does my PPPoE connection always seem to be getting disconnected by my DSL provider? I thought this was supposed to be an "always on" connection.

The Fix: The Point-to-Point Protocol over Ethernet (PPPoE) connection is not a dedicated connection. It'll stay on while you're actively surfing the Web or downloading files but, like your DSL service provider, it can disconnect you after some period of inactivity. Once disconnected, you'll need to log on again to re-establish the connection.

Fortunately, Internet devices such as routers support PPPoE connection types, and provide you with options that help keep the connection up during prolonged idle periods. Consider a Linksys wireless router, for example. Access the unit's setup routine using a web browser, and choose the Setup tab. Set the Connect On Demand time to a longer timeout period (bump it up to 20 minutes), and set a Keep Alive Redial Period of about 20 seconds. Remember to apply any changes, then re-establish your DSL connection, if necessary.

DSL AND CABLE DISTANCES

The Annoyance: My instructions tell me to keep the DSL modem near the phone jack, but it would be so much easier to run a long telephone cord to my data jack across the room. Do I really have to move the PC and DSL modem to the other side of the room?

The Fix: I understand your conundrum: do you put the modem near the phone jack and string a long Ethernet cable to the PC, or do you keep the modem near the PC and string a long telephone cord to the wall? The answer is to keep the DSL modem near the phone jack, and use the shortest telephone cord possible to connect it to the wall jack. This minimizes the length of the DSL loop (even if it's only by several feet), and reduces the potential for interference from other devices such as cordless phones. Once the DSL modem is connected, you can run a category 5 Ethernet cable to the PC. Ethernet cables are much better constructed and shielded than ordinary telephone cords, plus you can run an Ethernet cable between two points up to 100 meters apart.

DSL INTERNET CONNECTION FREEZES

The Annoyance: My DSL Internet connection freezes, but the link LED on the modem stays on. This usually happens when I'm downloading a file. Any ideas?

The Fix: This type of snafu frequently affects DSL connections when the MTU (Maximum Transmission Unit) setting in the Windows Registry is set too high. While a normal MTU setting for PPPoE and PPPoA is 1492, reducing the MTU value to 1430 or 1400 will often resolve the problem. Check with your DSL service provider first to see whether they have a recommended setting. Next, use a broadband tweaking utility like SpeedGuide's TCP Optimizer utility (*http://www.speedguide.net*). This free program supports Windows 9x through XP, and does not require installation (see Figure 7-13). Just download it and run. Remember to reboot the computer and reset the modem after making any changes to your broadband settings.

DUN ERROR WITH DSL CONNECTION

The Annoyance: I use DSL to access the Internet, so why do I keep getting a DUN error when I launch my browser?

The Fix: Most likely you need to reconfigure your web browser. Start Internet Explorer, select Tools → Internet Options, and click the Connections tab. In the "Dial-up and virtual private network settings" area, select the "Never dial a connection" radio button (see Figure 7-18). Now click the LAN Settings button and check the "Automatically detect settings" box. Click OK, apply your changes, and restart the browser. It should no longer produce a DUN error.

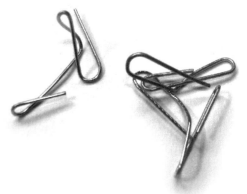

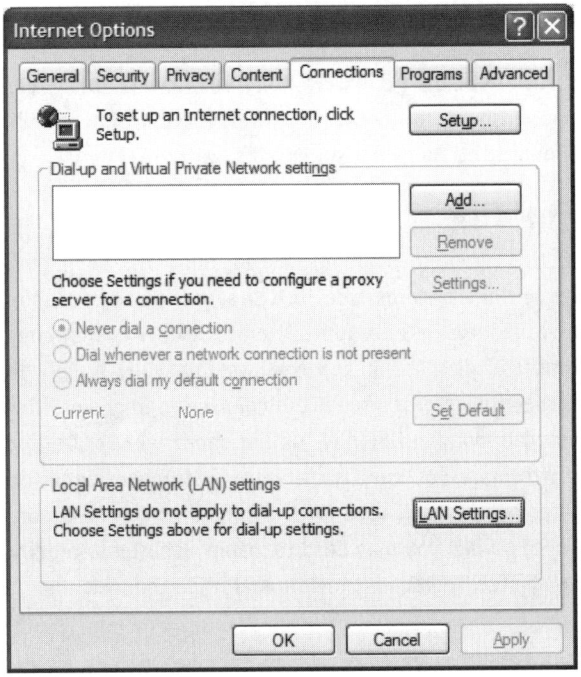

Figure 7-18. Eliminate DUN errors in cable/DSL connections by selecting "Never dial a connection."

DSL ROUTER IS INACCESSIBLE

The Annoyance: I've got a few PC workgroups in my small office. I installed a DSL router so that they could share Internet access, but I can't get the PCs to connect to it.

The Fix: First, check the router's power and signal cabling. Next, make sure each PC is assigned an IP address within the range of the router (192.168.1.2 to 192.168.1.524 using a subnet mask of 255.255.255.0, for example). If not, the networked PCs may appear to be on a different segment than the router, which will prevent them from communicating properly. You can correct this by manually assigning suitable IP addresses to each computer, or by enabling the router's DHCP feature. The latter option allows the router to assign IP addresses to your networked computers as long as you configure each PC to obtain an IP address automatically.

To do this, open the Network Connections control panel, right-click your network connection, and choose Properties. Now select the Internet Protocol (TCP/IP) entry and click the Properties button. Be sure to select "Obtain an IP address automatically" and "Obtain DNS server address automatically" (see Figure 7-19). Click OK to save your changes.

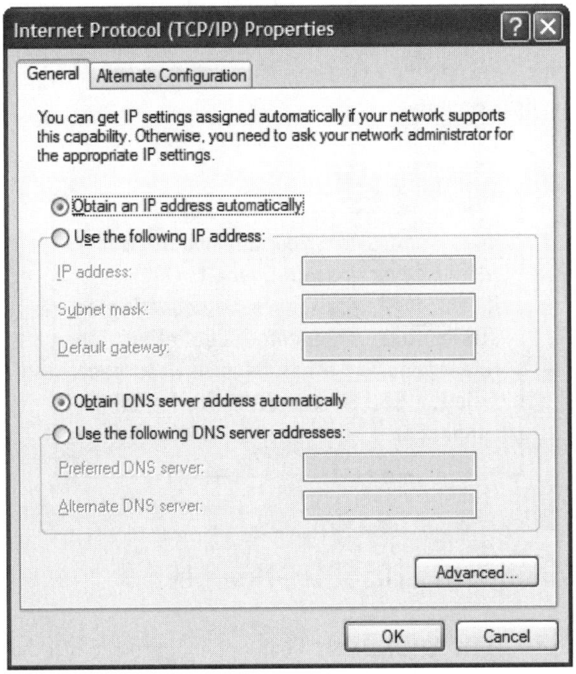

Figure 7-19. Configure each computer to obtain IP and DNS addresses automatically.

LINK LED WON'T STAY ON

The Annoyance: The link LED on my DSL modem won't stay on continuously. What gives?

The Fix: A link light indicates a valid network connection. If the light won't stay on, then you have a connection problem. In this case, the problem is likely between the DSL modem and the wall jack. First, check the RJ-11 telephone cable between the modem and the wall jack. Make sure that both ends of the cable are inserted evenly and completely. If that doesn't work, try another telephone cord (they're cheap).

Next, check for stray filters. Remember that filters prevent signals from voice devices (telephones, fax machines, answering devices, and so on) from interfering with data signals; however, you don't want a filter on the DSL jack, so be sure to check it. You'd be surprised how often users forget to remove the filter when they move the DSL modem from one jack to another. Finally, contact your DSL provider and have them line test your service as well as check the status of your account.

> Keep in mind that you may need to add a filter to every non-DSL jack in the house. If you don't, you may hear squealing or static (like a modem negotiation) on telephones and other telco devices each time the DSL modem attempts to make a connection.

DIAGNOSTIC LEDS SPELL TROUBLE

The Annoyance: I can't connect to the Internet using my DSL connection. When I check the DSL modem, I see that the diagnostic LEDs are illuminated.

The Fix: It's déjà vu all over again—your modem cannot communicate with the ISP. Again, the problem is probably due to a faulty telephone cord or errant filter. Reconnect both ends of the RJ-11 telephone cord, or try a new cord altogether. You may also have inadvertently installed a filter or line conditioner on the telephone cord that connects the modem to the telephone wall jack. Check the DSL jack and remove any filter components. Also, verify the status of your account with your DSL provider.

PHONES INTERFERE WITH DSL

The Annoyance: Why does my cordless telephone seem to interfere with my DSL connection? I thought the two were supposed to work together.

The Fix: Interference is the most common and perplexing problem plaguing DSL installations. Telephones, home alarm systems, satellite dish systems, game consoles, and fax machines are just some of the devices that could interfere with a DSL modem. Systematically disconnect suspect devices and see if the connection improves. If so, you can install a DSL filter on the phone jack in question. If necessary, you can try installing a stronger (higher dB) filter on the jack used by the offending device. If that doesn't work, you may need to install a splitter in order to completely segregate the data and voice channels.

WIRELESS NETWORKING ANNOYANCES

CORDLESS PHONES INTERFERE WITH WIRELESS

The Annoyance: I lose my wireless signal every time someone runs the microwave or uses the cordless phone. Can't I surf and make microwave popcorn at the same time?

The Fix: The problem is radio-frequency (RF) interference between the wireless access point and your wireless NIC. Wireless devices conforming to the 802.11b and 802.11g standards use the 2.4GHz radio frequency band. Unfortunately, that's the same band used by some cordless telephones. To make matters worse, other appliances (such as microwave ovens) often emit unwanted RF signals in that band.

The best way to deal with unwanted interference is to move the signal source farther away or remove it altogether. For example, try using a conventional, fixed-wire phone rather than a cordless phone, and stash the microwave in another room. If you must use a cordless telephone, try a 900MHz or 5.8GHz model instead. Of course, you can also tinker with the position of your wireless access points and search for locations that may be less sensitive to interference. In any case, correcting the trouble will take some experimenting on your part.

DEALING WITH WIRELESS SIGNAL PROBLEMS

The Annoyance: I helped a friend install a wireless access point in her office. She's a psychologist who shares a practice with five doctors, all of whom are wireless laptop users. We connected the wireless router/access point and got it up and running, but ran into signal problems for a laptop in one particular office. It works fine in some places, but not in others.

The Fix: The problem is almost certainly an issue with the building design and layout. If the wireless connection works in one location, you've proven that there's nothing wrong with the setup; it's all about range now. Offices have a lot of walls and other barriers that can impair wireless signals. Since you're working in an office, I'd take a serious look at the location of metal file cabinets. Although devices compliant with the 802.11b and 802.11g standards typically do a decent job of penetrating certain types of walls (as long as there aren't any metal supports or mesh screens in the way), metal obstructions like file cabinets are virtually impenetrable. Unfortunately, short of an expensive RF site survey or major furniture shuffling, the only effective way to work around the problem is to add another access point in the troublesome location. When installing another access point, locate it centrally in the area (say, the middle of the room), mount the access point (or an antenna for it) at ceiling level so that it's above most obstructions, and remember to pick a channel that will avoid interference with other wireless devices in the area.

KEEPING YOUR WIRELESS CONNECTIONS PRIVATE

The Annoyance: I've got a new wireless router for my broadband connection, but I foolishly told my neighbors about it. How do I keep them from logging on and sucking up all my bandwidth?

The Fix: Like any radio signal, wireless networks can be recognized and used by any device that is listening, which obviously opens a huge security problem. There's no way to prevent your wireless signals from reaching your neighbor's house if it's within 100–150 feet of your access point. However, you can protect your wireless setup using the Wi-Fi Protected Access (WPA) feature of your wireless devices. WPA applies encryption to your wireless signals, so only those PCs authorized to use your wireless network (and the same encryption key) can gain access to the network.

> **tip**
>
> Before you enable WPA, make sure you download the latest driver for your NICs. WPA routers and access points may also require the latest firmware update for best performance. Note that Windows XP requires Service Pack 1 for full WPA compliance.

To enable WPA on your existing wireless connection, open the Network Connections control panel. Right-click the Wireless Network Connection icon, click Properties, and select the Wireless Networks tab. Double-click the SSID of your wireless network in your "Available wireless networks" area (such as "linksys"). When the SSID Properties dialog opens (see Figure 7-20), set the "Network Authentication" option to WPA-PSK. Set the "Data encryption" option to the same encryption scheme used by your wireless network (such as TKIP), which you will find in the user's guide. Type the WPA shared key into the "Network key" and "Confirm network key" entries. Click OK to save your changes. This should enable WPA on your wireless devices. You'll need to configure each wireless network user the same way.

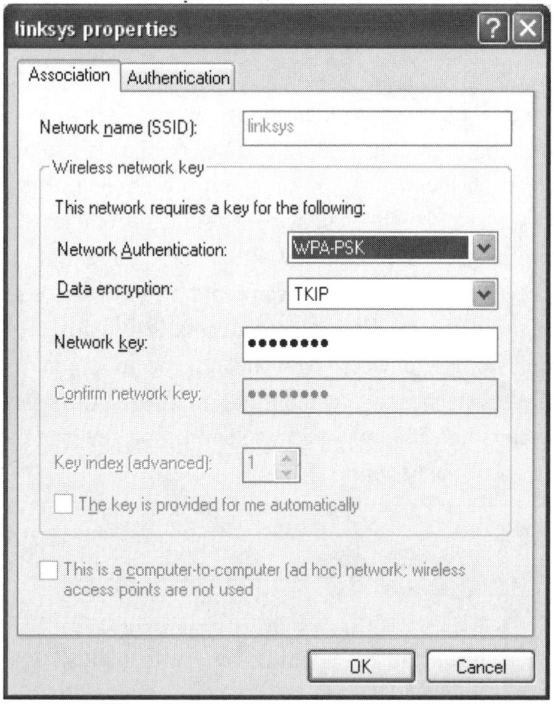

Figure 7-20. For maximum privacy, configure your wireless network to use WPA encryption.

> **t i p**
>
> Turn off the SSID (Service Set Identifier) broadcast feature of your wireless access points. This will make your wireless network "invisible" to unauthorized users.

STRONG SIGNAL WON'T CONNECT

The Annoyance: I've got plenty of wireless signal strength, but still can't consistently get online with my laptop.

The Fix: Your laptop is probably using a different SSID or the wrong encryption settings. Both are easy to check. Access the configuration applet for your router or access point and note the SSID and encryption settings. You'll need these to add your PC to the wireless network.

Open the Network Connections control panel. Right-click the Wireless Network Connection icon, click Properties, and select the Wireless Networks tab. Make sure your PC is configured to use the same SSID as your wireless network. If not, update the SSID and save the changes. Otherwise, double-click the SSID of your wireless network to see its properties (see Figure 7-20). Uncheck the "The key is provided for me automatically" box. If your wireless network uses encryption, enable encryption and enter the appropriate keys (see the previous annoyance, "Keeping Your Wireless Connections Private"). Your PC's settings should match those for the rest of the wireless network. If your wireless network is not using encryption, make sure "Data encryption" is disabled on your PC. Click OK to save your changes and reboot the PC.

NO WIRELESS SIGNAL STRENGTH

The Annoyance: I installed a wireless NIC, but I can't connect to the access point. Why isn't there any signal strength?

The Fix: Your PC might be too far away from the wireless router or access point, or it could be configured to use a different wireless channel. Start by checking the range between your PC and access point. It's simple—just move the two devices closer together. If range isn't the issue, access the configuration applet for the wireless router or access point and determine the current channel, encryption key, and SSID settings. Next, open the PC's wireless device properties and match the channel, encryption key, and SSID to your existing wireless network. Reboot the PC, and voila. If the problem persists or if you can't access the PC's wireless properties dialog box, your wireless NIC may be defective.

WIRELESS ACCESS POINT DOESN'T RESPOND

The Annoyance: I installed a Linksys WPC54G under Windows XP, but I can't get the unit to work. I can't even get to the Wireless Networks tab in the Wireless Network Connection Properties dialog box.

The Fix: You've probably installed unnecessary vendor software (such as the Linksys WLAN monitor) or disabled the Wireless Zero Configuration service in Windows XP. Remove any monitoring programs using the Uninstall utility in the Start menu (for example, select Start → All Programs → Wireless-G Notebook Adapter → Uninstall). Once it's gone, disconnect the wireless unit and reinstall it from scratch as recommended for Windows XP.

If the problem persists, click Start → Run, then type **msconfig** in the Open field and click OK. Next, select the Services tab and scroll down to find the Wireless Zero Configuration entry (see Figure 7-21). Make sure that the box is checked, click OK, and restart the computer if necessary. This should allow your wireless NIC to work properly.

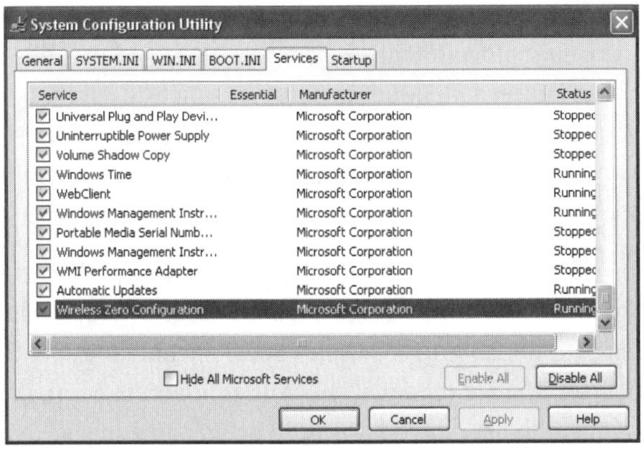

Figure 7-21. Use msconfig to check for the Wireless Zero Configuration service under Windows XP.

CAN'T CONNECT TO AVAILABLE NETWORKS

The Annoyance: I plugged a Linksys WPC54G wireless NIC into my laptop. Now it keeps telling me "One or more wireless networks are available." How do I just get the thing to work?

The Fix: In most cases, the wireless NIC is not detected or is improperly configured for your network. Start by cycling power to the PC and wireless NIC (turn your PC off and then on again). You can also try powering down your router or access point for 60 seconds, then reboot the device so that it can detect the wireless NIC properly. If the problem continues, make the following adjustments to your wireless router or access point (Figure 7-22 shows the Setup dialog box for the Linksys WRT54G Wireless G router):

- Set Wireless MAC Filtering to Disable.
- Set the Beacon Interval to 50.
- Set the Fragmentation Threshold to 2304.

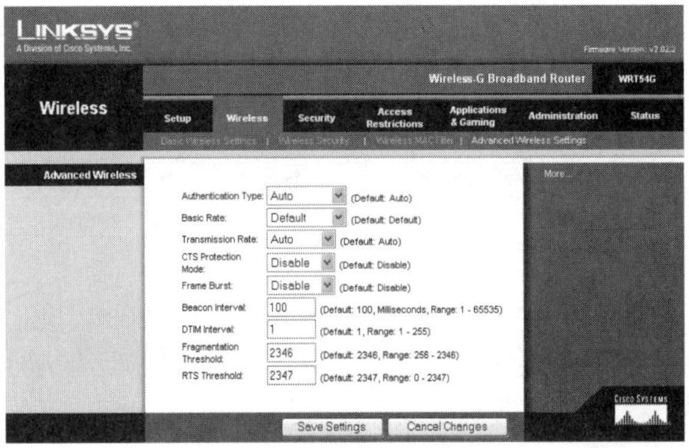

Figure 7-22. Make advanced configuration changes to your wireless router or access point.

NO IP ADDRESS FOR WIRELESS USB NIC

The Annoyance: I connected a wireless USB NIC to my PC, but can't get a valid IP address even though there's plenty of signal power. What's going on?

The Fix: Your PC's firewall software sometimes cuts off communication between a NIC and the network, and by doing so prevents assignment of an IP address. Try disabling the firewall temporarily to see whether the problem clears up. If so, you may need to reconfigure or reinstall your firewall software to accommodate the new wireless NIC.

Otherwise, you can try some configuration changes at the wireless router or access point. Access the wireless router or access point through your web browser, select the Setup menu, and choose your basic wireless options page. Make the following configuration changes (Figure 7-23 shows these setting for the Linksys WRT54G Wireless G router):

- Set the Wireless Network Mode to Mixed.
- For the Wireless Network Name (SSID), select a unique name (not the manufacturer's default).
- For Wireless SSID Broadcast, choose Enable.
- Disable the Wireless MAC Filter.
- Disable the Wireless Security.

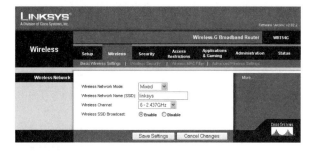

Figure 7-23. Make basic configuration changes to your wireless router or access point.

If the trouble persists, check the configuration of your wireless NIC. Open the Network Connections control panel. Next, right-click the Wireless Network Connection icon and choose View Available Wireless Networks from the shortcut menu. Highlight the SSID, and make sure it matches the SSID of your router or access point. Finally, check the "Allow me to connect to the selected wireless network, even though it is not secure" box and press the Connect button. You should now have a valid IP address.

XP HOTFIX KILLS WIRELESS

The Annoyance: I lost my wireless connection right after I installed a hotfix for Windows XP. What a drag!

The Fix: Surprise—this nasty little gotcha is usually associated with Windows XP hotfix Q815485. Although the hotfix allows you to use WPA encryption, you *must* enable WPA (or older WEP) encryption once the hotfix is installed. If not, your wireless connection will be completely cut off. If you don't want to use encryption, you'll need to completely uninstall the hotfix using the Add or Remove Programs wizard.

SHARED CONNECTIONS SEEM SLOW

The Annoyance: Although my 802.11b connection is usually fine, it slows to a crawl when my business partner logs on to the network. What's he doing that slows me down?

The Fix: Once again, limited bandwidth comes back to bite you in the behind. Remember that 802.11b networking hardware maxes out at 11Mbps (and often doesn't exceed 4–5Mbps in actual practice). Even though your wireless network may support multiple clients simultaneously, chances are that you'll run out of bandwidth long before a wireless network reaches the maximum number of clients.

The best way around this problem is to upgrade your wireless network to a 54Mbps 802.11g configuration. Of course, this will require a new router or access point, not to mention new wireless NICs, so be prepared to shell out some cash. In the meantime, protect your bandwidth by avoiding demanding tasks (such as watching streaming media), or arrange to "time share" the bandwidth with your partner.

SELECTING ONE OR TWO ANTENNAS

The Annoyance: Will I get better results using a wireless router with one antenna or two? If I replace an omni-directional antenna with a unidirectional antenna, does the new antenna have to be the same brand as my other wireless products?

The Fix: Sensitivity is the only tangible advantage offered by two-antenna devices. Many wireless devices include an "antenna diversity" feature that will automatically switch to the antenna with the stronger signal (which is not an option that you can control), and may give you slightly better data rates at greater distance. However, this is not a compelling enough reason for you to opt for a two-antenna device over a one-antenna version. The bottom line: as long as the antenna is designed for the correct frequency band (such as 2.4GHz for 802.11b/g) and has a suitable connector, you can use either style.

GENERAL NETWORKING ANNOYANCES

LINK LED ON AND OFF

The Annoyance: Why does my Internet connection keep cutting in and out?

The Fix: You've probably got a bad Ethernet cable that is wreaking havoc with your network connection. If you watch the link LED at your Ethernet port, I'll bet that you see the light flicker on and off. Simply replace the damaged Ethernet cable. You could also try connecting the NIC to a different port on the switch or hub.

DIAL-UP AND BROADBAND TOGETHER

The Annoyance: Why can't I receive faxes or voice mail over my new broadband connection? I don't have trouble with either when I use dial-up.

The Fix: Although ordinary DSL should continue to provide your current phone services, broadband cable connections do not include phone services. Once you establish a broadband connection, you should not require a dial-up modem. However, if you intend to continue faxing and receiving messages at your PC, you'll need to keep your existing analog modem in place. You've merely transferred the

Internet-related tasks (such as email, web surfing, and file downloading) to the high-speed connection.

HARDWARE SHARING REQUIREMENTS

The Annoyance: I connected several PCs in my home to a hub, and then connected the hub to my cable modem. Why can't I get the PCs to share Internet access?

The Fix: You can't just plug a hub into your cable/DSL modem and expect to give the networked PCs Internet access. To do that, you need a router, which is a device that connects networks together. The router replaces all of the unique IP addresses of the PCs on your network with a single IP address that is seen by the ISP. The router also keeps track of which data packets go to which PCs on your network, something a garden-variety hub cannot do. However, you can use a switch or hub behind a router. Just connect your PCs to the hub, then run an Ethernet cable from a hub port to the router. In fact, most routers incorporate several switch ports so that you can wire several PCs directly, which saves you the expense of buying a separate hub or switch.

PREPARING TO SHARE CONNECTIONS

The Annoyance: When I add another PC to the network so that it can share Internet access, do I need to make any changes to the router configuration?

The Fix: No, just connect the new PC to a switch port on your router (or a hub or switch behind the router). If the router is configured to act as a DHCP server and the PC is configured to receive an IP address automatically (see Figure 7-19), the router should see the new PC and assign an available IP address automatically.

If this process doesn't happen automatically, make sure the new client PC has a valid network connection. Open the Network Connections control panel, and make sure you can see at least one Local Network Connection. If not, you'll need to reinstall the Ethernet card or TCP/IP protocol stack, then reconfigure a valid network connection. Your PC's or router's User's Guide typically details this process for you, so I won't take 10 pages to do it here.

CREATING A VPN CONNECTION

The Annoyance: I need to create an incoming VPN connection, but I can't figure out how to set the darn thing up.

The Fix: Virtual Private Networks (VPNs) are important tools used to ensure the security of remote access network connections. If you're providing remote access to your company network for external users elsewhere on the Internet (perhaps a salesman needs to access files from the field), you can use the New Connection Wizard under Windows XP to create a VPN server interface.

Open the Network Connections control panel and create a new connection. Follow the New Connection Wizard to the Network Connection Type page, and choose "Set up an advanced connection." When you see the Advanced Connection Options page, choose "Accept incoming connection and click Next. On the "Devices For Incoming Connections" page, select any optional devices that you wish to use for incoming connections. When you see the "Incoming Virtual Private Network (VPN) Connection" page, choose the "Allow virtual private connections" option and click Next (see Figure 7-24). On the User Permissions page, select the users that are allowed to make VPN connections, and then click Next.

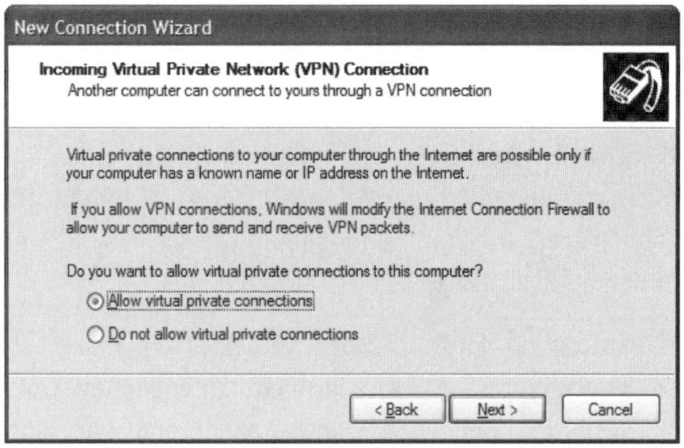

Figure 7-24. When configuring a VPN, be sure to allow virtual private connections.

But you're not done yet. Now you should see the Networking Software page. Highlight the Internet Protocol (TCP/IP) entry and click Properties. Check the "Allow callers to access my local area network" box (see Figure 7-25), click OK to return to the Networking Software page, and then click Next. Complete the rest of the wizard and click Finish to create the new connection.

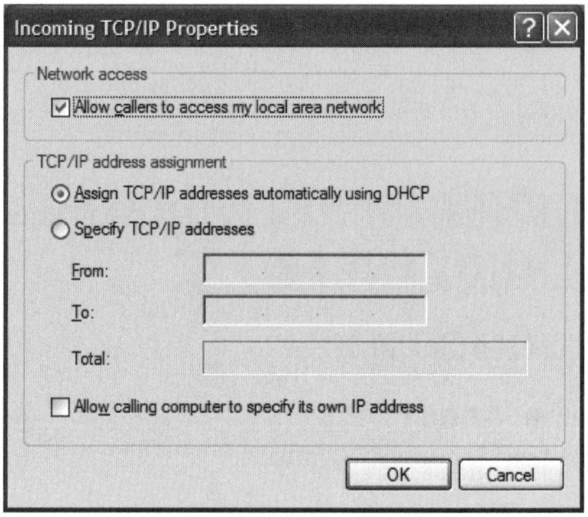

Figure 7-25. Allow VPN callers to access your local area network.

Now that you've finished setting up your new VPN connection, locate the connection in the Network Connections dialog, right-click it, and select Properties. If you see a note telling you that there is no hardware capable of accepting calls, choose the option to select the network card as your VPN.

DISABLING MESSAGE SPAM

The Annoyance: Is there any way for me to stop these annoying pop-up spam messages in Windows XP?

The Fix: When Microsoft introduced their Alerter service in Windows 2000/XP, they probably didn't foresee that spammers could abuse the feature to send pop-up messages to broadband users. The service is enabled by default, so the only way to secure your PC against this type of obnoxious attack is to disable the service. Many firewalls now do a good job at blocking the service, but it's better to be safe.

Simply click Start → Run, type **services.msc** and click OK. When the Services dialog opens, locate Messenger in the list and double-click it. Click the Stop button to halt the service immediately (see Figure 7-26), then select Disabled from the "Startup type" drop-down menu. This will prevent the service from starting each time you boot the computer. Close the Services dialog box, and you're done.

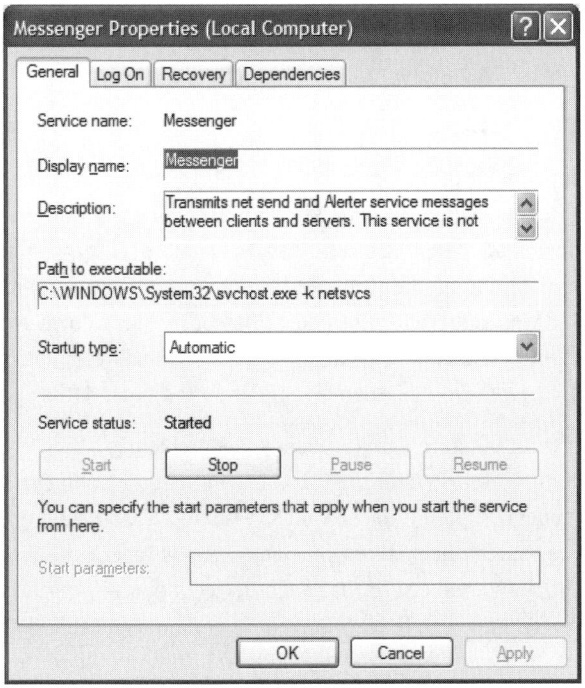

Figure 7-26. Use the Services control panel to shut down the Messenger service.

NETWORK CANNOT GET SYSTEM TO POWER UP

The Annoyance: Why won't my system power up when I try to exchange files through my LAN connection? I was under the impression that I could access a remote PC even if it's powered off.

The Fix: Easy peasy—you just need to configure the Wake On LAN (WOL) feature, which allows one PC to revive another one. For example, you can use WOL to turn on a host PC from another client PC. To make WOL work, you'll need an ATX motherboard with a WOL connector, an ATX 2.01 (or later) power supply, and a WOL-compliant NIC with its own WOL connector. You'll also need the latest drivers for your WOL-compliant NIC and a BIOS version that supports WOL (you'll see a WOL option enabled in your System Setup). Otherwise, check the motherboard manufacturer for a BIOS upgrade.

Make sure that the WOL connectors for the NIC and motherboard are compatible. If not, you could damage the power supply.

The trick is to keep the NIC in standby mode (which keeps the NIC "awake" so that it can "wake up" the rest of the PC) once the PC powers down. To test whether you've correctly set up WOL, power down the PC and check the NIC indicators (such as the link LED); if indicators are on, you're good to go.

If not, power up the PC again and try configuring the NIC. Open the Network Connections control panel. Next, right-click the Local Area Connection, select Properties, and click the Configure button. Select the Power Management tab and see that the "Allow this device to bring the computer out of standby" box is checked. Now click the Advanced tab (see Figure 7-27) and enable the "WakeUp on Link Change" property. Also, select the "NDIS Driver Version" property and set its value to NDIS 4 and enable the "Wake on Magic Packet" property if included. If the Advanced tab is missing, you'll need to update the NIC drivers. Click OK to save your changes, then reboot Windows.

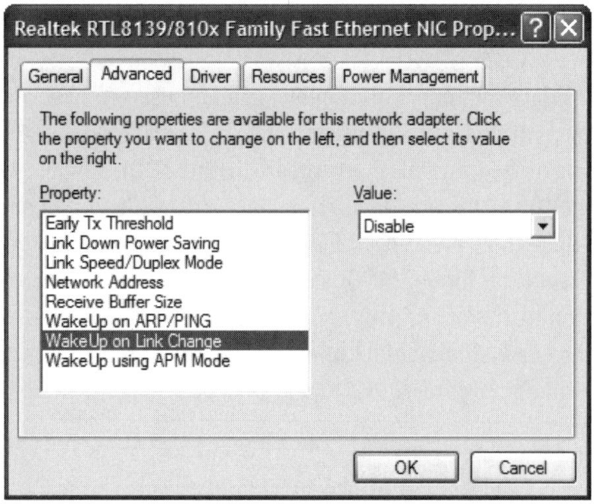

Figure 7-27. Remember to enable the WOL feature of your NIC.

IDENTIFYING NEW PCS ON THE NETWORK

The Annoyance: I added another PC to my network, but other networked PCs can't see it. How can I get these PCs to talk to each other?

The Fix: If the other PCs can see and communicate with each other, chances are that the new one isn't connected or configured properly. Before you do anything else, reboot the new computer and check to see whether the link LED between the PC and your hub or switch lights up. If not, then the cable is damaged or disconnected.

> **t i p**
>
> Check for an IP connection with an existing Windows utility such as Winipcfg or ipconfig. Make sure the new PC uses an IP address and subnet that places it in the same domain or workgroup as the other PCs.

If the new PC still doesn't appear, open the Network Connections dialog box and make sure that there's a valid network connection available. Open the Network Connections control panel. If you don't see a Local Area Network connection, click "Create a new connection" and follow the wizard. Right-click the new connection, then select Repair to let Windows try to fix it automatically.

If the problem persists, try accessing the new computer from another local client. To do this, open Explorer from one of your working PCs. Type the name of the missing computer in the address bar, preceded by two backslashes (\\newpc or \\johnsys, for example). If you still can't see the new PC, reboot the hub or switch, or try connecting the unit to a different hub or switch port. The port itself may be defective.

HANDLING WEB TIMEOUT ERRORS

The Annoyance: Why do I get a timeout error when I type a URL or IP address into my browser?

The Fix: Be careful with this one, or else you might spend a lot of time chasing your tail. Try several different URLs (or known IP addresses) and see whether you can download their web pages. If so, the trouble is likely at the remote end of the web site that gave you grief. Perhaps the web server is congested or has been taken down for maintenance. Double-check the URL or IP address that is giving you trouble, then give up and try it again later.

If you can't access *any* web sites, the problem is a bit more complicated. Reboot the PC, hub/switch, router, and cable modem. If the PC doesn't receive a valid IP address from the router, check all of your connections (check the link LEDs) and make sure that each device along the chain is receiving power. Replace any loose or damaged cabling. If the PC is receiving a valid IP address back from the router, you can assume that the local network is working up to the broadband modem, so check with your ISP to find out whether they are experiencing any technical difficulties.

REPAIRING NETWORK CONNECTIONS

The Annoyance: My system crashed, and now my PC won't connect to the LAN. Although the link LED next to the NIC port is properly lit, I can't figure out how to repair my network connection.

The Fix: If you're running Windows XP, you can easily fix common network interruptions by running the "repair" tool. Simply open the Network Connections control panel. Right-click the troublesome connection and select Repair. After a few seconds, the repair should be complete, and you can try the network connection again. You can often tell that the repair has been successful if you see a valid IP address or other evidence of a normal connection. If you're not running Windows XP, use the Network Troubleshooting wizard to help you isolate and correct the trouble.

CONFIGURING A STATIC IP ADDRESS

The Annoyance: I'm serving some FTP files from a PC, so I need an IP address that doesn't change. Is there any way to keep an IP address from changing each time I reboot the PC?

The Fix: The trick to using a static IP address is to select an address that is outside of the router's DHCP dynamic addressing scheme. For example, if the router is configured to manage dynamic IP addresses from 198.168.1.100 to 192.168.1.150, you'd need to select an IP address between 192.168.1.2 and 192.168.1.99 or between 192.168.1.151 and 192.168.1.254. Check your router's DHCP configuration to determine the exact dynamic range, then pick an IP address outside of that range.

To assign a static IP address to a PC, open the Network Connections control panel. Right-click the Local Area Connection and select Properties. Highlight the Internet Protocol (TCP/IP) and click the Properties button. Now enter the desired IP address for that system, and enter a Subnet Mask of 255.255.255.0 (see Figure 7-19). Use the router's IP address as the Default Gateway. Now opt to "Use the following DNS server addresses" and enter the Preferred DNS Server and Alternative DNS Server IP addresses (these can be provided by your ISP). Click OK to save your changes, and reboot the system if necessary.

ENABLING SERVICES BEHIND A ROUTER

The Annoyance: How do I allow a web server to work behind my high-speed router?

The Fix: This can get a little tricky if you haven't done it before. Basically, you'll need to set up the "port forwarding" feature of your router so that any requests to your web server are passed directly through the router to the corresponding port (such as port 80 for HTTP, portfor FTP, port 25 for SMTP outgoing mail, and port 110 for POP incoming mail).

Figure 7-28 shows the port forwarding page for a Linksys router. First, you need to enter the port range for each service you want to use. For example, a web server would use a range from port 80 to port 80. Next, you select the protocol(s) you want to use (TCP, UDP, or both). Now set the IP address of the PC that should receive the port request (e.g., the PC running the web server). If you configured the web server with an IP address of 192.168.1.101 (see "Configuring a Static IP Address" earlier in this chapter), make sure you enter that IP address. Finally, enable the port services you want to use. Remember to apply your changes and reboot the router if necessary. From this point forward, any requests to port 80 will go directly through your router to the web server.

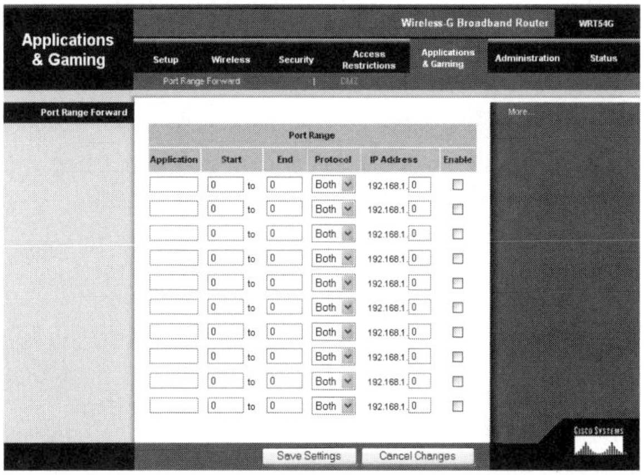

Figure 7-28. Use port forwarding to pass requests to services behind your router.

ACCESSING A ROUTER WITHOUT A PASSWORD

The Annoyance: I need to adjust the configuration of my router, but I forgot the password.

The Fix: Guess what? Most routers ship with a default password, which you can find in the installation and setup documentation that came with your router. Linksys, for example, uses "admin" as the default password. If you haven't changed the default password, that should be enough to should get you going. If you are vigilant about security, then you will change the password. That's the best way to prevent unauthorized users from making unplanned changes in your router's configuration.

Still, if you forget the new password, most router manufacturers let you reset the password (and, unfortunately, all the other factory settings) simply by resetting the router. Usually, all you need to do is press the Reset button for 15–30 seconds, which clears the router and resets it to its factory default settings (including the default password shown in the unit's documentation). Once you can access the router again, reconfigure it according to your network needs, and change the password to something you'll remember.

DISABLING PPPOE IN BROADBAND

The Annoyance: I've been using dial-up to access the Internet, but now I've got a DSL broadband connection. Do I still need to hassle with PPPoE settings on my PC?

The Fix: It depends on how your broadband connection is established. If you're using a single PC connected directly to a DSL modem using a PPPoE account, then yes, you'll still require PPPoE credentials when connecting to your DSL provider. However, if you connect through a router (in case you're using a shared DSL connection), then you will need to disable the PPPoE logon on each PC that shares the connection. Instead, configure the router to handle the PPPoE settings for you.

To do this, access your router and select the PPPoE connection type (see Figure 7-29). This changes the setup to receive your username, password, and connection maintenance settings—the same entries you've used on the individual PC.

![Linksys Wireless-G Broadband Router WRT54G setup screen showing Internet Connection Type set to PPPoE with User Name, Password fields, and Optional Settings including Router Name WRT54G, Host Name, Domain Name, and MTU set to Auto.]

Figure 7-29. Use the router to handle your PPPoE configuration when sharing a DSL connection.

Once the router is configured to support your PPPoE connection, disable the settings on your PC. Open the Internet Options control panel, click the Connections tab, click the LAN Settings button, clear any checked boxes, and then click OK (see Figure 7-30). Now select the "Never dial a connection" radio button. This will prevent any PPPoE dial-up prompts.

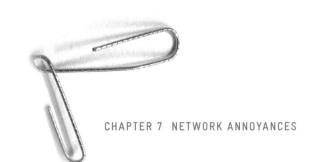

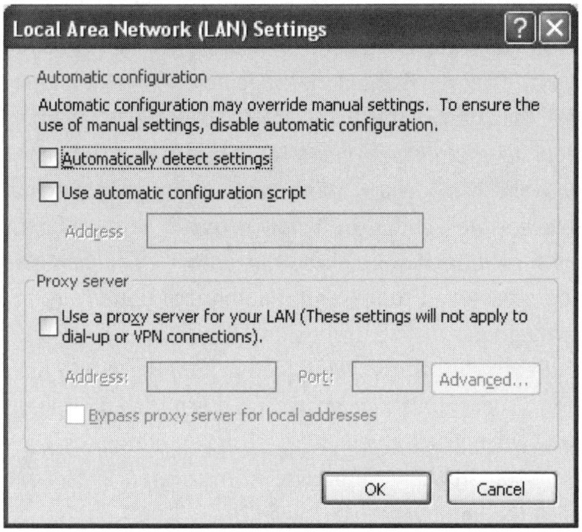

Figure 7-30. Disable the proxy server settings when removing PPPoE dial-up support from your PC.

HANDLING NETWORK FAILURES

The Annoyance: I can't get my new PC on the network. When I ran my NIC's internal diagnostic utility, it reported a network failure.

The Fix: A "network failure" can mean a million different things, so don't jump to any rash conclusions. Start by inspecting the cable between your NIC and the local hub or switch. Remember that a link light will appear on the Ethernet port whenever there's a good connection. If the link LED is out, the cable is loose or damaged, or you need a different cable type (such as a straight-through rather than a crossover cable). Also, try connecting the Ethernet cable to a different port on the hub or switch.

Open the Device Manager and check the entry for your network adapter. To do this, open the System control panel, click the Hardware tab, and then click the Device Manager button. Expand the Network adapters entry, right-click the NIC, and select Properties. The "Device status" entry on your General tab should tell you whether the device is working properly. If not, you should update the network driver or replace the NIC.

PRINTER AND FILE SHARING ANNOYANCES

TRASH THROUGH A PRINT SERVER

The Annoyance: I connected my printer to a print server so that all the PCs on the network in my house can share the printer. It was a fine idea in theory, but now the printer spits out garbage regardless of what I try to print.

The Fix: Attaching a printer to the network through a print server is an excellent way to allow printer sharing, so take heart. The first thing that I'd suspect is a cabling problem. Perhaps the USB or parallel port cable is loose. Maybe the cable chose this particular opportunity to manifest wiring problems. Make sure that each end of your printer cable is secure, and if that doesn't work, try another cable. If you need to replace the cable, make sure that the replacement cable is relatively short (less than 6 feet; even shorter for a USB cable). Long cables can introduce all sorts of data errors that result in printing problems, so avoid them at all costs.

Drivers are critical for both networked and local printers. When you installed the print server on your network, you should also have installed a driver that allows your PC to "see" the print server. Make sure that you've installed this driver on your PC, and on every networked PC that will access the print server. Don't forget that you eliminated the local printer when you attached the printer to the print server. Therefore, you'll need to reinstall the printer as a network printer. Use the Add Printer Wizard to install the printer over your network. Open the Printers and Faxes control panel and choose "Add printer" (see Figure 7-31). Repeat this process on every networked PC that will use the printer. Be sure to use the latest printer driver for your specific make and model. Old or incorrect drivers can cause a host of problems, and could account for the garbled output.

Figure 7-31. Use the Add Printer Wizard to configure a network printer for each networked PC.

SHARING FILES AND FOLDERS

The Annoyance: I want to access a folder of photographs on my son's PC. I can see his PC in My Network Places, but how do I get to the folder?

The Fix: In order for one PC to access resources on another, you need to enable file and print sharing on both PCs. You also need to share the resources that you want to access. I know it sounds like a mouthful, but it's a simple process to check.

First, check the file and print sharing on each system with resources you want to share (systems that aren't sharing do not need sharing setup). Open the Network Connections control panel, right-click your Local Area Network connection, and choose Properties. The General tab will list the items used in that connection. Look for the "File and Printer Sharing for Microsoft Networks" item (see Figure 7-32).

If the entry is there, you're all set. If not, click the Install button and install the file and printer-sharing feature (you'll need the OS installation CD for this step).

Now it's just a matter of sharing the folder with your photographs. Use Explorer to locate the folder that you want to access. Right-click the folder and select Properties, then choose the Sharing tab (see Figure 7-33). In the Network sharing area, check the "Share this folder on the network" box. If you want to edit or delete photos in that folder as well, check the "Allow network users to change my files" box. If you choose this option, don't forget to add a password to prevent unauthorized users from accessing your files. Enter a share name for the resource, and then click Apply. The folder will appear with a little "hand" beneath it to indicate that it is a shared resource. Now when you see your son's PC in your network places, you should be able to browse to the shared folders and open the photos that you need.

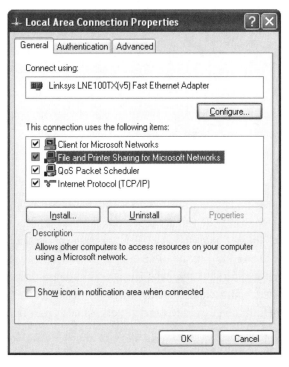

Figure 7-32. Remember to install file and printer sharing to access one system's resources from another.

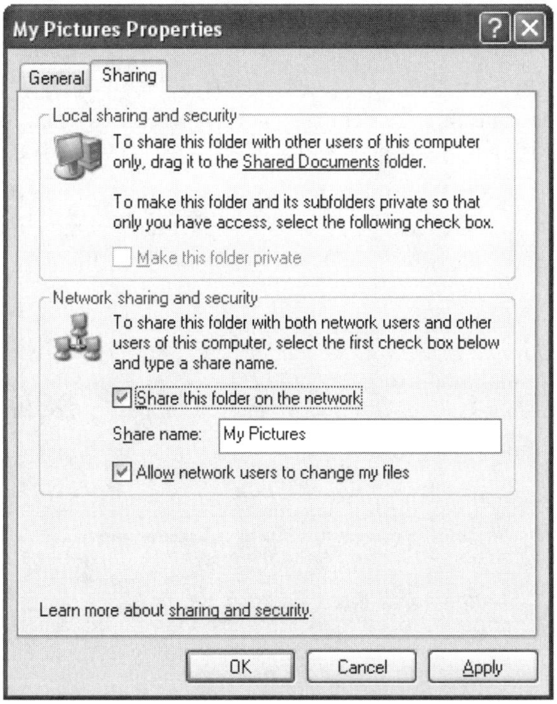

Figure 7-33. Be sure to share the folder so that other network users can access the resources.

RESOLVING PRINT SERVER IP CONFLICTS

The Annoyance: Why does my print server have an IP address conflict with other devices on my network?

The Fix: There are two things to look out for here. One common oversight is a DHCP allocation glitch—if the print server is on while the DHCP server (such as your Internet router) is turned off, the print server will typically retain its IP address, but does not communicate that to the DHCP server when the server reboots. As a result, the DHCP server may unknowingly assign the same IP address to another device on the network, which results in the conflict you described. In other instances, the newly added device has the same default address as another device on the network. For example, the print server may use the same default address as the router. The easiest way to resolve this issue is simply to cycle power to the print server while the DHCP server is running. This will cause the print server to obtain a new IP address (if not, you can also change the IP address manually).

You can also run into address conflicts if you assigned a static IP address to a network device that falls into the IP range used by your DHCP server. For example, if you assign a static address to your web server, but that address falls within the range of dynamic addresses used by the router's DHCP services, the router may assign the same IP address to your print server, which will result in a conflict. The solution is to assign the print server a static address that is outside of the dynamic range.

PRINTER TAKES A LONG TIME TO START

The Annoyance: Since I started sharing my printer on my home network, it seems to take a long time for it to start print jobs—especially complex jobs. Is there anything that I can do to speed it up?

The Fix: This kind of irritation is often a matter of printer spooling. Remember that a PC must send a substantial amount of information to the printer in order to specify text and graphic elements. When the printer is connected through a 10/100 Ethernet cable, the printer data must travel across the network to the printer before the job can start. If the network is very busy (e.g., lots of collisions and retransmissions), or if the link is only operating at 10Mbps (perhaps you're using an older print server or the print server is sluggish), it may take a noticeably long time to transmit the print job across the network.

One quick solution is to configure the printer so that it starts printing after the first page (rather than the last) is spooled. Open the Printers and Faxes control panel, then right-click the network printer and select Properties. Click the Advanced tab and select the "Start printing immediately" radio button. Apply your changes, click OK, and try printing again. If you don't mind spending a few bucks, another solution is to improve the performance of the printer's network segment. For example, use a 100Mbps print server rather than a 10Mbps print server, or add bandwidth (perhaps with a gigabit NIC and a switch, although that can become an expensive alternative) to reduce the network congestion.

WPS PRINTER WON'T PRINT

The Annoyance: I've connected a WPS-enabled printer through a print server, but it won't accept a print job.

The Fix: The trouble is with the WPS (Windows Printing System) architecture. WPS printer drivers poll the printer before sending print data to it. Because the printer is networked, the printer isn't found nor is any data is sent. To fix the problem, you'll need to reconfigure the network printer to work around the snafu. Delete the network printer and launch the Add Printer Wizard from scratch. When you elect to attach the new printer as a networked printer, enter a dummy value for the network path (such as `\\MyNum\P2 for LPT2`), and then select Next. The wizard won't see the printer, and will tell you it's offline. Opt to install the printer anyway.

When you're finished with the wizard, open the Printers and Faxes control panel. Your printer will be grayed out. Right-click the network printer and select Properties. Click the Ports tab and select your Print Server. Next, Apply your changes and click OK. Right click the printer again and verify that you see "Use printer offline" in the menu (if you see "Use printer online," click the entry to bring the printer online). The printer should no longer be grayed out, and should be ready for use.

FIREWALL ANNOYANCES

FIREWALLS ON THE CHEAP

The Annoyance: I want to use a firewall to protect my network, but I'm too cheap to buy one. Is there a free product I can use?

The Fix: Actually, there is—Windows XP includes a built-in firewall. Although the firewall is disabled by default, it's easy to activate. Just click Start, right-click My Network Places, and select Properties. Now right-click your Local Area Connection and click Properties. Click the Advanced tab and check the "Protect my computer and network by limiting or preventing access to this computer from the Internet" box (see Figure 7-34). Click the Settings button and select any particular Services, Logging, or ICMP features that you need. I won't bore you to tears with a lengthy explanation of those features here—you can always check the firewall's Help feature for more details and "how-to" information. Now click OK to save your changes, and reboot Windows if necessary. This activates the native Windows XP firewall.

Figure 7-34. Windows XP provides its own basic firewall for network and Internet protection.

If XP's firewall isn't reliable or versatile enough for your taste, there are other inexpensive firewall solutions such as ZoneAlarm from Zone Labs (*http://www.zonelabs.com*). You can download a free version of the firewall and install it on your system in a matter of minutes. ZoneAlarm offers comprehensive monitoring and logging as well as individual program control (see Figure 7-35).

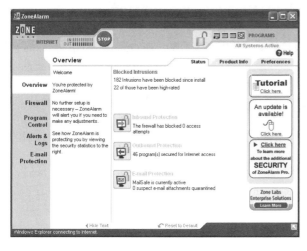

Figure 7-35. A free version of ZoneAlarm can be obtained directly from Zone Labs.

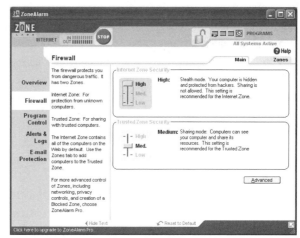

Figure 7-36. Configure the firewall to allow trusted PCs to access your computer.

STREAMLINE FILE SHARING

The Annoyance: I installed a firewall, but now I can't share files with other PCs on the LAN. What's the deal?

The Fix: Firewalls protect your computer by limiting the communication that takes place between your PC and other systems on accessible networks, including the Internet. By default, the firewall cuts off all communication with other PCs. Fortunately, firewalls like ZoneAlarm use a simple, two-step process to allow trusted computers to access your system. First, add the network subnet (or the IP address of each trusted computer) to the Trusted Zone page. Second, set the security level of your Trusted Zone to Medium, as this setting allows trusted computers to access your shared resources (see Figure 7-36). For tighter security, set the security level of the Internet Zone to high.

Other firewall products may appear differently, but most products offer comparable features.

DOMAIN SLOWS LAN STARTUP

The Annoyance: Ever since I installed a firewall on my network, it takes several minutes longer for the LAN startup to finish. How can I speed it up?

The Fix: Normally, a networked computer needs access to the network's domain controller to complete its startup and login processes. If the firewall blocks the domain controller (which is what happens when you forget to add the domain controller to the Trusted Zone), it often takes much longer than usual for the network's startup processes to finish. By adding the host name or IP address of the network's domain controller to the Trusted Zone, you'll whack several minutes off of the startup time.

FIREWALL CUTS OFF THE INTERNET

The Annoyance: I hate my firewall. I haven't been able to connect to the Internet ever since I installed it.

The Fix: This is one of the most common problems you're likely to encounter when you install a new firewall.

Remember, firewalls are intended to restrict unauthorized communication between your PC (or LAN) and the Internet. Firewalls like Zone Labs' ZoneAlarm accomplish this by detecting applications that communicate across known ports, then block those applications until you specifically give them permission. Chances are that your firewall cut off the dial-up software or another application (e.g., the web browser).

The easiest trick here is simply to disable your firewall. To do this, temporarily close the firewall application. (The process varies a bit for each firewall application, but for ZoneAlarm, just right-click the "ZA" icon in the System Tray and select "Shutdown ZoneAlarm.") Now try your Internet software again. If you still have problems getting online, the problem is not with your firewall. But if you can now access the Internet normally, you'll need to reboot the computer and reconfigure the firewall to allow access. For example, open the ZoneAlarm control panel and select the Program Control page (see Figure 7-37). Locate the offending program on the list and modify the settings to allow that program to connect to the Internet. Close the control panel and try your Internet software again.

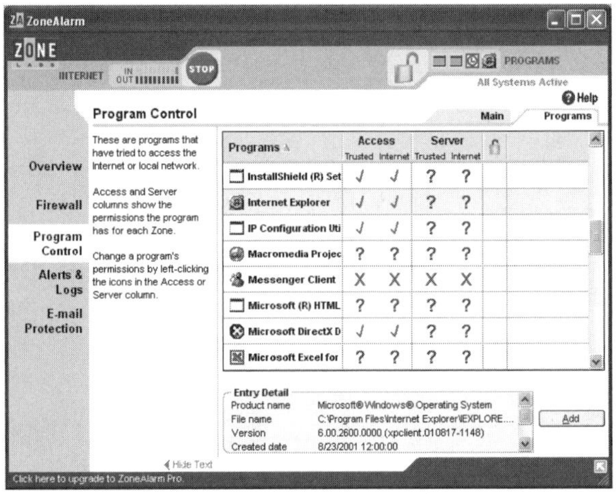

Figure 7-37. Configure your firewall to allow certain trusted programs to access the Internet.

MAINTAINING AN ISP HEARTBEAT

The Annoyance: Why does my ISP disconnect after just a few minutes? I didn't have this problem until after I installed a firewall.

The Fix: The problem could well be with your ISP "heartbeat" signals. Many service providers periodically ping their client connections to determine which clients are online and which are not. ISPs frequently consider clients that do not respond to this "heartbeat" test to be offline, freeing an assigned IP address for use elsewhere. Since most firewall products will block external pings by default, the ISP may fail to see you online and unexpectedly cut off your Internet access. To prevent this from happening, you'll need to identify the server sending the "heartbeat" messages and add it to your firewall's trusted zone. Alternatively, you can configure the Internet Zone to allow ping messages.

First, you must identify the server that your ISP uses to check your connection. You'll find this in the alert you received at the time you were disconnected. You can also usually find this information listed in the firewall's log or alert record. If necessary, contact your ISP and get the heartbeat server IP address directly from them. Now add the heartbeat server's IP address to your trusted zone.

> **tip**
>
> It's better to allow your ISP to ping you from a specific IP address than to allow general pings (sometimes called ICMP redirects). Hackers often use pings to probe your PC, so allowing general pings may open you up to a greater security risk than simply allowing pings from your ISP's known server.

RESTORING A DISABLED VPN

The Annoyance: I lost access to my VPN right after I installed my new firewall. How do I get back that access?

The Fix: A firewall can affect three services: resources, permissions, and protocols. A Virtual Private Network (VPN) connection can be disabled if any of these items is blocked. To check whether the firewall is at fault, disable the firewall temporarily and verify that your VPN access returns to normal (see "Firewall Cuts Off the Internet" earlier in this chapter). If the firewall is the culprit, reboot the computer to reload the firewall, then follow the firewall's instructions to add VPN-related resources (such as your VPN server) to the trusted zone (see Figure 7-36). Now, grant firewall permission to your VPN client and any other VPN-related programs. Finally, be sure to allow VPN protocols. Once you've allowed for VPN resources, applications, and protocols, try to access the VPN again.

MAKING THE MOST OF SECURITY SETTINGS

The Annoyance: Okay, my router includes a firewall with High, Medium, and Low security settings. The problem is that I need to share some files, and I'm not sure which level lets me do that while still maintaining adequate security. How do I tell what level to pick?

The Fix: A high security level is by far the most restrictive setting. It typically hides the maximum number of ports, and is often used as a "stealth" setting because it makes your client PCs very difficult to see from the Internet. High security also restricts file sharing and other common communications activities, which may prevent you from completing everyday Internet tasks such as web surfing or picking up your email. The medium security level generally strikes a balance between security and functionality. It allows common tasks while closing and hiding other expendable resources such as unused ports.

Low security offers a minimum of protection, closing few (if any) ports and allowing virtually unrestricted communication. As a rule, high security is recommended for the Internet (or WAN) area, and medium security is suggested for the local (LAN) area. All firewall products provide custom settings that allow you to tailor the firewall for the most appropriate security level for your network, so be sure to review your product documentation for specific options.

ENABLE VOIP ACROSS THE FIREWALL

The Annoyance: How can I get my VoIP program to work across my firewall? I haven't been able to get it to work.

The Fix: This is an easy one. You'll need to configure the firewall to give permission to the VoIP application(s), and add the VoIP provider's server IP address to the firewall's trusted zone. The address is not as critical for outbound originated requests, but you will need to configure the TCP and UDP ports specific to the VoIP application. The precise steps needed to complete these tasks vary a bit from firewall to firewall, but the objectives are the same (see ZoneAlarm in Figure 7-37).

AVOID FIREWALL AND ANTI-VIRUS CONFLICTS

The Annoyance: Why are my firewall and anti-virus software fighting over my email? I get error messages from both applications when a questionable attachment or file is downloaded, and it's driving me nuts.

The Fix: This type of problem occurs with increasing regularity as firewalls and anti-virus products incorporate overlapping features. For example, the Mail-Safe feature of ZoneAlarm can conflict with the email protection features of anti-virus software such as McAfee VirusScan. Fortunately, you can customize these applications to operate in a complementary fashion.

Here's a typical scenario. Set your anti-virus program to scan all files on access, and disable the email scanning option. Leave the MailSafe feature enabled in ZoneAlarm (see Figure 7-38). This will cause MailSafe to quarantine suspicious email attachments, and warn you when you try to open them. If you elect to open an attachment anyway, your anti-virus software will still scan it, then report on and disinfect any viruses that it finds.

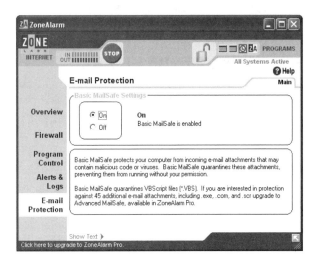

Figure 7-38. Email protections such as ZoneAlarm's MailSafe are a good first line of defense against common viruses.

NORTON WON'T LOAD DURING BOOT

The Annoyance: I uninstalled and reinstalled TCP/IP, but now my Norton Internet Security software won't load during boot.

The Fix: This happens when you remove and reinstall TCP/IP on systems running Norton Internet Security (NIS) or Norton Personal Firewall. Once you reinstall TCP/IP, you'll find that features such as ad blocking and information blocking no longer work because the load order has changed. When your firewall software runs its installation program, it configures the firewall to load after network protocols (e.g., TCP/IP). When you removed and reinstalled TCP/IP, its position in the load order changed, which in turn caused the firewall to load before TCP/IP.

This change in order prevents the utility from seeing the protocol. Fortunately, the fix is fairly easy. Just remove the firewall software and then reinstall it from scratch. This restores the original load order, which should make the special features in your Norton software work again. If for some reason NIS still gives you trouble, remove it and install an alternate firewall such as ZoneAlarm.

NIS BLOCKING OUTLOOK

The Annoyance: I installed Norton Internet Security, but now I can't get to my email through MS Outlook XP. What a pain!

The Fix: A pesky pain that crops up with Office XP once Norton Internet Security (NIS) or Norton Personal Firewall has been installed. When you open Outlook to get your email, you see an error such as "Outlook is unable to connect to your incoming (POP3) e-mail server." While the firewall software has default rules set for Outlook connections, chances are you didn't automatically scan for Outlook during the firewall installation. To work around the problem, just run the firewall's application scan feature and be sure to select all of its options to enable Outlook.

If the problem persists, you may need to reconfigure Outlook manually. To do this, open the ISP Properties window in Outlook and change the POP3 server entry to the real name of your POP3 server (available from your ISP or network administrator). With Outlook running, select Tools → Accounts → Mail. Select the account to configure and click Properties. Now select the Servers tab and examine the "Incoming mail (POP3)" box (see Figure 7-39). If the entry is something like pop3.norton.antivirus or pop3.spa.norton.antivirus, change it to the real name of your POP3 server. Apply the changes and click OK, then restart Outlook and try receive mail again. If NIS continues to give you problems, uninstall NIS and try an alternate firewall such as Zone Alarm.

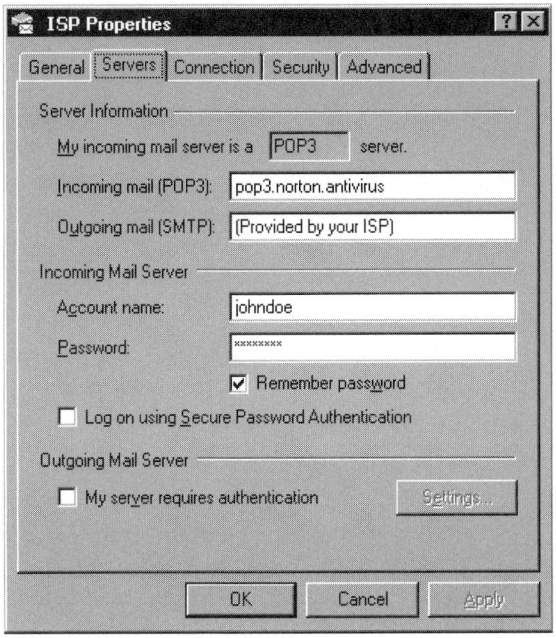

Figure 7-39. Reconfigure the POP3 entry to reflect your true mail server address.

NIS CUTS OFF SECURE WEB SITES

The Annoyance: I just added Norton Internet Security, but now I can't seem to access any secure web sites. That's a big price to pay for security.

The Fix: This is a known issue with the year 2002 versions of Norton Internet Security (NIS) and Norton Personal Firewall. A patch is available to eliminate this problem in the 2002 versions. However, don't be surprised if this annoyance also crops up with other versions of your firewall software if you don't enable access to secure (HTTPS) web sites. To get around it, launch the control panel for NIS or the firewall, select the Privacy Control, and click Configure. Select Custom Level and make sure that the "Enable secure connection" option is selected. Save the changes and close the control panel along with the browser. Now open the browser and try accessing the secure web site again.

TOOLS OF THE TRADE

A wealth of utilities exists to help you get the most from your Internet connections. Here are some particularly helpful programs that go the extra mile and are worthy of your attention:

SiSoft SANDRA (http://www.sisoftware.net)
> A utility that can identify the hardware, software, and configuration settings of your system

Hank Volpe's Modem Doctor (http://www.modemdoctor.com)
> A versatile utility that identifies and diagnoses dial-up modem issues in Windows

SpeedGuide TCP Optimizer (http://www.speedguide.com)
> Lets you tweak the Windows Registry settings for the optimal broadband connection speed

SpeedGuide Security Scan (http://www.speedguide.com)
> An online resource that tests your client PC for any common security flaws

Steve Gibson's Shields Up (http://www.grc.com)
> A detailed online resource that carefully inspects the security condition of a client PC's ports

CableTraffic 2.1 (http://www.cabletraffic.com) from AOTR, Inc.
> A utility that monitors your cable modem service and tracks the quality of your Internet connection.

Zone Labs ZoneAlarm (http://www.zonelabs.com)
> A popular and versatile firewall program; a free version is available from Zone Labs.

Printer and Scanner
ANNOYANCES

I can remember the old daisy wheel and dot impact printers grinding away in tiny, glass-enclosed computer rooms, systematically deafening everyone in the immediate area—ah, the memories! My first Panasonic KX-P1124 printer churned out a few precious pages per minute, though it made more noise than my brother's Harley-Davidson motorcycle.

New technologies such as laser and ink-jet printing quieted our obnoxious computer peripherals, while dramatically improving their print speed and quality. Suddenly, people were using laser and ink-jet printers to produce high-quality documents and crisp, high-resolution images. Today, color ink printers are an indispensable part of our multimedia diet, producing high-quality photographs, attractive greeting cards, and more. Scanners have also come a long way over the past few years, offering unprecedented connectivity, resolution, and performance. Yet, for all their speed and quality, printers and scanners still behave like the wayward children of the PC world. This chapter delves into setup and configuration issues, covers a series of performance problems, and solves some perplexing maintenance headaches.

SETUP ANNOYANCES

ENABLING A STUBBORN PRINTER

The Annoyance: I turned on the printer, but I still can't get it to print.

The Fix: Before you can print, a printer must be available to the computer. Take a look at the printer and its connection to your system. Make sure that the printer has power (a Power indicator is usually available), and check the parallel or USB cable to the host system. Loose cables can easily interfere with printing, so try reconnecting the cable at both ends.

Still, connecting a printer is just the beginning. The system still needs to "see" the printer and install the correct drivers for it. Otherwise, you may receive an error such as "printer not found." Open the Printers and Faxes control panel to display the printer and fax devices configured for your system (see Figure 8-1). If there is no entry (icon) for your printer, it's not installed. Click "Add a printer" and follow the wizard to install the drivers for your particular printer.

Figure 8-1. Verify that your printer is installed and ready.

Next, make sure you select the correct printer from your software's File → Print menu. For example, if you installed both a monochrome laser printer and a color photo printer, but only the laser printer is connected at the moment, you can't select the color printer (if you do select the printer, an error will occur when the spooler times out).

Finally, if your printer displays a grayed-out icon, the printer isn't ready. Perhaps the printer is out of paper or media (such as toner or ink). Also see that any external printer covers are securely closed. For example, you might have lifted the top cover to replace an exhausted ink cartridge; however, if the cover is left up (or doesn't close completely), the printer may remain unavailable.

NEW PRINTER ISN'T IDENTIFIED

The Annoyance: The PC does not identify my new photo printer during its initial installation. It's as if nothing is connected at all.

The Fix: Most printers are Plug-and-Play devices that are automatically identified by the operating system, but there are cases where a new printer can be a bit finicky. Disconnected or loose cables can kill a printer, so start by checking the power and USB (or parallel) connections to the host PC (see Chapter 1 for USB port annoyances).

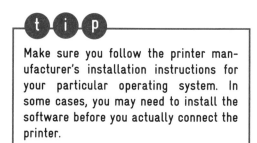

Make sure you follow the printer manufacturer's installation instructions for your particular operating system. In some cases, you may need to install the software before you actually connect the printer.

Once connected, the PC should generally "see" the printer (even if it's identified as just a new generic device). If not, there's trouble with the cable or the port on your PC. Try another cable, or enter the System Setup and see that the parallel port or USB ports are enabled. If the printer still isn't identified, launch the Add Printer wizard and install the printer drivers manually. Once the printer icon appears normally (as in Figure 8-1), you can try printing.

Still stuck? Try another printer. If a different printer installs and operates normally, your new photo printer may be damaged, or incompatible with your host PC. If you can't get other printers to work, the trouble may be with the port. Try installing the printer on another USB port, or try exchanging a parallel port printer for a USB model.

WAKENING A NETWORK PRINTER

The Annoyance: I just setup a home LAN for the family, but my kids (and especially the wife) still need me to print everything for them—I have the printer connected to my own PC. How can I get a printer set up for the network before I jump off the nearest bridge?

The Fix: Network printing throws a couple of wrinkles into the mix. For example, "true" network printers often incorporate a parallel port and USB port in addition to a native 10/100 Ethernet port. Some network-capable printers (such as HP commercial printers) implement an Ethernet port through an add-on card. In addition to the standard common-sense checks of your power and connections (see "Enabling a Stubborn Printer"), make sure that the Ethernet port is actually enabled and configured properly for your network. For example, a network printer at 192.168.0.50 won't work on a different network segment (e.g., 192.168.1.x or some other subnet). Checking this can typically be done through a series of front panel controls as described by the printer manufacturer.

If your printer doesn't have a built-in Ethernet port, you can still network the printer using a commercial print server. However, the print server typically requires software on every network client PC, so recheck the print server's installation and see that it's installed properly before attaching a printer.

If you're networking the printer through a client PC—that is, you're opting to "share" the printer through a PC rather than set up the printer independently—make sure you configure the printer as a working local printer, and see

that the client PC has a valid network connection. Open the Printers and Faxes control panel, right-click the printer you want to share and choose Properties. Click the Sharing tab and configure the printer for sharing (see Figure 8-2). Select the "Share this printer" option and enter a unique "Share name" for the printer.

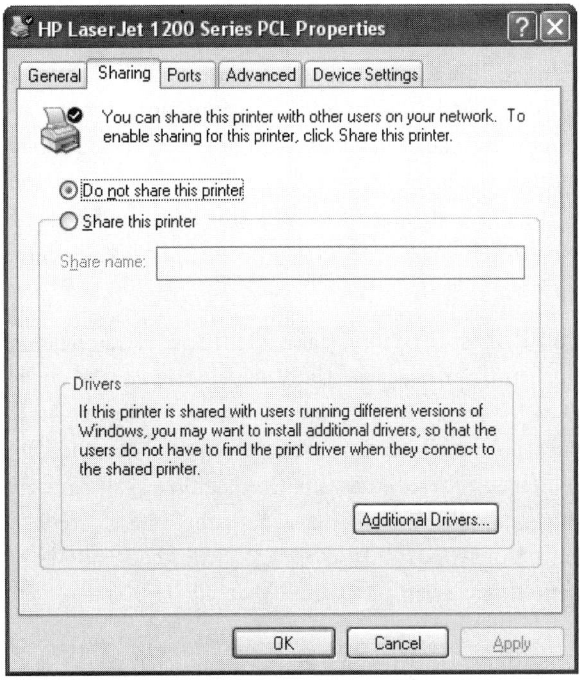

Figure 8-2. Be sure to share local printers through their client PCs.

WEIGHING A DRIVER UPDATE

The Annoyance: My printer maker says a driver upgrade is available. Is it worth going through the trouble to upgrade the printer driver? How do I even know what driver is currently installed on my system?

The Fix: As with most software updates, printer driver upgrades typically fix bugs, improve printing performance, and smooth compatibility issues with certain operating systems and ports (such as USB 2.0). In other cases, a manufacturer-specific driver may enable special printer features not supported by the default class of drivers under Windows XP.

tip

A printer may also benefit from an internal firmware upgrade rather than an operating system driver update, so check with the printer manufacturer for firmware upgrades as well.

However, the cardinal rule of computer troubleshooting is "if it ain't broke, don't fix it." So just because a manufacturer pumps out a driver update doesn't mean you should automatically rush to update it. First, check the related text file or web page to see what the driver update actually fixes. If you'll benefit from the fix, then it's worth the update.

Still, it's best to confirm your current driver version before jumping to a new one. Open the System control panel, click the Hardware tab, and then click the Device Manager button. Expand the printer entry, right-click the printer, select Properties, and click the Driver tab. Note the driver manufacturer and version number (see Figure 8-3). For example, my HP LaserJet 1200 uses the Windows XP default driver Version 5.1.2600.0 dated 7/1/2001.

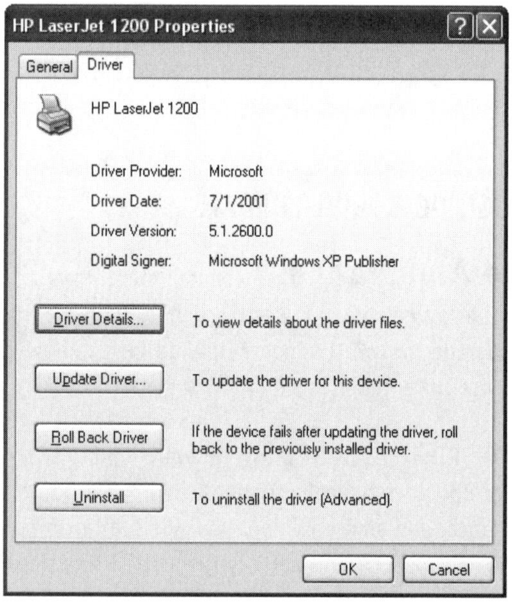

Figure 8-3. Check your current driver version and source before you implement a driver update.

Cleaning Toner Spills

Toner can make a huge mess—the microscopic powder gets everywhere, and it's very difficult to clean up. You can wipe up toner with cold water on a paper towel. Do *not* use hot water! Toner is designed to melt at high temperatures, and once it melts and sets, you'll never get it up. Also, do not vacuum residual toner without a bag intended specifically to hold microscopic granules. The toner particles will blow right through an ordinary filter bag and make an even bigger mess.

SPECIAL CABLES NOT NEEDED

The Annoyance: My printer maker sells cables with their printers. Do I need to buy the manufacturer's recommended USB or parallel port cables, or can I buy cables elsewhere?

The Fix: Don't pay a premium by buying cables from the printer manufacturer. Any good-quality USB or parallel port (IEEE 1284) cable should work just fine. If you don't get a suitable printer cable with the printer itself, save some cash and buy your cables from Staples or CompUSA. Just be sure to watch the cable length. For best results, keep parallel (IEEE 1284) cables under 6 feet (about 2 meters), and keep USB cables under 4 feet. Make sure you select shielded cables to reduce data errors due to noise and crosstalk from other nearby electrical devices.

FINDING THE RIGHT SIDE OF THE PAPER

The Annoyance: Someone told me that photocopier paper has a preferred side for laser printing. Is that true? How do I tell? Will it damage the printer otherwise?

The Fix: If you're worried about which side of the paper goes up in your laser printer, don't sweat it. You can safely print on both sides of the paper.

Ink-jet paper, on the other hand, is a slightly different animal. It tends to include an ink-absorbing coating on just one side (usually a shiny appearance). Although you can safely print on either side of ink-jet paper, printing to the "wrong" side may allow the paper fibers to absorb too much ink, resulting in a slightly dull or faded appearance. Glossy photo paper is an extreme example of this, so always print to the glossy side of photo paper.

PRINTER OUTPUT CUTS CORNERS

The Annoyance: My printer is supposed to print wavy lines as a border around some text, but the wavy lines come out as solid lines instead.

The Fix: This problem actually traces all the way back to Word in Microsoft Office XP. Depending on the combination of printer and operating system, some text, paragraph, and table borders that use dots, dashes, multiple lines, or wavy lines may print as solid lines. Fortunately, you can correct this annoyance with Office XP Service Pack 1 from Microsoft (*http://support.microsoft.com/default.aspx?scid=kb;EN-US;298953*).

You may also encounter this problem if you use the incorrect printer drivers (e.g., using an HP LaserJet 3020 driver with an HP LaserJet 3015 printer, or using an incorrect Postscript or PCL driver type). Double-check your driver and make sure you're using the latest driver version for your exact printer make and model.

PRINTER PUMPS OUT BLACK PAGES

The Annoyance: I connected my printer to the parallel port, and now it pumps out blank pages.

The Fix: The printer is getting bad data, so start by checking your selected printer, and see that the printer is using the latest driver from the manufacturer. For exam-ple, suppose you replaced your Canon printer with a new HP printer. If you don't change the default printer setting, your printing apps (such as Word) will still default to the Canon. Because HP uses a different command set than the Canon, the printing app will not talk to the HP properly, send bad data, and potentially cause this snafu. This problem can also happen if you install PostScript drivers for a PCL printer.

Next, check the parallel port settings in the BIOS (unless, of course, you're using a USB printer). Today's BIOS typically supports "standard," ECP, and EPP modes. Standard mode is the conventional bi-directional printing mode at 150KB/s. The ECP (Extended Capability Port) mode offers faster printing (up to about 1MB/s), and the ability to address unique devices on the parallel port cable. The Enhanced Parallel Port (EPP) mode runs up to 2MB/s and incorporates more device intelligence than the other port modes. Today, most printers run in standard or ECP mode. However, printer problems (such as blank pages) may indicate an incompatibility with ECP or EPP modes. Open the System Setup and disable ECP, or swap the mode to EPP or standard.

> **t i p**
>
> Setting the parallel port to standard mode will reduce printer performance, but often provide the best compatibility for diverse printers.

PRINTER DISCOVERED ON EACH BOOT

The Annoyance: Every time the PC boots, it "discovers" my Hewlett-Packard printer all over again, and prompts me incessantly to install the printer. If I cancel all the prompts, the printer works fine.

The Fix: This glitch seems to occur with some printer models under Windows XP. The first solution is to download and install any patches or hotfixes for Windows XP directly from Microsoft (*http://support.microsoft.com*, or use the Windows Update feature).

Once you've updated Windows XP to its latest revision level, download and install the latest drivers for your printer. In some cases, you may need to remove the printer through the Device Manager first, and then re-install it from scratch using the latest drivers.

SHARING PRINTERS THROUGH A NETWORK

The Annoyance: Now that I've got a few PCs on my home network, it would be nice to share my printer. Is there an easy way to do this? Can printers be shared without leaving all the PCs on?

The Fix: If you don't want to spring for a pricy Ethernet printer, you can use a print server to interface a parallel or USB printer to your Ethernet network. Linksys (*http://www.linksys.com*), Netgear (*http://www.netgear.com*), and D-Link (*http://www.d-link.com*) offer a selection of print server products for parallel and USB printers. Some print servers actually support two or more printers, so you can install a selection of conventional printers on your network. By taking your printer off its local PC and putting it on a print server, you don't need to leave a PC on all the time, and you also don't risk data by allowing other PCs to access the printer through a PC.

> **t i p**
>
> You'll need to have the print server driver CD and the printer driver CD when performing your installation on each networked PC.

PRINTER POPS UPS BREAKER

The Annoyance: How come the circuit breaker on my UPS pops when I connect my laser printer?

The Fix: An uninterruptible power supply (UPS) provides battery power to computer equipment when the AC power fails. However, a UPS can only provide a limited amount of power (watts) to drive attached equipment. A laser printer—especially large business-quality laser printers—can draw too much power when combined with the load from your PC and monitor. The circuit breaker pops to protect the UPS. This is an important protective feature; don't even *think* about defeating it unless you want to see your home or office burn to the ground.

You should leave high-load devices such as laser printers on a surge-protected outlet (rather than a UPS outlet). Who cares if the printer powers down in an outage? A UPS is intended to give you precious minutes to save your files and close your applications in a safe fashion. You can always repeat the print job when the AC power returns.

MULTIFUNCTION UNIT WON'T RECEIVE FAXES

The Annoyance: I set up a home office and bought an HP OfficeJet multifunction printer. It works great for the most part, except I can't receive faxes.

The Fix: Specialized services from your telephone company can sometimes block incoming faxes. Voice mail, privacy blocks, security screens, anonymous call rejection, and privacy managers can impair fax reception, so contact the telephone company and see if they can temporarily disable those services or suggest other solutions.

Also, make sure you configure the multifunction to receive faxes automatically. For example, enable automatic answering, or set the unit to fax or fax/telephone-answering mode (if you set the answer mode to "telephone," the unit will expect voice messages rather than faxes). Try removing any answering machines or other telephone devices on the fax line. Finally, the multifunction may require a firmware update.

NEW PRINTER RAM NOT RECOGNIZED

The Annoyance: My HP LasrJet1300 failed to recognize the new memory I installed. Now I'm totally disgusted because I still can't print my CAD drawings.

The Fix: First, tell the printer to deliver a test page, which should list the total amount of installed RAM (check your printer manual for instructions). If the new RAM doesn't appear, power down the printer and recheck your installation. Make sure that the RAM module(s) are installed evenly and completely, and verify that their orientation is correct. It's also worth trying the new RAM module(s) in other slots (if multiple memory slots are available).

No luck? Check the RAM manufacturer's part number against the supported modules listed in the printer's documentation or on the support web page). If the printer manufacturer does not recommend the new RAM, it may not be fully compatible with the printer. Or, one of the new memory modules might be defective. In either case, try a memory module tested and approved by the printer manufacturer.

> **tip**
>
> Check the printer manufacturer for firmware upgrades that may help to overcome expanded memory compatibility or performance issues.

RESOLUTION IS LIMITED

The Annoyance: I've got an older printer with a 600×600 resolution and no Windows XP drivers. The native Windows XP drivers only offer a 300×300 resolution. It doesn't even seem that the manufacturer intends to provide XP drivers.

The Fix: This exact situation occurred with the NEC 1260 laser printer. The 1260 supported 600×600 resolution with Windows 98/SE drivers. However, the drivers do not work under Windows XP. Although Windows XP does provide a native driver for the 1260, it's limited to 300×300 resolution. No problem, you say? Just upgrade the drivers? Well, that's the right thing to do; unfortunately, it seems that NEC doesn't offer XP drivers for the 1260, and no XP

drivers appear to be forthcoming—effectively ending NEC's support for the product.

Check with the printer manufacturer to see if there are any other Windows XP drivers for similar printers that might be compatible with your model. A similar driver may not support every feature, but it may offer the features you need (such as extended resolutions). Sadly, there's not much you can do when the manufacturer discontinues their driver support. You can stick with the native XP drivers, or you can choose to upgrade the printer to another make and model. Fortunately, you can buy a decent laser printer for under $300 today, so a new printer won't break the bank.

PERFORMANCE ANNOYANCES

CLEAR THE QUEUE

The Annoyance: I had five minutes to print my report, drink my coffee, make a phone call, and get to a meeting across town. Plenty of time. But when I tried to print my document, I got an error telling me that the network printer queue is full.

The Fix: A full print queue typically means that the maximum number of print jobs is already waiting for the printer. The easiest workaround is to get a second cup of coffee and try the print job again later (once several jobs have been completed and left the queue). If this becomes a persistent problem for you (and other network users), it might be worth increasing the amount of memory in the printer. Busy network printers could also benefit from an internal hard drive. More RAM and disk space will hold more jobs, effectively giving you a larger queue.

GETTING TOP PRINT SPEED

The Annoyance: I work in a large office and it takes me 20 minutes (okay, 15 minutes) to get from my cube to the printer. However, when I finally reach the printer I still have to wait for my documents to print.

The Fix: Several important factors affect print speed. The document complexity itself is a big issue. Simple text memos will queue up and print much faster than complex drawings or CAD layouts, which can take considerable time to download from the host PC. If you want more speed from "draft" printouts, simply lower the printing resolution (then restore the original quality levels for your final print job).

For example, open the Printers and Faxes control panel, right-click your printer, and select Properties. Click Printing Preferences on the General page, and then click the Advanced button (see Figure 8-4). Reduce the Print Quality (e.g., from 600dpi to 300dpi). You can also try disabling Advanced Printing Features.

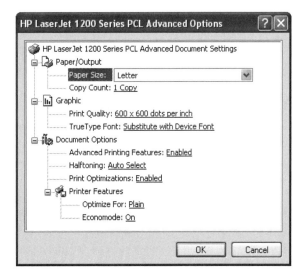

Figure 8-4. Reduce print quality to speed up draft print jobs.

Another possible trick is to change your print spooling preferences. Return to the printer properties dialog and click the Advanced tab (see Figure 8-5). Make sure that the "Start printing immediately" option is selected. The printer will deliver pages as soon as each page is available. The other option (Start printing after last page is spooled) will wait until the entire job is spooled before printing. Changing this option can make a radical difference with long and complicated print jobs.

Finally, if you're trying to print the maximum number of pages per minute, check with the printer manufacturer for firmware or driver updates that will enhance performance.

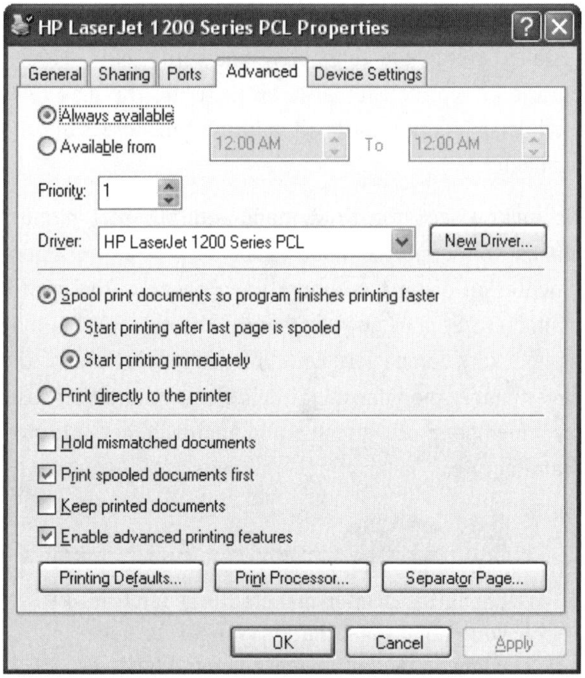

Figure 8-5. Spool your documents so that the printer churns out pages as soon as they are available.

GETTING THE MOST FROM TONER AND INK

The Annoyance: I got a nice little ink-jet printer with my new PC. I thought it was a great deal until I started printing photos. I've already spent more on ink than the printer is worth. What can I do?

The Fix: Considering that you almost need a second mortgage to afford toner and ink for today's printers, you can save some real cash by using the printer's "economy" or "draft" modes when running off nonessential print jobs. Open the Printers and Faxes control panel, right-click your printer, and select Properties. Click Printing Preferences on the General page, and then click the Advanced button (see Figure 8-4). For example, the Economode on my HP LaserJet

1200 should be set to On. Other printers will provide similar options for toner/ink reduction. When you're ready to print a "final" copy of a picture, report, or other document, remember to turn the economy mode off.

Here's another notion for your noggin. Lots of toner and ink is wasted printing graphics and text that aren't really needed. For example, suppose you want to print a map from a travel web site, but don't need the copious text directions that appear on the same page? A utility such as PrintMagic creates a virtual printer that lets you drag and drop only the content you're interested in printing. Although originally developed for the Mac, PrintMagic is now available for Windows (98 to XP). Download an evaluation version from *http://downloads-zdnet.com.com/3000-2088-10145322.html*.

THE PRINTER SPEWS GARBAGE

The Annoyance: My printer spews out incorrect characters, bad fonts, screwed up images, and all kinds of garbage. What can I do to fix this?

The Fix: Check the parallel or USB cable connection at both the printer and PC ends. Replace cut, scuffed, or damaged cables. Also, make sure you use the shortest possible cable—long and poorly shielded cables can allow electrical noise to affect the printer data.

If the problem persists, make sure you're using the latest driver for your particular printer make and model (see "Weighing a Driver Update"). If you've installed multiple printers, be sure you select the current printer in your printing application. For example, if you have a laser and color ink printer installed, but only the laser printer is attached at the moment, make sure you select the laser printer from the File → Print menu.

STOPPING MULTIPLE COPIES

The Annoyance: My laser printer spits out multiple copies of a page even though I only selected one copy in the Print dialog box. I usually recycle or reuse the extras copies as scrap paper, but it still seems like a waste.

The Fix: The printer itself may be configured for multiple copies. Check the printer's LCD menu-driven control panel and set the internal copy setting to 1 (check your printer manual for instructions). If the setting is more than 1, it will typically print that number of copies regardless of the application's copy setting.

HALTING AN UNWANTED PRINT JOB

The Annoyance: I accidentally hit the Print icon in Word when working on a huge file. I immediately went to the printer icon in the System Tray and cancelled the job, but it kept printing.

The Fix: This annoyance happens a lot, and it's surprisingly hard to stop. When you tell an application to print a file, that file is spooled to the hard drive, and then sent off to the printer's memory. Plain documents can spool with startling speed—before you know it, the document is already at the printer. When you start a bogus print job, just turn off the printer first, and then clear the PC's print queue by double-clicking the printer icon in the System Tray and deleting the job. When the queue finally empties, remove any paper still jammed in the unit, then restore power to the printer. You may also need to reset the printer (according to the manufacturer's documentation) to clear any jobs still internally queued in the printer's hard drive (if one is installed).

HTML UPSETS PRINTING

The Annoyance: I like to print recipes and maps from the Web, but often the margins get all screwed up and I end up missing an important ingredient or turn.

The Fix: This problem occurs because HTML pages know nothing about paper margins. Most of the time, the browser will render HTML pages with excessively wide margins (wider than 8.5 inches). It also uses other formatting commands that can cause the page to print wrong. Click the Properties button in the Print dialog box and choose "Landscape" orientation to print sideways on the page and capture content that might otherwise be lost. In other cases, look for HTML pages with "printer-friendly" versions specifically formatted to fit within regular paper margins.

Recycle Toner and Ink Cartridges

Toner and ink cartridges can take up a lot of space in the local landfill, and that's not good for the environment. Most printer manufacturers will accept returns of spent toner and ink cartridges for refurbishment and recycling. In many cases, the cartridge box can serve "dual duty" as a free return-shipping container for your exhausted media. Contact your printer manufacturer to learn about their current recycling programs.

REVERSING MIRRORED PRINT

The Annoyance: When I print PDF and Photo-Shop files, the document or photo appears mirrored (reversed).

The Fix: A poorly designed driver can cause this problem when you try to print certain file types. Click the Properties button in the Print dialog box and return the driver to its default setting. For example, click the Advanced tab in the HP LaserJet 1200's properties dialog box, and then click the Printing Defaults button (see Figure 8-5). If the problem continues, download and install the latest printer driver for your specific operating system.

DEALING WITH INSUFFICIENT SPACE

The Annoyance: I upgraded my printer driver, but now I get an error that tells me there is insufficient space to print the job.

The Fix: This is a compatibility problem with the new printer driver. As a workaround, open the System control panel, click the Hardware tab, and then click the Device Manager button. Right-click the printer (it will be located with your printer ports or USB ports depending on your printer's interface) and select Properties. Next, choose the Drivers tab, and then click the Roll Back Driver button and follow the wizard to restore the earlier driver. Alternatively, open the Printers and Faxes control panel, right-click the printer, and select Properties. Choose the Advanced tab and click the New Driver button. Then reinstall an older driver.

CLEANING UP DIRTY FONTS

The Annoyance: Some of my fonts appear dirty or broken when they print, or the characters print incompletely.

The Fix: Forgot to have the maid dust the printer, eh? Well don't worry. In most cases, the printing application distorts the text and causes it to appear dirty or broken. Check with your software maker for any available patches or updates. An upgraded printer driver may also help.

You can also change the print quality through the application. For example, in Microsoft Word, select File → Print, click the Properties button, and then click the Advanced button. Next, increase the print quality to a higher resolution, or use "Substitute with Device Font" (using the printer's internal fonts) rather than download the font data to the printer as "soft fonts" (see Figure 8-4).

PRINT JOBS DON'T CLEAR THE QUEUE

The Annoyance: I'm trying to print to my HP LaserJet across a network. The jobs print, but don't clear the queue. The job even prints again if I reboot the system.

The Fix: This little gem of a migraine pops up in HP LaserJet printers, and may be due to HP's printer management software running in the background. The print spooler doesn't work properly with the printer manager software, causing the print job to hang in the queue (even though the job may print fine). Try disabling bi-directional printing. Open the Printers and Faxes control panel, right-click the printer icon, and select Properties. Next, click the Ports tab and uncheck the "Enable bidirectional support" box (see Figure 8-6).

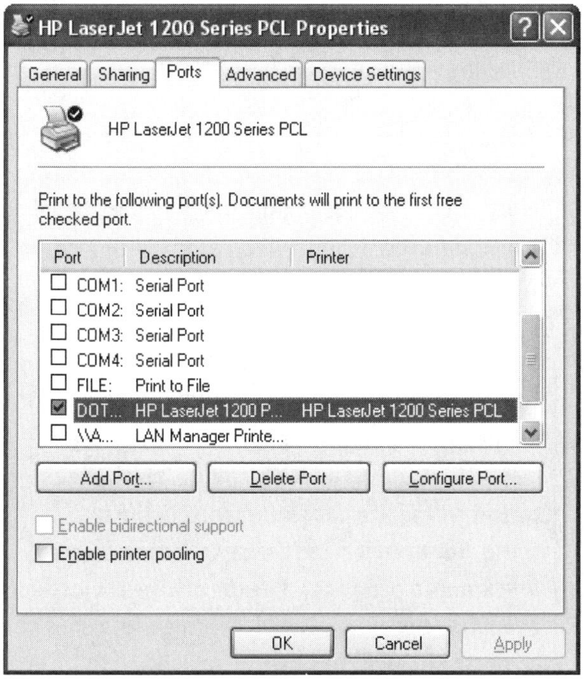

Figure 8-6. Disable bi-directional support to cut off communication between the print spooler and management software.

If the problem persists, update the driver and then disable bi-directional support as described above. As a last resort, try the native Windows XP driver rather than the manufacturer's (possibly uncertified) driver.

MAINTENANCE ANNOYANCES

NEW DRUM STILL WANTS REPLACEMENT

The Annoyance: I replaced the electrophotographic (EP) drum in my printer, but I still get a message telling me to replace the drum. Ugh!

The Fix: When you replaced the drum, did you remember to reset the page counter? If not, then dig those drum replacement instructions out of the trash (or wipe the cobwebs off of your printer manual) and make sure you reset the printer's page counter as directed by the manufacturer. The printer uses the page counter to keep track of the drum's age and remind you when it's time for a new one.

OVERCOMING PERSISTENT TONER ERRORS

The Annoyance: I replaced the toner cartridge in my laser printer, but I still get an error telling me that the toner is empty.

The Fix: Remove the cartridge and gently shake it back and forth to distribute the toner, and then reinsert the cartridge. If the problem persists, clean the corona wire—a high-voltage wire used to place a charge on the drum and attract toner. Over time, the wire may corrode slightly or attract debris and cause light/white streaks down the page. (Note that if you replace the toner cartridge, it will not replace the corona wire, unless the toner supply is part of the EP assembly). Remove the EP drum from your printer and locate the primary corona wire (see your printer manual for the exact location). In many cases, drum assemblies already include a little plastic cleaning tab that you can simply run back and forth along the wire a few times. Return the tab to its locked position and reinstall the drum.

SMOOTHING OUT LIGHT STREAKS

The Annoyance: I bought a laser printer so I could print out more professional looking documents, but each page has a light streak down the middle. The laser printer isn't telling me to replace the toner.

The Fix: Toner cartridges usually do a great job of telling you when they're exhausted, but don't always distinguish low points very well. If your printed pages look correct—except for a light/blank streak running the length of the page—your toner may simply be low in a spot. Remove the toner cartridge and gently shake it back and forth, then reinsert the cartridge. If the problem returns later, simply replace the toner cartridge.

If, however, you shake the toner cartridge and the streaks persist, remove the EP drum assembly. Next, clean the transfer corona wire (not the primary corona wire) as suggested by the printer manufacturer. The transfer corona wire applies a charge to the paper, which pulls toner off the drum. If any part of the transfer corona is fouled, a charge may not be applied to the page in that area and result in a light/blank streak. As a last resort, replace the EP drum assembly outright.

CLEANING UP INK SPILLS

The Annoyance: Yuck! I've got a bad cartridge that's dribbling ink all over the place. What's the best way to clean up this mess?

The Fix: Ink is notoriously difficult to clean up. It's a truly rare occurrence with factory-fresh ink cartridges, but it can happen frequently with cartridges damaged by one too many ink refills. First, protect your hands and clothing (i.e., put on junky clothes and use latex gloves) or you might ruin your new office power-tie or make your hands look like the "swamp thing." While you're at it, gather up some paper towels, a bagged trash barrel, a lint-free cloth, and some isopropyl (rubbing) alcohol.

Open the printer and remove the hemorrhaging ink cartridge(s). Use some paper towels to soak up the majority of the wet ink. Make sure you remove ink from any electrical ink cartridge contacts and the platen where the cartridges pass over the paper. Now wet the cloth with a 50/50 mix of isopropyl alcohol and water and clean up any stubborn residue. Remember that you don't have to be perfect here, just get the ink off the paper handling area, and dry everything before you install a new cartridge and print again.

CLEANING INK-JET CARTRIDGES

Ink-jets eject minute droplets of ink from the microscopic nozzles of an ink cartridge. Ideally, ink cartridges require no maintenance. In the real world, however, leaving the cartridge uncovered for extended periods of time can dry the ink just enough to clog nozzles and leave fine white lines across the page. Most times, regular printing tasks will free minor clogs, and printers typically include a "purge" feature intended to work any stubborn clogs free. If your cartridge still suffers from clogged nozzles, remove the cartridge and sit it (nozzles down) in a shallow bath of isopropyl alcohol (no more than 1/8 inch—just enough to kiss the nozzles). Wait 24 hours, dry the nozzles gently on a paper towel, reinstall the cartridge, run a purge or cleaning cycle, and try your print job again.

When it comes to ink-jet refills, success depends on the quality of your refill ink and cartridge. A typical refill process involves filling a small syringe with a quantity of ink, then inserting the needle into the cartridge (through either a pre-existing hole, or a small hole that you drill yourself), then slowly pushing the ink from the syringe into the cartridge. You can buy refill kits at stores such as CompUSA, as well as over the Internet, for about $20 (*http://www.compusa.com/products/product_info.asp?product_code=299371&pfp=SEARCH*). When performed properly with suitable ink, a refilled cartridge should work about as well as a new cartridge. However, printer manufacturers typically frown on refilled ink, and may not honor your warranty if you return a printer with a refilled ink cartridge installed. Check your warranty closely for ink cartridge exemptions.

If you would rather not hassle with refills, opt for remanufactured ink cartridges (an ink cartridge that has been refilled and certified to work by the cartridge maker or a third-party recycler). Search the printer manufacturer's web site and see if they support remanufactured cartridges. If so, you can usually save a few dollars per cartridge.

Another alternative is a "continuous ink" system from a manufacturers such as Niagara Systems (*http://www.mediastreet.com*). These systems replace the ink cartridge on certain Epson and Canon printers with a semi-permanent nozzle system leading to a series of tanks located off the printer. This setup can be a very economical solution when printing lots of color.

INSTALLED INK CARTRIDGES ARE MISSING

The Annoyance: An error message says an ink cartridge is missing, but I just installed brand new cartridges in the printer.

The Fix: Replaceable ink cartridges have a bevy of electrical contacts on their backside (opposite the "labeled" side), and each of these little electrical contacts must mate exactly with the corresponding contacts on the printer. Recheck your installation and make sure you snapped the ink cartridges in their correct locations (you generally don't want the Cyan cartridge in the Magenta holder).

Over time, the electrical contacts may corrode slightly and interfere with the connection. Remove the pesky cartridge(s) and gently clean the contacts with a little isopropyl alcohol on a cotton swab (clean both the carriage and cartridge contacts). Let the alcohol dry completely and reinstall the cartridge(s). If the problem persists, replace the cartridge.

THE JAM THAT WOULDN'T DIE

The Annoyance: My laser printer stopped because of a jam. I cleared the stuck page, but the printer still reports a jam. What did I miss?

The Fix: Clearing paper jams can get a little tricky when you start tearing up the pages. You probably left a little fragment of paper in the printer, which is covering the paper sensor and prolonging your torture. Open the printer and take a careful look around. Perhaps another page started into the printer from the paper tray. Check the entire paper path for lingering paper fragments. You may need to remove the toner cartridge and EP drum to view the entire paper path.

JAMS IN THE DUPLEXER

The Annoyance: My laser printer jams every time I use the duplexer.

The Fix: A duplexer lets you print on both sides of the paper, but anytime you add complexity to the paper path, you also increase the possibility of jams. Open the duplexer and look for paper or label fragments that may be obstructing the paper path—one little paper fragment can knock a page off course and cause a jam. Also, make sure you properly attached the duplexer to the printer.

Next, check the media (e.g., paper, labels, and transparencies) limitations of your duplexer. For example, a basic printer may easily print on 50lb card stock, but the duplexer may not support paper heavier than 30lb. Try ordinary 20lb paper and see what happens. Other factors, such as excess humidity in the summer (or insufficient humidity in the winter), may also adversely affect the media. If all else fails, replace the duplexer.

TONER RUBS OFF

The Annoyance: When I pick up printouts from the laser printer, a little toner seems to rub off the pages, which gets on my hands, and then on my shirt, and then… well, you get the idea. What can I do to lower my dry-cleaning bill?

The Fix: Laser printers heat the toner particles to a high temperature, then squeeze the molten toner into the paper fibers. Any unusual media or loss of temperature can cause some of the toner to remain in its particle form—free to rub off onto subsequent pages or your fingers. The paper (media) itself may be your biggest culprit. Specialty papers, coated papers, or unusually thin paper may not allow for proper fixing. Try some regular 20lb paper.

If the problem persists, there may be an issue with your printer's fixing unit (the twin rollers that heat and squeeze the toner). Crack open your printer manual and look for a temperature adjustment feature and tweak it upward in small increments until you fix the problem. If your printer lacks this feature, contact the manufacturer. They may need to replace the failing fixer (sometimes called a "fuser") module.

> ### HOW LASER PRINTERS WORK
> A laser printer works by placing a uniform electrical charge onto a light-sensitive drum. A laser beam then sweeps back and forth as the drum rotates and "draws" the text or graphics onto the drum. Toner jumps to the areas of the drum hit by the laser beam. The toner is then transferred onto the page where it is heated and squeezed to fix the toner to the paper. Some laser printers provide a separate toner cartridge and electrophotographic (EP) drum, while other printers integrate the toner supply and drum into the same replaceable assembly.

PAGES SEEM GRAY AND DINGY

The Annoyance: It took me almost 20 minutes to clear a pesky paper jam from my laser printer. I put everything back properly (toner cartridge, EP drum, etc.), but now the pages seem dark and grayed out.

The Fix: This problem (also known as "fogging") occurs when you expose the EP drum to light (especially sunlight through a nearby window) for 15 minutes or longer. EP drums are extremely sensitive to all types of light, though intense light (such as sunlight) is most damaging. If you leave the drum exposed, you can "poison" its light-sensitive coating, which makes it much harder for the drum to accept a toner-resistant charge. Viola! Dark pages with crummy contrast.

Fortunately, your drum will usually recover from "fogging" in 24 hours (48 hours at most). If not, you'll need to replace the drum assembly outright. In the future, always place the EP drum in a dark container if you remove it from the printer. A heavy-gauge garbage bag would work, or you can use the dark bag that covered the drum when you first installed it in the printer.

DEALING WITH HP DRIVER ERRORS

The Annoyance: When I try to print to my HP 930C printer, I get an HPF9XDR0 error.

The Fix: You're looking straight down the barrel of an HP driver error. An HPF9XDR0 error frequently occurs with major programs, such as Word, Paint, Photoshop, and PrintMaster. In most cases, your driver version is old or incompatible with the software. Download the latest printer driver for your specific printer model. If the problem persists, disable or uninstall the HP printer monitoring software.

Also, check for unexpected or specialized fonts. For example, according to HP, the BD Denver.TTF (True Type Font) installed with ByDesign software may conflict with the HPF9XDR0 driver. For this particular wrinkle, update the troublesome font file or uninstall the ByDesign software.

COLOR PRINTER ANNOYANCES

FIXING NOZZLE MISFIRES

The Annoyance: Why do I see white lines in my printed photos?

The Fix: Over time, nozzles may fail or clog and cause fine white (missing) lines in your photos. To correct this problem, clean the ink cartridge(s). Ink-jet printers typically include a "cleaning" feature designed to loosen any clogged nozzles (see the sidebar "Cleaning Ink-jet Cartridges" earlier in this chapter). If you still can't get the cartridge to fire on all cylinders, try another ink cartridge. You need not discard the old cartridge—just relegate it to secondary tasks, such as draft or text printing. Of course, if your printer uses a separate print head and ink tank, return it to the manufacturer for service.

Many ink-jet printers include a pattern check as part of the test page. It often appears as a grid, solid block, or other pattern that can clearly illustrate the presence of missing nozzles.

OPTING FOR DEEP CLEANING

The Annoyance: My printer offers a print head cleaning cycle and a "deep cleaning" cycle. What's the difference?

The Fix: Almost every ink-jet printer provides some type of automatic cleaning cycle to clear clogged nozzles. However, some printers, such as the Canon S9000, offer a "deep cleaning" feature to clear out any stubborn clogs. Of course, this drives the ink nozzles harder and longer, and wastes additional (expensive) ink. When you clean the nozzles, always start with a basic (or light) cleaning cycle. This will clear most clogs and waste the least amount of ink. If your nozzles don't clear in one or two cycles, the cartridge may be defective, so replace the cartridge (keep the old cartridge for draft or text printing).

HEADS WON'T ALIGN

The Annoyance: The photos I printed on my HP All-In-One look a bit ragged and disjointed.

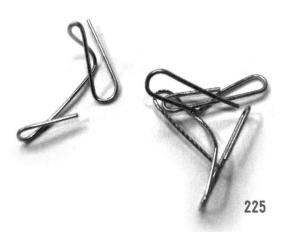

The Fix: Your printer has an alignment problem. Normally, ink-jet printers include an alignment feature that produces a test page with an array of symbols (each using a different offset factor). When you run the alignment cycle and receive the printed array, you select the number corresponding to the "best" alignment, and enter it into the printer driver. You may need to repeat the alignment cycle each time you replace the ink cartridges.

If you can't find an appropriate alignment factor, chances are that you're using a third-party ink cartridge that doesn't meet the exacting technical specifications of the manufacturer's original design. Still stuck? Contact the printer manufacturer to arrange service or replacement.

COLORS SEEM WRONG

The Annoyance: I just got back from my honeymoon and started printing out some photos for the family. The problem is that my beautiful sunset shots just don't seem to capture the moment—the colors seem wrong. Any ideas?

The Fix: Remember, the colors you see on your monitor do not always reflect the colors produced on your ink-jet printer. Only a few printer setups include a color monitoring/matching unit. Otherwise, the color printer driver simply attempts its best interpretation of your color image. Bottom line: printed colors may deviate a bit from the colors shown on the monitor. If your printer driver provides support for color profiles (see Figure 8-7), you can tweak your printer's colors based on the media and printer configuration. You can also use a photo-editing program such as Adobe Photoshop Elements to tweak the image colors.

If you notice even more subtle problems—such as ink splotches of poor color mixing—it may be time to clean the ink cartridges. Run a complete cleaning cycle on the ink-jet printer and try another print job. Compare the two print jobs and see if the cleaning cycle made a difference.

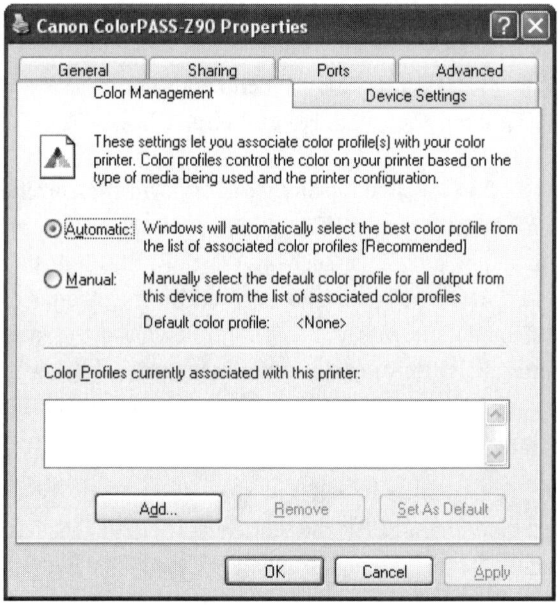

Figure 8-7. Use color profiles to tweak printer colors for your media and hardware configuration.

COLOR IN THE GRAYSCALE

The Annoyance: I see traces of color in the grayscale images I print. Did the color red suddenly become a shade of gray?

The Fix: Most color ink-jet printers use four colors: black, cyan, magenta, and yellow. When you opt for black (or a shade of gray), the printer should employ only the black ink cartridge. However, you can also combine cyan/magenta/yellow inks to produce black (and grays). Some printers let you switch between "true" black and "combined" black. When you print grayscale images, make sure you choose the former. If not, the printer will attempt to use your color components (resulting in a far more expensive print). If your printer relies on a color cartridge to emulate black and grays, replace the color cartridge with a black cartridge before you print grayscale images.

COLORS APPEAR GRAY

The Annoyance: I snapped a photo of the most amazing sunset. The sky was ablaze with all shades of yellow, red, and orange. Of course, you would never know it by looking at the print because my color printer only spits out black and white images all of a sudden. What gives?

The Fix: Open the Printers and Faxes control panel, right-click your printer, and select Properties. Click the Printing Preferences button and then click the Paper/Quality tab, and select the "Color" option (see Figure 8-8). Of course, this option may appear differently for other printer types and driver versions, but you get the general idea.

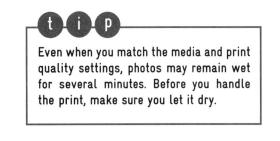

Figure 8-8. Make sure you select the Color print option rather than the Black & White option.

STOP INK FROM SMEARING

The Annoyance: When I print photos, the ink just smears into a line—it's like there's a paintbrush just running the colors together.

The Fix: If enough dust, pet hair, and other debris accumulate on the cartridge, it can actually act like a paintbrush—wiping one wet color into another—and ruin your print. First, remove the ink cartridges and clean away any debris from the cartridges and carriage holders.

This problem can also arise if you use the wrong media, print quality, and paper type settings. Plain paper, coated ink-jet paper, transparencies, and glossy photo paper all absorb different amounts of ink. For example, if you tell the printer that you're using glossy photo paper, it may spray more ink to create a bolder, brighter image. The problem is that if you actually loaded transparency or uncoated media into the printer, the excessive ink might cause the colors to run or bleed. Always make sure your paper and print quality settings match the media (paper) in the printer.

> **tip**
>
> Even when you match the media and print quality settings, photos may remain wet for several minutes. Before you handle the print, make sure you let it dry.

INK DOESN'T FILL PROPERLY

The Annoyance: My ink-jet printer works OK, but the ink doesn't seem to fill my text and graphics completely. For example, when I print out real estate listings, the photos have color gaps, and the descriptions and detail text seem a bit broken.

The Fix: Manufacturers designed ink-jets to print on flat surfaces. Textured papers (such as a canvas print paper) create a lot of "hills and valleys" that just won't fill properly. Try printing on standard, 20lb plain paper found at your local office supplies store. If you absolutely must print on coarse or rough-surfaced papers, make sure you select a "normal" or "high quality" print mode and force the printer to spray the maximum amount of ink.

Watch your ink cartridges also. White (missing) lines in the print may indicate a clogged ink nozzle (see the previous annoyance "Fixing Nozzle Misfires"), so run a cleaning cycle on the ink cartridges and try to print again.

DISCARDING INK CARTRIDGES

The Annoyance: I print a lot of photos of the ocean. As a result, my inkjet, which uses a single CMY color cartridge, runs out of cyan ink faster than the other colors. Ink is very expensive, and discarding a CMY cartridge when only one of the three colors is exhausted seems like a terrible waste of money.

The Fix: Unfortunately, you have precious few options. One popular option is an ink refill kit. Select a color refill kit appropriate for your make and model of print cartridges and add some ink to the exhausted color in your cartridge. However, ink cartridge refills are not always reliable. Users often damage the cartridge in the refill process, and most cartridges can only be refilled a few times. If you use a poor quality refill ink or the wrong one, it may also result in frequent nozzle clogs (or excess leaking).

> **Warning...**
> Never try to coax more ink from a cartridge by introducing solvents or other chemicals to the ink container. Solvents will thin the residual ink and the cartridge will likely leak.

Still, it's not all doom and gloom. Virtually all color printer manufacturers provide some kind of recycling program, and some manufacturers may offer a respectable discount on remanufactured ink cartridges (check for special offers from your particular printer manufacturer).

> Buy an ink-jet with separate cyan, magenta, and yellow cartridges rather than a single combined CMY cartridge. This way, you only need to replace the exhausted color.

MORE INK FOR THE MONEY

The Annoyance: Where can I find oversized or bulk ink systems for my printer? Are these any good? Do I really save any money?

The Fix: Two great sources for bulk ink systems are MediaStreet (*http://www.mediastreet.com*) and CIS, Inc. (*http://www.nomorecarts.com*). Bulk ink systems typically use a series of external ink bottles (each holding between 4 and 128 ounces) to feed a substitute cartridge, and provide enough ink for hundreds (even thousands) of pages. Unfortunately, bulk ink systems are not available for every printer type. MediaStreet's Niagra systems only support Epson (and some Canon) printers. The Continuous Inking Systems from CIS, Inc. support a variety of Epson printers (see Figure 8-9).

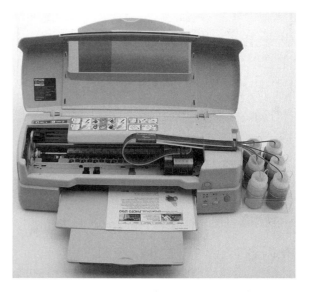

Figure 8-9. An Epson Stylus Photo 1290 printer with a CIS inking system attached.

Is it worth the money? To estimate your cost savings, you need to know the cost of your own ink cartridges, the amount of ink in ounces, and the number of pages you can print. Then you can calculate the rough cost per page. Now look at the cost of the ink system and the bulk ink, and figure the rough cost per page. Compare the two figures and you'll see your savings.

PAPER ANNOYANCES

AVOID BAD PAPER TYPES

The Annoyance: My printer supports an amazing variety of paper textures, weights, and finishes. In fact, I find the overabundance of options annoying. Got any tips on which papers to avoid?

The Fix: There are few hard rules to follow, but here are some tips to help you decide:

- Paper-handling mechanisms can handle a limited number of paper weights—avoid excessively light and heavy paper weights. For example, 50lb card stock frequently misfeeds because it can't make the tight twists and turns in most paper handing paths. Thin papers also cause misfeeds because the paper-handling rollers can't grasp the pages securely.

- Ink and toner typically don't adhere well to oddly coated papers, such as wax or metallic. The coatings can also cause the pages to slip (and contaminate your rollers) and cause misfeeds or jams.

- Textured papers (e.g., canvas finish) may work with certain printers, but not all. For example, an ink-jet printer may use a canvas finish page to produce a professional photo-quality print, but a laser printer may not be able to transfer toner to such a rough paper surface. Make sure you use paper products tested and recommended by the printer manufacturer.

Some manufacturers (such as HP) sell maintenance kits, which let you replace items such as rollers and fusers without returning the printer for service. Check the printer manufacturer's web site for replacement assemblies and service options.

SEVERAL SHEETS FEED AT ONCE

The Annoyance: Sometimes when I try to print long documents, the sheets stick together and jam the printer.

The Fix: First, make sure you use a paper type and weight recommended for your printer (see "Avoid Bad Paper Types"). Unusually light or coated papers tend to stick together and cause misfeeds. Extremely dry environments (especially a dry New England winter) can cause static cling and keep pages stuck together. Do not overload or underload the paper tray. Also, make sure you fan the paper before you insert it into the tray.

STOP ENVELOPE CRUMPLING

The Annoyance: When I try to print envelopes they come out all crumpled or jam in the printer.

The Fix: Check your printer's documentation for recommended weights and sizes. Oversized or overweight envelopes may simply not work well in your particular printer model (see "Avoid Bad Paper Types"). As with other papers, environmental conditions such as excess humidity (or even a lack of humidity) may adversely affect the envelopes and cause unexpected jams. Excess humidity can also wreak havoc with your envelope adhesive in a laser printer. The combination of heat and humidity can actually seal your envelopes and force you to pry open the sealed flap. Keep your paper and envelopes in a dry, cool place.

SCANNER ANNOYANCES

PC DOESN'T SEE THE USB SCANNER

The Annoyance: My PC fails to recognize my USB scanner. Other USB devices work just fine.

The Fix: First, make sure your system meets (preferably exceeds) the minimum system requirements for your scanner. For example, you may need an OS upgrade before you connect the USB scanner.

Next, make sure the power and USB cables are attached securely at both ends. Many USB devices also require you to install drivers and other supporting software (such as scanner management software) before you attach the actual hardware. In this case, detach the scanner, remove any unknown entries from the Device Manager (Open the System control panel, click the Hardware tab, and then click the Device Manager button), then install the scanner software as recommended by the manufacturer.

If the scanner is still AWOL, test the USB port by attaching another USB device (such as a mouse) to the port to see if it works. If not, connect the scanner to another port or troubleshoot the original USB port (see Chapter 1 for some tasty USB annoyances). If the USB mouse works, you know the port works (although it never hurts to try a different USB port anyway). Next, try the scanner on another PC. Still no luck? Then you should return the scanner to the place of purchase or contact the manufacturer.

Here's one more trick for techie-types. Because systems often power-down idle USB ports, but don't always allow the port to re-awaken itself when a device is attached, you could try rebooting the PC and attaching the USB scanner immediately. You could also access the USB Root Hub corresponding to your port and prevent a power-down. To do that, open the System control panel, click the Hardware tab, and then click the Device Manager button. Expand the "Universal Serial Bus controllers" entry, right-click the corresponding "USB Root Hub," and

select Properties. Click the Power Management tab and uncheck the "Allow the computer to turn off this device to save power" box (see Figure 8-10).

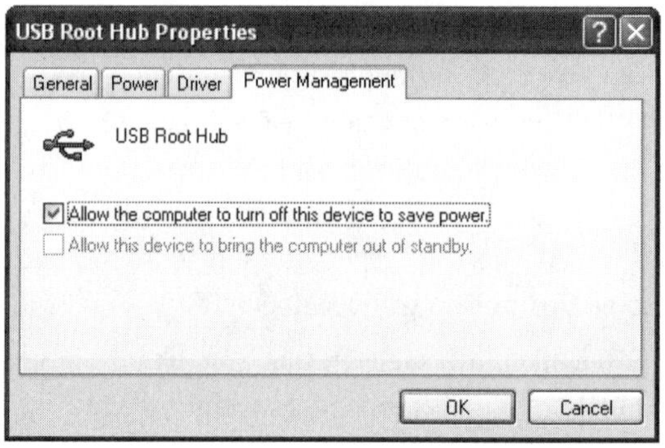

Figure 8-10. Prevent the host computer from automatically powering down your USB ports.

> **tip**
>
> If you use a USB hub, try connecting the scanner directly to a USB port on the PC.

SCSI CONNECTION CAN'T INITIALIZE SCANNER

The Annoyance: When I connect my SCSI scanner I get an error that says "scanner cannot be initialized."

The Fix: This surprisingly common annoyance often relates to the configuration of your SCSI host adapter. First, check the SCSI cabling and termination between the scanner and SCSI port. Also, make sure you terminated the last external SCSI device—almost always the scanner.

Here's a wrinkle. You may need to unterminate the SCSI host adapters if you attached both internal *and* external SCSI devices. Remember that the *ends* of a SCSI chain must be terminated; hence, you normally terminate the

SCSI host adapter and the last internal drive. However, with both internal and external devices attached, the SCSI host adapter winds up in the middle of the SCSI chain, and therefore should not be terminated. Also, make sure you assign the scanner a unique SCSI ID.

Whew! Now check for updated drivers for your SCSI host adapter and SCSI scanner. Install any SCSI host driver updates first, and then try any new SCSI scanner drivers.

Another problem may be in the SCAM (SCSI Configuration Automatically) feature of your SCSI host adapter. SCAM automatically assigns a SCSI ID to each device on the SCSI host adapter (rather than fixed IDs set by hand). Unfortunately, some SCSI devices may receive different IDs each time you start the PC. If the scanner receives different IDs, it may appear or work properly on some startups, but not others—it depends on which ID it receives. Disable SCAM through the SCSI host adapter's BIOS and set the SCSI IDs of each device manually.

THE SCAN BUTTON FREEZES THE PC

The Annoyance: When I press the ScanTo button on my HP All-In-One unit, the PC freezes and then I've got to reboot the whole thing. What a pain in the you-know-what.

The Fix: Many of today's scanners include buttons designed to automate common actions. For example, the ScanTo button can launch your scanning application and preview the image with one-button ease—removing much of the drudgery involved with launching the software and starting a scan manually. However, the host PC must meet (preferably exceed) the minimum system requirements for the scanner. Patch or update your operating system if necessary. Low disk space or RAM can also allow the system to crash when you use custom buttons. Close any unneeded background applications to free some extra RAM. Ultimately, a RAM upgrade or a larger hard drive may be required to use the scanner's onboard controls correctly. Finally, check with the scanner manufacturer for updated drivers and application software, which may eliminate this bug on your particular PC platform and operating system.

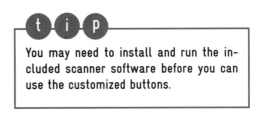

You may need to install and run the included scanner software before you can use the customized buttons.

SCANNING OPENS ANOTHER APPLICATION

The Annoyance: When I press the Scan button, some photo-editing program opens instead of the scanning software.

The Fix: The software on your host computer configures the buttons on your scanner. When the PC sees a function button (such as Scan), it automatically follows a task configured in the scanner driver or scanner management software. The photo-editing software probably found your scanner and changed the scanner's default scanning/editing application. To reconfigure the Scan button and launch a different program, refer to the scanner's manual for instructions.

GETTING MORE RAM FOR SCANNING

The Annoyance: When I try to scan full-page images, I get a memory error.

The Fix: Scanning is a memory-intensive task—there's no way around it. Just imagine an 8.5×11 inch scan at 300dpi in 16-bit color. That's 90,000 dots per square inch. Since the 8.5×11-inch image has 935 square inches, we're talking about 84,150,000 pixels. At 16 bits per pixel (two bytes), that's 168,300,000 bytes (168.3MB) for the complete uncompressed image. Even for a PC with 512MB, 168.3MB is a huge chunk. A 32-bit color scan would take twice that (336.6MB). It's easy to run short of RAM—especially with multiple applications open.

Start with a quick memory test. Quit your background applications to free up more RAM (and stop possible software conflicts that may be causing your error). Try the scan again. If the problem persists, try a small scan, lower the color depth, or drop the resolution. Any of these three options will reduce the RAM needed to hold your scans. If the memory error goes away, you need to add more RAM.

Don't forget about virtual memory. PCs normally set aside some hard drive space to emulate RAM. When real RAM runs short, the PC will use virtual memory. Open the System control panel, click the Advanced tab, and then click the Settings button in the Performance area. Click the Advanced tab and look at the "Virtual memory" area (see Figure 8-11).

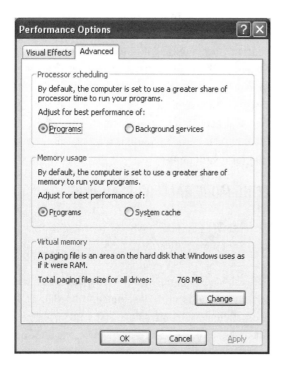

Figure 8-11. Check the amount of virtual memory allocated for your system.

By default, Windows XP uses about 1.5 times the total RAM for virtual memory. For a system with 512MB, the system will set aside 768MB. If this option is disabled (or considerably less), click the Change button (see Figure 8-12). Opt to customize the amount of virtual memory, or let Windows handle it automatically. Once ample virtual memory is available to your scanning software, your memory errors should disappear.

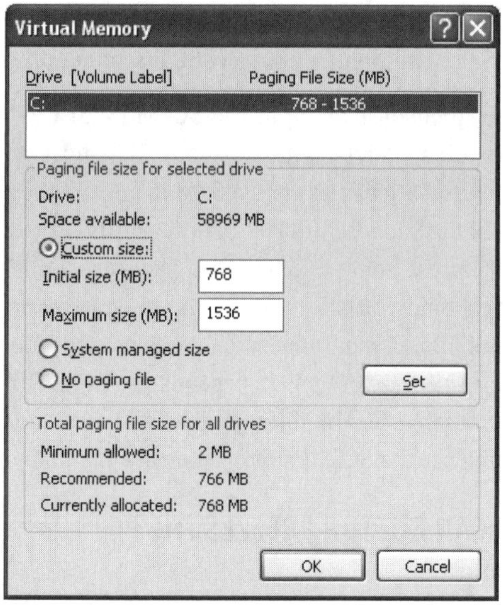

Figure 8-12. Configure an ample amount of virtual memory manually, or let Windows manage VM automatically.

MANAGING THE SCANNING LAMP

The Annoyance: My HP ScanJet takes its own sweet time before it starts a scan. It takes 45 seconds or more just to scan a page into the PC. Can I get the scanner to run faster by increasing the light output?

The Fix: Normally, scanners operate in a power-saving mode—the scanner turns off when idle to conserve its internal lamp. When you start a scan, the lamp needs to warm up for 30 seconds or so to ensure uniform light intensity and color purity across the tube. Scanners such as the HP ScanJet 6200C let you disable the economy mode to keep the lamp on at all times. Open the Scanners and Cameras control panel and double-click the scanner's icon. Click the Lamp tab, select the Faster Scan mode, and then click the OK button. Keeping the lamp on eliminates the warm-up period, and starts the scanning cycle faster.

Reduce RAM

When you want to scan an image, open your photo-editing program and use its own internal scanning (or Acquire) feature to run the scanner directly. This shortcut saves you both time and RAM because you no longer need to open the scanning software and cut and paste the scan into another program.

SCANNING TO UNCOOPERATIVE APPLICATIONS

The Annoyance: I want to scan some newspaper articles, but the scanning applet doesn't list my Microsoft Works application as a valid destination.

The Fix: This common problem occurs with older scanners and OCR (Optical Character Recognition) programs. In some cases, it may be possible to patch or upgrade the native scanner software (and destination application if necessary) to achieve compatibility. If your scanner and application just won't play nicely together, you can usually approach the problem as a two-step process. First, use the scanner's native software to generate a scan and save the scan as a standard image file (such as a *.BMP* or *.TIF* file). Second, open the scan as an import from the desired application (such as your image editor or OCR software).

MANAGING MOIRÉ

The Annoyance: Why do I get little squiggly lines through my scanned photos?

The Fix: You're probably seeing the effect of moiré— a kind of distortion that occurs when you try to scan or display images with fine detail (such as delicate patterns or texturing). First, make sure you properly align the image on the scanner bed. Next, use a scan/display resolution equal to (or higher than) the original image. If you use a lower resolution, the difference between the original photo and the scanned photo can cause an optical illusion and create concentric circles or crosshatched patterns. Finally, check your scanning software for a "moiré reduction" feature.

GETTING THE BEST PHOTO SCANS

The Annoyance: I scan a lot of documents for work. The scans never look very good, but at least they get the job done. However, now I want to scan and archive my family photos to CD-RW. What can I do to improve the quality of my scans?

The Fix: The following tips will help you get the best scans of your B&W and color photos:

Consider your original photo. Faded or out-of-focus images will not improve in a scan. Creases and stains will also transfer to the scanned image. However, a good image-editing program such as Adobe PhotoShop Elements lets you manage brightness, contrast, red-eye reduction, and other common photo maladies.

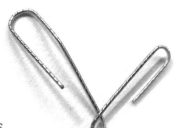

Different scanners will give you different results. Use a scanner that offers the resolution and color acuity needed for good-quality photo scans. Scanning at a higher resolution and color depth will result in larger image files, but will help bring out the detail and subtleties in your original print (high-resolution scans will also let you enlarge photos for printing later). If your scanner uses a different horizontal and vertical resolution, try rotating the photo 90 degrees and see if it looks better in the other orientation. Scanning in slightly lower resolutions, on the other hand, may help mask minor imperfections in some prints.

Clean the scanner. Remember that dust, pet hair, and other debris on the scanner bed will appear in your scans (see the "Cleaning a Scanner" sidebar earlier in this section).

Let the scanner warm up. Scanners use intense light sources (usually quartz halogen or fluorescent lamps) to illuminate the item being scanned. However, lamps take up to 30 seconds to reach their full brightness and stabilize at their proper "color temperature." If you scan with a "cold" bulb, the scan may appear dark or dull, and the scanned colors may seem wrong (see "Managing the Scanning Lamp" earlier in this chapter).

Save images in "loss-less" formats. Each file format (BMP, PNG, TIFF, JPEG) offers a tradeoff between file size and compression. Some formats (such as JPEG) use "lossy" compression, which saves file space but sacrifices fine image detail. You may notice the loss of detail more when you print the saved image. If you want top-quality images (and can spare the storage space), use a loss-less file format such as BMP or PNG.

> **tip**
>
> To test the image quality, scan and save copies of the image in several different file formats. Now compare the sizes and image quality of each saved file.

Cleaning a Scanner

To clean dust from the glass surface of your scanner, use an ordinary lint-free cloth. You can remove fingerprints and smudges with an ammonia-based glass cleaner (such as Windex). Don't spray the glass bed directly—wet a lint-free towel instead.

SCANNING FOR WEB PERFORMANCE

The Annoyance: I'm scanning a shoebox full of photos for my family's web site. The images scan great and look really nice, but when I stick them on my web page, the page seems to take forever to load. I know that the photos are probably too big, but what's the best way to get them smaller for faster web page loading, but still keep the images looking good?

The Fix: When you're scanning images for use on the Web, follow these steps:

- Select a resolution of 75dpi (higher resolutions do not appear better on a computer monitor).

- Shrink the image file size by using 16-bit rather than 32-bit color.

- Use a high-compression format such as JPEG, GIF, or FPX to save the image, instead of a loss-less format, such as TIFF or BMP. (Note that some scanning programs provide a "Scan to Web" option, which configures your resolution and file format automatically.)

WHITE DOTS ON THE SCAN

The Annoyance: When I scan photos, white dots and splotches appear in the image.

The Fix: If you printed the original photo on non-glossy paper (such as matte, luster, or canvas), it can catch reflected light and cause anomalies, which appear as white dots or small patches. If, on the other hand, you use smooth, glossy photo paper, the scanner captures the light reflected directly from the photo.

One common solution is to rescan the photo in a different orientation. For example, change the photo from a portrait to a landscape, or flip the photo 180 degrees. Now use your scanning software to rotate the scanned image. Rotation changes the directions of light reflection, and often reduces the occurrence of white dots. Of course, you could also reprint the original photo from its negative on standard glossy photo paper.

GETTING CRISPER SCANS

The Annoyance: I accidentally scanned my drawing twice using the same exact settings. The first scan looked okay, but I wanted to adjust the contrast to see if it made a difference. Oddly enough, the second scan looked brighter and crisper even though I used the same settings by mistake.

The Fix: Your second scan probably benefited from a warmed up light source. Remember that the scanner is basically a solid-state device, but the quartz-halogen or fluorescent light source remains an "analog" element. The characteristics of that light source will change slightly as the lamp warms up. It usually gets a bit brighter, and its "color temperature" changes (resulting in slightly better color fidelity in the scan).

If you need to tackle a lot of scans, use the scanner driver or management applet to turn off the scanner's economy feature and keep the lamp on all the time. Also, let the scanner warm up for several minutes before you scan your first drawing (see "Managing the Scanning Lamp" earlier in this chapter).

MATCHING COLORS IN THE SCAN

The Annoyance: I scanned a beautiful color photo of my cousin's wedding, but the colors on my monitor don't match up with the colors in the photo—the sparkling blue sky seems grayish, and the clouds look dark.

The Fix: Ideally, the colors in your scanned image should match the colors in your original drawing or photo. In practice, however, this doesn't always happen. For example, colors may vary due to scanner inaccuracy caused by a cold or failing light source (see the earlier annoyance "Getting the Best Photo Scans"). Your scanner's brightness, color, and contrast settings, as well as subtle differences in the way your display driver interprets color information in the scanned image can also have an effect. The following tips will help you improve color fidelity:

- Let the scanner's lamp warm up for several minutes, and use the scanner driver or scanning applet to set the brightness, contrast, and color balance controls to their "neutral" settings.

- Check with the scanner manufacturer for updated drivers and application software patches intended to improve color fidelity. Check for updated graphics card and monitor drivers as well. Also, make sure your display adapter is configured for your specific monitor (rather than a generic Plug-and-Play monitor).

- Try a color correction file. Just as you can employ color correction files between a PC and a color printer, you can also employ color adjustment files between a PC and a scanner. Open the Scanners and Cameras control panel, right-click your scanner and select

Properties. Click the Color Management tab and select an available color management profile that will help to correct your colors (see Figure 8-13).

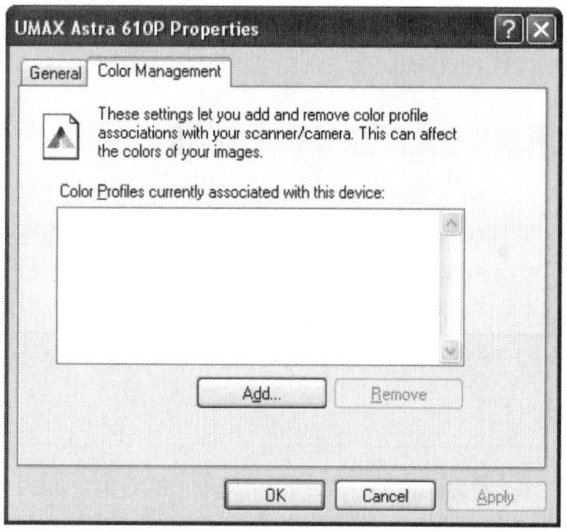

Figure 8-13. Use the scanner's Color Management tab to employ color matching profiles.

- Some high-end scanners (such as the HP ScanJet 8200) include a calibration feature that allows you to directly match (calibrate) the scanner and monitor to ensure proper color fidelity in the scanned image.

TOOLS OF THE TRADE

Printer manufacturers typically include the drivers, management software, and other essential utilities in the box. However, the following third-party utilities deserve a place in your toolbox:

PrintMagic (http://downloads-zdnet.com/3000-2088-10145322.html)

Lets you drag and drop only the content that you want to print, saving paper and toner/ink

InkSaver (http://www.inksaver.com)

Helps you control the amount of ink used by your inkjet printer, making your ink cartridges last longer

IntelliScribe (http://lpr.brooksnet.com)

A PC-based TCP/IP print client for Windows that lets you efficiently send print jobs to network or host system printers

Color Converge (http://www.redweathertech.com/products/colorconverge/index.html)

A digital, color-matching utility that improves the color fidelity across different printing devices

ThumbsPlus (http://www.cerious.com)

A photo database and graphic editor utility that works quickly and offers numerous format and compression options

Index

Colophon

Our look is the result of reader comments, our own experimentation, and feedback from distribution channels. Distinctive covers complement our distinctive approach to technical topics, breathing personality and life into potentially dry subjects.

Genevieve d'Entremont was the production editor and proofreader for *PC Hardware Annoyances.* Derek Di Matteo was the copyeditor. Patti Capaldi, Melanie Wang, and Genevieve d'Entremont did the typesetting and page makeup. Colleen Gorman and Claire Cloutier provided quality control. Mary Agner provided production assistance. Julie Hawks wrote the index.

Volume Design, Inc. designed the cover of this book using Adobe Illustrator and produced the cover layout with Adobe InDesign CS using Gravur Condensed and Adobe Sabon fonts.

Patti Capaldi designed and implemented the interior layout using Adobe InDesign CS. The text and heading fonts are Rotis Sans Serif, Lineto Gravur, and Myriad Pro; the code font is The Sans Mono Condensed. Julie Hawks converted the text to Adobe InDesign CS. The screenshots and technical illustrations that appear in the book were produced by Robert Romano amd Jessamyn Read using Macromedia Freehand MX and Adobe Photoshop 7. The cartoon illustrations used on the cover and in the interior of this book are copyright © 2004 Hal Mayforth.

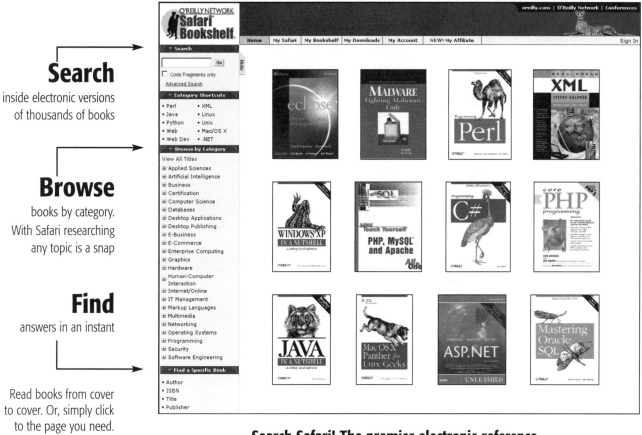

Related Titles Available from O'Reilly

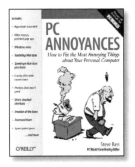

Windows Users

Access Cookbook, *2nd Edition*

Access Database Design & Programming,
3rd Edition

Excel Hacks

Excel Pocket Guide

Outlook 2000 in a Nutshell

Outlook Pocket Guide

PC Annoyances

Windows XP Annoyances

Windows XP Hacks

Windows XP Home Edition:
The Missing Manual

Windows XP in a Nutshell

Windows XP Pocket Guide

Windows XP Power User

Windows XP Pro:
The Missing Manual

Windows XP Unwired

Word Hacks

Word Pocket Guide, *2nd Edition*

Keep in touch with O'Reilly

1. Download examples from our books

To find example files for a book, go to:

www.oreilly.com/catalog

select the book, and follow the "Examples" link.

2. Register your O'Reilly books

Register your book at *register.oreilly.com*

Why register your books?
Once you've registered your O'Reilly books you can:

- Win O'Reilly books, T-shirts or discount coupons in our monthly drawing.
- Get special offers available only to registered O'Reilly customers.
- Get catalogs announcing new books (US and UK only).
- Get email notification of new editions of the O'Reilly books you own.

3. Join our email lists

Sign up to get topic-specific email announcements of new books and conferences, special offers, and O'Reilly Network technology newsletters at:

elists.oreilly.com

It's easy to customize your free elists subscription so you'll get exactly the O'Reilly news you want.

4. Get the latest news, tips, and tools

www.oreilly.com

- "Top 100 Sites on the Web"—PC Magazine
- CIO Magazine's Web Business 50 Awards

Our web site contains a library of comprehensive product information (including book excerpts and tables of contents), downloadable software, background articles, interviews with technology leaders, links to relevant sites, book cover art, and more.

5. Work for O'Reilly

Check out our web site for current employment opportunities:

jobs.oreilly.com

6. Contact us

O'Reilly & Associates
1005 Gravenstein Hwy North
Sebastopol, CA 95472 USA

TEL: 707-827-7000 or 800-998-9938
(6am to 5pm PST)

FAX: 707-829-0104

order@oreilly.com
For answers to problems regarding your order or our products. To place a book order online, visit:

www.oreilly.com/order_new

catalog@oreilly.com
To request a copy of our latest catalog.

booktech@oreilly.com
For book content technical questions or corrections.

corporate@oreilly.com
For educational, library, government, and corporate sales.

proposals@oreilly.com
To submit new book proposals to our editors and product managers.

international@oreilly.com
For information about our international distributors or translation queries. For a list of our distributors outside of North America check out:

international.oreilly.com/distributors.html

adoption@oreilly.com
For information about academic use of O'Reilly books, visit:

academic.oreilly.com

O'REILLY®

Our books are available at most retail and online bookstores.
To order direct: 1-800-998-9938 • *order@oreilly.com* • *www.oreilly.com*
Online editions of most O'Reilly titles are available by subscription at *safari.oreilly.com*